ON BECOMING CARL ROGERS

Delta Books by Carl Rogers

CARL ROGERS ON PERSONAL POWER

BECOMING PARTNERS

ON BECOMING
Carl Rogers

by Howard Kirschenbaum

 A DELTA BOOK

A DELTA BOOK
Published by
Dell Publishing Co., Inc.
1 Dag Hammarskjold Plaza
New York, New York   10017

For information address Delacorte Press, New York, New York.
Delta ® TM   755118, Dell Publishing Co., Inc.

ISBN: 0–440–56607–X

Reprinted by arrangement with Delacorte Press
Printed in the United States of America

First Delta printing—January 1980

Grateful acknowledgment
is made to the following
for permission to quote
from copyrighted material:

The American Psychological Association

Houghton Mifflin Company

Charles E. Merrill Publishing Company,
A Bell & Howell Company

Carl R. Rogers

Excerpts from *Carl Rogers on Encounter Groups*
by Carl R. Rogers,
copyright © 1970 by Carl R. Rogers,
used by permission of
Harper & Row, Publishers, Inc.

CONTENTS

To my mother and father,
whose congruence, empathy
and positive regard
made this book possible

INTRODUCTION

When Carl Rogers was a small boy he was a great reader of adventure stories. One novel told of the hero who, in one episode, would be fighting pirates, in another riding across the desert, in another exploring uncharted forests, and so on, in each chapter a different adventure. As a boy Rogers could not quite believe that one person could be involved in so many different walks of life. Ironically his own career, which has spanned half a century, is not unlike that of the fictional hero. He has made contributions and left an indelible influence on so many of the helping professions, here and abroad, that many people, knowing only one part or another of his long career, do not realize the scope of his contribution.

You may have read one of his many books in the fields of psychology, education, or human relationships. You may have been counseled by someone who was a "Rogerian," or heard a tape on which Rogers was the counselor. Maybe one of your psychology teachers told you an anecdote of how nondirective Carl Rogers nodded acceptingly as one of his clients jumped out the window. You might have seen a film of him leading an encounter group. If you are of a scientific bent you might know him as one of the first persons to conduct serious research on the process of psychotherapy. Or you may have come across his

articles in a journal of nursing, social work, pastoral psychology, semantics, or education.

In these pages I want to convey the fullness of Rogers' contribution
to the helping professions and to society. Yet, at the same time, the
process of "becoming Carl Rogers" (to borrow from the title of his
best-known book) has been an integral part of his professional philosophy and practice. So I hope equally to portray Carl Rogers the person.
As those who know him are wont to comment, with this particular man,
his life and work are impossible to separate.

Most biographers, wanting to maintain objectivity and not wanting
to distract the reader's attention from the main character, assume an
anonymous role. Except in personal biographies *(My Life With _____)*
any attention the storyteller calls to himself or herself is regarded as
an egotistical and impertinent intrusion, not to mention poor literary
form. Without belaboring the point that no biography can be entirely
objective, since the author's biases inevitably color many decisions
about the selection and interpretation of events, the traditional pose
of being solely an "omniscient observer" did not seem to me the most
appropriate one for a biography of Carl Rogers.

Consequently, you, the reader, will occasionally be reminded of my
presence in the course of the book—not so often, hopefully, that you
will be distracted from the narration, but often enough so you are
reminded that there is a storyteller, and that he is making decisions
about what to tell and has opinions and feelings about the subject. As
you read on and see how Rogers' own writing style changed over the
years, my rationale for occasionally using the first person should become apparent.

This project began when I wrote to Rogers in the spring of 1970,
introduced myself, requested his help on the biography, and sent
along some samples of my published writings. This began a correspondence which led to a meeting that summer. We quickly established
mutual trust and Rogers promised his cooperation in helping me work
on his biography. The help was varied and is worth describing, since
it says a good deal about the sources of data for the biography.

First, he gave me copies of any books or articles I had not previously
gathered in my own library research. As some of the books were out
of print and some of the articles in obscure journals long since defunct,
this enabled me to complete my set of all Rogers' published writings
—some fourteen books and almost two hundred articles and research
studies.

Second, he opened his files and library to me, regretting only that when he moved from Wisconsin to California in 1963 he had thrown away a great deal of material which would have proven very valuable for a biographer. Still there were hundreds of letters, memos, diaries, unpublished essays and tapes, articles written by colleagues, photographs, book inscriptions, and assorted pieces of information that have been invaluable in filling in many of the spaces left by the published materials. Helen Rogers was also very helpful in this respect, sharing with me, for example, scores of love letters she and Rogers exchanged during their courtship.

A literary decision I had to make was how many footnotes and references to these published and unpublished materials to include. I did not want to distract the reader with a mountain of reference data, but I did want people to be able to check my sources or satisfy their curiosity about a reference. My solution was to eliminate all but a few footnotes in the text and to provide a list of Rogers' major publications at the end of the book, along with information on where researchers might look for additional source material.

Third, Rogers gave me the names and addresses of some three hundred colleagues, relatives, friends, and "enemies" who had worked with or known him over the years. He also wrote a covering letter, which I was able to duplicate and send to all these people, affirming that I was working on the biography with his cooperation and support and requesting that they help me with my research, feeling free to share their negative memories and impressions as well as their positive ones.

This was invaluable help. It led, first, to personal interviews with Rogers' older sister, one of his two living brothers (the other wrote me a seventeen-page letter in lieu of an interview), the Rogers' son and daughter, four of their six grandchildren, and many other colleagues. I sent a questionnaire to all the others and received over a hundred replies. Many of them sent long letters or tapes sharing their experiences with Rogers, and often enclosed from their own files memos and letters going back many years that provided data on different periods in Rogers' life. It would take too long to identify all these people by name, but they have my greatest appreciation for the enormous contribution they have made to this biography.

Carl and Helen Rogers also made themselves available for extended interviews and visits. I spent a total of about six weeks with him or them in a wide variety of settings. I've had meals and spent the night at their home; attended staff meetings at the Center for Studies of the Person; accompanied him on consulting trips and at various conferences and workshops; observed a long editorial session with him and one of his publishers; and driven together with him on several long car trips. He has spent the night with my wife and me at our cabin in the woods, and he and I have spent many hours together taping interviews in his study.

Finally, both Carl and Helen Rogers have read every chapter in every draft of my manuscript and commented freely as to matters of fact and interpretation. They caught many errors, clarified many ambiguous points and, above all, whether they agreed or disagreed, never imposed upon my freedom to interpret the material as I saw fit.

In addition to the Rogers and the other sources previously cited, there are four people who deserve my special thanks for their participation in this biography. These are my friends and colleagues Larry Krafft, Rodney Napier, Leland Howe, and Rockwell Stensrud. Their early support and encouragement for this work, their ongoing contribution of helpful ideas and their editorial assistance on earlier versions of the manuscript have all contributed substantially to the final product. They have my sincere and lasting appreciation.

Given my close relationship to the Rogers during the research and writing of this biography, it is natural to wonder whether my interpretation of Rogers' life and work is not unduly biased. As far as I can tell, it is biased, but not unduly so.

It is biased because I had some very specific reasons for contacting Rogers and asking for help in writing his biography. As I told Rogers in my first letter to him, I thought his biography could accomplish four goals: (1) to give the student or layperson an interesting introduction to the world of psychology and education, (2) to challenge the thinking and practice of professional helpers, (3) to give the reader a deeper faith in his or her own attempts at personal growth, professional experimentation, and intellectual exploration, and (4) to encourage teachers and leaders to give their students and group members more freedom to pursue their own educational, professional, and personal goals. In short, I find Rogers' life and work a fine example for persons in and out of the helping professions. The years spent on this book would not have been possible were it otherwise.

Still I tried to present a balanced picture of the man. In addition to the critics of Rogers whose names and addresses he gave me, I asked the several hundred people to whom I wrote or spoke for the names of other Rogers critics they knew. I tried to contact all these people. Unfortunately Rogers' friends and colleagues over the years were much more willing to take the time to share their thoughts and experiences than were his critics. Still, I think I got enough of a sample of negative opinion from these sources, from critical book reviews and essays on his work, and from the frequent negative viewpoints one hears around academic settings, to represent both sides of the story.

With some emotional distance and some historical perspective, we can perceive things that Rogers could not—just as Rogers perceived things thirty years ago that many of us are only beginning to understand and assimilate today. We can love someone and still see him or her objectively, the good and the bad, separate from our own projections. This is what I have attempted to do—neither hide my affection for the man and his ideas, nor gloss over the occasions when he was not at his best, as a scientist, as a practitioner, or as a person. If I have failed to maintain this balanced perspective throughout, my error is surely on the side of affection.

ON BECOMING CARL ROGERS

CHAPTER 1
Childhood and Boyhood
1902-1919

Unlike most of the better known psychologists with whom Carl Rogers' name is often associated—Maslow, Perls, Frankl, Buhler, Fromm, etc. —who are European emigrants, Carl Rogers is a product of midwestern America. His roots go far back into United States history.

His grandfather, Alexander Hamilton Rogers, left the area around Glens Falls, New York, before the Civil War. He left behind a family which, in two generations, as emigrants from England, had firmly established itself in the community, several becoming lawyers and judges, others farmers and businesspeople. Traveling along the recently completed Erie Canal, which opened the Northwest Territories to new settlers, and then the Great Lakes, he eventually stopped in Milwaukee. Still later he moved to Wauwatosa, Wisconsin, where he raised five sons. There is still a Rogers Avenue in Wauwatosa; their house, the Damon House, is an historical landmark. Alexander's second son, Walter Alexander Rogers, was born there in 1868.

Matthew Cushing, also of English descent, crossed the Atlantic in 1638 and settled in Hingham, Massachusetts. The *Genealogy of the Cushing Family*, compiled by James S. Cushing in 1877, shows again a family that made many contributions to the community and to the new country. Like the Rogers, a branch of the Cushings moved west along the

1

Erie Canal and settled in Wisconsin. In Delafield, Wisconsin, there stands a memorial to three Cushing brothers killed in the Civil War. After the war one of the Cushing family purchased a farm in Brookfield, about six miles from Wauwatosa. There Julia Margaret Cushing, one of three daughters, was born also in 1868.

Walter Rogers and Julia Cushing knew each other as children. The Cushings had moved into town, a block away from the Rogers, so they met at various school, church, and social occasions. On New Year's Day the five brothers would dress up and "go calling" on the three sisters.

Walter attended the University of Wisconsin and was graduated with the class of 1888. At a time when college education was not widespread, he remained for a year of graduate work in engineering and mathematics, completing his formal training as a civil engineer. He was the first Fellow in the University's Cement Laboratory, which had just been established. While there, he developed the concrete "briquet," for testing the tensile strength of concrete—an important contribution to that field. At the University he also resumed his acquaintance with Julia Cushing, who attended college there for two years. They must have found much in common: they were the same age, they came from the same home town and from similar farming and religious backgrounds, and they attended the same college. They were married in Wauwatosa on July 1, 1891. As the local paper announced, "After the wedding, Mr. and Mrs. Rogers left for their home in Livingston, Montana."

For the next ten years Walter struggled to establish himself in the engineering field. He was often away from home, supervising the construction of track, bridges, and tunnels for different railroads across the country, especially the Chicago, Milwaukee and St. Paul. Thus it was that they spent the beginning of their marriage in western Montana, where he was supervising several construction projects. A short time later they moved back to Elgin, Illinois, near Chicago. Their first three children, Lester, Margaret, and Ross, were born there in 1893, 1895, and 1899, respectively. Around the turn of the century they rented a bigger house on Clinton Avenue in Oak Park, a few miles away. Here their fourth child, Carl Ransom Rogers, was born on January 8, 1902. Two more sons, Walter and John, came later, in 1907 and 1908.

Carl was a rather sickly child—slight, shy, prone to tears, often the target of jokes and teasing by his older brothers. With his father often away from home on business trips, he developed much warmer feelings for his mother. The baby of the family for over five years, he received considerable attention from her and the older children, who taught him to read at about age four. He seemed to take easily to the world of books and before long was reading many of the thick volumes on the family's bookshelves, especially a book of Bible stories called *The Story of the Bible from Genesis to Revelation Told In Simple Language Adapted to All Ages, but Especially to the Young,* which he read from beginning to end many times, to the approval of his religion-minded parents.

Business continued to improve for Walter Rogers, so that when Carl was almost five the family moved to a new house at 547 North Euclid Avenue, on the other side of town, the "suburbs" of Oak Park. This was a large house which Walter designed and on which he supervised the building. The lot ran clear through the block to the other street and had a barn for the horses and buggies, chickens, and the tools for Julia's large vegetable garden. Although the move was exciting for Carl it marked the first in a series which would repeatedly interrupt the friendships he had barely begun to establish. But he quickly made new playmates in the neighborhood and soon was quite happy in the new house.

It was an upper-middle-class neighborhood, and when Carl was ready to begin school at the age of six years and nine months, he attended the Holmes School. Ernest Hemingway, who lived three blocks away, and the children of Frank Lloyd Wright were also attending Holmes at the time. (Dr. Hemingway, Ernest's father, taught the nature-study classes.) On his first day in school he was placed in Miss Ely's first-grade class. She seemed like a very stern teacher to little Carl, and he was relieved when Miss Ely alerted the principal, Miss Hood, that he was too far advanced for the first-grade reader. Helen Elliott, one of Carl's classmates then, later recalled how, on the second day of school, a small boy was ushered into her second grade classroom and asked to read to the class from the second-grade reader. His performance was so fluent that he also read to the third and fourth grades that day; but it was decided that the second grade would be far enough along for Carl to begin school. He found Miss Littler, the second grade teacher, to be a nice young woman and soon felt very fondly toward her.

With Miss Littler's and subsequent teachers' encouragement, his love for reading increased. Father Rogers also encouraged this at first. Carl's sister Margaret recalled how "Father would get these exciting

Indian stories. The Indians were just coming over the hill and we'd be breathless . . . then father would close the book and say, 'It's time to go to bed.' " Consequently Carl devoured all the books he could get his hands on, mostly novels and adventure stories—tales of Indians, wars, pioneers, and pirates—and he came to love more and more the fantasy world created through his reading. James Fenimore Cooper was a great favorite. One history book he loved and read through many times was *The Sinking of the Albemarle.* This told of the exploits of Willie B. Cushing, one of his mother's family, who became a Civil War hero when he took a small boat with a torpedo on it and, with a small crew, went up one of the coastal rivers and blew up the Confederate Ironclad *Albemarle,* which at that point was sinking many Union ships. When no other books were available, he would read the encyclopedia or even the dictionary, occasionally trying to gain sex information through these sources. Like most parents then, his own never provided this; the subject was taboo.

In addition to being an avid reader of adventure stories, Carl seemed to have a talent for creating stories himself. When he was in the second grade, one of his stories—a fantasy about leaves talking to each other and finally falling off the trees—was posted for visitors to see. A few years later he would keep his younger brothers, Walter and John, entertained for hours with war and adventure stories that he would make up on the spot.

Although his parents were both college educated, and although his father was partly responsible for his love of adventure stories, they soon began to frown upon his reading habits and his fantasy world. They were somewhat anti-intellectual and very practical people. Bible reading, of course, was to be encouraged, as were technical and how-to books, but when there were chores to be done, reading and storytelling for their own sake were considered unproductive, self-indulgent, practically sinful. One of his mother's frequent reprovals was, "There you are again with your nose in a book," and many were the times when he would be embarrassingly startled out of his dream world to remember, "Oh, gosh, I was supposed to do this or that and I never once thought of it." (Years later, as a college professor, it took him some time to overcome feelings of guilt when he read in the morning.) Brother John remembered a sign on Carl's dresser, in large print, reading, DO IT NOW!

In the family Carl's tendency toward dreaminess was the source of many jokes and barbs. It was a teasing family, and, as he later recalled, the teasing could be vicious at times. "You just took digs at everybody and everybody took digs at you." Thus he was dubbed with many nicknames, like "Mr. Absent-Minded Professor" and "Mr. Mooney," the latter after a comic strip character of the time who might be described as a Mr. Magoo with adequate eyesight. Margaret remembered how "those boys nearly tore each other limb from limb in their arguing, but after they were over with it they were good friends again. That was the sort of fellowship we had. It was really rough at times but you stood your own ground or you knuckled under, but then you were friends afterward." Years later, after Carl described his family in an autobiographical essay, Walter, John, and Margaret Rogers all insisted that Carl had exaggerated the negative quality of the teasing. They saw it mostly as being in good fun, and John and Margaret seemed almost offended that Carl would characterize the family in this way. On the other hand, they all agreed that Carl was the most sensitive of the children. So whatever the reality, the picture emerges of Carl as a vulnerable child, tender and easily hurt, yet feisty and even sarcastic in his own way, since this was necessary to survive in the family repartee.

Walter and Julia Rogers were exemplars of the Protestant work ethic, with a bit of Calvinism and fundamentalism thrown in. His family had been Congregational, hers Baptist. On Sundays the family all climbed into the larger of their two horse-drawn buggies (the smaller one was for shopping), and Walter drove the family to the Congregational church in Oak Park. In the cold Illinois winters they piled on layers of blankets to keep warm. When they got their first automobile, an Argo electric model with isinglass curtains, a charcoal-burning foot warmer in the back seat helped provide additional heat in the uncovered car as they drove the several miles to church. Later father Rogers served as Chairman of the Board of Trustees of the First Congregational Church in Glen Ellyn, Illinois, where they dedicated "the Rogers chapel" out of gratitude for his generous help in their building program.

Carl later wrote, "My Mother was a person with strong religious convictions, whose views became increasingly fundamentalist as she matured. Two of her biblical phrases, often used in family prayers, stick in my mind and give the feeling of her religion: 'Come out from among them and be ye separate'; 'All our righteousness is as filthy rags in Thy sight, oh Lord.' (The first expressed her conviction of superiority, that we were of the 'elect' and should not mingle with those who were not so favored; the second her conviction of inferiority, that at our best we were unspeakably sinful.) My father was involved too in the family prayers, church attendance and the like, but in a less emotional way. They were both devoted and loving parents, giving a great deal of time and energy to creating a family life which would 'hold' the children in the way in which they should go. They were masters of the art of subtle and loving control. I do not remember ever being given a direct command on an important subject, yet such was the unity of our family that it was understood by all that . . . 'Other persons behave in dubious ways which we do not approve of in our family. Many of them play cards, go to movies, smoke, dance, drink, and engage in other activities, some unmentionable. So the best thing to do is to be tolerant of them, since they may not know better, but to keep away from any close communication with them, and to live your life within the family.' For some reason, swearing was not quite so strictly tabooed—perhaps because father would, on occasion, vent his anger in that way."

One religious ritual which existed as long as any of the Rogers children can remember was that of morning worship. Following breakfast the whole family would sit in a circle and each take turns reading verses from the Bible. This went on seven days a week, whether there were guests or not. After the reading they would all kneel by their chairs and Walter, if he were home, or otherwise Julia, would offer a prayer—not a ritual prayer, but something different each day. Carl and Walter always thought that their mother was the more religious of the two, with Father going along to please her. But John thought "both parents were in a very close relationship in their feelings toward God. They could talk to Him. It gave them assurance and conviction. They were unafraid."

Another value of the family was that of work. There was little that good hard work would not cure, and the children were all expected to do their share of the chores. One of Carl's responsibilities was feeding and caring for the chickens out behind the house. This was the traditional "business enterprise" of the Rogers children, and while in elementary school Carl took over the job of selling eggs to his mother and the neighbors. His parents encouraged this type of activity. He would be near home, away from possibly bad influences, and engaged in productive work. He had to make out bills, keep records, and do most everything required of a small businessman. If he did not submit a bill to his mother for the eggs he sold her, he simply would not get paid. When the children were youngsters, father Rogers would empty his pockets when he came home and have them put the pennies, nickels, and other coins in similar piles; or he would have them put his canceled checks in numerical order. Both father and mother encouraged that kind of practical knowledge wherever they could. Father would often take his children on trips with him to broaden their experience in the real world; then he would urge them to keep a journal and describe what they had seen. In 1914, for example, he took the family to British Columbia, where Lester and Ross were working on one of his construction sites. They were in Winnipeg the day the First World War began, and Carl swam in a hot spring pool in Bampf, Alberta, in a July Fourth snowstorm. Aside from their educational value, John thought there was another reason his father took the children on trips. "Since he was away so much of the time during World War I, this gave him an opportunity to further enjoy his children. If he couldn't stay home, he'd try to take someone with him when possible."

Helen Elliott, his classmate since the second grade, lived a block away from Carl in Oak Park. Along with several other boys and girls from the neighborhood, they walked or rode their bicycles to school together and would often play together on the block, riding or playing tag, pom-pom-pullaway, "three old cat," and other games. But Carl was expected home right after school and so did not develop as deep friendships with the others as he might have. Helen remembered him then as a "shy, sensitive, and unsocial boy, who preferred to live in his books and his dream world rather than encounter the rough-tumble of the play yard or enter into competitive sports. He went directly home after school and while we lingered to bat the ball in a softball game, he was feeding his chickens or selling eggs to the neighbors." He remembers* having "one fairly close friend, the girl next door," but beyond that, the other children were only acquaintances.

Living in a world of books as he did, he was an excellent student, always getting among the highest grades in the class. He was the pet of several teachers, anxious to do well and please them. They encouraged his reading and intellectual curiosity in ways his parents did not. He had another crush on his fifth grade teacher, Miss Kuntz, and one of his first minor acts of personal independence was to stay after school frequently, helping her with tasks around the classroom. He once cheated on a test that year, so scared was he of failing. Other than being something of a teacher's pet, he did nothing to alienate his fellow students; but neither did they know him very well or particularly

---

*Rogers' recollections in unpublished interviews and correspondence with the author are described in present tense, e.g., "Rogers recalls. . . ." All other recollections of Rogers or others are phrased in past tense, e.g., "His brother agreed," "Rogers wrote," etc.

like him. He had only one fist fight in elementary school and later wrote of it, "I was frightened to death but did my best in what ended as pretty much of a draw." Walter and John, on the other hand, were often getting into fights with their classmates. "Carl would come on us fighting and stop it. Walt would say, 'The kid started it.' Carl would ask why. I would say, 'Walt was the reason.' After a series of these came the nicknames: John, the Kid; Carl, the Lad; Walt, the Reason. So we were The Kid, The Lad and The Reason."

When Carl was in the eighth grade, his father had to leave on a trip to several construction sites in the South and the East. He was invited to go along, and allowed to miss school for two or three weeks with the understanding that he would write a report about his "educational trip," including Chicago, New Orleans, and Norfolk, Virginia. At some point it began to occur to him that his father was trying to interest him in the construction business. Later he realized that this was not necessarily the main motive, as his brothers Lester and Ross were already interested in that business; nor was it entirely "educational." It was more that his father was concerned with his withdrawn, dreamy, and impractical nature and wanted to interest him in something outside himself and his books, something in the "real" world. The trip failed in that regard, but Carl did come the closest he had ever been to his father, from whom he usually felt somewhat remote, and toward whom his attitude was more respectful than affectionate. This trip afforded them the chance to enjoy themselves together and contributed to a feeling of camaraderie that Carl had not experienced before. By contrast Carl's younger brother Walter always felt very close to his father. "Once, when I was isolated in bed for three months with the scarlet fever, the old gent would come home each night and come up and read to me for an hour at a time. . . . He was a sweet man . . . he loved his grandchildren," Walter told me many years later, and the fondness was apparent in his eyes as he said it. Margaret, too, the only daughter, remembered her father with the greatest fondness and admiration.

The parents were stern disciplinarians, but also tenderhearted and warm. Though they exercised tight control over their children's behavior, there was still much fun and laughter in their home. Margaret remembered, "One time my brother Ross who just loved horses—and I didn't care a bit about them—encouraged me to ride this old horse that had been on the construction jobs and was farmed out to pasture at home. Well, I did, and I got scared and screamed and Ross came and . . . well, anyway, I didn't ride again. But the next morning my verse at worship was that in Proverbs which said, 'A horse is a vain thing for safety.' Of course that broke the family up."

Realizing that perhaps they could hold the family together more if their children's social events took place at home, Walter and Julia also tried hard to make their home a comfortable place for their children's friends. They installed a tennis court out back. Carl's oldest brother Lester often invited friends to the Euclid Avenue house, and Carl remembers lots of parties with the older children laughing, singing popular songs, playing approved of games like pin-the-tail-on-the-donkey, and thoroughly enjoying themselves. There was also a good deal of music in their home. Red Seal records of operas and classical music were often played, and although he didn't keep up with it in later years, Carl learned to play the piano quite well. The parents' concern was to keep the children from the contaminating influences of suburban living. When Carl was just beginning high school, his parents went even further in this direction. They moved the whole family to a three-hundred-acre farm, about twenty miles away and twenty-five miles west of Chicago.

Although he grew up in a town, Walter Rogers always had a love of farming; but for twenty years the engineering and construction business had kept him too busy to think of beginning any major new projects. He had been working as Assistant Chief Engineer for Bridges and Buildings for the Chicago, Milwaukee and St. Paul, with Mr. Onward Bates as Chief Engineer, when the two men decided to go into business together. They would build the projects themselves, under contract to the railroad, rather than just supervise the construction. On April 1, 1901, they established the Bates and Rogers Construction Corporation, with headquarters in Chicago. Mr. Bates dropped out a few years later because of ill health, so it was essentially Rogers' company (Carl's brothers Lester and John would each later become president of the company, which celebrated its seventy-fifth anniversary in 1976). They began with bridges and tunnels and, as business flourished, expanded into all kinds of construction work, especially hydroelectric power plants and dams and, with the coming of the automobile, concrete roads across the country. By 1914 Walter Rogers was well established and could think about taking on an expensive and time-consuming avocation. John remembered him explaining the move to friends by saying it was a good place to raise his four lively boys who were still at home.

He bought the farm near Glen Ellyn, Illinois, in the only rolling area immediately west of Chicago. For the summers of 1914 and 1915 and weekends during the fall, the family lived out there in a large barracks his construction crew had erected. The "Shanty," as they called it, was a T-shaped building such as Walter's crews built as temporary headquarters when they were out on a job. The four older boys had one room, where Carl slept on a double-decker bunk bed; Margaret and little Johnny had another. There was no indoor plumbing, and the water had to be heated by a fire built under a coil of pipes coming from the pump outside. Saturday night baths became quite a ritual, with the family taking turns as to who would bathe in the big washtub first and so get the cleanest water. One night in the Shanty the whole family was awakened by horrible, raucous, and eerie noises emanating from a closet. Carl, it turned out, had found a hoot owl that day and thought it would be more comfortable inside. On another occasion, when a mother pig died, the boys bottle-fed the babies and kept them inside. They would run around the Shanty tripping everyone up, much to the boys' delight.

Combining his interest in farming with his practical nature and education, father Rogers began to read about scientific agriculture and hired a man to run the farm according to his directions. Fred Landorf, the farm superintendent, stayed with the family for forty years. He also hired Frank and Mabel Smith as chauffeur and caretakers. Walter loved the farm. He loved the cows, walking in fields, administering the operation both as a hobby and a business. Julia had mixed feelings. She liked it there, especially the gardening; but now that all the children were of school age, she didn't relish the idea of getting tied down again to a farm. On the other hand she had no taste for the social life of the suburbs. Both parents agreed the farm environment was better for their children, since it was away from all the corrupting influences of city and suburbs. Julia taught the boys how to use tools and to garden. They loved it. Things were working out so well that Walter soon began building a substantial new brick home there.

It is widely known that Carl Rogers grew up on a farm, but not so widely known that the farm house had a slate roof, tile floors, eight bedrooms and five baths, and a clay tennis court behind the house. Just before Christmas 1915 the family sold their house in Oak Park and moved to the farm to live year round. After a family meeting and vote they named the farm-estate "Warwood," the first three letters being Walter Alexander Rogers' initials and the last four acknowledging the wooded areas around the farm.

Carl had just started high school in Oak Park, so when the family moved at Christmas time he transferred to the high school in Downers Grove. Whatever friendships he had begun to develop in Oak Park had to be discontinued; nor was there much of a chance for new ones in Downers Grove. Each morning he and his brother Ross would go three miles by horse and buggy or car, over rough roads, to Lisle and then take the train five miles to Downers Grove. In order to get home in time for chores and supper, they had to leave right after classes. As if this weren't enough to prevent him from developing his own friendships, after a year and a half at Downers Grove, a change in the train schedule forced him to transfer again and so he completed his last two years of high school in Naperville.

In Carl's case, then, his parents' desire to keep the children close to home seemed to be working very well. He spent his high school years socially isolated from his peers. Since dancing was not allowed for the Rogers, and that was what the young people mostly did at parties, he had practically no social life. He had only one "date." This was a result of his having been elected junior class president, probably on account of his good grades and of his not belonging to any of the class cliques —an ironic compensation for having no close friends. As class president he had to attend the one social event of the year, a dinner to which it was necessary to bring a girl. Later he remembered "the agony I went through in inviting an auburn-haired lass whom I had admired from a distance. Fortunately for me, she accepted. If she had not, I don't know what I would have done."

And so he turned back to his own family for the companionship he needed. Lester, the oldest brother, was in his twenties and away from home when the Rogers moved to the farm. Carl had always admired and respected him, but they were too many years apart to be real friends. During the war, when Lester scored the highest grade of any soldier ever tested at Camp Grant on the Army's Alpha Intelligence Test, Carl was so proud that he clipped the newspaper article and kept it all his life. Margaret was also considerably older than Carl and not a likely friend for a young boy. Her attitude toward him had always been more maternal than chummy. Ross, only three years older, was perhaps the most likely companion in the family, but the two brothers never got along very well. While Ross may have been jealous of Carl, who had supplanted him as the "baby" of the family years before, Carl believed that his parents favored Ross, and for a while he got attached to the notion that he had been adopted. "One Christmas the folks gave Ross and Carl a set of boxing gloves. While Mother was getting dinner ready and Father was someplace else, they decided they'd try out the gloves. Soon it got to be a pretty hot fight, and Walt and I hid behind chairs to keep out of the way. They stopped after a while in about a draw, but the gloves got a real good initiation."

So his brother Walter, five and a half years younger, became his closest comrade and conspirator, and John, a year and a half younger still, usually tagged along, getting teased in the typical family fashion. Fighting in the house was absolutely forbidden. The parents' response to it was characteristic of their noncoddling, practical child-rearing: "Go outdoors and beat your brains out if you want, but don't come screaming to me when you get hurt." "By the time we got outside," Walt recalled, "we had usually cooled off anyway."

Carl loved to play in the woods behind the farm, learning the names of the animals, birds, trees, and shrubs. To him the eighty acres of woods and underbrush was a veritable forest, a wilderness that shielded an Indian behind every tree. All the fantasy tales from his reading came alive, and he led his brothers in many an adventure, expedition, or battle against their imaginary foes. "Carl was the guy who dreamed up all the fancy stuff to do," Walter remembered. "He was a great one for reliving the life of the pioneers in the woods. One time he had us out shooting some pigeons, then we built a big brush fire, encased the pigeons and potatoes in wet clay and threw them in the ashes—which, according to Carl, was the proper procedure. . . . We'd go around finding big hornets nests. We'd throw rocks at them, and when they swarmed out, we'd run like hell." Or, as John remembered, "When the young heifers were feeding in the woods beyond the fenced-in yard, Carl and Walt thought it would be great sport to ride one bareback. Our heifers were very tame, so we went up to them and patted them. Quickly my two brothers were astride their pets and just as quickly they were off, as the young cows whirled and drove in under a thorn-apple tree, with the rest of the herd dashing along behind." They also had fun and took pride in exhibiting their animals and pets in the local fair at Lisle where they won many blue ribbons.

It wasn't all fun by any means. There was always work to do on the farm, and the children were expected to do their share, and then some. Using a hatchet Carl helped clear out the underbrush in the woodlot. While attending high school he would be up at five o'clock or earlier to milk a dozen cows every morning and again at night. As a result his hands and arms were continually stiff, prickly, and "asleep" during much of the school day. In the winter for a time he had also to care for the furnace—shake the grates, shovel in the coal, regulate the damper. During the summers he often drove the milk truck to town and one summer was in charge of all the pigs on the farm. Also during the summer he often rode the cultivator all day long. He was assigned a section of the farm very distant from the house. This portion of land was entirely in his care, with the decisions and action about repairing the equipment, caring for the team, figuring on the soil and weather conditions left solely in his hands. It was a lonesome task.

The farm work, however, helped him overcome his early childhood sickliness, and he developed a strong, wiry, and sturdy frame. Although he wasn't much of an athlete, he enjoyed playing softball when he could and was fairly good at tennis. From then on, with only a few exceptions, his health was excellent and his capacity for long hours of untiring work rarely diminished. Another important result of his responsibilities on the farm was that he developed a lifelong love of the outdoors, of working with his body and hands, and of watching and helping natural things grow. Years later, when I interviewed Carl, Margaret, and Walter Rogers, Carl showed me his begonias, Walter gave me a tour through his greenhouse filled with numerous kinds of cacti, and Margaret proudly conducted me through her garden. The farm apparently had a similar effect on all of them. When he went away to college, Carl would write, "Oh! how I long to be home and feel the cool breeze brush my hot forehead as I work outdoors. I can hardly keep myself at work."

When he was about thirteen he developed another hobby that was very important to him and to his later development. At the time, Gene Stratton-Porter's books—*Freckles, Girl of the Limberlost, Moths of the Limberlost* and others—were very popular. These books described the world of nature, especially the large night-flying moths, and were a combination of technical and fictional writing. Carl had read the whole series. "So I was in a responsive mood when I discovered in the woods close to home, against the dark fissured bark of a black oak tree, two lovely luna moths, just emerged from their cocoons. These beautiful pale green creatures, large as a small bird, with long 'swallowtail' wings spotted with purple, would have intrigued anyone. They fascinated me. I began my first 'independent study project,' as it would be termed today. I obtained books on moths. I found and raised their caterpillars. I hatched the eggs and raised caterpillars through their whole series of moults, into the cocoons, until the 12-month cycle was complete and they emerged again as moths—Polyphemus, Cecropia, Prometheus, or one of the dozens of other varieties I came to know. I even 'tied out' a female moth on the roof to attract males—a very successful experiment—and was continually busy getting leaves of the special sorts which the caterpillars demanded as food. In my own very small and specialized field I became something of a biologist."

His reputation as a biologist soon spread. Neighbors would often call, saying, "We've got a big bug over here, do you want it?" And he would go over to see if it was a new variety to include in his carefully mounted collection. This was the first serious, spontaneous interest that was entirely his own and that was tied to the world of reality. The interest lasted until he left for college and marked the beginning of a scientific inclination toward careful observation, collection, and organization of objective data. Bird watching, which had many of these characteristics, was another hobby of his.

Having thus commenced his scientific career at age thirteen, Carl soon developed a second and related interest, this time in the field of agriculture. Because Walter Rogers wanted to run the farm in the most modern way, he frequently had experts from the university out to advise him, the foreman, and the herdsman about the best methods. Carl often listened to these experts but, at first, had little interest in the subject. Then he began to read many of his father's books, magazines, and catalogues on farming. Just as he had learned to play chess by reading the *Encyclopaedia Britannica,* it was rather typical of him then that he would become interested in farming through books, rather than through face-to-face contact with the adults on the farm or the consultants who were called in. Later he recalled, "I can remember reading these books—particularly the heavy scientific one by Morison on Feeds and Feeding. The descriptions of all the scientific experiments on feeding, on milk and egg production, on the use of different fertilizers, different varieties of seed, of soil, etc., gave me a thorough-going feeling for the essential elements of science. The design of a suitable experiment, the rationale of control groups, the control of all variables but one, the statistical analysis of the results—all of these concepts were unknowingly absorbed through my reading at the age of 13 to 16."

"He practically memorized Morison's *Feeds and Feeding,*" Walter said. After a while he sent away to some of the seed companies for several varieties of oats, barley, and corn and planted these in some informal experimental plots to see what might happen. The plants grew and so did his interest in farming. Soon Walter and John joined him in the venture and their father gave them a couple of acres to use as they liked. The farm foreman prepared the ground for them in the spring, but they did the planting and set up some good experiments using various types of seeds, soils, and fertilizers. The "Rogers Bros." even sold some of their produce to the local market and declared dividends at the end of the year. Unfortunately the whole experiment ended prematurely, when Walter, Sr. and the foreman decided they needed those few acres after all and wanted to combine the smaller plot into a larger adjoining field. Compared to the satisfaction he and his brothers were getting, his father's reasons seemed weak to Carl. He protested vigorously, argued, reasoned, wept, and finally lost one of the biggest fights he could ever remember with his father. It was at about this time, age thirteen, that he began to question the thinking of his parents. "I never rebelled in behavior very much, not until much later. But in a sense I did feel that nobody was going to dominate me."

This may help to understand why it was so difficult for him to ask for help. On one occasion "Father sold the sheep on the farm but there were, as I recall, eleven lambs which were too young to sell and he gave them to myself, Walter, and John. We raised them on bottles for as long as necessary and then fed them, pastured them, cared for them, and so forth. It never would have occurred to me to ask any of the farm workers how to go about this. Instead, I wrote and got Government bulletins about the care of sheep. When it came time to butcher one of the lambs again I would have scorned any practical advice. I read up on how to butcher a lamb from a Government bulletin and did so. I did everything 'by the book.' And I realize as I look back that I certainly avoided asking advice whenever possible."

Brother John added, "Carl neglected to tell of the technique used in butchering the lamb. He read that in a slaughter house a man swung a heavy mallet to stun the animal, then another would stick it with a knife, then hang it up to skin it and dress it out. Since we didn't have such a mallet, he elected to use our Louisville Slugger baseball bat. Well, the first crack wasn't hard enough; the second was. Walt and I were his helpers until Walt started to turn green and left for the house. So Carl and I were the two who butchered the lamb. Walt later went on to become a leading O.B. and gynecologist in Pasadena."

Carl soon realized he wanted to become a farmer. Beyond loving the outdoor work, he had been stimulated by the possibilities of scientific agriculture. His agricultural readings had challenged his intelligence and, like his father, he now looked forward to running the farm in the most modern manner. To do that, of course, he would have to go to college to learn all the latest developments in farming and farm management.

High school seemed rather dull compared to his own educational pursuits on the farm. But like many bright students he did not let the irrelevance of his education prevent him from working hard at it. His parents held Lester's and Ross's achievements up as models to the three younger boys. Walter considered Carl the most competitive member of the family. "He's never been satisfied unless he was number one. If he didn't come home with all A's he was depressed." Soon Carl, too, was being mentioned as one of the models for Walter and John to emulate.

He did his best in English and science. The course he liked best was taught by Miss Graham, "a spinsterish teacher of English at Naperville High School. Though she was a strict disciplinarian and rarely if ever smiled, she had a true scholarly interest in her work. I somehow felt that she would understand what I wrote, so for themes in English I wrote personal accounts as well as rebellious papers on 'Shakespeare as an over-rated author'. . . . She helped me realize that it was alright to be original and unique."

On the day of his high school graduation Carl was given his first diary, in which he wrote:

> I don't think I shall use this book as I am supposed to. Some days I have so much to write about and then for days and days I'll have nothing to write at all so I will write when I please and put down the date. Besides, when I write, I want to write enough to look at. I am not like Mrs. Bryant, who when William Cullen Bryant was born wrote in her diary. Nov. ____ Stormy. N.E. wind churned. Seven in the evening a son born. . . . She must have had an ultra practical mind.

Just after Carl's graduation Walter Rogers was going to take the family to Estes Park, Colorado. At the last minute he was called to Philadelphia to finalize plans with the government about some construction work in Panama City. So the trip west became a trip east, and Carl saw the sights of Philadelphia, Atlantic City, New York City, and Washington, D.C.

Although the Rogers were by now quite prosperous, it was expected that Carl would work during the summer to help put himself through college. Thus he spent the summer of 1919 in Kenmore, North Dakota, working in one of the chain of lumberyards owned by his three uncles. He worked a full day at the yard, unloading lumber, filling customers' orders, shoveling coals, unloading bricks, and learning the ins and outs of the lumber business, which impressed him no more than the construction business had. He also lived and slept there, being the only one on the premises after work hours were over. "I get pretty lonesome," he wrote in his diary, "but I have a fine time with my new books."

With forty-three dollars of a fifty-dollar graduation present from his parents he had bought a set of chessmen, a kit of toilet articles, and, typically, twenty-two books, including works by Carlyle, Hugo, Dickens, Ruskin, Stevenson, Emerson, Scott, Poe, Dumas, and many others. After hours, as he had often done as a boy, he compensated for his lack of social contacts by losing himself in the world of literature. He wrote in his diary:

> I have come to love my books a great deal. Dickens, with his humor and his indignation at oppression of any kind, and his wonderful characters, is a very good friend. Mark Twain with his chuckles can always knock out my homesickness. I listen to Scott's tales with a wide open mouth. I have somber discussions with Emerson and Van Dyke, but one author has utterly captured me in his spell, and his name is Victor Hugo. He speaks nothing in whole chapters, and then suddenly volumes spring forth in sentences. Far far back he begins, picking up each separate thread of each separate life and I grow almost weary watching him trace each one. Then suddenly, several of them cross and he certainly makes the most of every dramatic situation. Then at last at the crisis every loose fact comes together with a flash that almost blinded me and the whole beautiful story stands complete. I came to the crisis of the story Mon. night and this is how it affected me:
>
> In three hours I read 300 pages. I knew nothing of time or external things. When at last I reached the apex of the story and laid down the book I could not remember what day it was, or what I had been doing. It was 15 minutes before I knew what I had been doing, etc. For three hours he had utterly fascinated me. Les Miserables is one of the most wonderful bugle notes of truth that I have ever read as well as the most fascinating story. Hugo is a wonder.
>
> I have had lots of time to think this summer and I feel that I have come much closer to God, tho there are thousands of things that still perplex and baffle me.

Back home again, shortly before leaving for college, Carl reflected on the previous two months. "As I look back over the summer," he wrote, "I feel that I have really gained a great deal in many ways. . . . I have learned to love farm life better thru absence and I fully intend to be a farmer."

CHAPTER 2
The Wisconsin Years
1919-1924

In September of 1919 Carl packed his bags, said good-bye to his family, and traveled the 120 miles to Madison, Wisconsin, to enter the largest freshman class yet enrolled at the University of Wisconsin. Although his major was scientific agriculture, and Wisconsin had an excellent school of agriculture, this was not the main reason for his choice of college. The Rogers had *always* gone to the University of Wisconsin. Both parents and his older brothers and sister had studied there; there simply was never any question that Carl would study there, too. Consistent with the Rogers' tradition of "sticking together," he moved into the campus Young Men's Christian Association and roomed with his brother Ross, who was student president of the campus Y.M.C.A. chapter. During his sophomore year he roomed with a cousin.

Although he did well in his subjects, the first two and a half years at Wisconsin had little permanent impact on him academically. Among several autobiographical essays and interviews, Rogers has made only one reference to the classroom for this entire period: "One of the things I remember best was the vehement statement of an agronomy professor in regard to the learning and use of facts. He stressed the futility of an encyclopedic knowledge for its own sake, and wound up

18

with the injunction, 'Don't be a damned ammunition wagon; be a rifle!' "

Of far greater importance were Carl's extracurricular experiences during these years. With his religious background and his eagerness to meet people and make friends, it was natural that he would join the "Ag-Triangle," a group of agricultural students meeting under the auspices of the Y.M.C.A. Professor George Humphrey was the adult leader of the group of twenty-five or so young men. Carl saw him as a well-intentioned man, but rather weak. Whether or not Humphrey knew what he was doing in leaving everything up to the group, his was an example of the facilitative leadership that Rogers was to advocate years later. Left to their own devices, the group set up its own curriculum, organized social and educational activities, conducted business in parliamentary fashion, discussed topics deeply, and became a very closely-knit group.

The Ag-Triangle was an extremely important experience for Carl. Having come from a cloistered background, never having had real friendships outside his family, he was here able to interact on a deep and trusting level with many other men from different backgrounds. In February, writing his journal, he summed up his first semester in glowing terms: "As I look back, it seems to me that it has been the best and richest five months I have ever had. I have learned more from the hearts and lives of men. I have made the first friend I have ever had and hosts and hosts of fine acquaintances."

Another outcome of the Ag-Triangle experience was a lasting understanding and appreciation of parliamentary rules. During Rogers' career he would serve as president and chairman of many professional organizations. The skill he developed in the Y.M.C.A. group in using parliamentary procedure always proved useful to him, and he never felt fearful later about chairing any type of parliamentary assembly. He also assumed leadership roles in the Ag-Triangle and became a Boys' Club leader, organizing and directing boys' activities both in Madison and at summer camp in Sturgeon Bay.

It was not for religious or social reasons, however, that Carl's parents were putting him through college. He had come to the University to learn to be a successful farmer in what was rapidly becoming a modern industry. But once away from home, surrounded by new people and fresh ideas, presented with many new alternatives for his life's direction, he began to realize that his becoming a farmer was not an accomplished fact and that many other possibilities were before him. His growing uncertainty and ambivalence was reflected in an October entry in his journal. "This whole year," he wrote, "everything that has happened during vacation and in school has impressed on me the wonderful opportunities before me, and I sometimes wonder—well, anyway, I'm going to be a good farmer first, because that's the work I love and am fitted for, and if a bigger better job comes, I hope and pray that I'll have the sense to take it and the guts to make good."

Whether agriculture did not have the emotional commitment the young man was seeking, or whether it did not sufficiently challenge his intellect, he quite rapidly moved away from his previous decision to be a farmer. By November of his freshman year his life's work was clearly an open question. Again in his journal:

> I have just come from a fine Fellowship meeting. "Dad" Wolfe spoke on "Selecting a Life Work." Oh, it's wonderful to feel that God will really lead me to my life work, and I *know* He will, for never has he deserted me. Just the same, tho, it is an awesome thing to think that a wrong decision will wreck my life, but oh, how I'll try and keep my life in tune with God, so that He can guide me. I have plenty of ambition, in fact I sometimes think I'm too ambitious, but if I can only keep that terrible swelling force within me in the right path, I know all will be well. The most wonderful promise in the Bible for me is: Ask, and it shall be given you; seek and ye shall find; knock and it shall be opened unto you. Lord, I ask Thy guidance; I am seeking the kingdom of Heaven; and the door at which I knock Thou alone knowest beside myself. Lord help me to see in the right spirit that I may obtain. Amen.

As the year drew to a close, religion came to consume an increasing amount of his emotional and intellectual energy. Under "Plans for 1920" he wrote, "I intend to live closer to God, to form a more intimate friendship with Him and to spend more time and effort in communion with Him. I spend time cultivating my friends and count it time well spent. How much better should I count the time spent when I am cultivating God's friendship. . . . I intend to earnestly seek and follow the great trial which God has staked out for my life."

Then in the last days of 1919 and the first days of 1920 Carl traveled to Iowa to attend the Des Moines Convention, a series of meetings organized by the International Y.M.C.A. devoted to educating and inspiring young people to spreading the Christian gospel throughout the world. The Des Moines Convention was a turning point for eighteen-year-old Carl Rogers:

> A Great Flame! That to me was the Des Moines Convention. A great consuming flame which for a few great moments burned away all dross

and showed the world and also my soul, not as they look but as they are! A great lifting hand which bore us up, up, up, until the world was below us, a great field white for the harvest, a great multitude of starving faces, looking for the Christ love, a great pot of molten metal, dross on top but pure gold underneath.

And the cry is "Men! give us men!" Men to reap the white fields, men to let the Christ love shine thru their lives, men to sweep the dross from the pot and help shake the gold.

We cannot always live on the mountain top and see that view, but we can never forget once we have seen it. This is what I wrote after Sherwood Eddy's third great speech:

> "During Eddy's morning speech I almost made up my mind to go into Christian work and during his afternoon speech I made my final decision. God help me keep it! All my previous dreams seem cheap now, for I have volunteered for the biggest, the greatest work on the globe. I have found what I never found before, the peace of God which passeth all understanding. I never dreamed that simply enlisting for Christ could make me feel so right with the world. It is wonderful."

Despite this and other occasional moments of certainty, his decision to make Christianity his life's work was not yet absolute. For two or three years he wavered, but he began to guide his life more and more in the direction of the ministry. He helped organize campus religious conferences, traveled to meetings in other states, shifted his major from agriculture to history—an area he felt would better prepare him for the ministry—and continued to lead his group in the Boys' Club. At one Y.M.C.A. conference he attended at Lake Geneva, Wisconsin, in June, 1921, his religious vision was extended beyond the theological, and he began seriously to consider the need for "Christianizing industrial, political, social and international relationships." He also joined the college debating team, which considerably bolstered his confidence in speaking before groups. By the end of his sophomore year his decision was becoming increasingly firm. "I am more positive than ever I will go into Christian work, and feel quite convinced that it will be the ministry, whether rural or not I do not know."

In the summer of 1921 he was the leader of a barracks of eight high school counselors and one hundred poor boys from Milwaukee who spent the summer at a cherry pickers' camp at Sturgeon Bay, Wisconsin. The boys, mostly of Italian descent, ordinarily would not have had the chance to spend the summer in the country. The camp enabled them to work at picking cherries for part of the day to pay their expenses, while during the rest of the day they had a more typical

Y.M.C.A. camp program. Carl took his leadership position very seriously. He felt responsible not only for their recreational lives, but also
for their moral development. On one occasion there was a theft in the
camp and a boy everyone suspected of being the thief. "We got him
alone behind one of the buildings and talked with him and threatened
him and prayed over him . . . whether he fessed up or not I don't
remember, but we were trying to use all the leverage at our disposal,
including the divine."

Because of his considerable involvement in Christian youth work,
Carl met many leaders in the evangelical movement and impressed
them with his sincerity, intelligence, and leadership ability. Nevertheless he was amazed and even wept upon learning that in December of
1921 he had been chosen to be one of the ten United States youth
delegates to the World Student Christian Federation's Conference in
Peking, China, that coming April. At the time, he wondered if his
parents' ability to finance the trip were not a significant factor in his
selection. This was not the case. The selection was made by Ray Sowers, then State Secretary for the Y.M.C.A., who was later to become a
well-known Wisconsin educator.

Fifty years later Sowers himself recalled how "I immediately thought
of the many able and promising leaders in the twenty student Y.M.-
C.A.s in the state, but I could think of none who would be more
representative of Wisconsin youth than two brothers, Ross and Carl
Rogers, at Wisconsin University in Madison. Ross, the elder brother,
had been president of the University Y.M.C.A. and was recognized as
an outstanding leader on campus. Carl while younger showed equal
promise. I discussed the matter with Fred Wolfe and the Dean of the
Law School who was then serving as the faculty advisor for the Y.M.-
C.A. We all agreed that either of these two students would make an
excellent choice, but because Ross would be leaving the campus at the
end of the year and Carl would remain on campus for several years,
we decided to nominate Carl. . . . Next came the matter of financing
the trip. While the Rogers family was in better than moderate financial
circumstances and could have afforded the expense, we felt that the
members would feel more that Carl would be their representative if
they assumed responsibility for raising a major proportion of the expenses. We therefore set out to secure the funds by popular subscrip-
tion . . . and in short order the money was raised from students and
faculty interest in the project."

Although the conference would last only a week, the trip would
involve six months away from home, including travel in many countries

and meetings and speaking engagements throughout China and the Orient. The trip would mean missing the last semester of his junior year, but this loss seemed insignificant compared to the experience ahead. "Why? Why?" he asked himself. "That is the question of my life. Surely God wants me for some great task, something that he is saving for me alone. I feel as David must have felt when he was anointed by Samuel, and may it be true of me, as it was of David; 'and the Spirit of the Lord was upon him from that day forward.' Surely God's hand is visible in this last and greatest opportunity and responsibility that has come upon me. May I be big enough to meet it. . . . I am 20 years old today."

On February 15, 1922, Carl left Wheaton, Illinois, near his farm home, on the Overland Limited, to begin the trip that five months later he would call "the greatest experience of my life." On the eve of his departure he wondered "how much the trip will change me and whether the Carl Rogers that comes back will be more than a speaking acquaintance of the Carl Rogers that is going out."

The Carl Rogers who came back was considerably changed, and we are fortunate in having detailed records on the six-month trip to help shed light on his evolution. In addition to an enormous correspondence that he carried on during the trip ("Part of the morning I wrote letters, but I had finished most of the seventeen the evening before. . . ."), Carl faithfully kept a journal, which he called his "China Diary." The voluminous correspondence and the eighty-six-page, typed, single-spaced "China Diary" show that, as early as age twenty, Rogers had an intense drive to communicate his observations and reflections.

This need to communicate can hardly be separated from his drive to work, to produce—a strong part of the family upbringing. On three different days, just after leaving Illinois, he noted: "I read for about an hour and a half after I got on board, finishing about 110 pages of Prof. Ross' book on 'The Changing Chinese,' " "I was the last one to bed and the first one up, and have finished about 150 pages of a book on Japan, as well as having looked at the scenery a lot, and read several descriptive pamphlets on the scenery we are passing through," and "This morning I read 130 pages of a book on China before 11 o'-clock." Beyond reporting "the facts," his pride in his own productivity is evident. He maintained this throughout his life. Forty-eight years later he circulated a two-page paper called "A Day in My Life," in response to numerous inquiries as to how "an old man spends his time." After describing a staggering array of activities for the day, he concluded, with obvious irony, "As you can see, it is a very boring life."

Two other qualities that have always contributed to Rogers' productivity are his generally excellent health and his very high energy level. As the boat left San Francisco in a heavy gale, ninety percent of the passengers became so seasick that they did not even come to the dining room for supper. Carl was among the other ten percent. While others in the various delegations occasionally became ill due to the variations in dietary and climatic conditions throughout the Orient, he was in perfect health the whole time. He sampled all the new foods possible, slept in unlikely places, and traveled by train and boat thousands of miles throughout Hawaii, Japan, Korea, China, Hong Kong, and the Philippines. His health and energy were again revealed on the return trip when he was worried that he might miss his only chance to climb Mt. Fujiyama, the highest mountain in Japan. So, anxious to cram every new experience possible into his trip, and while most of his companions were asleep, he spent all night climbing the 12,368 foot "Fuji," arriving at the top just in time to see the sunrise.

One of the major changes Carl went through during the trip was the liberalizing of his religious views. Until that point his exposure to religious orientations other than his own had been very limited. At home his mother had been the chief source of his spiritual guidance. The students he met at Wisconsin reflected a similar Midwestern, rural, conservative, religious background. His influences at the Des Moines Convention, where he had first decided upon a religious life, were also highly evangelistic and traditional.

Imagine, then, young Carl's experience on the three-week voyage across the Pacific, when he had a chance to hear, question, debate and discuss numerous religious questions with students, scholars and religious leaders from all parts of the country and from all types of background and experience. Five days into the voyage he wrote, "We have had many discussions already on lots of the doubtful points, and I am thankful beyond words that we are with a group of leaders who are all forward-looking, young minded people, who are still building up their own faiths, not dogmatists who are sure that their own interpretation is the only one. The more we talk and think, the more I am finding it possible to define what I myself believe, and what I consider non-essential."

The next day ". . . we got started on a discussion of whether a man had to believe in the deity of Christ to be a Christian, and that led to 'What is a Christian?' and we sat at the table thrashing things out and trying to thrash them out until ten o'clock. That is the beauty of this life on shipboard, that when we get into a profitable discussion, none of us have to quit, so that we either keep on until we are worn out or else have arrived somewhere."

By the return voyage home he was able to write:

> Naturally all these friendships, and this eye-opening trip, and the time to think that I have had on shipboard, etc., have tremendously changed me. Most of all perhaps, I have changed to the only logical viewpoint— that I want to know what is *true*, regardless of whether that leaves me a Christian or no. Since taking that attitude (and it has been a gradual step, starting before I left home) I have found the most wonderful new riches in the life of Christ and in the Bible as a whole. It is a tremendous relief to quit worrying about whether you believe what you are supposed to believe, and begin actually studying Christ to find whether he is a personality worth giving your life to. I know that for myself that method of approach has led me to a far deeper and a far more enthusiastic allegiance to Him. For the first time in my life, I find myself anxious to tell people what I believe about Him, and about His wonderful Kingdom that he came to establish. I don't wonder that His early disciples simply couldn't keep from telling the "good news."

For Carl's family back in Illinois, it was hardly good news that they were receiving in his letters. Beginning with the ocean voyage and continuing on throughout the trip, his letters revealed that his religious views were becoming increasingly different from theirs. To even entertain the idea that Christ was not a deity but a man was unthinkable for Julia and Walter Rogers. Yet this is what their son had come to believe, writing home that "Jesus himself was a man who came nearer to God than any other man in history." Most of Carl's family regarded his new ideas as "queer" and "unsafe," and he was sorely grieved that they had not shared the experiences that had helped change his thinking.

Moving away from the family's views, fortunately, did not involve much of the internal conflict, guilt, and rebellion that often accompany achieving independence from one's parents. The transcontinental and transpacific mails were so slow in 1922 that his parents' reaction to one of his letters might not arrive for two months after his own letter was written. By then two months more of living had ensued, and whatever imminent changes he had discussed in the earlier correspondence were all but solidified. By the time he returned home in August there was an intellectual and emotional gap between him and most of the family that would never be bridged. The next few years were not without their conflicts and heated discussions in the Rogers home; but "from the date of this trip, my goals, values, aims, and philosophy have been my own."

The Peking conference itself was an exciting week of forums, committee meetings, general sessions, speeches, debates, and informal meetings and discussions among the two hundred foreign and six hundred Chinese delegates. As Carl described it in his first published article, on the front page of the Y.M.C.A.'s *Intercollegian*, "From the Orient, and from the Occident, from Czecho-Slovakia and Poland, from Burma and Ceylon, from white and black and yellow races, students came together at Tsing Hua College, for the purpose of understanding one another, of comparing and discussing their problems and their opportunities, and in the hope of binding together in a real and vital fellowship the Christian students of the world."

This was the first such gathering to take place since the New York conference in 1913, and, with the First World War having come and gone, one of the liveliest topics of debate was the position of the world's Christian youth regarding war and pacifism. The Indians and Australians argued that Christianity and pacifism were inseparable. The Europeans disagreed, arguing that some wars could be justified. One student of the latter persuasion tried to gloss over the differences in the room by saying that, after all, the group had a spiritual unity which transcended their differences. To which Carl noted in his journal: "How can he say that we have a spiritual unity that goes deeper than our differences, when he knows that if we all believed the same as he does, we would be shooting each other tomorrow if our governments ordered us to?"

Carl participated actively in all the General Sessions and served on two subcommittees, deliberating over the membership composition of the World Federation, the attitude the student Christian movement should take toward members of other religions, how to present Christ to students, the goals and purposes of the international Christian youth movement, and whether, in fact, it really was a youth movement or one controlled by adults. His faith was strengthened as he saw a common bond, Christianity, able to keep people working together for common goals. "In spite of differences of race and nationality," he wrote, "in spite of sore spots in the relations of many countries, never, even in the hottest committee discussions, have I seen any of the delegates show anything but the finest kind of spirit . . . it has been an education for a narrow, provincial middle westerner like myself to find what splendid men may be hidden behind different labels of nationality, or wrapped up in packages of different color. I have made a good many friends during this period, and that alone has made the conference worth while."

After the conference Carl spent almost three months traveling through China, first as part of a delegation that included in addition to himself a student each from Germany, France, England, and China. Later he accompanied Professor Kenneth Latorette, a former missionary to and expert on China and Japan. Visiting Hankow, Nanking, Shanghai, Canton, Foochow, and numerous other towns and cities unfamiliar to most westerners, he took in the sights and snapped photographs like many tourists, but he also had unique experiences unavailable to most travelers. In each city Y.M.C.A. representatives or local missionaries offered the visitors their best hospitality, which included introducing them to local friends and officials and giving them specially guided tours of the area.

Thus Carl was able to see the inside of an old Chinese prison ("the filthiest, lousiest hole that I ever care to see. . . . The poor wretches just kow-towed and grovelled on the ground when they saw us. I suppose they thought we could do something to help them"); talk politics with the military governor of the Philippines, General Wood ("If the American people knew all that he told us, I think that there would be a considerable reaction"); ride through the streets of Yokohama in a ricksha ("It is a queer feeling to ride behind a human draft animal. It is something that I am afraid I would never get used to. I couldn't help but think of the fact that he was a man, not an animal, and that he had a home, no doubt, and possibly a family"); spend a good deal of time traveling through China with an American black man and an American Indian ("there have been groups of people who nearly ruin their eyesight staring at us"); hear hair-raising stories of brutality from an escapee of a Russian prison camp that had not been informed that the war was over ("The whole dinner seemed like a dream. . . . Think of eating dinner in a Chinese house, in Peking, talking to two of our late enemies, the Austrians, and hearing about men suffering up in Russia who didn't even know that the war was over"); and get trapped on a sabotaged railroad line in the midst of a regional civil war ("We found an empty boxcar and we all piled in and held on to that boxcar and kept other people out until we got to Nanking").

He was able also to show eight Chinese students the sights of Nagasaki, Japan ("I had the time of my life helping them translate the menu into language they can understand"); visit a children's hospital in the Philippines ("We saw there poor little kiddies whose legs and arms were simply bones with the skin hanging on in folds and flaps. I have seen lots of sights, but this was honestly the worst I have ever seen. There was one little girl eight years old, who weighed 25 pounds. Her case was complicated by tuberculosis. I wish that I could forget some of the things I saw there"); and see countless examples of fantastic poverty and squalor ("I wouldn't advise you to look very long at this beggar we are passing—I'm afraid that you might not sleep very well. Can the ragged, warped, deformed thing, holding out his hand and making a pitiful moaning sound, be made in the image of God?").

More and more he began to juxtapose his religious beliefs with the social and economic realities around him. Visiting a Chinese silk factory, he saw six- and seven-year-old girls, some of whom had just had their feet bound—causing permanently deformed, yet, according to the tradition, more feminine feet—working over tubs of steaming water all day long.

> Somehow silk will never look quite the same to me [he wrote]. It has lost considerable of its luster. . . . Anyone who could see those tiny little kids (some of the poor little tykes were just having their feet bound and stood first on one foot and then on the other to ease the pain)—anyone who could see those little kids, and say that such things were all right, is not a Christian, by my definition. I don't care whether he believes the whole Bible from beginning to end or whether he believes every orthodox doctrine that ever was—I couldn't call him a Christian. These kids came to work at four thirty in the morning, and go home at a quarter to eight at night. . . . Think of kids seven years old working fourteen hours and a quarter every day! I don't know how it makes other people feel, but it makes me see red, and I wish I had a gun. I no longer wonder that people turn Bolshevik. I consider it mighty fortunate that I have all my life seen the other side of the question, for even with that, it sometimes seems as if the best thing to do were to send the whole____system to____, where it came from [sic].

> One of the Hankow mills which declared a 40% dividend besides putting a large sum in the sinking fund . . . had not twelve hour days for women and children, but a fourteen hour day! God knows that we have given them splendid examples in our own history. The U.S. Steel Corporation, the Standard Oil, the packers, the Colorado Fuel and Iron—goodness knows that they have done [worse] things than have yet been attempted in China, and I suppose that we can't blame heathen China too harshly for following Christian America and England.

Nor did he attempt to avoid his own responsibility. At Nagasaki, before returning to San Francisco, he witnessed a human conveyor belt made up of women passing twenty- to twenty-five-pound baskets of coal up from the dock into the hold of the ships. "If you want to know what people mean by a 'sense of guilt' I think you ought to stand as I did for a couple of hours and watch those women slave away in the blazing sun, grimy and dirty, without a chance to rest even for a moment, and then meditate on the fact that *you* are partly responsible for those conditions. Those women are submitting to those conditions, and slaving their lives out, simply to get *you* across the ocean, and yet *you* go calmly ahead and let them do it, without a thought for anything but your own comfort. That to my mind, is a good example of the fact that we are each one of us responsible to a certain extent for the unchristian conditions that we find around us."

Although neither he nor anyone else would have used the term then, his views were developing an "existential" slant in religion and morality. A person is a Christian not on the basis of her words or beliefs, but in her actions. He came to believe that good works were more important than ritual or doctrine in Christianity. One must take responsibility for one's actions. References to being "chosen" to do God's work or God's "leading" him were replaced in his letters and diary by indications that he, Carl, was going to have to do the choosing; the responsibility was his own.

Thus his views on many religious, political, social, and economic questions changed considerably as a result of his trip to the Orient. Although he never actually became a pacifist, he did seriously consider joining the Fellowship of Reconciliation, an ecumenical, pacifist-activist organization whose members often made sacrifices, including going to jail, for their principles of peace and brotherhood. The social conscience he developed on the China trip lasted throughout his career; for example, thirteen years later, in the depths of the Great Depression, when prominent in the social-work field, he would criticize the profession for being "reluctant to face the fact that by and large the interest of social workers favoring the welfare of each individual and the more equitable distribution of wealth and income, is more or less opposed to the interest of the business and taxpayers groups." He also maintained sympathy for the peace movement throughout his life and was outspoken in his opposition to the Vietnam War.

Another important consequence of the China trip for him was a significant increase in his self-confidence. At the Peking conference, the shy midwesterner was selected by his delegation to represent the Christian youth of the United States before the World Federation. Throughout China and the Orient he gave dozens of formal speeches and informal talks to groups of hundreds of students and adults. He debated religion, politics, and economics with men much older and more experienced than he. He impressed many adult missionary workers and was offered a job on the Y.M.C.A. staff in India, which he declined in order to continue his education. He even did some personal counseling with students in trouble.

In reading the "China Diary," Rogers' first lengthy, though unpublished, manuscript, I was struck immediately by his literary style. Especially when describing agriculture and nature, which he did frequently, there is omnipresent both an artist's and scientist's concern for detail. For example, in China he wrote,

> As we got higher, the whole Foochow basin lay in a panorama below us—the long island, with a silver strip of river on each side—the bevy of dusky winged junks coming upriver on the incoming tide—the little clustered villages scattered over the plain, with a few wisps of smoke hanging over each one—the clean little rice paddies, cut here and there with little threadlike canals—and off to the right, the close packed city of Foochow, with a crowd of anchored junks at the river bank. Frame all this flat basin with an irregular ring of mountains, extending range behind range as far as you can see, and hang a wine red sun just over the westernmost range, so that it lights up the clouds and the mountains with a strong tinge of red, and you have some faint idea of the view that we had from old Kushan.

Rogers concluded the "China Diary" with a description of his nighttime climb up Mt. Fujiyama, on the eve of his return to America.

> . . . About nine or nine thirty we got above the timber line, and from there on the trip was wonderful. All the clouds and mist had cleared away, and the stars seemed so close you could almost reach up and touch them. . . . We stopped every now and then at the rest houses along the way, and about ten thirty stopped for a meal, and laid down to sleep until . . . a little before twelve. . . . The climb was getting steeper and steeper, and the rarity of the air was beginning to bother the other two fellows. . . . A slender silver crescent of moon began to show up about twelve thirty, adding to the light of the stars, and making our pathway considerably plainer. At three o'clock we stopped at the sixth of the nine stations. Phelps had told me that we should be at the eighth station by four o'clock if we wanted to see the sunrise from the top, so that at three thirty, I got the bunch started again, but their pace was entirely too slow. I wanted to get to the top, so I took a few sandwiches from the pack that the guide was carrying, and started out at my own pace. It was very cold now, and we had to keep moving to keep the sweat from freezing. The east was just beginning to show a few streaks of light, and I knew that I would

have to hurry. When I was a little above the eighth station, the view in the east became so wonderful that I watched it for some time. The country around the foot of the mountain, as far as one could see in every direction, was covered with a thick blanket of billowing white clouds, looking for all the world like a great expanse of foaming ocean breakers, frozen silent in mid-air. On the eastern edge of this expanse, there was a great glowing light coming up from beneath that colored the sky all colors of the rainbow. There was a perfect prismatic scheme of colors, blue, fading into purple, green, yellow and red. It was one of the most beautiful sights I have ever seen, looking across that snowfield of clouds. In a little while the light became brilliant, and more brilliant, and then —Hurrah! the SUN. I wish you could have heard the shout that came from the many pilgrims at various stages of the climb, when the sun finally shoved its white-hot brim up thru those soft clouds. And I shouted too, and waved my cap. We had seen a tremendous event.

Fired with enthusiasm, filled with great goals and plans, and bolstered by an increased self-confidence, Carl returned to the United States in August 1922. Shortly after his return he began to suffer from abdominal pains which had troubled him, from time to time, since age fifteen. The problem turned out to be a duodenal ulcer, which became so serious that it demanded five weeks in the hospital and a year away from college to recuperate. Interestingly, three of the six Rogers children suffered from ulcers at some time during their lives, a fact which Carl attributed to a "gently suppressive" atmosphere at home, in which emotional displays were inappropriate and hard work was the solution to all obstacles and frustrations. "It'll get well before you're married," was a typical response of their parents to many of the children's complaints. Even during his period of recuperation he was expected to do his full share of physical work around the farm. He also worked in a local lumberyard for two months, driving back and forth between work and home in his first car, a second-hand Model T Ford, for which he had paid eighty-five dollars. On one occasion the car was wedged in a tight parking space at the lumber yard. Rather than ask for help he lifted the back end by himself, moved it over a few inches, and strained his back.

While working at the lumberyard he took a correspondence course from the University of Wisconsin in introductory psychology. It was his first formal introduction to the subject and, using William James as the text, he found it rather dull. "The only portion of the course I remember is that I got into an argument by mail with my instructor as to whether dogs could reason. It was his claim that only human beings could reason. I was quite able to prove to my own satisfaction that my dog, Shep, was definitely able to solve difficult problems by reasoning."

There was a good deal of tension at home, which Carl ascribed to his mother's "increasingly fundamentalist views" and her inability to accept the changes in him. Brother Walter thought differently. He saw both his mother and father becoming increasingly more accepting of new ideas as they grew older and as the children left home. All the tension of that transition seemed to center around Carl. Carl was the first to dance and to join a fraternity, for example, and had to contend with his parents' resistance in doing so. But once the deed was done, the parents found it easier to accept such behavior in the younger children. In fact, once it was clear the dancing battle was lost, they invited a dance instructor to Warwood to teach Walter and John. If they were going to dance, they were going to do it right, and under parental supervision.

Walter thought Carl and his mother very similar temperamentally. "Carl found disagreement with her to be very uncomfortable, and visa versa." Yet, "Carl would go out of his way to do battle . . . he would argue vehemently with our parents. Vigorous arguments over interpretation of scripture. . . . Both Carl and Mother are somewhat Billy Graham types at heart. This is where the fireworks occurred." Why couldn't he leave well enough alone and go his own way when he disagreed, as Walter learned to do? "I think he felt the need of Mother's approval; he felt closer to her than Father. It was a serious attempt on his part to communicate." When the barriers to communication proved too great, he more or less gave up. When he finally left home, he did not keep up with his parents as much as the other children did. They didn't offer him as much help as they did the others, nor did he accept as much as they of what was offered. Only later in life was Carl able to communicate better with his mother, after his own sense of identity was long established and his listening and helping skills well developed.

Back at the University, stimulated by all he had seen, heard, and done in the Orient, he plunged into scholastic work with a new relish. While in China, he had received word that he had been elected to Phi Beta Kappa—a high honor under any circumstances, but especially so for a junior in college. Against his parents' wishes, he now joined the Alpha Kappa Lambda fraternity, noted for its scholastic excellence, and lived at the fraternity house during his junior year. He was very impressed by Wisconsin historians Carl Russell Fish, George Sellery, and Eugene Byrne and developed a great respect for scholarship and historical research. Unlike many students he used the term paper as a vehicle for exploring his own interests. In one paper, "The Soul of a Troubadour," he showed how St. Francis of Assisi placed far greater emphasis on doing good works and following the example of Christ than on a mystical union with God. In "The Pacifism of Wyclif" and "The Development of Luther's Idea of Authority in Religion, 1518–19," he explored two other themes which were important to him. Throughout the former paper he seemed to sympathize with Wyclif's views on war, writing: "A summary of his principles . . . put into modern language, will show this: It is wrong to kill, either through hate or fear. War cannot be reconciled with love, the central principle of Jesus' teaching. It is impossible for love to be the motive of war. The best defense is not a military offense, but a resistance of love and patience and suffering to force. To deny the foregoing principle is to admit that Christianity is not practicable—that force is stronger than love, evil stronger than good. The virtues of which war is the mother are the virtues of the hangman. Conquerors have not title to their conquests unless they rule justly. The approval of the church does not make war right. Indeed, it is worse for the church to approve war than for any other organization. . . . The above summary, as far as its ideas are concerned, might be the brief of a pamphlet published last week or last month in London, or New York, or Chicago, by some 'dangerous' group of radicals. It is most interestingly modern in its outlook and in its underlying thought."

Throughout most of his professional life, a basic tenet of Rogers' has been the importance of the individual's trusting his or her own experience. Concluding the Luther paper in 1923, he wrote, "Fortunately for later generations, he . . . dared to set the authority of his own reason and his own clear conscience above any other, be it Church, or Pope, or a rigid interpretation of the Bible. As Dr. McGiffert says, 'He really substituted for all external authorities the enlightened conscience of the individual Christian. The Bible he read for himself and admitted the claim of no council or body of men to read it for him. This, in principle, though he never fully realized it, and seldom acted upon it, meant the right of private judgment in religious things, and in it lay the promise of a new age.' "

He was learning to gather data from other scholars to help him clarify and support his own thinking and to set this down for others

to see. This skill would play an important part in his later professional
writings; at this point they merely impressed his instructors. On the
Luther paper, his bachelor's thesis, Dean Sellery wrote "Ex/First rate
work" and on the Wyclif essay "Excellent/High grade work."

During these later years at the University Rogers also resumed his
involvement with college debating. "I found it both surprising and
thrilling," he wrote, "to realize that I could tackle a subject on which
I knew nothing—in this case the compulsory arbitration of labor disputes—put in eight solid hours a day working at it over a period of
weeks—and come out reasonably 'well informed.' It somehow gave me
a feeling of confidence in my own ability to tackle a new intellectual
problem and to master it."

For Rogers, then, the second half of his undergraduate career
was very different from the first. Earlier his courses had not interested him much. His real learnings and important involvements
came through extracurricular religious and social activities. The last
two years continued to offer extracurricular involvements; but now
academic life became important to the young man, desiring as he
did to learn as much as possible in order to become a more effective agent in Christian work. Ray Sowers, the Y.M.C.A. leader,
remembered how "on two or three occasions when I would be at
the University, Carl would indicate that he felt a bit frustrated at
times, because he found so few of his classmates with whom he
could share 'the long thoughts of youth'—their concerns and occu-
pations were primarily transient and trivial. . . . Because of these
encounters with Carl, I gained the impression that he was well on
his way to a level of perception and maturity which had great
promise for the future."

Rogers also had a business going which had great promise for the
future, if he cared to develop it. When he returned from China he had
brought with him a variety of Chinese jewelry and handicrafts which
his friends and relatives very much treasured. Mrs. Taylor, wife of the
dean of the Peking Union Medical School, had offered to shop for him
on a commission basis. So he sent her twenty-five dollars with a small
order for various Chinese crafts. The duty came to another twenty-five
and, to his surprise, he had no difficulty selling the lot for a hundred
dollars. Seeing the chance to help pay his way through school (his
parents were supplying half of the cost), he began ordering more items
in larger quantities. There were strings of beads and other jewelry
made of all kinds of material—ivory, agate, cornelian, carved olive bits,
glass, crackled glass, and so on. He also sold finely embroidered Chi-

nese linen, and napkins, bridge sets, Mandarin rugs, *cloisonné* bowls and vases, and a whole range of Chinese handicrafts—some twenty items in all.

The Christmas season of his senior year was his most daring venture. He had sent an extremely large order to China, and when it didn't arrive he became frantic. Finally the goods came, around December first. He practically dropped all his studies and spent his time classifying, pricing, and labeling his products and selling them. For weeks he banked from one hundred to four hundred dollars per day, half of it profit. In all, he earned several thousand dollars profit from his brief importing career, enough to help pay his way through college and the first year of graduate school.

During his freshman year at the University, Carl had several dates with Helen Elliott, one of his childhood playmates, the girl from Oak Park who had seen him read before her second-grade class. Since the Rogers and Elliotts lived a block apart in Oak Park, Carl and Helen had known each other throughout grammar school. When the Rogers moved to the country, they didn't see one another for four years; but meeting again at the University, he found Helen "tall, graceful and very attractive. . . . She was my first date in college, largely because I was too shy to date a stranger." Later, as he did date a few other girls, he came to appreciate "her gentleness, her straightforwardness, her thoughtfulness—not a brilliant academic glow, but a willingness to think openly about real issues, while I was caught up in the desire to appear scholarly. I can remember being ashamed of her sometimes in social groups because she seemed lacking in general and academic information."

As each exposed the other to new interests, their friendship deepened. On hikes and picnics Carl showed Helen the world of nature that he loved. She taught him to dance and derive some enjoyment from social events. He began writing to her in the summer of 1920, and they continued to date throughout the following year at Wisconsin. Busy with his school work, Boys' Club, and religious activities, he confined his dating almost exclusively to Helen, while she continued to date several others. At the end of their sophomore year he noted, ". . . tho I haven't been such a fool as to fall in love, I must say that I like Helen very well. I hope, surely hope she will change her present plans and decide to come back next year, because I'd like to carry the thing a bit further."

Helen did not return the next year, but "the thing" did go a bit further. In November he wrote, "I have found a small portion of myself missing; it seems that a piece, at least, of my heart is in the slender hand of a certain young lady named Helen. It is a great life, I imagine, if you follow Emerson's advice, and 'give all to love.' I think I will try it someday."

Helen had been an art student at the University. She had considerable talent in painting and design—a talent she continued to cultivate throughout her life. After two years at Wisconsin she transferred to the Chicago Academy of Fine Arts to learn to be a fashion artist and thus earn a living. It was a two-year course of study, and she lived at home in Oak Park during that time. Except for vacations and occasional weekends, then, Carl and Helen's courtships had to be carried on through correspondence. In December of his junior year he wrote in his journal:

> I am making a particular effort these days to keep any thought of Helen out of my mind as much as possible, and get my work done. I appreciate, I think, that my life is mine to forge out, and I've got to forge it out now while it's hot, into the kind of a weapon I plan to make it. I'm bound that that is going to be my main business and everything else is incidental, as far as I can make it so. . . . But while uttering these noble sentiments, I may add that if I don't get a letter from Helen tomorrow, I'll be as dejected as I was when I didn't get one today. Goldarn that little cuss without any clothes that goes around with a bow and arrow!

By January, at about the time he discovered he would be going to China, he also had discovered the full extent of his feelings for Helen: "She is a splendid girl, fine looking, with a beautiful face that is a good deal more than pretty—she has a great fund of common sense, that priceless article—she is bright, rather deep thinking than witty—she is neat and has excellent taste in everything—she is a good housekeeper —she is a fine Christian girl. . . . In short, I love her, and I love her very deeply, tho not with as fine and deep a love as I hope we may have some day, when I am sure it is mutual."

He proposed to her before leaving for China. She put him off. She was quite fond of Carl, but she was also a practical person. It seemed fairly certain that Carl was heading toward religious work and probably the ministry. She did not feel cut out to be a minister's wife; feeling neither as spiritually or intellectually inclined as she imagined the role called for. Yet she liked him a lot and was undecided. So she asked that they postpone a decision until after his return from the Orient.

Having always been a shy person, Carl had little confidence about his relationships with women in general, and Helen in particular. While he knew he loved her, he hardly dared hope that the feeling was mutual. They corresponded heavily throughout his trip. For Helen the correspondence was a help to understanding and appreciating Carl as never before. He, not knowing this, sometimes wondered if he had been wise to tell her of his feelings. "Since then there have been times when I felt sure she loved me, and times when I have felt she only cared for me as for any other friend. The real truth, I think, lies somewhere in between." In words that he might have used years later to describe the therapeutic relationship, he added, "It is a wonderful experience, this exploring, with fear and trembling, the depths of another personality. It is wonderful what unexpected riches we sometimes find."

During the period of recuperation after his hospitalization, Carl lived at home and was therefore able to see Helen quite frequently, although it meant a twenty-five mile drive, each way, over terrible roads. During this time the love became mutual. In late fall he wrote in his journal, "Two weeks ago last night, Oct. 29th, the world changed. The most wonderful miracle in the universe took place—for Helen told me that she loved me." Love, in that era of courtship, went hand in hand with marriage; they were engaged that night. In later years Carl described that evening and the feelings that went with his realization of their mutual love as one of the peak experiences of his life.

For the next two years, Carl and Helen saw each other as frequently as possible. Although distance often kept them apart, and the telephone was considered too expensive a means of communication, a two-cent stamp was sufficient to carry their love long distance. From 1922 to 1924 he wrote her 169 letters and she sent 85 to him. Their love continued to deepen, as he described in his journal three months after the engagement. "There have been times when we have been together—like last Wednesday night—when it has just seemed to both of us that we have loved each other with an intensity that simply couldn't be measured—when mind and soul and body are just flooded in a mighty tide of love. And then there are often times when we have opened the secret chambers of our personalities to each other, and oh, the treasures I've found hidden in those inner sanctuaries! And there are other times when our love means simply the satisfying companionship of two lovers who understand each other. But in all its aspects and variations, it is growing more beautiful, more precious each day. And she is, too."

During the half year at home, after his hospitalization, he wrote, "At home, there is continually, whether spoken or unspoken, the clash of different types of personalities—liberal vs. conservative—and it has been a joyous relief to have a lover who is as deeply sympathetic as Helen. I have at times stood in great need of just such a safety valve."

Their correspondence shows what a safety valve she was. He explored his feelings and ideas with her on far-ranging topics, from the tensions at home to the world situation. Some excerpts from his letters illustrate vividly many of the significant themes in his life at that time.

The moving away from his parents. Referring to a letter from his mother he wrote,

Her letter sounded tired, and she said she had been in bed Tues., Wed., and Thurs. And the thing that worries me is that the letter I wrote her about Walt probably arrived Monday. Cause and effect? Je ne sais pas. I don't know whether I feel more like crying or more like swearing about it. I wrote that letter so carefully I thought it couldn't possibly hurt anyone's feelings, and all I did was to beg that they should try and see things from Walt's point of view, because if they didn't he *would* be apt to drift away from them. He and I are so much alike I know how he feels. And then in order to meet one of Mother's pet answers—that she's sorry she hasn't brought us up more as we think we ought to be brought up —I added that nothing I said was any criticism of our bringing up. It was because all of us, Walt included, have been brought up to be *men,* that we do try and stand on our own feet intellectually as well as in other ways. I was fool enough to think that the letter might clear things up a bit. I might have known better. Towards the close of her letter Mother says, "Thank you for your letter regarding Walt—Am sorry you feel as you do about your early life and home." That is all. But she couldn't have slapped much harder. . . . Oh well, what does it all matter? I'm an ass to think I can change things at home, or that I can ever do anything to make father and mother anything but unhappy. And I certainly have no reason to bother you with all of it, but I have no apology to make. I had to talk to somebody. It's lots of fun to be a black sheep.

His self-concept. After quoting a letter of recommendation to graduate school, which described him as "one of a very small group of the most promising men I know in the present student generation who are headed for the ministry . . ." and added, "To unusual qualities of mental keenness and fearlessness, he adds still rarer qualities of heart and spirit that, in my judgment, qualify him unusually for religious leadership in the coming generation," Carl told Helen how the writer "quite outdid himself in trying to make them believe I was somebody.

And like all pats on the back, it makes one feel for a little while that possibly he is good for something. Even tho he may know better."

His fun-loving, robust side. At the fraternity initiation "they had a bunch of crazy stunts, tests for us to pass through, etc. Some of them were dandy, and in one of them I had a corking time. It was a blind-folded boxing match between two of us pledges. After a few seconds of fighting I got what proved to be a brilliant hunch. I slipped past my real opponent and started pummeling one of the active members who was helping to form the ring to keep us in. Before they could shove me back into the ring I had given several of them some dandy swats, pretending that I thought I was fighting my opponent. I sure did have fun during the two rounds."

His commitment. Just back from a campus YMCA meeting, he wrote,

All their plans seemed so trivial . . . his deepest idea of change in Y policy was that we should fix up a parlor for members only and arrange for other privileges. Oh *Hell!!!* . . . And then at great length plans for the frosh mixers were discussed, and how we could entertain the frosh, and what we should do about the freshman banquet, etc. . . . The churches are split wide open on the questions of whether a man can think in modern terms and still be a Christian. Martial law is on in Oklahoma because a large body of Protestant "Christians" [the Ku Klux Klan] believe that the only solution for the Catholic, Jewish and alien problem is to flog out of the state those other groups. Europe is breeding hell for future generations because France thinks that the way to insure peace is to throttle Germany until she pays her last cent. An editorial writer in the Trib condemns the latest modern language New Testament because the old St. James version is good enough. And yet with the thousand and one problems of our day begging for a Christian solution, we sit around and twiddle our thumbs and wonder whether an old Haresfoot act would be entertaining for the frosh, or whether we can't find some clever fellow who can put on a little act of his own.

His empirical side, his desire to find the truth.

And the one big thing both of us must do now is to bend every effort to finding out something about this old, old riddle of Life and what it is all about. There will be plenty of time for affirming things later on, but the preparation for that will be to question clear to the bottom every doubt we have. If there is a doubt about God let's follow it out into every ramification we can until we have settled whether, for us, God does or does not exist. If there is a question about prayer let's ferret the thing out until we know either that prayer has no value, or that it has some value in releasing latent power already within us, or that it supplies us with power from outside. If there is some doubt as to whether the principles of Jesus will work, let's observe in our own lives and in the lives of others, and in the history of nations and peoples, whether they do or do not work better than the methods he condemned.

Most of all, the letters reveal Carl's caring and loving side. Excerpts from two letters and a poem he wrote for Helen capture the flavor.

I'm so thankful I have a girl whom I can love in so many ways. It makes me gasp sometimes when the realization of what a sweetheart I have grips me. I like some girls because they are practical. I like some because with all their education they are still unselfish and thoughtful of others. I like some girls because they are capable of big things, full of semi-dormant possibilities. I like some girls because they are good looking and some because they are good sports. And I like some because they are strong minded and strong in character, not afraid of other opinions, nor afraid to express their own. And when with all that, one finds a girl who has the dearest gray eyes, and slender tapered hands which handle things just as the mind behind them handles problems—delicately, yet with the sureness and firmness that ought to go with an artist's touch—when one finds all that, I say, how can one do otherwise than say with all that is in him—*I love you.*

The poem is one of several he wrote during this period.

To A Gray-Eyed Goddess

In Sappho's time and Sophocles'
The gray-eyed goddess men sought to please
And lyrics, rhymes, and satires keen
They dedicated to fair Athene.

No lofty lyrics mine—yet deep
Within my heart of hearts, I keep
Love, and hope, and great desires,
The stuff, I think, for lyric fires.

And if from that heap a flickering light
Lifts a white arm to the night
And smoky threads of fragrance rise,
I dedicate them to your sweet gray eyes.

Finally:

If you had a sweetheart that meant all the world to you, and that sweetheart had a birthday, what would you say? Would you try and tell her how deliciously sweet her kisses were, or would you try to describe that joyous dancing love-smile that lights her face when she is completely happy in the arms of her lover? Of course if you were a poet there would be no question about what to do. A dainty little lyric that would sing like my heart sings when I think of her, and the long cool hands of her, and above all in the precious, precious heart of her,—that would be the very thing—if one were a poet. For if you take the coolness and freshness of the April breeze—yes, and the occasional gray sky of April, too; and add the vigor and strength and upward-pushing courage of all that lives in April; and sweeten it with the breath of the woodsy may-flower and make it soft as the underside of a thrush's wing—there you have my sweetheart. Why you couldn't help being born in April, Dearest. It's the very month most like you.

A half century later, when Helen Rogers sent me all these letters, she wrote, "When you read all the passion we poured forth in these letters, you won't believe that we never once went to bed together. I can hardly believe it myself. But that was how it was for us then—it simply had to be *legal.* " It was a different age then in many ways, as one last excerpt indicates. In this letter Rogers unknowingly predicted what much of their life together would be like.

I had the most glorious time last night, although I thought my heart would bust for wanting you. You see I went to bed early, about 10:30, and a little after midnight I was awakened by singing. At first I couldn't imagine where it was but gradually realized that the Varsity Glee Club was serenading the Kappa Delts across the street. I've forgotten the first song, but the second was 'The Bedouin Love Song.' I've always liked that as a poem, but when the words are sung to a haunting melody that carries in it the breath of the desert and the very heartbeats of love— well, they could have sung it over fifty times and I wouldn't have been satisfied. . . . I'm afraid the Bedouins went to my head last night. . . . May we always live as Arabs—never unwilling to fold up our tents—either material or spiritual—and move onward to new lands of promise if we feel the urge.

In his senior year Rogers applied to and was accepted at Union Theological Seminary in New York. He and Helen had every intention of going together. The families disapproved. Married people, they felt, ought to be settling down, with the man holding a steady job and the woman raising a family. The idea of four years of schooling *after* marriage was positively scandalous. Besides, Carl's graduate studies toward the ministry would be demanding enough, without adding to them the obligations and distractions of marriage. Both families thought highly of the match but advised the young couple to wait.

The couple, deeply in love, would not wait—at least, not for their parents' reasons. Helen was somewhat reluctant to give up the promising career as a commercial artist which she had begun six months before. But she finally agreed with Carl that since so much was likely to happen to him during his four years in New York, unless they could share these experiences together, they would very likely grow in different directions. Against their parents' advice, they were married on August 28, 1924, at Helen's sister and brother-in-law's home in River Forest, Illinois. For their honeymoon, they piled all their belongings into Carl's new Model T coupe and drove east to New York City.

CHAPTER 3
The New York City Years
1924-1928

Driving to New York City in their own car was a great adventure for the new couple. Before the wedding Carl had given Helen a book on sex and marriage—an avant-garde thing to do at the time. Nevertheless both partners were extremely naive. "Whether in spite of or because of our lack of sophistication," Rogers later wrote, "we had a delightful honeymoon."

The Morningside Heights area on Manhattan's Upper West Side was (and it still is) a center of university life when the Rogers arrived in 1924. Broadway separated Barnard College and Union Theological Seminary to the west from Columbia University to the east. Dormitories for married students were practically nonexistent then; but arriving just before classes began, they managed to find "the world's smallest apartment in New York" on the ground floor of the Cathedral Ayrcourt Apartments at 540 West 123rd Street. A large vacant lot of solid rock (now the site of the Jewish Theological Seminary) and Broadway separated them from Union, while six flights of stairs separated them from the roof of their apartment house, where they would dry their clothes and, later, the diapers.

For about four and a half dollars both of them could have a splendid evening on the town. They would begin with a full course dinner for a dollar apiece at their favorite French restaurant on Amsterdam Avenue, and then ride the subway, for a nickel each, down to Times Square. On Monday nights they could get theater tickets at half price at Gray's Drug Store, where, if they were lucky, they could get two of the cheapest seats for a dollar and seventy-five cents. A pound of their favorite peppermint patties, for fifty-nine cents, would top off the evening.

The city proved to be an exciting place for them both. Helen wrote that "the thrill of exploring the big city with its many cultural advantages of the theatre, the Art Museums, the Bohemian area of the Village—as well as the intellectual stimulation of studying under such giants in education as Kilpatrick, Dewey, Fosdick, and McGiffert—had a very freeing quality for two young provincial midwesterners."

Rogers chose Union Theological Seminary because "it was the most liberal in the country and an intellectual leader in religious work." His parents had wholeheartedly opposed this decision, believing "their fundamentalist journals which told them that [Union] was the devil in disguise. . . . My father even tried to bribe me . . . he told me that if I should happen to choose to go to Princeton Seminary, which was of course the outstanding Fundamentalist seminary at the time, then he would be able to pay my way." Rogers resented the offer and indignantly rejected it. "Instead, I took some competitive examinations and won a good scholarship at Union Seminary and we made our plans for going there. My parents were more generous in gifts to help us get underway [they gave the couple a twenty-five-hundred-dollar wedding gift], though it was still necessary for me to earn a considerable amount of money for our expenses."

Rogers had a great deal of respect for Arthur Cushman McGiffert, then head of the Seminary. "He created an exciting philosophical climate at Union Seminary. . . . You were there to do your own thinking and there was no pressure toward an orthodoxy of any kind." McGiffert was also "a remarkable teacher and a profound scholar. His course on 'Protestant Thought before Kant' and other similar courses introduced me to a new level of teaching excellence. As we heard him present the thinking of one philosopher or theologian, we in the class would become convinced that, 'Aha! This is the person with whom he really agrees.' The next week he would present someone else with equal conviction and persuasiveness."

Rogers later wondered if McGiffert "could have done such a beauti-

ful job of presenting others' points of view if he'd had any of his own";
but in the end his students had to think for themselves, which was of
course what McGiffert intended. With experiences like this, Rogers
found Union "a stimulating and exciting place. I made friends, found
new ideas, and fell thoroughly in love with the whole experience."

Helen audited many of Carl's classes, which enabled them to grow
together. One was taught by the famous Harry Emerson Fosdick and
gave them "a feeling for a modern and liberal religion." In the courses
and on their own they read many books together, attended shows, and
discussed all the new ideas to which they were exposed.

Rogers' term papers that year reflected his increasingly liberal thinking. Had his parents read them, their worst fears would have been
confirmed. In a paper he wrote for "Systematic Theology 1," he concluded that Christianity had primarily three dimensions: the person
and life of Jesus of Nazareth, a lofty system of ethics, and an inherent
tendency toward social improvement. "These are the three contributions which I would suggest as the most valuable Christianity has
made. We could now question—do these things give a basis for hailing
Christianity as in any sense the universal or final religion? By no
means. Other religions have given to the world great personalities.
Other religions have high ethical standards. Other religions and quasi-
religions (e.g. Communism) have high social vision. It seems to me
typically Western and very tragic that we have persisted in viewing
Christianity as the one and only religion."

In another paper, written for "Church History 9," he went so far as
to say there was no such thing as Christianity. In an impressive *tour de
force,* he compared Jesus, Peter, Paul, Marcion, Ignatius of Antioch,
Augustine, Hildebrand, Francis of Assisi, Savonarola, John Huss, Eras-
mus, Martin Luther, and Ignatius Loyola on their attitudes toward
public worship, prayer, doctrine, the Church, Jesus Christ, the Bible
and religious authority, immortal life, the Spirit, and the Christian life.
He showed how all these Christian leaders had widely divergent attitudes on almost all of the issues. Thus he concluded: "The Christian
religion has satisfied very different psychological needs in different
men. . . . The important thing is not the religion but the man. . . . The
third conclusion is closely linked with the first two, and forces itself
upon me as I consider the data. It is this; there is no such thing as the
religion of Christianity—the term is simply a name with which we cover
a multitude of religions. No one religion can possibly cover the vast
number of directly opposed ideas which we have uncovered. It is a
confusion in terms to call it one religion. Let us rather seek among this

jumble of religions for a faith which will enrich and vitalize our own lives."

The first year at Union Seminary also reintroduced Rogers to the world of psychology. Harrison Elliot and Grace Loucks Elliot were on the Seminary faculty and very involved in working with individuals and in the group discussion approach. Through them Rogers recognized for the first time that "working with individual persons in a helping relationship could be a professional enterprise." But his major influence in psychology that year came through a young man who was to become a lifelong friend and an extremely important figure in his early professional career.

Goodwin Watson was only a few years older than Rogers and came from a similar midwestern background with strong religious values. As a student at the University of Wisconsin, Watson had known Carl's older brother Ross when the latter was president of the campus Y.M.-C.A. Watson moved to New York and became an Instructor in Religious Education at Union Theological Seminary. In 1925 he moved across the street to Teachers College, Columbia University, where he became an Instructor in Educational Psychology. Throughout a long and distinguished career, in addition to making significant contributions as an educational and social psychologist, Watson served as a key figure in the development of the T-Group and laboratory method of human relations training and of the Union for Experimenting Colleges and Universities, based in Yellow Springs, Ohio.

In 1925 Rogers and Watson were not aware that their careers would parallel and interweave in so many ways. Their first meeting came when Watson crossed back over Broadway to teach a course at Union, with the psychiatrist Joseph Chassell, on "Working with Individuals." Union, Teachers College and the Columbia Graduate School had a very freewheeling exchange program then; faculty and students teaching or taking courses at the neighboring institution was not at all unusual. Watson and Chassell invited many prominent people in New York City to the class to discuss their interest in psychology and their particular type of work with individuals. Whereas a few years earlier, in his correspondence course, Rogers had found psychology to be a dull and lifeless field, now it seemed alive and exciting. The course proved to be a turning point in Rogers' career.

In the summer of 1925 Carl and Helen went to East Dorset, Vermont, where for several months Rogers assumed the position of pastor of a tiny church. This was a customary part of the seminarian's training at Union. Many rural churches could not afford a full-time minister, and in the winter months they often had to share one with several neighboring communities. Union arranged for its students to take over full-time summer pastoral responsibilities in these small churches. The communities were grateful, and the seminarians received important, practical experience.

Rogers' eleven sermons that summer were filled with the latest developments in modern religious thinking. This being the summer of the famous Scopes "Monkey Trial," in Dayton, Tennessee, in which William Jennings Bryan and Clarence Darrow battled over the teaching of the Darwinian theory of evolution in the public schools, Rogers chose to teach his little church something of the "higher criticism." In one sermon, "Three Stories of Creation," he showed how the Book of Genesis contained not one, but *two* stories of creation; therefore, why not recognize the Darwinian theory as a third story and acknowledge the meaning and beauty of all three? On another occasion he preached, "I may doubt whether God spoke as directly to Moses as the naive writer of the book supposed, but I cannot doubt that the message he gave is the message of the universe to every nation. . . ." His sermons (as Jesus' were) were filled with rural and agricultural images and analogies that reflected his own background; but they were also full of his new learnings from psychology. "The psychologists tell us . . ." and similar phrases were frequent.

"I worked very hard on my sermons," Carl later wrote. "Each was a decidedly polished and scholarly product, not particularly appropriate for a small village. I found it absolutely impossible to make my sermons longer than 20 minutes, a fact which disturbed me but for which my congregation was doubtless thankful. . . .

"Helen and I were very much welcomed by the village. The town drunkard had given up his house for the summer in order that we might have it. . . . Helen taught the girls softball and other games that they had never known. I took the boys on hikes and inaugurated a number of activities such as a men's club. We were both involved in many new experiences.

"One of these new experiences was my first encounter with death. A parishioner died of cancer and I thought that I would have to console the family and conduct the funeral services. I was enormously relieved that a neighboring minister was invited to undertake the task and I was not called upon to meet this ultimate problem. I also recall my surprise that the dull son in the family (ten or twelve years of age) became hysterical and went racing around the house laughing at the top of his voice as his reaction to his mother's death.

"Up the road from our house lived a confirmed alcoholic who brought different women into his home at different times. Still further up the road was a woman who was completely psychotic, living with her very unstable son. All in all, this summer gave us a real acquaintance with the range of psychological and personal problems which exist in the ordinary community. It also gave me an increasing interest in understanding these problems, though at that time my understanding was very limited indeed."

During his second year at Union (1925–26) Rogers registered for several courses at Teachers College. Building on his new interest in psychology he took his first course in clinical psychology with Leta Hollingworth and found it fascinating, especially because she seemed to him to be so interested in children and people in general. He also had his first real exposure to progressive education, through the famous William Heard Kilpatrick. Kilpatrick, a student of John Dewey, was the greatest translator and popularizer of his teacher's philosophy. According to historian Lawrence Cremin, "He was by all reports a master at working with classes numbering in the hundreds, managing to engage individuals to the point where both their ideas and their teaching techniques changed radically. And however much he personally detested indoctrination, he seems to have been extraordinarily effective in making disciples. In all he taught some 35,000 students from every state in the Union at a time when Teachers College was training a substantial percentage of the articulate leaders of American education."

Consistent with this description, Rogers found his "Philosophy of Education" course with Kilpatrick "very stimulating indeed—not only the lectures and question and answer periods, but also the small group discussions which were a part of the course." Twenty years later, when students from across the nation would flock to Rogers' huge lecture courses on counseling and psychotherapy at the University of Chicago, his students would describe him in much the same way that he and Cremin described Kilpatrick.

Kilpatrick's and the progressives' influence on Rogers, however, came sooner than that. During his two years at Union Seminary, in order to supplement the income from his scholarship and savings, he worked weekends as the director of religious education at the First

Congregational Church in suburban Mt. Vernon, New York. The community was well educated and middle class and the church modern in its thinking. Average church attendance was about three hundred, average church school attendance a bit more than half of that. When Rogers took over as religious education director, he found the worship services dull and rather sterile. To involve the church school youngsters more in the service and to make the service more gripping and human, he introduced processionals, more organ music, robes for the Choir, and reports from the religious education classes on their projects—all of which helped. But in some of his reading for Union Seminary he noted criticism of the type of worship service that aimed primarily at an emotional-psychological effect, instead of some sort of commitment to social action. He began to doubt the usefulness of the changes he had introduced. On one of his examinations, for "Religious Education 22," he explored some of his new thoughts: ". . . If however one holds the Dewey-Kilpatrick type of educational philosophy, then the meaning is: The work of the church is a type of social education, and the task of the workers is to enrich the experience of those within the group, and make sure that each experience leads out into richer fields. . . . Personally I hold the latter view, and I have done considerable thinking as to what it involves. In the first place it means helping people to solve the immediate problems which they are facing, in the best possible way. For the life of me, I cannot see that there can be any distinction as to the type of problems we help them solve. If their real problem is one of sex adjustment, we cannot turn them toward some problem about God, because that is 'religious.' It means that we regard all of life as our field of education. . . . In the second place this type of approach means that we will encourage a scientific facing of such problems as they bring. When it is realized that this means the facing of the current standards of morality, the belief in God and in religion itself, all as mere hypotheses, and the examination of the evidence for and against, we realize some of the radical ways in which this educational approach is bound to work out."

Again the worship service at the Congregational Church changed its focus, and Rogers encouraged religious education classes to use the group problem-solving approach of the progressives. During the week the children would tackle real problems in their lives and in the community. On Sunday the worship service would be a time of sharing and reflection on these efforts, a time for renewal of faith in their ethical mission, and a time to build a sense of community which comes from group efforts. Rogers thus anticipated by some forty years the changes in church services which would occur widely in the 1960s—primarily the renewed sense of celebration and of community sharing and involvement.

Even his recommendations for the training of religious education teachers showed the influence of the progressives. "Put not your trust in Teacher Training courses as they are presently offered," he wrote in May 1926. "By beginning with the immediate problems of the teachers, by sharing experiences between the new teachers and those who have been longer at it, and by developing further the interest which all have in certain common problems, I believe one will accomplish more actual education than through a formal course. Furthermore, the reading that is done when a person asks for help on a particular problem, is of much greater value than the very small amount of routine reading that is done for a standard Teacher Training Course."

A fellow graduate student, Theodore Newcomb, began to think of Rogers as "an educational radical." Although for the next thirty-five or so years he did not turn again to education as a *primary* focus, it is apparent how deeply Rogers' own teaching style and his subsequent educational thinking have been rooted in the progressive tradition.

While he developed his views on education, religion, and religious education, however, he also became increasingly perplexed by an unavoidable dilemma. If, as he stated above, religious education is primarily progressive social education, and if a scientific examination of all the foundations of religion is essential, then, he wrote, ". . . it seems to me that the policy works itself into a hopeless tangle. In the first place, its scope becomes so wide that it includes almost exactly the territory of the modern school. When the question arises as to which is better equipped to handle this sort of education, it seems to me that the modern school has all the arguments, and that the only excuse for the continuation of the church school is that in many localities there is as yet no conception of modern education in the public schools. In the second place, I am inclined to wonder whether the thoroughly scientific attitude is compatible with the idea of religion. I am afraid that without some "Eternal Verity" which it was unwilling to question, there could be no such thing as religion. Throughout history, religion has struggled to beat off the advances of science, but unsuccessfully. It scarcely seems fair now to say that all that has historically been religion is something else. To me at present it seems suspiciously close to being an unwillingness to face unpleasant facts.

"It is impossible to make plain my position in such a short space and without more time to think it out, but as a summary of my appraisal of this educational approach to religious leadership I should say something like this. From the point of view of social progress, and ultimate human welfare, I should say that it represents a sound and valuable contribution. From the point of view of religion I should say that it was quite subversive of anything that might be called religion, and that it was a grave question as to whether it had any right to work under the aegis of religion."

Rogers' instructor wrote on this paper, "This is a very clear analysis of the problem. Some day I'd be glad to talk with you further on your conclusions." But "some days" are hard to find, and Rogers and several of his peers at Union Seminary were left with many distressing questions. The young men needed answers if they were to remain in their calling. The situation led to what Rogers later described as "an amusing but highly significant venture."

"Knowing universities and graduate schools as I do now—knowing their rules and their rigidities—I am truly astonished at the freedom which was granted us at Union. A group of students, of which I was one, felt that ideas were being fed to us and that we were not having an opportunity to discuss the religious and philosophical issues which most deeply concerned us. We wanted to explore our own questions and doubts and find out where they led. We petitioned the administration that we be allowed to set up a seminar (for credit!) in which there would be no instructor and in which the curriculum would be composed of our own questions. The Seminary was understandably perplexed by this request but they granted our petition. The only restriction was that in the interest of the Seminary a young instructor was to sit in on the course but to take no part in it unless we wished him to be active. This seminar was deeply satisfying and clarifying. It moved me a long way toward a philosophy of life which was my own. The majority of the members of that group, in thinking their way through the questions that they had raised, thought their way right out of religious work. I was one. Theodore Newcomb was another. Various other members of the group have gone on in sociology and psychology. The whole seminar was very freewheeling. It took up profound philosophical, religious and social problems. My own reason for deciding at that time to leave the field of religious work was that although questions as to the meaning of life and the possibility of the constructive improvement of life for individuals were of deep interest to me, I could not work in a field where I would be required to believe in some specified religious doctrine. I realized that my own views had changed tremendously already and would very likely continue to change. It seemed to me that it would be a horrible thing to have to profess a set of beliefs in order to remain in one's profession. I wanted to find a field in which I could be sure my freedom of thought would not be limited."

So, in the fall of 1926, Rogers again crossed Broadway to Teachers College, this time to stay. He had scored highest in his group on both the Thorndike intelligence test and the content examinations required of applicants. Majoring in clinical and educational psychology, he was now able to continue his graduate work at Columbia.

His parents' worst fears had proven true. From the liberal Union Theological Seminary, Carl left the church never to return to any formalized religion. It is a shame, though, that Walter and Julia Rogers did not live until 1967; for if they had, it might have been some small consolation to see their son receive the Distinguished Contribution Award from the American Pastoral Counselors Association.

Their first child, David, was born on March 17, 1926, when Carl was finishing his work at Union. At about this time his ulcer began bothering him again, and they realized that expert medical attention was needed. Consequently Carl, Helen, and David traveled to Rochester, Minnesota, to the Mayo Clinic, where several of the Rogers had been treated and which had the family's highest confidence. A successful operation, a gastro-enterostomy, was performed. Helen rented a room for herself and David near the hospital; so, by running back and forth, she could look after both her recuperating husband and their three-month-old son. They received no help then, financial or otherwise, from Carl's family, a fact which, looking back on the episode, was puzzling to them, as finances were no problem to his parents and as Rochester was not very far from Illinois. Carl's recent decision to leave Union Seminary probably was a factor in the family's remoteness, as well as his history of refusing their help when it was offered.

Still recovering from the operation, Carl and Helen left David with Helen's mother, and went to the Y.M.C.A. Camp in Estes Park, Colorado. There they both conducted a short workshop-course on marital and sexual adjustment. The group with whom they worked was very grateful for the chance to talk freely about their concerns in this area. It was a daring enough venture at that in 1926; but Carl and Helen also passed out a questionnaire to elicit some facts about the participants' sex lives and to generate topics for discussion. They were amazed to discover that the questionnaire, falling into hands outside the group, created quite a stir and almost lost the Y.M.C.A. the support of one of its major contributors.

One reason the Rogers had felt competent to lead the course was the sexual awareness that had recently taken place in their own marriage. Many years later he described how he had become "very dimly aware that though our sexual relationship was great for me, it was not great for her. I realize, though, how little I understood the deeper meaning of her phrases: 'Oh, not tonight'; 'I'm too tired'; 'Let's wait 'till some other time.' There is no doubt the situation could have led to a crisis.

"At this point sheer luck gave us a break, though like most good luck, it needs to be used. In my graduate school, I learned that a psychiatrist, Dr. G.V. Hamilton, needed a few more young married men to complete a research study he was engaged in. Probably there was some pay involved, which would account for my snatching the opportunity so promptly. (Actually the study was a more personalized forerunner of the Kinsey researches, and very well done, though never widely known.) I went to Dr. Hamilton's office for two or three lengthy interviews. He questioned so calmly and easily about every aspect of my sexual development and life, that I gradually found myself talking with almost equal ease. One thing I came to realize was that I just didn't *know* whether my wife had ever had an orgasm. She often seemed to enjoy our relationship, so I *assumed* I knew the answer. But the most important thing I learned was that the things in one's private life which cannot *possibly* be talked about, *can* be talked about, easily and freely.

"So then came the question, could I translate this into my personal life? I began the frightening process of talking—*really* talking—with Helen about our sexual relationship. It was frightening because every question, and every answer, made one or the other of us so vulnerable —to attack, to criticism, to ridicule, to rejection. But we weathered it! Each learned to understand much more deeply the other's desires, taboos, satisfactions, and dissatisfactions, in our sexual life. And while at first it led only to greater tenderness, and understanding, and improvement, gradually it led not only to orgasms for her, but to a full, continuing, satisfying and enriching sexual relationship—in which we could talk out new difficulties as they arose."

Or as Helen wrote, "What I feel was the most fortunate for me was Carl's ability to be open and frank and truthful in facing all our problems, including our sex life. We were able to establish a free communication with each other, never allowing misunderstandings or hurts to fester. It gave us a basis for growth and closeness which has lasted through the years. His ability to listen and be empathic was there in the very first years of our marriage."

As parents they followed the Watsonian behaviorism which was popular then—strict scheduling, little emotional or physical contact, and the like. "It was a period when you were supposed to let a child cry for four hours, if he was on a four hour feeding schedule, no matter what his feelings were. We were influenced by that, though I'm glad to say we didn't always follow it. . . . Fortunately, Helen had enough common sense to make a good mother in spite of all this damaging psychological knowledge." David was an active toddler, and they put him in an experimental nursery school at Teachers College at eighteen months—a rather modern idea which Helen had some guilt feelings about, but which they both thought would be good for him, and would also give them more freedom.

America's first major educational psychologist, E.L. Thorndike, was teaching at Columbia when Rogers transferred there in the fall of 1926. Because of Thorndike's considerable reputation he was eager to take a course with him. He found the lectures interesting, although he was not particularly interested in the subject, the testing of mathematical aptitude. The science of psychology was still in its infancy in the twenties, and the psychology department at "T.C." was dominated by a strong interest in testing. Freud was generally regarded as a dirty word in academic circles. Thorndike and his colleagues saw measurement as being fundamental to the growing science. Intelligence testing was relatively new and quite the rage, as was the creation of new tests and measures for any psychological phenomenon one wanted to study. Goodwin Watson, for his dissertation, had developed a *Measurement of Fair-Mindedness.* Rogers, too, for his dissertation, would develop a new psychological test.

Naturally he had to take his share of statistics courses. When he went to register for the first such course, however, he found it was offered at a very inconvenient hour. Always confident in his intellectual abilities, he decided he could probably bypass the introductory course, and managed to get permission to enroll in the second statistics course, with Professor Ruger. Here he found the lectures terribly abstruse and confusing, and for the first time knew the feeling of not being able to grasp the material. Although he worked hard on his own, he knew there was a strong likelihood of failing the final exam and the course.

He did as best he could on the exam, but was quite certain he had failed. Figuring that under the circumstances he had nothing to lose, at the end of his examination blue book he wrote a scathing criticism of the course and the instructor's method of teaching. He passed, but never knew why.

Testing also played a part in his second course in clinical psychology with Leta Hollingworth. "It was under her supervision that I first came in actual clinical contact with children—testing them, talking with them, dealing with them as fascinating objects of study, helping to make plans for their welfare." He worked especially hard on his first "case" in this practicum, giving the boy many psychometric tests, interviewing him at length, and writing a long and eloquent analysis of the whole situation. Several years later the boy's father telephoned Rogers, explaining that his son was seeing another psychologist and that Rogers' original report would be very helpful. Rogers no longer had the actual report but, as with first love, could not forget his first client. He typed out another lengthy analysis, from memory, and sent it on, shortly thereafter receiving a thank-you note from the psychologist who was impressed, not only that Rogers remembered, but that he had been so perceptive in his observations.

Leaving his studies at Union Seminary had created a financial problem, for he could no longer continue as religious education director in Mt. Vernon. Fortunately, just when he needed it, Rogers received an attractive job offer from Goodwin Watson, whom he later called his "brilliant young sponsor. . . . He was a very good teacher, but I particularly appreciated the fact that he was quite willing to let me go my own way in my graduate work and research."

As Watson described Rogers' job, "The one in which Carl assisted me was entitled 'Orient and Occident: An Opinion Survey.' It was financed by the Institute of Pacific Relations and designed to explore attitudes of numerous American groups (students, business men, farmers, club-women, prisoners, etc.) on domestic and foreign issues relating to China and Japan. Our sampling techniques weren't very sophisticated but we got several thousand replies and tallied them by hand. This was rather typical of the exploitation commonly practiced when graduate students were available as cheap labor. Why was Carl selected? Bright young man, needed to earn money, hard-working, wholly trustworthy, friendly and cooperative."

Rogers remembers how Watson "always had many irons in the fire, and he turned over to me almost complete responsibility for an extensive survey he had initiated. I employed a sizable group of research assistants, conducted the analysis of some very complex material, and organized and wrote the presentation, all under pressure of an unyielding and imminent deadline."

Rogers' training at Teachers College strongly reinforced and advanced his belief in and understanding of the scientific method, which had existed for him ever since his early agricultural experiments. The training also instilled in him a strong respect for the concept of intelligence and for intelligence testing. Over the next decade of working intensively with children, he frequently used terms like "dull," "dull-normal," "average," and "superior" to describe the intelligence of children he had studied. Later on, when he abandoned psychological testing in his clinical work, he stopped using these terms. But even forty years later, describing a "revolutionary program for graduate education," he included "intelligence, perhaps more specifically defined as a high degree of ability in problem solving," as one of the three criteria for selection of students into the program.

Late in 1926 Rogers applied for a Fellowship at the about-to-be-formed Institute for Child Guidance in New York City. In addition to providing a valuable intern experience that would enable him to complete his training as a psychologist and do much of the research on his doctoral dissertation, the Fellowship also carried a salary of twenty-five hundred dollars—just enough to support his family. He won the appointment for the 1927–28 school year; but shortly before the year began, he received "an embarrassed letter from Dr. Frankwood Williams, the psychiatrist who headed the selection committee. He had just discovered that psychiatrists were to get $2500. The Fellowships for psychologists were to be only $1200. It was the financial rather than the professional insult which roused my dander. I wrote him a very strong letter, saying essentially that the Fellowship had been awarded, I had been informed of it, I had made all my personal plans on this basis, I needed the money to support my family. On the strength of my letter he made an exception and I received a $2500 Fellowship."

Throughout his career psychiatrists would often complain that Rogers, a psychologist, was encroaching on their territory. Thus he later commented, "It is interesting and symbolic that I started my professional training—through a fluke—on the same level with psychiatric residents."

Just before beginning work at the Institute, Carl, Helen, and David spent the summer of 1927 in Willoughby, Ohio, where Rogers served both as camp counselor and psychologist at Camp Wawokeye, the summer camp for "problem boys" from the Cleveland Child Guidance Clinic. Theodore Newcomb, one of the members of the student-directed seminar at Union Seminary and later a famous social psychologist himself, was also a counselor at Camp Wawokeye that summer. Newcomb remembered how "One of their recurrent 'problems' was bed-wetting. I remember that all five of my charges, who slept with me in the same tent (on straw mattresses) were so afflicted. The camp had almost no money, and Carl decided to make a 'project' of building a rowboat, with some assistance from the boys. As it was nearly completed, the question arose of what name to give the boat. Although it eventually turned out to be properly seaworthy, as well as goodlooking, it was still untested. I believe it was I who therefore proposed that we name it the S.S. Enuresis—and so it was. Carl, of course, was instantly dubbed 'Captain of the S.S. Enuresis.' "

"Child guidance work was just coming into its own," wrote Rogers, "and an elaborate Institute for Child Guidance was established by the Commonwealth Fund in New York City in order to provide training for such clinical workers." The facility was lavish and impressive, and the Institute employed a large and excellent staff (when the Great Depression came a few years later, the Institute folded). Dr. David Levy, chief of staff, introduced the Rorschach method to this country and was a pioneer in using play therapy with children. Rogers found E.K. Wickman, the chief psychologist, "thoughtful, balanced, a good research worker, genuinely interested in discovering the truth" and always admired his "open-mindedness." The well-known psychiatrist Lawson Lowrey was director of the clinic staff and, along with Levy and Wickman, was helpful to Rogers.

As he described the Institute in his dissertation, "The Institute for Child Guidance offers almost ideal facilities for carrying on any type of research among difficult children. . . . Problem-children in large numbers, widely varying in age, mentality, and behavior, are brought to the Institute for study. Harassed parents, baffled teachers, and perplexed social workers keep its offices filled with youngsters whose behavior is to be diagnosed and treated. . . . The child receives a complete study from the psychiatric, psychological, and physical angles. An exhaustive social history, obtained by competent workers, chronicles the child's behavior and family background as completely as it is possible to do so. This wealth of data about each child is of first importance in conducting research. The large staff of the Institute represents a wide variety of experience and training. They do not represent any one school of psychological thought."

At the Institute, Rogers had considerably more exposure to Freudian thinking than before. It was only eighteen years earlier, in 1909, that Sigmund Freud had first come to America to lecture at Clark University, after which Dr. A.A. Brill worked indefatigably to translate Freud's voluminous writings into English and to popularize his views. Just before the war Freud and the "new psychology" was *the* topic of discussion in Greenwich Village and among New York's intelligentsia; but psychoanalysis caught on much more slowly in medical circles. Rogers characterized the Institute's philosophy as "an eclectic Freudianism," representing many "different shades of psychoanalytic thinking and other psychiatric and psychological views." Although he had a brief interest in psychoanalysis and occasionally used some analytic techniques in his "remedial work" with children, for the most part he was never much impressed with the complex theoretical and analytical system.

He had a variety of experiences at the Institute. Under the supervision of trained psychologists he made complete psychometric examinations of children, utilizing tests as different as the Stanford Binet Intelligence Test, Healy Picture Completion Test, Ferguson Form Boards, Porteus Maze, Gates Primary Reading, and Stanford Achievement. He helped conduct a psychological survey of a school. He took part in case conferences. He was exposed to the many different points of view of the various psychologists, psychiatrists, psychoanalysts, and social workers who were invited to speak to the Institute's staff. "Alfred Adler lectured to us, for example, and shocked the whole staff by thinking that an elaborate case history was not necessary. I remember how misinformed I thought he must be, since we routinely took case histories 50 to 70 pages in length."

On another occasion, early in his stay at the Institute, he and the other interns were meeting in a seminar with staff member Dr. Marion Kenworthy. The interns wanted to make some changes in their program or, at least, discuss certain problems of concern to them. Kenworthy, instead of dealing with their questions, chose to interpret their behavior to them. It was natural, she said, that they would feel somewhat rebellious in a new situation, in having to deal with a woman, and so on. It was kindly but, as Rogers saw it, "a definite indication that we were small boys and we would get over it and she knew best, etc. Being on the receiving end of that kind of interpretation, which had some truth in it, showed me how demeaning and degrading it was. We might have been willing to give in a bit up to that point, but after that we wouldn't give in come hell or high water."

"I also began to realize that I had real clinical skill, both in dealing with individuals and with colleagues. I remember one case conference with an uncooperative caseworker from outside, discussing a boy with whom I had been working. I was late because of a sleet storm that morning. When I arrived the conference was obviously stalemated because the outside worker was totally unsympathetic and uncooperative. I won her over by my explanation of the situation, though I was the youngest and least experienced member of the conference group. It was this boy who was the first individual with whom I carried on regular therapy (though when psychologists did it, it was called remedial work or some such name). I made real progress in helping him, though I was full of the psychoanalytic theories which I was trying out at the time."

His year at the Institute was "extremely stimulating," but not without its conflicts. While Teachers College, where he was still taking courses, emphasized measurement and statistics, the Institute for Child Guidance emphasized emotions and personality dynamics. Having to resolve the tension between the two forces—understanding the person from the outside through objective testing versus understanding from the person's own perspective through sensitive interviewing —was very important in Rogers' growth. His resolution was to combine both emphases, as he did in his doctoral dissertation, *Measuring Personality Adjustment in Children Nine to Thirteen Years of Age.* Using and adapting many of the questions that psychologists and psychiatrists normally would ask children in clinical interviews, he constructed a paper-and-pencil test which helped reveal the child's attitude toward: (1) himself and his abilities, (2) his relationship to his companions, (3) his family, and (4) all of these, as revealed by the content of his daydreams and fantasies. There were separate test forms for boys and girls. He gave the test to about two hundred children, developed norms for scoring, measured its reliability and validity—in short, created an instrument which the Institute for Child Guidance found useful and practical and which Teachers College judged as being objective and scientific. The following excerpt from his dissertation is part of a "preliminary diagnosis" of Edward L., Anglo-Saxon, Age 9, Grade 4A, I.Q. 115, based solely on the boy's test responses. It presents a fairly good picture of the nature of the test. The boy scored third highest in Rogers' sample on overall maladjustment, but as Rogers wrote,

No scores are necessary to show that Edward is a badly adjusted boy. His test is full to bursting with unusual and abnormal responses. His three wishes are to be stronger, brighter, and better looking, and this evidence of personal inadequacy is borne out by a great many bragging responses. He is evidently sensitive about his looks and feels he is not at all good-looking. He refuses to answer the question in response to which he would rate himself on his brightness. He is extremely anxious "to be a very great person, and to do great things that people will talk about."

Edward brags not only of his accomplishments, but also of his lack of them, especially when answering questions in the realm of social adjustment. He admits that he does not know how to play games, and says he has no wish to be different. He is not popular and he does not care. When asked how many friends he would like to have he replies, "None." . . . On the other hand he says, "I just can't stand it if people don't like me."

A daydreaming tendency is indicated by his rather extravagent ambitions—to be a movie star, a cowboy, an aviator—and by his imaginary companions, preference for solitary play, etc. He gives considerable evidence of a tension in the family area. He likes his mother best, his youngest sister next, and his father comes third in his affections. However, he would prefer to go with his father to the circus.

The test gives a picture of a boy who feels very inferior personally, who seems almost completely isolated socially, who evidently indulges in a good deal of fantasy, and is not entirely happy at home. He seems to be a very serious case.

This preliminary diagnosis made from the test was later confirmed in almost every respect by an extensive case study on the boy. The test proved to be a useful instrument. It was published in 1931 by Association Press, the YMCA publishing house, along with a manual for its administration. Right away several clinics around the country began using it, as did many schools and private clinicians. As of 1971 over 430,000 copies of the test were sold, and even when the test was forty years old, it continued to sell over 15,000 copies a year, not including the Australian, Portugese, French, and Italian editions.

Rogers had gathered most of the data on the test by 1928, shortly before leaving New York City. However, "in the excitement of a new job and all, I came very close to not finishing up my degree. Goodwin Watson jolted me on that finally . . . in late '29 or '30, I suppose . . . said if I was ever going to get my degree I better get the darn thing out of the way. I had all the data but I had never worked it up or written my thesis. So I finally did that while I was working in Rochester and got my Ph.D. in '31."

* * *

In the spring of 1928 Rogers was looking for a job. Positions for psychologists were not plentiful, and at one point he felt he might have to accept a position at Culver Military Academy in Indiana. In mid-April, leaving David with Helen's mother, who had moved to New York City after her husband's death, Carl and Helen drove to Rochester, New York, for an interview at the Rochester Society for the Prevention of Cruelty to Children.

Besides leaving David, they also left springtime and tulips behind in New York City. They encountered snow, slush, hazardous driving conditions, and even a frozen radiator when they stopped for the night on the way up. While Carl spent the day interviewing, Helen hunted around for a suitable apartment, should the job work out. David was two and very, very active, Helen was again pregnant, and they wanted an apartment with a roomy yard, big enough for the children to romp in and for a flower and vegetable garden.

He was offered the position, which involved working with delinquent and problem children—diagnosing their difficulties, making plans for their treatment, and perhaps conducting some "treatment interviews" with them. He was a bit depressed by the Children's Shelter or detention home where many of them would be staying while he worked with them; but all in all the job followed logically from his training and he thought he would like the work. That he would be isolated from university life and from stimulating professional contacts did not deter him; nor did the twenty-nine-hundred-dollar salary, low even in those days. Throughout his career Rogers has tended to follow his instincts about job moves, operating on the assumption that if he were doing work he enjoyed, everything else would fall into place. He accepted the position.

Helen had mixed reports to give on her day. She had not succeeded in finding an apartment or house to rent, but she did find a house she wanted to buy. He went back with her to survey the situation. They had not come to Rochester prepared to buy a house, but the builder trusted them. With a twenty-five-dollar cash deposit and their names on the dotted line, they were the proud future owners of a brand-new little eighty-five-hundred-dollar Dutch Colonial home, with a big yard in the back.

It had been quite a weekend—a new job and a new house in the space of a few hours. Their parents and, in fact, many of their friends were appalled at the haste with which both decisions were made. Such impetuosity, however, was rather typical of them both. As Rogers described them, "Both of us have clear (though often intuitive rather than conscious) feelings as to what we want. When we examine something—a position, a home, a plan for a trip, a piece of furniture—it either 'clicks' or it does not. Our independent reactions are nearly always similar, and when we both feel that something is 'right' we have rarely been mistaken. When it does seem 'right' we make an immediate decision and move ahead. Neither of us has ever been troubled by backward looks, or by regrets. We have, in some significant psychological sense, always seemed to 'face forward.' "

Although Rogers' parents disapproved of their taking on a big mortgage, they eventually offered to help; but he would have no part of it. Rochester, New York, it would be—for the next twelve years—on their own.

CHAPTER 4
The Rochester Years
1928-1939

The early 1900s had seen enormous growth in the fields of psychology, psychiatry, and social work.

In psychology the two major thrusts were, first, testing and measurement and, second, experimental work in the laboratory, using animals to explore various theories of learning. Clinical psychology, the treatment of people with problems, was just coming into its own, but was still a minor part, if any part at all, of most psychologists' work. Psychological testing usually played an important part in clinical work; psychotherapy, however, was not widely used.

In psychiatry, in the late 1800s, most M.D.s, psychiatrists, psychopathologists, alienists, and neurologists were still seeking organic causes for the various neuroses, psychoses, hysterias, and anxieties in humans. They used shock treatments, drugs, medications, and hypnosis as the primary means of treatment. Freud graduated from these practices and went on to revolutionize our thinking about the causes of psychological problems and the manner of treating them. His disciples, in America and abroad, often modified his theories and techniques, and various schools of analysis and therapy were formed. By the late 1920s, through the efforts of this small minority of the medical profession, psychoanalysis and psychotherapy had achieved a firm foothold in several metropolitan centers along the eastern seaboard of the United States.

Along with psychology and psychiatry, the field of social work was achieving professional status and developing its techniques in a more rigorous fashion. In the nineteenth century, social work had moved through several phases, emphasizing charity work, institutional care, and socioeconomic legislation. By the turn of the century the number of social agencies dealing with children's problems had proliferated dramatically in almost every large city. The courts, hospitals, orphanages, "shelters," "reform schools," foster homes, school systems, religious institutions, youth clubs, settlement houses, charity organizations, psychological and psychiatric clinics all had resources to offer the child in trouble.

But the poor or troubled family rarely knew about all these available resources, let alone how to go about using them. A professional person was needed to serve as a liaison between the child or family in trouble and the helping agencies of the community. She (for it was predominantly women who entered this field) would need a background in sociology, economics, psychology, and child care, a knowledge of the new techniques of diagnosis, placement, and counseling, and considerable skill in working with people under stress. Thus the roles of "case worker" or "social case worker" and later "psychiatric social worker" came into prominence, and social work came to be viewed, more widely than ever before, as a legitimate new profession. In the first quarter of the century many colleges and universities instituted departments or schools of social work, and the beginnings of scientific research in the field were undertaken.

In many clinics and institutions the three fields of psychology, psychiatry, and social work joined forces in diagnosing and treating individual problems. This was the case in Rochester, New York, when Carl Rogers joined the Child Study Department of the Society for the Prevention of Cruelty to Children, thus situating himself at the confluence of three new professions, each in its infancy, each presenting opportunities for pioneering research on methods of helping children and their parents in trouble.

And troubled children there were. Each year an average of six to seven hundred children, mostly lower- to lower-middle-class whites, came or were sent to the Society for help. They were referred by dozens of social agencies throughout the community: parents, the social worker,

Children's Court, the schools, private charitable organizations, medical authorities, and the like. They represented every behavior and personality problem imaginable: enuresis, stealing, lying, extreme sex curiosity, sex perversions, sadism toward animals or younger children, extreme withdrawal or aggressiveness, incest, stammering, eating dirt and worms, and numerous other comparable problems.

To help these children were five departments within the Society. "Intake" made the initial contact with the child and filled out the required paperwork. The Medical Department gave each child a complete physical examination. When exploitation or neglect was part of the problem, the child would be seen and the case investigated by the Protective Department. Child Placing supervised the foster homes, adoptions, and the temporary placements of children. In almost every case the child also would visit the Child Study Department of which Rogers was a member in 1928 and the director by 1929.

His first introduction to a given child might be no more than a few words or phrases on the referral card forwarded by Intake to the Child Study Department.

"Stealing, truancy from school, sex play."
"Boy has thrown knife at mother, threatens to kill her—"
"Child mentally retarded (?) and deaf; present foster mother finds him unmanageable."
"Girl very promiscuous. Is she committable?"
"Needs vocational guidance."
"Delinquency (purse-snatching)."

These descriptions conveyed little of the actual circumstances. From talking with the child and perhaps the parent, Rogers or his co-workers would soon understand more about the child's situation. Dick was one boy Rogers interviewed shortly after coming to Rochester. He later described him in a case study:

An eight-year-old boy backed into a corner of the schoolroom, face livid, eyes partly closed, hatred in every line of his body, hurled an eraser at his teacher and shouted, "You shut your mouth! You can't make me do it!"

This particular tantrum on Dick's part was caused by the teacher's request that he go to his seat. Other tantrums, equally violent, made him a very difficult problem in school. Dick's diagnosis of the situation given in one of his better moments was "Satan had my father. I have a temper just like him. It's better to have a temper—you need it. When the Devil comes around, I just have to get mad." Dick had other satanic afflictions. He had a mania for knives and slept with one under his pillow, often threatening what he would do with it. He had always had night terrors, which would waken him screaming with fright. He showed a deeply sadistic streak, enjoying cruelty to pets and small animals and continually poking, teasing, and pinching children at school.

Needless to say, there was ample home background to explain Dick's behavior. The mother, an attractive woman, had spent most of her childhood in an orphanage, and her adult years were given over to compensating for the boredom of the institution. Her promiscuity engendered a deep jealousy in Dick's father, and his fearful temper storms gave the boy the pattern for his behavior. The father's cruelty was known throughout the rural neighborhood, and his almost insane torture of some of the farm animals makes gruesome reading. More than once he threatened to kill his family, and his beatings terrorized the children. When he was sent to the penitentiary on a charge of rape, the mother became even more promiscuous and also more religious. She joined a revival mission, taught the children large portions of the Bible, and became a very earnest worker. The whole situation was so extremely unsatisfactory for the children that they were removed by court order. . . .

Another boy Rogers saw during his first years in Rochester was John. We will hear more of both Dick and John later.

John came from a slovenly home in which there was little or no discipline. At the time that he and his sister, aged seven and ten respectively, were removed from their mother because of her flagrant immorality, most of John's life had been spent in "running wild" in a very questionable neighborhood. The home situation had been such as to stimulate in the boy an overwhelming curiosity in regard to sex. The mother had lived with several men, and John had spent hours at the keyhole watching his mother and her latest companion, or the actions of the boarder and his sister. An atmosphere of filthy sex talk in the home added further elements to his fund of information, and even this was supplemented by spying on older boys and girls in the neighborhood. John early learned that his sex knowledge gave him a source of power and he was not slow in using it. He achieved a reputation among children of his own age, not only for his talk, but for his actions. He had persuaded several of the small girls in the neighborhood to engage in sex experiments with him. A complaint was lodged with the police when he initiated two other boys in various sex perversions. His language was a scandal in the neighborhood, so much so that even the firemen, with whom John loved to lounge about, chastised him on several occasions as an aid to public morals.

When seen in the clinic, it was felt that John was more saturated with an unwholesome and smutty attitude toward sex, and was more aggressive in sex matters, than any boy who had ever entered the department.

Within a few moments after his introduction to the psychologist, he was inquiring whether that gentleman was married, and whether he slept with his wife!

What could be done to help these children?

There sat the young clinical psychologist, confronted by real-life problems and responsibilities that went far beyond his training. The helping professions themselves were not much older than twenty-six-year-old Carl Rogers, who looked around him and saw that for every twenty books which explained the causes of behavior problems, there was only one that dealt with their treatment. There were several other comparable clinics around the country, but each of these, too, was trying in its own way to develop effective techniques, and none had any definitive answers.

For Rogers, then, the Rochester years were a decade of experimentation. Will this work? Is it effective? These were the questions he asked himself and his staff, again and again, throughout the years. The principle that guided his efforts was *pragmatism,* a quality nurtured by his childhood experiments with scientific agriculture. Any method of helping children was worthy of consideration if it seemed potentially effective. The theoretical base of a helping approach was far less important to him than the results the approach yielded. Whether the professional was a psychologist, psychiatrist, or social worker mattered little if that person had insights or techniques which could be of help.

Almost universally accepted at this time was the belief that the first step in helping problem children was to understand thoroughly the nature of the problem. Rogers was so convinced of the critical importance of diagnosis that, early in his stay in Rochester, he was wont to tell PTA and community groups that their clinic was "rather similar to a garage —you brought in a problem, received an expert diagnosis, and were advised how the difficulty could be corrected."

Friendly questioning and a look at the child's records might reveal a great deal about the child and the family background; but the child's mental and emotional life might still remain mostly concealed. Given his Teachers College background, Rogers believed that psychological testing could reveal many of the hidden factors, and such tests were used as a matter of course in the Child Study Department. No one set of tests was administered; rather, depending on the particular child, tests were selected that would help elucidate his particular problems or situation. Intelligence tests were used most frequently, along with reading and mathematical achievement tests, mechanical aptitude tests, interest inventories and, beginning in 1931, when it was published, Rogers' own Personal Adjustment Inventory.

The more diagnoses he made, however, the more dissatisfied he became with the process. He wanted a consistent, organized, diagnostic approach—not one based on the personal intuition or guesswork of the psychologist or case worker. He also wanted an approach toward diagnosis that went beyond the ideological biases of various schools of thought. Freudians, for example, tended to give enormous weight to early childhood influences. Sociologically inclined workers gave greater weight to the neighborhood, school, and peer group. Other psychologists relied almost entirely on psychological testing. In an attempt to cut across ideological boundaries and take into consideration *all* the factors that could significantly be influencing the child's present behavior, Rogers developed a new method of diagnosis—the "component factor method."

In the component factor method, eight factors influencing the child's development and present behavior were considered: Heredity, Physical factors, Mentality, Self-Insight, Family emotional tone, Economic and cultural factors, Social experience, Education and supervision. On each factor, children were rated on a seven-point scale (minus three to plus three), based on how the child compared to seven standardized descriptions for that factor. The psychologist's ratings would be placed on a grid with an "x" to indicate how the child was rated on each factor at the time of diagnosis. Then an arrow would be drawn to indicate what degree of change would be realistic to expect, given the situation. A year or more later the actual changes which had occurred in the child's situation could be compared to the predicted results, on each of the eight factors.

The component factor method is a good example of that eclectic pragmatism which often led Rogers to transcend older ideologies and techniques. His eight-factor method did not deny Freudian or behavioral or sociological theories; it simply incorporated them. The approach also shows Rogers' concern for science and the scientific method. He was not content with vague thinking about the causes of children's problems. He wanted every possible factor clearly spelled out, so that it could be considered, and so that one psychologist's ratings could be open to the scrutiny of other professionals who might want to double-check the work. Finally, the method illustrates Rogers' lifelong concern with evaluating the results of his work. By using the factor chart again a year or more after the original ratings workers could evaluate not only the validity of the original predictions, but also the efficacy of the treatment. By averaging many individual cases on one chart, the results of treatment for large numbers of children could be determined, too, thereby assessing the efficacy of an entire clinic.

Although its validity, reliability, and usefulness were clearly demonstrated, and Rogers and his colleague Chester Bennett publicized the method in several well-received speeches and a paper, the component-factor method never caught on. Whether clinical workers were reluctant to give up their biases about the primary causes of children's problems or whether they did not want to look at their actual, possibly disappointing results or whether they did not want to invest the time or energy that follow-up work required, one may speculate. Nevertheless the method enabled Rogers and his colleagues to examine much more critically the work *they* were doing. Just how effective is our treatment? What degree of change is realistic to expect along the different factors? Why are our predictions consistently overly optimistic on this factor and overly pessimistic on that factor? What is the significance of this surprising trend we have just discovered? How do our results compare with those of other clinics? Important questions like these could be generated and sometimes answered by the component factor chart. "So far as diagnostic techniques are concerned," he wrote, "there is no best method; there are only methods which need testing and experiment and revision." His own work in this area set a good example.

After Rogers had talked with the child and parent, the psychological examinations had been administered, the case records had been perused, and the diagnosis seemed complete, the original question remained: How can we be of help to this child?

The answer was not provided by the psychologist alone. Once the child had been seen by the Child Study Department, a case conference was called, with a representative of each agency that had an interest in the child present. Thus, at one case conference, there might be the social worker, a foster parent, and a doctor. At another there might be a probation officer, the "cottage parent" from a reform school, and a member of the Society's Protective Department. In each case Rogers or one of the other psychologists from his department would conduct the conference, acting, as he described it, as "a catalytic agent . . . to bring out the pertinent experience of each conference member, and also contribute the findings of the clinic in regard to the child's abilities and attitude and the significant patterns evident in his behavior. . . . Rightly managed, such sharing conferences became the best and most practical means of using and strengthening the co-operative relationships, with a wide group of agencies offering a range of treatment services."

Years later Rogers noted that writing up these cases was "the experience which perhaps contributed most to my psychological writing [skill]. . . . Frequently these reports had to meet a deadline of a court hearing or agency decision. If they were to have any influence they had to be accurate, penetrating, comprehensive, persuasive in presenting the reasons for our recommendations, clear and interesting enough to read, and able to stand the test of time, since we would continue to be in contact with both the agency and the child, often for long periods."

The goal of the case conference, a strategy which Rogers had learned in New York City and then introduced in Rochester, was to arrive at an effective treatment plan for the child. Generally treatment fell into one or more of three categories—changing the child's living situation, modifying the child's living situation, or direct therapy. Each of these approaches constituted a major portion of Rogers' work.

The first two types of treatment were commonly thought of as "environmental" treatment or therapy. The more extreme of the two involved a major change in the child's living situation—to a foster home, from one foster home to another, to an institution, or a return to the child's own home. When Rogers introduced a research program to look more closely at the work they were doing in their clinic, one of the surprising findings was that one of the first steps in treatment for over half the children who came to them was to select a totally new environment for the child—a practice similar to that used in many other child guidance clinics at the time.

Dick and John, whose cases are described above, were both boys for whom Rogers and the case conference arranged foster home care. The boys were sent to the "Thompson home," one of the best foster homes in Rochester according to Rogers, who liked to tell an anecdote that illustrated Mrs. Thompson's ability to accept the children's feelings without being manipulated herself.

William, having "tried out" previous foster mothers so successfully that it had been necessary to move him several times, renewed his tactics in this home within the first few days of placement.

"I'm tough!" he said, slapping his chest.

"Are you?" answered mother. "I'm tough, too."

William looked decidedly surprised and in a somewhat lower tone of voice asked, "How tough are you?"

"I'm tough like you," confided the foster mother.

"Well," said William in a subdued voice after a thoughtful pause, "I'm not so tough."

How did Dick and John respond to foster home treatment? Rogers continued their case studies:

> After clinic study, a foster home was recommended—a home where the foster mother was strict and positive, and where Dick would be with other boys. It is interesting, in looking over the conference notes, to see that foster home placement was regarded as a forlorn hope, and it was the consensus of conference opinion that Dick would soon have to be institutionalized. His behavior was too extreme for lesser methods. To quote from the record, "Dick has an extremely disorganized personality. His temper tantrums have made him feared and disliked. He should be tried in a foster home before institutionalization is decided upon."
>
> Dick was placed in the Thompson home. At first he remained quiet, aloof, solitary. He seemed to be thinking and dreaming much of the time, which was quite unlike his former self. The foster mother encouraged vigorous activity, and gradually Dick began to mingle with the other boys. He began to join more in the conversation and seemed more contented. Six weeks after placement he had his first temper tantrum. It occurred (poor Dick!) when Mr. Thompson asked him to take his cod-liver oil as usual with the other boys. Dick refused, began to scream and kick, and then let out a burst of oaths which were remarkable for an eight-year-old. Without any hesitation, Mr. Thompson washed his mouth with bitter aloes. Dick quieted immediately, became quite contrite, and ceased his tantrum. Since that time there have been no violent tantrums and a decreasing number of temper outbursts of any sort. Within ten months of placement the foster mother reported that he presented no problem at all.
>
> At the present time (two and one-half years from date of placement) certain new difficulties are arising. Dick's mother—now on a salary with the revival mission and creating a scandal by her actions with the minister—visits Dick quite frequently and heaps presents on the boy as she coddles and kisses him. Dick is quite upset by her visits and by her talk of taking him to live with her. After these visits he becomes irritable and more inclined to temper spells. He also shows a tendency to lord it over the other boys because of his more numerous possessions. Were it not

for this outside influence, Dick would be making a completely satisfactory adjustment. Temper tantrums, sadistic impulses, vicious tendencies —all have disappeared.

Commenting on the case, Rogers wrote: "In Dick's case, as with some of the other boys, the greatest contribution made by the foster home is that of consistent control. Rewards and punishment follow with certainty on the heels of good and bad behavior. The child's universe comes to have a logic, a reasonableness, which was scarcely discernible in the riotous confusion and fear of the early home life."

Now, to return to John, the seven-year-old with the incredible sophistication about sex.

The psychological tests showed that John, in spite of his alert manner, was a very dull boy, and this, combined with his attitude toward sex, made the outlook most unfavorable. It was felt that whether he was placed in a foster home or an institution, he was certain to "corrupt" the children with whom he came in contact. It was as a very dubious experiment, and because of his extreme youth, it was decided to place him in the Thompson home.

The fear of John's influence seemed justified the first day of placement. Mrs. Thompson had been forewarned as to John's behavior, but even she was scarcely prepared to hear a burst of obscenity directed toward the social worker as that individual started to drive away from the home. John was using his best means of gaining attention and he was highly satisfied to see the gaping astonishment on the faces of the other children. Mrs. Thompson immediately talked to John alone and told him in a kindly, but firm manner that her boys did not speak like that and that if she ever heard such language again, she would wash his mouth with soap. This was the first and the last obscenity that John used as an attention-getting device. To be sure, when aroused, his swearing was extremely colorful, but this, too, gradually came under control. He did try other means of getting attention, as might have been expected. He began to tell "tall tales," which the foster mother met by replying with even wilder statements and then laughing away both as jokes. She refused to consider them as lies, and hence made it easy for John to give them up. She also gave him ample opportunity to gain attention in other ways; she asked him to perform little tasks for her; she praised him liberally when he brought home a good school paper; she told him of the improvement he was making.

In four months Mrs. Thompson was able to report that John was no longer swearing and was very proud of his progress along this line. She could also say that at no time had sex talk or sex practices constituted a problem with John. When his previous behavior is recalled, this seems nothing short of astounding.

A year after John's placement in the home, he was re-studied at the clinic. Without a knowledge of his past, it would have been impossible to recognize this jolly, healthy, eight-year-old, full of amusing stories about life at "home," as the grave problem of the previous year. He told of earning his spending money, of the fun they had at Christmas, of his responsibility for wiping the dishes, in a frank, spontaneous fashion that seemed to have nothing in common with the smirking, sophisticated attitude of his first clinic contact. Even the memory of his own home seemed to have become dimmed and uncertain. He told the interviewer confidentially that he had had "another home," but regarded Thompson's very definitely as his "real home." To cap the climax of the transformation, John spoke with genuine horror of a boy on their street who actually swore!

Three and a half years have slipped by and John's excellent record continues. Nearly eleven years old now, he has developed into an attractive, friendly boy, with a very winning smile. He is truthful and dependable, though he is full of life and has to be handled with a firm and consistent hand. He is in fourth grade, doing "D" work, which is all that could be expected of a boy of his mentality. He has developed an interest in nature study, and enjoys working with tools.

This foster home, however, was not utopia. Rogers described how, on one occasion, "when the foster mother was very new in the work, two of the boys were found masturbating. The goddess of mental hygiene must have wept to see their punishment—two small boys, solemnly washing their hands for thirty minutes." Nor was foster home placement successful in all cases. "If we could fully explain why Donald has failed to adjust while the other boys have successfully adjusted, we should have the solution to much of the mystery of human nature."

Yet, he could not deny what he witnessed, time and time again, in the lives of hundreds of children. Extreme behavioral, psychological and emotional problems would often disappear or be reduced to a minimum in a healthy environment. The child has within him the drive, the need to grow and mature. To create an environment that supports growth is to *allow* the child to be healthy.

What constitutes this healthy, supportive environment? Rogers, thinking of the foster parent, listed four conditions, which are noteworthy in that they contain the roots of much of his later thinking. "It seems clear," he wrote, "that the suitability of a foster home for the care of problem children depends more upon certain types of attitudes than on any external factor. These attitudes might be summarized as follows:

"1. An attitude of intelligent understanding. This involves the ability to look at the child's behavior as a natural result of his makeup and experience, rather than as an infraction of moral rules, or a deviation from adult convention. It also requires the creative imagination to understand the way the child feels and the motives for his acts. . . . 2. A consistency of viewpoint and discipline. This element of stability in management gives the child the comforting feeling of knowing where he stands with reference to some standard. The consistency of viewpoint seems more important than the actual type of discipline itself, since every clinic or child-placing agency can point to successful homes with very diverse views on discipline. . . . 3. An attitude of interested affection. It is the moderate type of affection which seems most helpful, not the glowing enthusiasm of the emotionally starved parent. 'Fundamental interest and affection' is perhaps the best descriptive phrase. It is a primary factor in the child's security. . . . 4. Satisfaction in the child's developing abilities. Only if the foster parent finds this satisfaction will he wisely reward the youngster for achievement, and permit the child more and more freedom to grow in independence."

The foster home was only one environmental change which Rogers and the Child Study Department used to help children. Institutional care was another, although it was employed much less frequently, especially during the Depression, when the delinquency rate throughout the country fell off dramatically. From his experiences with institutions and from the great amount of research he read on the subject, Rogers came to see that regimented, military-style institutions rarely lessened but usually exacerbated emotional problems which led to delinquency. On the other hand he was very impressed by a few institutions he visited or read about that provided individual treatment for the delinquent and dependent children. In his writing and his speeches before community groups, he advocated institutional structures that gave the young men and women significant choices to make as part of their reeducation.

In addition to using methods of changing the child's environment, Rogers and his staff frequently recommended "treatment through modifying the environment." This often involved working with the parents to change parental attitudes (psychotherapeutic methods were sometimes used here). It also might mean working through the schools —perhaps recommending remedial work or a change in the child's program.

Another means of treatment through modifying the environment was through the intelligent use of camps, groups, and clubs. After three summers as a leader at the Y.M.C.A. camp in Wisconsin and at Camp Wawokeye near Cleveland, Rogers knew that these activities could be an important, positive influence in the lives of children. Though it was not directly connected with his duties as director of the

Child Study Department, he served as consultant for Camp Corey, a Y.M.C.A. camp, and helped organize a "farm camp," an effort by the Society for the Prevention of Cruelty to Children to provide a meaningful work experience for teenage boys during the Depression. He played a significant role in its direction and growth.

Readers who are familiar with Carl Rogers' later contributions to the field of psychotherapy may be surprised to see how his earliest treatment efforts revolved primarily around environmental therapy—foster homes, institutions, schools, and camps. The importance of total treatment was underscored most strongly in his second published professional article, in 1931. Coauthored with a co-worker, Mitchell E. Rappaport, "We Pay for the Smiths" is an interesting, if depressing, case study of a welfare family with thirteen children—a family which was already in its third consecutive generation on Rochester's relief rolls, and which had already cost the city well over fifty thousand dollars. The authors' conclusion would probably bring a chuckle to B.F. Skinner, Rogers' later-day sparring partner on many psychological and social questions. "Deep laid social ills," they wrote, "of the sort the Smith's represent will not be cured by new ways of relief giving, by an analysis of the emotional situation between worker and client, or by new systems of keeping case records. They call not only for refinement of method, but for bold, farsighted policies of social planning and social control."

Although Rogers' own interests moved toward intensive psychotherapy during his years in Rochester, he remained very much impressed with the power of environmental therapy. "The changing of parental attitudes, the manipulation of the school and social environment, the use, in serious situations, of a completely new and therapeutic environment outside of the home, have all been suggested as means of attacking the causes of problem behavior. There has been in some quarters, a tendency to look down upon such methods of treatment as being in some way inferior to direct methods of psychotherapy, which deal with the child himself. This viewpoint is both unrealistic and unfortunate. We shall not be inclined to look down upon treatment involving the manipulation of the environment, if we recall the fundamental axiom upon which it is based, namely, that most children, if given a reasonably normal environment which meets their own emotional, intellectual, and social needs, have within themselves sufficient drive toward health to respond and make a comfortable adjustment to life."

This "fundamental axiom," in my opinion, represents the basis of

all Rogers' subsequent work after he left Rochester. Later on, some of
his most important work went into supporting his theory that human
beings, like animals and plants, have an innate "drive toward health"
which can be nurtured by the right type of environment. Even when
he was in Rochester the basis of this "axiom" was dramatically illustrated by a small research study conducted by the Child Study Department. It involved a fifteen-month follow-up study on children for
whom the case conference had recommended some kind of environmental treatment, usually a change of residence. Each child was rated
as "adjusting" or "failed to adjust." Rogers and his staff found that "of
the 89 cases where the court had followed the treatment plan mapped
out by the clinic conference, one was a failure and was transferred from
the recommended institution to another. Of the 6 cases where minor
changes had been made in the plan, one was a failure. Of the 19 cases
where the court had adopted some totally different residence plan than
that suggested, 12, or 63 percent, were failures within the fifteen
months."

"As a mode of treatment," Rogers wrote in 1939, "the selection of
a place of residence which will have a therapeutic effect does not
necessarily appeal to the imagination. Such a choice has about it none
of the mysterious elements or technical verbiage which make some
types of therapy so alluring. It is nevertheless the only sound foundation for all the more subtle or more refined sorts of treatment which
we shall proceed to consider."

For about one fifth of the children who came to the Child Study
Department, "treatment interviews" or "direct therapy" was conducted. Rogers had come to Rochester with an open mind about
psychotherapy. Although he had been exposed to psychoanalysis in
New York, most of his own work was in the area of psychological
testing and the analysis of case studies. With respect to psychotherapy
he was quite willing to learn from his experiences in Rochester. Again,
the principle which guided his explorations into the various schools of
therapy was pragmatism. Is this method effective? Will it work?

Unfortunately, as he looked for professional guidance on the subject, there was little help to be found in the literature. "A verbatim
record of intensive psychotherapy with one child, giving in full all the
conversation of both child and therapist, would be a new and valuable
contribution to our thinking," he noted. But no such account was
available. Nor was there any substantial scientific research on the dif-

ferent approaches to or outcomes of psychotherapy. "In this realm where so much depends on the personal interactions and responses of worker and child," he wrote in 1939, "we find more the skills of an art than the technique of science. Nevertheless there is reason to hope that even these subtle relationships may be helpfully studied by scientific means and more accurately known and guided. As a preliminary to such a study we shall endeavor to describe and classify some of the methods used with children."

He distinguished between those treatment interviews which used "deeper therapies" and those which did not. By deeper therapy he meant "those therapeutic methods which aim toward giving the child self-insight, or in which the emotional relationship between child and worker is a very strong one." Among these he included psychoanalysis, interpretive therapy, and relationship therapy. Among the less-deep therapies were educational therapy, persuasion or suggestion, and release or expressive therapy. He tried out every one of these approaches. His Rochester years were a period of experimentation, during which he gradually came to formulate his own ideas on the process of psychotherapy. This led eventually to Rogers' founding a new school of therapy that would have a profound impact on the helping professions.

One example of educational therapy is the case of Philip, who was referred to the Society for the Prevention of Cruelty to Children by Children's Court. Rogers saw the boy* and wrote the following report:

> Philip was an overgrown Polish boy of 14 when he came to the clinic on a serious delinquency charge. He had broken into the house of his next door neighbor in the middle of the night, had made his way to the room of the 18-year-old daughter, and had attempted to strike her over the head with a crude lead pipe blackjack. Fortunately the blackjack struck the head of the bed, the girl awoke and screamed, and Philip was captured. The situation as it revealed itself was plainly an acute personal-

*In Rogers' early writings almost all the case studies presented are case studies of boys. This has several possible explanations. All of Rogers' camp and group experiences had been in boys' camps and groups. The excellent foster home Rogers wrote about most frequently was a foster home for boys. Boys far outnumbered girls in referrals to the Rochester S.P.C.C. However, although these factors partially explain the imbalance, Rogers did have considerable experience working with girls, too. So one is left wondering. Interestingly, once he began to work primarily with adults, this phenomenon disappeared, and case studies of women appear in his writings as frequently as or more frequently than studies of men.

ity problem. Philip was an inarticulate, shy boy of better than average mentality. He was much the youngest of four children and associated little with his older siblings. His father was dead, and his relationship with his mother was one of obedience rather than trust and confidence. He was not at all social, but did have two good friends, both of them very respectable boys. He was gifted along mechanical lines. Everyone knew him as a very quiet, very colorless, well-behaved boy. He had literally no sex information, and no sources of such information. As he became adolescent, he mulled over his perplexities about sex. The girl next door, whose bedroom window was visible from his own, became the object of his daydreams, and time after time he concocted imaginary means of disrobing her in order to answer his fundamental questions regarding female anatomy. Finally he acted out one of these daydreams.

In treatment of Philip the whole aim was educational. Throughout a number of contacts with the boy very complete sex education was given, in as matter-of-fact a manner as possible. Male and female anatomy, intercourse, reproduction, the birth process, masturbation, boy and girl relationships were discussed with more than usual thoroughness. Because he was so inarticulate himself, this was a somewhat one-sided process. Later after a period of a few months, these topics were brought up again to make sure he had assimilated the information. This was practically the only type of treatment used, with the exception of some reassurance to the mother that her boy was not abnormal. It was not felt safe to interpret to the mother the full significance of her boy's actions, since she was herself too repressed.

Because Philip found it difficult to verbalize his conflicts, this treatment was used without too precise a knowledge of the content of his fantasies or perplexities, save that they were sexual. It may well be that there were aspects of his problem which we did not know and which remained untreated. Three years have elapsed, however, and there has been reasonably satisfactory personal adjustment without further delinquent behavior.

There were educational techniques other than information-giving. The therapist might also help children in difficult choice situations clarify the alternatives available and their likely consequences. From his experience Rogers concluded that the educational therapies could be helpful "where ignorance of facts is a source of mental conflict or emotional tension . . . no matter how deep-seated the problem may seem."

His experience also taught him the limitations of the educational approach. Deep-seated emotional problems would scarcely be touched by education. And even when ignorance of basic facts was an important part of the problem, emotional conflicts often interfered with the individual's ability to accept the facts. Rogers described an example of this in an interview he had with a parent.

A mother requests help with her child, a girl of 11, who is difficult to manage and has never been allowed to attend school. It needs little more than a glance at the child to recognize that she is the type of mental defective known as Mongolian, and a brief examination establishes her mental development as approximately that of a three-year-old. The obvious step for the clinician seems to be to educate the mother as to the nature of mongolism, to point out to her that there is no known cure or remedy for the condition, that she must face the tragic fact that her child can never develop much beyond this point, and that institutional care is the only sensible and kind procedure for the welfare of both child and parent. Recognizing that this information may be upsetting and disappointing to the parent, there would seem to be no difficulty in at least conveying the simple facts regarding the condition and the experiences of others with similar children. We find, however, that this mother, of at least average intelligence, is quite unable to digest this information. She insists that the child can read and write at the very moment that the youngster is making unintelligible sounds to indicate its wants, unable to formulate a complete sentence. She is sure that the child has shown great improvement in the past, then shifts to the notion that she will show great improvement in the future. In spite of the explanation of the nature of mongolism, she states that the child's condition is due to the refusal of the educational authorities to let her attend school. Finally she reveals that four other competent physicians and psychologists have examined the child in the last five years and have given her substantially the same diagnosis and suggestions as are being given to her now. Although she reports this, she seizes upon some minor circumstance or statement of each examination to fortify her own viewpoint. She leaves, having gained nothing from this attempt to "educate" her, nor, it would seem, from any of the four previous attempts.

Another form of therapy was that of persuasion or suggestion or the therapist's use of personal influence. Although these techniques were widely used by therapists with varying orientations, Rogers noted that they were no longer being explicitly advocated as they had been in earlier treatises on psychotherapy. Interestingly enough, one of the explicit proponents of this approach was Dr. Samuel Hartwell, whom Rogers had employed as the consulting psychiatrist for the Child Study Department when he became director. Hartwell argued that one of the psychiatrist's goals was to achieve a rapport with the child in which the child would become increasingly suggestible to the psychiatrist's guidance. At the deepest level of rapport, Hartwell wrote, "he is suggestible to the greatest possible degree. He considers things in the light of my emotional response to them rather than his own. . . . [The child] wants his psychiatrist to be his best friend. He wishes to please him more than he wishes to do anything else. Out of loyalty to his friend he is perfectly willing to alter his emotional life as far as it is possible for him." On one occasion Hartwell encouraged a boy to join some group activities the child was afraid of by saying, "I want you to do it because you're my kid."

Rogers had a great deal of respect for Hartwell. He envied Hartwell's ability to put a child on his lap and, in a fatherly way, establish an immediate rapport. While unquestionably friendly and sincere, Rogers was more emotionally reserved at this time in his life and would not have felt comfortable enough to do this. He was also caught up in the techniques of interviewing, trying to decide the "right" thing to do. "Hartwell was more himself, and therefore more therapeutic," Rogers commented years later. But in spite of his respect for and admiration of Hartwell's fashion of relating to children, he was not impressed by the direct persuasion Hartwell and others sometimes advocated and frequently used as a therapeutic technique. He acknowledged that suggestion could serve some good purpose. As with Hartwell's "kid," mentioned above, if the persuasion had "served to tide the boy over the initial difficulties of group adjustment, he would then find social contacts satisfying in themselves. In such instances personal influences may be likened to a hypodermic given as a temporary measure, either to inhibit or stimulate behavior of a certain type until the more lasting therapeutic influences can take place."

This statement also suggests Rogers' misgivings about the use of persuasion and suggestion in therapy. The results were only temporary, wherever deep-seated emotional problems were present. Persuasion was based on the therapist's supplied motivation, not the child's. Once away from the therapist's influence, the original emotional conflicts would begin operating again, and the original problem symptoms or new ones would emerge. Rogers' growing distaste for persuading or "pushing" the child in a given direction is reflected by Louise Johnson, then a counselor at the University of Rochester. "I was working with a student whose problem was too complex for me to handle, so I, with her permission, approached Carl to ask him to see her. When I attempted to arrange an appointment with him for the student, he checked me saying, 'Let the student call me—and we can go on from there.' "

One experience which helped confirm Rogers' pessimism about persuasive therapy involved a very intelligent, very insecure eleven-year-old boy being treated for his enuresis. After he was placed in a foster home which seemed to meet some of his deeper emotional needs, it was decided to attack the bed-wetting directly by means of hypnosis.

The treatment was carried on by Dr. Griffith Williams, who was an expert in hypnotic therapy, and Mr. Gordon Riley, a psychologist on the clinic staff. The hypnosis took place right in the Child Study Department and Rogers followed the case closely from the start.

> The boy was trained until he was able to go into a fairly deep trance and carry out post-hypnotic suggestions of a neutral sort. Then such suggestions were made as that he would ask the foster mother for a chamber to keep under his bed so that he could use it just before he retired. These suggestions were carried out post-hypnotically, but the enuresis continued in spite of more frequent use of toilet facilities brought about through suggestion. In later trances, as specific suggestions were made attacking the symptom more directly, such as suggesting that he would wake at intervals during the night, it became more difficult to gain the boy's cooperation, and finally it was impossible to induce a trance state at all.

Rogers was deeply impressed by what he saw. Everything, so it seemed, was operating in their favor—the boy's initial cooperation, his successful adjustment in the foster home, the expertise of the psychologists—yet the treatment was a failure. To Rogers the case demonstrated "a clear picture of the limitations of hypnotic suggestion, and the limitations of conscious suggestion and persuasion seem very similar. When suggestion or persuasion cuts definitely across the deeper emotional purposes and needs," he concluded, "it can hardly be effective."

The last of the "less-deep" therapies which Rogers employed during his Rochester years was "expressive therapy" or "release." He was more intrigued by the possibilities of this approach than by those already mentioned. To "talk out" one's feelings, to ventilate one's conflicts, to unburden oneself of concerns, anxieties and problems, Rogers felt, had considerable therapeutic value. "Such a catharsis," he wrote then, "even where the therapist is a listener only, has a constructive effect, since the child clarifies his feelings by verbalizing them. . . ."

Since Rogers often worked with young children, sometimes preschoolers, one of the expressive therapies that greatly interested him was "expression through play techniques." Dr. David Levy was a leader in this approach, which utilized clay, stuffed animals and other common toys, as well as dolls with amputatable legs, arms, heads, breasts, etc. Children would begin playing with the toys, the therapist would observe and ask the child questions, and before long the child would be using the dolls and toys to express many important feelings and conflicts that would have been difficult, if not impossible, to get to with words alone. Rogers described one of his own experiences with play therapy.

> Freddie, a hyperactive eight-year-old, was regarded as a serious school problem. . . . A series of interview contacts on a play basis assisted Freddie in dramatizing and acting out his feelings which he did not express with much freedom in words. To quote one such incident from the record, "Examiner gave Freddie modeling clay. He made a figure.
> 'Who is it? Guess.'
> Examiner: 'Your father? Me?'
> 'No, it's the principal. He's got flat feet.' He made a fist on the figure. 'Gee, he's mad.' Vindictively he knocked off the head and the fist, jumped the figure around the table singing, 'Poor Mr. W—— (the principal)' and gradually annihilated it."

Rogers often used play techniques with young children. Reared in an environment that discouraged the expression of feelings, he thought that the expressive therapies which encouraged catharsis, ventilation, and release were very promising. They could help children see themselves more clearly, accept themselves more easily, and, to some extent, cope with reality more effectively. But Rogers noted that, in terms of coping with reality, the various types of expressive therapies had not yet found ways to help the child really work through the conflicts and make a satisfactory adjustment in the real world. Thus he was sympathetic to the goals and methods of expressive therapy, but felt more work was needed to make it as effective as it might be. Interestingly, one of Rogers' doctoral students, several years later, probably did more than anyone else to bring "play therapy" to the attention of the general public interested in psychology. This was Virginia Axline, author of *Play Therapy* and *Dibs in Search of Self,* who wrote in the former book in 1947, "The principles of non-directive play therapy which are discussed in this book are based upon the non-directive counseling techniques which have been developed by Doctor Carl R. Rogers."

Although Rogers had experimented with psychoanalytic theories in some of the therapy he had conducted at the Institute for Child Guidance, he never was very impressed by the psychoanalytic movement. He did recognize Freud's great contribution to psychology—his exposure of the powerful psychological dynamics operating within the individual, his and his followers' insights into repressions and defense mechanisms, his legitimizing the therapeutic interview as an accepted professional procedure. But by nature and by training Rogers was a pragmatist and a psychologist. While he recognized Freud's historical importance, his whole nature and training were opposed to the elaborate theoretical superstructure and method of psychoanalysis which Freud had introduced.

For one thing, psychoanalysis was impractical. It took so much time and money that only a handful of those needing help could receive it through analysis. "One hundred analytic hours would be regarded by most Freudians as a minimum amount of time in which to complete the analysis of the child," he wrote. Meanwhile, in Rochester, he saw *hundreds* of children in need, every year. So he felt very impatient with analysis as a useful tool in his own work.

A second objection he had to psychoanalysis was that, with its emphasis on past and repressed material and events, it tended to ignore or to minimize the importance of the individual's present environment. In Rochester he learned just the opposite. He knew of too many examples of intensive individual help which failed because the unhealthy environment the child was in simply could not support the growth taking place in the clinic or the therapist's office.

A third fault he found with analysis was that "unfortunately, psychoanalysts have not favored the investigation of their methods by evaluative research." As a psychologist he had been taught and had come to believe in the importance of research and evaluation. As a pragmatist, he continued to ask himself, "Am I being effective? How can we improve if we don't see clearly what we are actually accomplishing?" As a scientist, he knew that careful research procedures were the only way to answer these questions honestly, minimizing the biases of the experimenter. Ironically, while psychiatrists and psychoanalysts have traditionally branded Rogers' theories and methods as "superficial," Rogers often felt condescending in his attitude toward psychoanalysis. This is in no small part due to the value he placed on careful research, one of his own lasting contributions to the field of psychotherapy.

Another reason for his somewhat superior attitude toward analysis was theoretical. As a psychologist trained in the scientific method, he had learned that one quality of a good theory is that it attempts to explain phenomena in the least complicated way. He saw psychoanalysis doing just the opposite. "The [psychoanalytic] interpretation," he wrote, "is not usually made on the simplest basis which will explain the facts but is made in terms of a preconceived ideology, frequently unverified, sometimes fantastic. . . ."

Rogers also objected to the mystique he thought psychoanalysis created about mental illness and the way it tended to exaggerate common problems. He wrote in 1937 that "too often in psychoanalytic and psychiatric literature any negative experience, any confusion of thought, any tendency to day-dream, or to feel inadequate to life is regarded as significant of abnormality. . . ." The psychologist's personality tests, Rogers believed, "helped to bring reason back into the situation by pointing out the degree to which the average and presumably normal individual shows neurotic tendencies or other personality difficulties." Later in his career he would go even further toward arguing that there is no qualitative difference between mentally "sick" and "healthy" people, the difference being essentially only quantitative, and that the same basic methods of helping could be used with the college student confused about his goals and the institutionalized schizophrenic.

It would be a mistake to construe Rogers' several objections to psychoanalysis as a conscious attempt to discredit analysis or its practitioners, or as a rebellion or defensive attack on the older "psychotherapeutic establishment." Unlike some of Freud's disciples, Rogers never had enough of an emotional or professional investment in psychoanalysis to openly rebel against it and thus form his own school of thought. In fact his reading of Freud was relatively shallow. He was always grateful that his thinking did not come from the teachings of one special mentor, nor out of the writings of one special person, nor out of endless philosophical debates on the merits of the various schools of therapy, or the nuances and changes in some "master's" thinking over the years. Rogers' ideas developed primarily from his own experiences—and from several other influences which shall be mentioned shortly. It was only in organizing and communicating his learnings that he bothered to invest time and energy in expressing his misgivings about psychoanalysis. Since at this time his primary concern was with children, and he noted that "from a quantitative viewpoint, the treatment of children's problems through psychoanalysis is negligible," he did not expect his opinions on psychoanalysis to be particularly controversial. Only in his last two years in Rochester did he become embroiled in his first major controversy between psychology and psychiatry, and by then his views on the latter profession had been long since established.

Given Rogers' views on psychoanalysis and, to some extent, psychiatry, the relationship between the psychologists and the consulting psychiatrist in the Child Study Department had real significance. As expressed in the 1933 brochure of the Society for the Prevention of Cruelty to Children, "When there are indications which might point toward mental disease or where further help is desired, the child, or the child and his parents, may be seen by a psychiatrist." Rogers reflected the same role definitions in the 1937 Annual Report of his department: "The psychiatrist is a physician trained in the prevention and treatment of abnormal mental conditions and insanity. He is especially helpful in dealing with the mentally disturbed individual, whether child or adult, and with any individual who shows symptoms indicative of neurological difficulty or mental disease. . . . The psychologist is trained to understand the normal child and the emotional, educational and behavior difficulties which such children present. He is skilled in the measurement of the child's developing mentality and personality traits. He is especially helpful in diagnosing and treating the behavior, personality, and educational problems of children who fall with the 'normal grouping' and are not definitely abnormal."

Rogers wrote this for political reasons, so that the psychiatrists and psychoanalysts in the community would not feel their territory was being encroached upon. During that same year Rogers was writing his first book, in which no such vague, oversimplified distinctions as "normal," "definitely abnormal," "mental disease," "insanity," and "mentally disturbed individual" are ever used in this way. In reality the Child Study Department often violated the separation between the psychiatrist's and the psychologist's roles as delineated above. While theoretically the prevention and treatment of "insanity" was to be left to the psychiatrist, another annual report dramatically shows the opposite happening in the case of Arthur who is ". . . diagnosed by his companions as just a bit 'goofy,' and while they stand in awe of his screaming, brick-throwing tantrums, they know nothing of the nightmares where he dreams of going insane. . . . Of the many elements in his treatment, those that were primarily environmental, such as a move to a new home and a transfer to another school, were left with the social agency. In addition, however, the boy needed skilled help in removing this basic fear, and this help was given through interviews with the psychologist in this department."

This blurring of distinct roles was probably facilitated by the consulting psychiatrist with whom Rogers first worked when he came to Rochester. Rogers described him as "a rather weak person and for the most part we told him what we thought he should say and he said it, thus giving our recommendations more force and authority." When Rogers became director and employed Samuel Hartwell as consulting psychiatrist, a man he really respected, the psychologists' freedom and scope of operation had already become a norm in the department. Still, Hartwell tried to persuade Rogers to take four to six years off to become a medical doctor and then a psychiatrist, so he could have more influence on the field. Rogers had neither the means nor the desire.

The issue illustrates a commonly held notion about the difference between a psychiatrist and a clinical psychologist. It is widely thought that the former professionals work with cases where the problems are "deeper" or "more serious." Rogers felt that this distinction between the two professions and the distinction between "normal" children's problems and "abnormal" children's problems were both spurious. However, the distinction between the professions still exists as a controversial issue a half-century later and would come back to plague Rogers on several occasions during his long career.

If Rogers favored any one deep, therapeutic approach when he came to Rochester, it was "interpretive therapy," the major goal of which is to help the child or parent achieve insight into his* own behavior and motives, past and present. Such insight presumably enables the child or parent to give up any symptoms of distress and to cope realistically with the future.

Interpretive therapy works toward insight in a rather consistent way. As rapport and trust are established, the child or parent feels increasingly free to tell (or in the case of young children in play therapy, to

---

*For the sake of equity and clarity, I have chosen to use the female pronouns to refer to those in the helping role (therapist, teacher, parent, etc.) and the male pronouns to refer to the recipient of help (the client, student, child, etc.). When quoting Rogers or others, I have retained their own usage. This decision reflects my dissatisfaction with the trend I see in publishing today: first, to acknowledge that the exclusive use of the male pronouns often leaves female readers feeling excluded and reinforces stereotypes; second, to point out how the continual use of "he or she," "s/he" or some such form is awkward and distracting; and third, to explain that, therefore, the convention of the exclusive male pronoun will be maintained, but now everyone should understand that the male pronouns are meant to include females, too. In lieu of a suitable impersonal pronoun, and considering the nature of the material, the present solution seemed the most appropriate.

show) the therapist a great deal about himself. As the therapist begins to understand the individual's behavior and psychodynamics, and as she feels the individual is ready for self-understanding, the therapist begins to interpret the individual's behavior to him. If relevant, dreams can be interpreted. Where the relationship of the child or parent to the therapist seems significant, this too is subject to interpretation. As with one of Rogers' clients:

> Treatment took the form of getting John to go over the events of his early history until he understood their influence on him: his first five years living with his grandmother, who favored and spoiled him, moving to the separate home which his parents then established and the coming of his baby sister, the competition with his sister, his repeated patterns of tantrum behavior to gain his own way, which he could remember clearly as far back as the age of eight. As he went over this material during several interviews he was able to laugh at himself and to see how his childish patterns originated. The psychologist also interpreted this material to him in clearer terms. Another means used to help John attain insight was to describe in concrete terms the dependency and egocentric tendencies of the child, and the ways in which those characteristics were changed in the mature adult, who is able to take responsibility for himself, whose interests are socialized, who is able to face reality. He was encouraged to analyze the ways in which he was mature, his reading interests, for example, and the many ways in which he was immature. From the time that treatment contacts began, the tantrums diminished greatly in number and severity until they were no longer a problem. John sometimes became upset by the dictatorial and unreasonable requests of his father, but in these instances his behavior represented a fairly normal reaction.

Implicit in the interpretive approach is an optimistic view of human nature—that, basically, people want to be healthy, to grow toward psychological maturity. Because they are also frightened by growth and its risks, they may erect many defenses against seeing themselves and their situation clearly; but if they can be helped beyond these defenses, they will, as they achieve insight and self-understanding, choose a healthy course for themselves.

Although he never abandoned this optimistic view of humans underlying the therapeutic process, Rogers gradually did develop mixed feelings, and then increasingly negative feelings, about interpretive therapy. Sometimes it worked. Sometimes it only seemed to work. The interpretation was "accepted" by the child or parent who, at the time, also seemed to "feel" the interpretation to be true. Yet, weeks or months later, the child or parent would seem to "forget" or be unable to act upon his new insight. Maybe there was more to therapy than having the child or parent accept and believe a valid interpretation.

Rogers' weaning from interpretive therapy was very gradual. He often illustrated his process of disillusionment by relating three of his experiences in Rochester.

Beginning with his training in New York he had been fascinated by the works of William Healy, one of the outstanding authorities at the time on delinquent and problem behavior in children. Healy, who had a Freudian orientation, felt that delinquency was often associated with sexual conflict, and that if the real conflict were uncovered, the delinquent behavior would cease. One or two years after coming to the Child Study Department, Rogers began working with a young pyromaniac. He held numerous treatment interviews with the boy in the detention home, tracing back the causes of the boy's behavior to his sexual impulses about masturbation, and gradually interpreting this understanding to him. The treatment was terminated and Rogers, feeling very proud of his skill in handling the case, was shortly thereafter amazed to find out that the boy, on probation, had been arrested again for setting fires.

Rogers was incredulous. Why had the therapy failed? Could Healy have been wrong about the causes of delinquency? Was he learning something that Healy did not know about therapeutic treatment? For Rogers this shock constituted a naive but important realization. Authorities in his field could be wrong. There was new knowledge yet to be discovered.

Shortly after he came to Rochester he was asked to lead a discussion group on interviewing techniques. As a catalyst for group discussion he brought in "a published account of an interview with a parent, approximately verbatim, in which the case worker was shrewd, insightful, clever, and led the interview quite quickly to the heart of the difficulty. I was happy to use it as an illustration of good interviewing techniques. . . ." Several years later he had a similar assignment and remembered this material. "I hunted it up again and reread it. I was appalled. Now it seemed to me to be a clever legalistic type of questioning by the interviewer which convicted this parent of her unconscious motives, and wrung from her an admission of her guilt. I now knew from my experience that such an interview would not be of any lasting help to the parent or the child. It made me realize that I was moving away from any approach which was coercive or pushing in clinical relationships, not for philosophical reasons, but because such approaches were never more than superficially effective."

The third experience occurred a few years later, near the end of Rogers' time in Rochester. "I had learned to be more subtle and patient in interpreting a client's behavior to him, attempting to time it in a gentle fashion which would gain acceptance. I had been working with a highly intelligent mother whose boy was something of a hellion. The problem was clearly her early rejection of the boy, but over many interviews I could not help her to this insight. I drew her out, I gently pulled together the evidence she had given, trying to help her see the pattern. But we got nowhere. Finally I gave up. I told her that it seemed we had both tried, but we had failed, and that we might as well give up our contacts. She agreed. So we concluded the interview, shook hands, and she walked to the door of the office. Then she turned and asked, 'Do you ever take adults for counseling here?' When I replied in the affirmative, she said, 'Well, then, I would like some help.' She came to the chair she had left, and began to pour out her despair about her marriage, her troubled relationship with her husband, her sense of failure and confusion, all very different from the sterile 'case history' she had given before. Real therapy began then, and ultimately it was very successful.

"This incident was one of a number which helped me to experience the fact—only fully realized later—that it is the *client* who knows what hurts, what directions to go, what problems are crucial, what experiences have been deeply buried. It began to occur to me that unless I had a need to demonstrate my own cleverness and learning, I would do better to rely upon the client for the direction of movement in the process."

Since psychoanalysis is one type of interpretive therapy in which the interpretation of facts fits into a particular school of psychological thought, it is interesting that Freud himself, during the course of his career, went through a process very similar to Rogers, in recognizing the limitations of coercive or ill-timed interpretation. As Freud wrote in 1924,

This answer of course involves a condemnation of that mode of procedure which consists in communicating to the patient the interpretation of the symptoms as soon as one perceived it oneself, or of that attitude which would account it a special triumph to hurl those "solutions" in his face at the first interview. . . . Such conduct brings both the man and the treatment into discredit and arouses the most violent opposition, whether the interpretations be correct or not; yes, and the truer they are actually the more violent is the resistance they arouse. Usually the therapeutic effect at the moment is nothing; the resulting horror of analysis, however, is ineradicable. Even in later stages of the analysis one must be careful not to communicate the meaning of a symptom or the interpretation of a wish until the patient is already close upon it, so that he has only a short step to take in order to grasp the explanation himself. In former years I often found that premature communication of interpretations brought the treatment to an untimely end, both on account of the resistances suddenly aroused thereby and also because of the relief resulting from the insight so obtained.

Although Freud never went as far as Rogers, who eventually abandoned interpretation altogether, Nathaniel Raskin has argued convincingly that Freud, too, even "with his fundamentally authoritative orientation found it necessary to reckon more and more with the attitudes of the patient and to depend less and less upon the will of the analyst, in order to make therapeutic progress."

Around 1936 Rogers became familiar with the work of Otto Rank and his students Jessie Taft and Frederick Allen, and he often acknowledged later that their work had a very important influence on his own professional growth. Their direction in therapy, more than any other discussed so far, eventually became a part of his own, unique approach.

Rank was, for many years, one of Freud's closest associate-disciples. His break with Freud became evident in 1925 after the publication of Rank's *The Trauma of Birth.* He came to the United States in 1926 and, for a short time, joined the faculty of the Pennsylvania School of Social Work, where he continued to work out his own therapeutic approach, known as "will therapy." Rogers' first real exposure to will therapy came through a former member of his staff who was analyzed by Rank. She wrote Rogers a long letter describing her therapy in great detail. He was very impressed by her description. The next exposure to Rank's work came through several social workers connected with the Rochester Society for the Prevention of Cruelty to Children. They had been trained at the Pennsylvania School of Social Work, and their use of Rankian methods kindled enough interest in Rogers and the other psychologists in the Child Study Department to invite Rank to Rochester to conduct a seminar for interested members of the helping professions in that city.

Rogers was not particularly impressed with Rank's theoretical formulations. To one already bored with Freud's ideology, Rank's substitution of birth for castration as the first trauma and source of anxiety, and the substitution of the breast for the penis as the first libido object, had little interest or significance. On the other hand Rogers was quite fascinated by Rank's description of his therapeutic approach. Nathaniel Raskin summarized some of the highlights of Rank's will therapy:

> The individual seeking help is not simply a battleground of impersonal forces such as id and superego, but has creative powers of his own, a will. . . . Because of the dangers involved in living and the fear in dying, all people experience a basic ambivalence, which may be viewed in various aspects. Thus, there is a conflict between will-to-health and will-to-illness, between self-determination and acceptance of fate, between being different and being like others, etc. This ambivalence is characteristic not just of neurotics, but is an integral part of life. . . .

> The aim of therapy, in light of the above, becomes acceptance by the individual of himself as unique and self-reliant, with all his ambivalences, and the freeing of the positive will through the elimination of the temporary blocking which consists of the concentration of creative energies on the ego. . . . In order to achieve this goal, the patient rather than the therapist must become the central figure in the therapeutic process. The patient is his own therapist, he has within him forces of self-creation as well as self destruction, and the former can be brought into play if the therapist will play the role, not of authority, but of ego-helper or assistant ego. . . .

> The goals of therapy are achieved by the patient not through an explanation of the past, which he would resist if interpreted to him, and which, even if accepted by him, would serve to lessen his responsibility for his present adjustment, but rather through the experiencing of the present in the therapeutic situation. . . . The neurotic is hamstrung not by any particular content of his past, but by the way he is utilizing material in the present; thus, his help must come through an understanding of present dynamics, rather than of past content. . . .

> The ending of therapy, the separation of patient from therapist, is a symbol of all separations in life, starting with the separation of fetus from womb in birth, and if the patient can be made to understand the will conflict present here, the conflict over growth towards independence and self-reliance, and if he can exercise the separation as something which he wills himself, despite the pain of it, then it can symbolize the birth of the new individual.

Unfortunately Rank was rather vague about what he actually *did* and did not do in therapy. "My technique," he wrote, "consists essentially in having no technique, but in utilizing as much as possible experience and understanding that are constantly converted into skill but never crystallized into technical rules which would be applicable ideologically."

Although Rank often condemned the techniques of education and interpretation, many of his statements seemed to justify interpretation. Rank said, "I unmask all the reactions of the patient even if they apparently refer to the analyst, as projections of his own inner conflict and bring them back to his own ego." The therapeutic hour "is the place to show him how he tries to destroy the connection with this experience just as he does with the past. . . . All the therapist can do is to take over with understanding the role falling to his lot, and to make clear to the patient the universal meaning of this experience (therapy) which comprehends in itself the whole man, yes, almost the whole of humanness. This explanation, however, can be given only in the individual terminology of the particular patient and not in a general ideology."

Apparently the distinction is one between the past and present. While it is forbidden to interpret to the patient the meaning of *past* content (earlier experiences, dreams, etc.), it is permissible to interpret to the patient the meaning of his behavior in the therapeutic relationship.

Rogers, from his own experience, had already come to distrust therapist interpretation of past *or* present events, feeling that this interpretation led to only superficial understanding and behavior change by the child or parent. So Rank's interpretation of the dynamics of the therapeutic relationship did not appeal to him. In other areas, however, Rank's thinking did influence him—but only indirectly. Rank's seminar in Rochester lasted for only two days. One searches Rogers' writings in vain for even a single quotation from Rank or even for more than three consecutive sentences on Rank's thinking. It was more through the influence of the social workers connected to his clinic and his reading of Rank's students Jessie Taft and Frederick Allen that Rogers came to incorporate Rankian views and methods into his own developing viewpoint. Taft and Allen, writing in English, were clearer than Rank and more explicit about what the therapist actually does. They also published several accounts of their therapy which provided detailed records of therapist and patient responses. Unlike Rank or Allen, Taft went so far as to abandon interpretation altogether, even interpretation of the dynamics of therapy. Rogers called Taft's book *The Dynamics of Therapy in a Controlled Relationship*, which was published in 1933 and which he first quoted in 1937, "a small masterpiece of writing and thinking." If one had to choose an individual who had the greatest influence on Rogers' evolving views during his Rochester years, it would be she, Dr. Jessie Taft.

Thus not so much Rank himself, but the Rankian school, contributed to and supported Rogers' own thinking. First, their emphasis on the patient's positive will as the source of growth in therapy was particularly attractive to Rogers. Referring to relationship therapy (Taft's term), in 1937, Rogers wrote, ". . . its major value may be . . . the fresh viewpoint of non-interference and reliance upon the individual's own tendency toward growth which it has emphasized." Stemming from this, the Rankian conception of the therapist, not as director of therapy, but as supporter and helper to the patient in his struggle toward health, was also very congenial to Rogers' thinking.

But perhaps most important was the Rankians' shift in emphasis from the analysis of past content to a focus on the patient's self-insight and self-acceptance within the therapeutic relationship. Of course, both of these elements—past content and the emotional dynamics of the therapy—were stressed in classical psychoanalysis. In analysis, however, working through the patient's resistances and transference in the therapeutic relationship were considered important primarily because this freed the patient to move ahead toward understanding his own psychological development—the *understanding* being the goal of the relationship. For the Rankians, the *therapeutic relationship itself* became the main goal. If the patient could develop the ability to live as a healthy individual in the therapeutic hour, they believed, this would be carried over into daily living. Jessie Taft was particularly eloquent in describing the therapeutic hour as a microcosm of life itself.

> The reaction of each individual to limited or unlimited time betrays the deepest and most fundamental life pattern, his relation to the growth process itself, to beginnings and endings, to being born and to dying . . . in accepting time, one accepts the self and life with their inevitable defects and limitations. This does not mean a passive resignation but a willingness to live, work and create as mortals within the confines of the finite . . . one might fairly define relationship therapy as a process in which the individual finally learns to utilize the allotted hour from beginning to end without undue fear, resistance, resentment or greediness. When he can take it and also leave it without denying its value, without trying to escape it completely or keep it forever because of this very value, in so far he has learned to live, to accept this fragment of time in and for itself, and strange as it may seem, if he can live this hour he has in his grasp the secret of all hours, he has conquered life and time for the moment and in principle.

It is difficult to provide one good example of relationship therapy, because there were many differences in the way Rank, Taft, Allen, and others in this tradition actually operated, once the door to the office was closed. The case of Edward, however, which Rogers once used to illustrate relationship therapy, contains elements common to most of the case reports published by the Rankian school.

> As he became more secure in the visiting-teacher relationship, he began to express more and more open and violent aggression. The situation was intensified because of the visiting teacher's carrying on treatment simultaneously with another child in his room, Daniel Allen, who happened to have the same name as his younger brother. The climax of his expression of hostility toward the visiting teacher came in the third month of treatment:

> . . . E. began making faces and guttural noises. "You're the dumbest cluck I ever saw," he said. V.T. said it must make him mad for other children to come to her office. He began a train of rapid talk—something about locking Daniel Allen in the gym at the "Y"; then he went into pantomime, pretending to draw a gun, saying, "Stick 'em up.". . . There were many noises and then, "I don't care if I yell—I'll get you fired, and then you can't bring other kids down." V.T. said, "It does make you mad for other kids to come down, doesn't it?" The play grew wilder, he picked up a box, saying, "I'll bump this over your head." There were many noises, twisting of his face, and then aiming at the wall, "Bing-bing, now you're dead." V.T. interpreted that she could see that he had pretended to kill her but that sometimes he liked her too. . . .

> In this excerpt from the interview we of course see E. expressing his inability to share the visiting teacher with other children just as in the home situation he was unable to share the mother with his siblings. In an interview a few days later he was physically ill on discovering that the visiting teacher was married and was helped to express his rivalry and resentment that he had to share her interest with a father-person, just as he had to share his mother with his father. This interview occurred the day before the Christmas holidays. In the next interview after expressing these feelings he was able to work through to an expression of his positive feelings also.

> . . . V.T. talked with him about the times before the vacation, saying that he must have been very mad with her and that she knew how he felt. E. began fussing with the file and said, "The only one I like is only you; they've had a lot of sissies around here." V.T. accepted this. . . .

Rogers' analysis of the critical elements in relationship therapy with parents is particularly interesting because all these elements would be a part of his own approach throughout his long career. "It applies only to those parents who have a desire to be helped . . . ," he wrote. "The relationship between the worker and the parent is the essential feature. . . . The worker endeavors to provide an atmosphere in which the parent can come freely to experience and realize his own attitudes. The worker creates this atmosphere by her acceptance of the parent, by her failure to criticize, by her refusal to impose on the parent any program or recommendations, and by her refusal to answer questions except when the parent genuinely desires an answer and is unable to answer for himself. . . . The effect of this relationship upon the parent may be characterized by the terms 'clarification of feelings' and 'acceptance of self'. . . . It is typical of relationship therapy that it does not aim toward such clarification and insight primarily as a means to the end that the individual will change his attitudes or personality. Their stress is very frankly upon the individual's full realization and acceptance of himself. Any changes will come from normal growth in personality once the parent can accept himself and his limitations."

While Rank called his approach "will therapy," Taft and Allen's approach was usually called "relationship therapy." In an interview many years later Rogers summed up these influences on his own thinking: "I became infected with Rankian ideas and began to realize the possibilities of the individual being self-directing. This certainly fit in with earlier ideas I had absorbed from Kilpatrick and John Dewey. I was clearly fascinated by Rankian ideas but didn't quite adopt his emphases for myself until I left Rochester. But the core idea did develop. I came to believe in the individual's capacity. I value the dignity and rights of the individual sufficiently that I do not want to impose my way upon him. Those two aspects of the core idea haven't changed since that time."

To one who is familiar with Rogers' later work in "nondirective" and then "client-centered" therapy, it may now appear as if Taft, Allen, Rank, Virginia Robinson and others in this school were the real founders of "Rogerian" therapy, and that Rogers was merely the one who was the best salesman for the approach and got most of the credit. A closer look at the two schools, however, to be taken in the next chapter, reveals some significant differences between the Rankians' and Rogerians' methods.

Carl Rogers spent twelve years in Rochester, the years of the Great Depression, learning a great deal about helping people, while actually helping thousands of children and their parents. In addition to environmental therapy he had varying degrees of personal experience with all the deeper, direct therapies discussed above. From this experience, shortly after he left Rochester, a new approach to therapy would emerge.

Before he left Rochester, Rogers wrote his first major book, *The Clinical Treatment of the Problem Child,* published in 1939. Leonard Carmichael, his editor at Houghton Mifflin, called the book "a progress report" on the field of child guidance. It was also a progress report on Rogers' own growth, describing and presenting the pros and cons of all the types of environmental and direct therapy he had worked with in Rochester. The book contained the seeds of his future work as well. Of special interest in charting his growth are two sections of the book —his description of the therapist's role and his references to scientific research.

Having experienced a great deal and read and heard a great deal about the various approaches to therapy, Rogers asked the question: What, if anything, do all these therapeutic approaches have in common? The one point he saw where the different approaches did converge was in the attitude of the therapist. Whatever his orientation, Rogers wrote, there were four qualifications required of all therapists.

First was *objectivity.*

> There is included in the concept a capacity for sympathy which will not be overdone, a genuinely receptive and interested attitude, a deep understanding which will find it impossible to pass moral judgments or be shocked and horrified. A person with this attitude differs on the one hand from the cold and impersonal detachment of the individual with Jovian tendencies, and differs quite as sharply from the deeply sympathetic and sentimental individual who becomes so wrapped up in the child's problems as to be quite incapable of helping. It is, to come back to the first description of it, a degree of sympathetic "identification" with the child sufficient to bring about an understanding of the feelings and problems which are disturbing the youngsters.

The second qualification of the therapist was a *respect for the individual.*

> . . . a deep-seated respect for the child's integrity . . . a willingness to accept the child as he is, on his own level of adjustment, and to give him some freedom to work out his own solutions to his problems. . . . Frequently in environmental therapy the worker does select the treatment goal and arranges circumstances so as to develop the child in that direction. In psychotherapy the aim is to leave the major responsibilities

in the hands of the child as an individual growing toward independence. The more this is and can be done, the more lasting and effective the treatment. It cannot be accomplished at all unless the therapist has the capacity to see the child as a separate individual, who has both a right and obligation to maintain his separateness.

The third qualification was *an understanding of the self.* The therapist must have

> . . . a sound understanding of himself, of his outstanding emotional patterns, and of his own limitations and shortcomings. Unless there is this considerable degree of insight, he will not be able to recognize the situations in which he is likely to be warped and biased by his own prejudices and emotions . . . the individual whose own life is reasonably well adjusted, and whose own emotional needs are in large measure satisfied, is capable of becoming a helpful counselor. Perhaps the outstanding quality of some of the lay and professional people who, without much expert knowledge, have acquired reputations as trusted advisers is the fact that they are "comfortable" people, with an acceptance of themselves and an adjustment to others which gives them freedom to be objective and helpful in regard to those in trouble.

In these three qualifications of the therapist are the roots of "empathic understanding," "unconditional positive regard" and "congruence"—three concepts which would be among Rogers' most important contributions to the understanding of helping relationships. Finally, he included *psychological knowledge,* "a thorough basis of knowledge of human behavior and of its physical, social and psychological determinants," and added, "It might seem more logical to put this qualification first, but the experience of every clinic would bear out the viewpoint that a full knowledge of psychiatric and psychological information, with a brilliant intellect capable of applying this knowledge, is of itself no guarantee of therapeutic skill. The essential qualifications of the psychotherapist lie primarily, as we have pointed out, in the realm of attitudes, emotions, and insight, rather than in the realm of intellectual equipment."

A second aspect of interest here in the *Clinical Treatment of the Problem Child* is Rogers' concern with scientific research. Throughout the book he referred extensively to previous research on dealing with problem children; equally important was his frequently repeated emphasis on the need for further research. This was not a widely accepted view. The science was in its infancy; the terms—like "mental illness," "neurosis," "insight"—were vague; and the techniques of therapy were in the early stages of development. Many therapists felt it was too soon for re-search. Others felt the time was right but despaired at the difficulty of the task. Still others, like Jessie Taft, believed that science could not be applied to therapy at all. To her the process was "purely individual, non-moral, non-scientific, non-intellectual—divorced from all hint of control." Rogers disagreed with all these viewpoints. "The psycholo-gist cannot agree that this relationship, whatever its results, is a pro-cess which goes beyond intellectual understanding. If it is a process, it is possible to analyze and describe it. If it produces results, as I think most of us would agree it does, it will someday be possible—horrible thought—to measure them. The psychologist is not impressed by the claim that this is something purely individual, beyond the domain of science, some almost mystical process which simply occurs. Undoubt-edly the psychologist will do his part in bringing the movement down to earth." Indeed the next twenty years would justify Rogers' faith in the methods of science and bring him worldwide acclaim and the American Psychological Association's Scientific Contribution Award for his researches in the field of psychotherapy.

For Rogers the Child Study Department proved to be a fascinating laboratory in which to experiment and learn. By no means, however, did he spend all his time in the laboratory. As he was learning himself, he began to teach others and, in so doing, gradually began to build a reputation.

Certainly in the Rochester area he came to be regarded as one of the major authorities in the community on children and youth and their problems. He was elected Chairman of Rochester's Conference on Youth Problems, a member of the board of directors of Rochester's Council of Social Agencies, Harley School, and Memorial Scholarship Fund, and President of the Rochester Psychological Society. He gave frequent talks before community groups and, as part of the depart-mental program which he established, he taught short courses to foster mothers, teachers in six different schools, an orphanage staff, a group of workers with boys, a staff of camp counselors, social workers, two groups at the YWCA, and the Mental Health Society of Utica. Both as Director of the Child Study Department and as a private consultant, his advice was sought frequently by social agencies and institutions concerned with youth.

In the summer of 1935 he was invited to return to New York City as a visiting lecturer at Teachers College, Columbia University. "I found this highly rewarding and ego strengthening," he recalled, "I was much surprised that the classes, even though enormous (150–300) seemed to respond to me very favorably and had good learning experiences. My approach at that time was to give a lecture but with ample opportunity for questions and discussion from the group. I particularly remember one course which was broken into thirds. I taught the first part, a much more experienced psychologist taught the second portion, and I was to teach the third portion of the course. When I returned for this last portion the class applauded loud and long when I came in. I was bowled over by the message that this contained, namely, that they were glad to see me back and really liked me better than the more experienced faculty member who had been teaching them. I began to realize not only that I loved to get people excited about new ideas and new approaches, but that they loved this too."

His reputation soon spread beyond New York State. Out of his years in Rochester came the publication of a dozen articles, many of them involving original research in the child-guidance field, several of them coauthored with colleagues. Most of these articles were first read at various professional meetings. For example he presented "Three Surveys of Treatment Measures Used With Children" at the 1936 meeting of the American Association of Orthopsychiatry in Cleveland; "The Clinical Psychologist's Approach to Personality Problems" at the 1937 meeting of the National Council of Social Work in Indianapolis; and "Needed Emphases in the Training of Clinical Psychologists" at the 1939 meeting of the New York State Association of Applied Psychology at Cornell University. After the conference the papers would usually be published in the official journal of the organization. In 1936 he was asked by Governor Lehman's office to represent New York State at the sixty-third annual meeting of the National Conference on Social Work in Atlantic City. Thus Rogers' face and name began to be visible at the conferences and in the journals of several helping professions. Publication of *The Clinical Treatment of the Problem Child* also added to his growing reputation.

During this period Rogers began to wonder just which helping profession he identified with the most. Although half of his articles were published in the journals of the social work profession, and although he referred to the "worker" as often as to the "psychologist" in *The Clinical Treatment of the Problem Child,* he still tended to think of himself as a psychologist. But, he wrote, "The University of Rochester made it clear that the work I was doing was not psychology, and they had no interest in my teaching in the psychology department. I went to APA

(American Psychological Association) meetings and found them full of papers on the learning processes of rats and laboratory experiments which seemed to me to have no relation to what I was doing. The psychiatric social workers, however, seemed to be talking my language, so I became active in the social work profession, moving up to local and even national offices. [Among other things, he was chairman of the Rochester chapter of the American Association of Social Workers, one of the organizers and first chairman of the New York State Council of the A.A.S.W., President of the Monroe County Mental Hygiene Society, and a member of the executive committee of the American Association of Social Workers.] Only when the American Association for Applied Psychology was formed did I become really active as a psychologist.

"I began to teach courses at the University on how to understand and deal with problem children, under the Department of Sociology. Soon the Department of Education wanted to classify these as education courses, also. Before I left Rochester, the Department of Psychology, too, finally requested permission to list them, thus at last accepting me as a psychologist."

During 1937 and 1938 Rochester's Council of Social Agencies decided that a community guidance center was needed to coordinate the work of all the helping agencies in the community. Since the Child Study Department was already fulfilling a good deal of this function with children and parents, the Council felt that the Department should be the core of the new guidance center, with Rogers as the director. "At this point," Rogers wrote, "my psychiatric friends made a strong case to the Community Chest, to my board of directors, and to all who would listen, that such a clinic should be headed by a psychiatrist. So far as I know there was little criticism of the job I had done. The argument was simply that a psychiatrist was in charge of almost all similar clinics in other cities, and must be in charge here." Undoubtedly behind this argument was also the feeling that, where depth psychotherapy was to be involved, psychiatrists and not psychologists were the professionals best suited to the task.

Judging from his later writings, tapes and films, people often picture Carl Rogers as a totally accepting, warm, and understanding person. While these characteristics certainly do describe him, they definitely do not comprise his entire repertoire of responses. Whenever Rogers' personal or professional interests have been threatened, he has been extremely tenacious about getting his own way, or in his own words, "capable of a dogged determination in

getting work done or in winning a fight." The fight over the direc-
torship of Rochester's community guidance center was the first of
many professional battles in his long career, a good many of them,
incidentally, with the psychiatric profession. This particular battle
encompassed a year of heated, often bitter, meetings, debates, and
letters. In 1939, however, Rogers became the first director of the
Rochester Guidance Center.

David Rogers was two years old when Carl and Helen moved to
Rochester in the summer of 1928, and their daughter, Natalie, was
born that fall. With the experience Rogers was getting in the clinic and
sharing with Helen, their opinions about proper child rearing practices
changed rapidly. As opposed to the strict Watsonian behaviorism they
had tried to practice in New York City, Rogers was now telling parent
groups how "the growing weight of evidence regarding the vital importance of deep emotional security and affection for the infant is
rapidly changing our parent education programs. No longer do we find
stress on rigid schedules, on the importance of definite rules, on the
hospital-like method of caring for infants. Instead there is a wholesome
stress on the infant's need of affection and cuddling, on the fact that
such emotional security is as important as cod liver oil."
Because of his active professional life Helen had the far greater
responsibility for rearing David and Natalie. Rogers credited her with
being the better parent. "I would rate myself only fair as a father then
. . . in those days I was more concerned with whether they were
disturbing me, than whether what they were doing was in the direction
of promoting their own growth." His children did not entirely agree.
Natalie told me, "I think he's much too hard on himself that way.
. . . We had a lot of times together which kids don't have with their
fathers." David thought his father exaggerated his preoccupation with
work. "Dad wasn't away on trips very often, was home almost every
night, was accessible, was always interested in how I was doing. . . . I
always felt secure that I could do what I wanted to, that he would be
pleased and proud of me." Carl's brother Walter also remembered
many occasions when the Rogers spent weekends together. Walter,
who was by now a physician, and his wife Elise lived in Rochester for
six years during this period—for two of those years only two houses
away from Carl and Helen. Walter and Elise joined them for Sunday
drives in the country, family picnics, games, bridge, and even the
building of a kayak together. They had always been close as boys, and

this period united the brothers again as adults and cemented their lifelong friendship.

There was lots of stimulation for the children at home. "Mother would have a table filled with art materials," David remembered, "and we'd all make mobiles or collages, and I remember everybody taking great pride and interest in what everybody else was doing. Nat was a good painter and, of course, Mom was superb. So I did sculpture. We all used to get very turned on by what we were doing. Mother gave very professional criticism."

Something of their parenting style and of the atmosphere in which Rogers was raised can be inferred from Natalie's recollections of their occasional trips back to Warwood. "I was terrified of my grandparents, particularly grandmother. Grandfather was kind of pleasant. He'd have a twenty-five or fifty cent piece in our jeans for us and joke around and be kind of jovial and fun, but Grandma Rogers scared me to death. There was something about going into their fairly formal living room and the fact that they said prayers every morning and I didn't know what it was about, and I was worried that I was going to make a mistake. It felt like everything was good or evil there and I couldn't win; it had to be evil. I felt I could never possibly perform like I was supposed to, I didn't know what the ground rules were. And while it was kind of a big adventure to go to what seemed like a big estate, it had such a different feel to it, I was frightened. . . . One time Dave and I had taken a bath together and then were running around nude. We were really young and this is how we acted at home. Then I remember Aunty Mags catching us and just laying it on so heavy. 'What *are* you doing?' I don't remember what she said exactly, but this whole feeling came over me that there was something wrong with the two of us running around nude and having a good time—like our bodies were horrible. It was my first concept of sin. I felt like just going into the closet and hiding for a long time. It was terrible, just awful."

David and Natalie attended the Harley School, a private school in Rochester. The choice reflected Carl and Helen's dissatisfaction with the public school they would have attended and the value they placed on their children's education. Natalie thought her parents "didn't have the kind of money that most of the parents who sent their kids to that private school had . . . they were certainly sacrificing, in the Depression years, in sending us to a private school." David felt somewhat ashamed of his father in that social context. "We lived in a smaller house than the other kids and Dad didn't have a typical business job. Plus he looked different. His collars were always sticking out from his shirt and none of the other fathers looked that way. . . . Later, at around 16 or 17, as I began to find out who he was and what he did, I felt so profoundly lucky compared to my contemporaries."

Their choice for their children of this fairly traditional private school indicates the importance they attached to classroom achievement; although Natalie, as a girl, experienced this less acutely than David. He recalled one time when he brought home a report card and was feeling pretty cocky about his grades. He was startled when his father got angry, pulled out a class roster (Rogers was on the board of directors of the school), and said, "Well, you think you're doing so well, let me just show you how you stacked up against your classmates." David remembered being so chagrined that he buckled down to work and got almost all A's for the rest of his educational career. The expectation was quite clear.

In fact, there were quite a few expectations like this. David felt, "You were expected to do well, to do things correctly, to be polite to your parents and others. My dad was just martinetish about that sort of thing. I remember one time going in and working at his desk on a pad —just a yellow pad—drawing pictures and so on. And I remember my dad calling me in and explaining very carefully how that was not *his* pad of paper, that it belonged to the University and that, if I wanted paper, then he would be glad to help me get some or I should buy it; but that it wasn't his pad. I thought of that many times, in terms of how far he carried that very, very exquisitely honest behavior.

"He was fairly meticulous. I remember him buying me a whole set of tools quite early on, and I think it was because he used to get fairly frustrated to find nicks in his chisels or his hammers where they shouldn't be. I don't ever remember him berating me about that; but he helped me build a bench and he got me my own set of tools, and they were *mine* and the others were *his.*"

This was fairly typical of his style of discipline—calm, reasonable, and firm. Strong negative feelings were not permitted to ruffle the waters, neither between the parents nor between parent and child. Years later David said, "I never saw Dad get mad at Mom; and the reverse only once. Mom had made some pudding which was cooling in the sink. Dad washed his hands in the sink. Mom got mad and cried." Natalie said she "was never aware of any conflict between them. I never saw any anger between them and I still don't. They were affectionate with each other in front of us—physically demonstrative, warm and affectionate. But I never had any models for how to deal with anger. . . . As kids we were sent to our rooms to deal with our feelings. . . . There wasn't facilitation of open feelings in the family by anybody. The way to deal with it was to go to your room and cool off or go out for a walk or essentially keep it to yourself—not to work it through. When it wasn't interpersonal in the family, when there was a problem at school, etc., then I felt listened to and understood and so forth. But not on the crucial ground which is in the home ground. For example, I don't remember anybody ever talking out loud about the fact that Dave and I were competitive and jealous and envious. That would have helped a whole bunch. It was too early in his or their life to apply what they were learning to the family situation."

With this combination of reason and affection characterizing the children's upbringing, his father was, as David put it, "a very reluctant disciplinarian. I never got spanked or got really berated for anything. There were a couple of times he got fairly sore at me, but they stand out as being such an unusual occurrence," such as when "for the umpteenth time I'd ridden my bicycle over to some little girl's house and hadn't appeared for supper, and it had gotten dark, and I called and explained where I was and asked if he'd come get me in the car. It had happened enough times before, but he was clearly sore when he got there and said something that I remember was very crushing. He said, 'You just never know when to quit, and I hope you never take a drink because if you do you'll be a drunkard.' It was about the harshest thing he ever said to me."

Rogers was by no means the only authority figure in the family. David realized his mother "was a big, strong gal and, if I ever got really sassy, she would haul off and let me have it—very rarely—but I always felt she was perfectly able to handle a discipline situation all by herself." One such occasion was when, at age eight or nine, David went to Camp Cory, near Rochester, for two weeks. "I got there and I was just desperately homesick. And I cried and cried and my cabinmates were so pissed off at me. I remember one day I came in the cabin and they were all standing there with paddles, and they said if I didn't stop crying they were just going to beat the hell out of me, and I couldn't stop crying, so they proceeded to beat the hell out of me. I remember calling home repeatedly and saying, 'Come get me!' and finally mother came down that week. She took me out for the night and I wept most of the way. And then she came in the next morning and said that I really ought to finish camp, that if I really wanted to be a man I had to finish out the two weeks. And I remember crying all over again and saying that I didn't want to be a man—all I wanted to do was go home. But she took me back to camp. I think the second week was better."

Many of the family's most memorable occasions during these years took place at Seneca Lake, about fifty miles from Rochester. Thirty years later, during the 1960s in the United States, a great number of young people returned to the country, to the land, often in communal living situations. Rogers, in his later years, has been intrigued by this phenomenon and has written and spoken frequently on the subject. This interest can be partly understood by a letter which Helen and Carl wrote in 1931 to several of their friends from Union Seminary and Teachers College who had decided to look for a summer place together.

> Dear Gang:
>
> We have found a marvelous piece of property—10 acres in all, of woods, bluffs and lake front on the east shore of Seneca Lake near the town of Valois. . . . It is very accessible yet it is isolated, it has both a glorious view and good bathing, it has woods and bluffs, and we think some flat land would be available for ball grounds, etc., and last but by no means least, it is within our reach financially. . . . On the property is a good house, one that could be made into a main building for the group. It has a kitchen and two other rooms downstairs . . . and enough room for at least three bedrooms upstairs. . . . It is well built and in good repair. . . . He will sell the house and one acre for $500, and will give us the other 9 acres for another $500. . . . We would say the land is from 300 to 500 feet deep and stretches along the shore about 900 to 1100 feet. If you don't know about Seneca Lake, it is the largest and most beautiful, we think, of the Finger Lakes. It is 40 miles long and about 3 miles wide, and not heavily populated. . . .

Four other families joined them and the property was purchased. While the families were building their own cabins or having them built, they used the main house as the communal dining area and dormitory. Carl and Helen personally built their own cabin and maintained it for many years, often living there quite primitively. It was here on summer vacations and many weekends that the children got to know their father best. Natalie commented, "It's true he wasn't around during the day, some evenings and so on; but he doesn't give himself the credit for how big an influence he was in the summers and the whole spirit of working together, building together, doing projects together and the values of self-sufficiency and appreciating nature and learning how to do for yourself and the fun and excitement of that."

Both children felt, as Natalie did, that "working on projects with him was the best way to communicate with him—not to sit down and talk." As David said, "a lot of my communication with Dad was doing things together. . . . We'd be involved building a cabin or a bridge or sailing or something like that. . . . As far as how to be a carpenter, or the outside world, or what trees were what, or how to make a bow and arrow or a shack I learned from Dad—the motor-active kinds of things." Helen recalled one of these physical, family projects. "Carl wanted a sailboat, so in the winter months which were long and snowy in Rochester, he designed and constructed 'The Snark'—a 12-foot flat-bottomed sturdy sailboat with centerboard, jib and mainsail. This was a project we both loved. I laid out the pattern for the sails on our living-room floor, cut and sewed the sail cloth, complete with grommets and binding and rope and together we built the neatest little craft that was ever launched on Seneca Lake (or, at least that was our conviction)."

Unfortunately, when the Snark was first put into the water, its proud captain did not realize that the centerboard, which provides balance and better maneuverability, had not yet been attached. He stepped confidently from the dock, and, as his weight shifted from dock to boat, the Snark tipped promptly to one side and dumped its captain headlong into the lake—an event that soon became a favorite family anecdote.

For Natalie, the sailboat left another set of memories. "As I have thought about my girlhood," she wrote in her late forties, "the metaphor that comes to mind is that of being crew in a sailboat. That I enjoyed sailing in the boat with my father and/or my brother is a simple, joyful recollection. That being the crew for one or two men skippers while Mom was on the shore making lunch, has become a metaphor that has much significance in my development as a female. I was proud to be a good crew: I knew how to keep the boat ship-shape to the requirements of the captains. It was a small, tubby boat that my father had made, so we were proud of its stability even though it was not the sleek racing boat that others had on the lake. Our boat could weather the storms. As crew, I was pleasing the men in my life, getting their praise for doing what was expected of me. It was exciting to me to be a part of their action. I was aware that I didn't have to take full responsibility for the boat. I liked that feeling, of being protected from the full responsibility, yet being part of the excitement. I used to think, 'Too bad for you, Mom, you're not out here with the adventure of making the boat heel, or of racing towards home before the squall comes up.' I must have felt proud to be included with the men and somewhat disdainful of the woman left on shore, yet glad that she was there with the warm soup, when we got back.

"It doesn't take an analyst to see that I was part of an acculturation for my role as a woman. . . . Whether the metaphor is literally true in detail or not, (I can hear my father and brother objecting), the truth for me is how I perceived my role. . . . Though I was appreciated and loved and included, the expectation seemed to be that I would not be capable of being captain of a ship. I would ask for a turn at the tiller with full knowledge that I could only be second best. They had the *real* understanding of how things worked. . . .

"As a model for being a wife and mother, my mother set very high standards. She was nurturing, supportive, always there to do things for us, feed us, take care of us. Although she had interests of her own, the message to me was definitely that 'children and husband come first, my own needs come last.' We prospered under this in many ways, but at what cost to her?"

At one point during these years, with the primary child rearing responsibility on her shoulders, Helen did begin to feel a bit "put upon," as she described it, "though not as put upon as many young women would feel today." So she began attending some night school classes, while Carl took care of the children. She also continued her painting and became quite actively involved in a cause that proved to be an intense, lifelong interest of hers—the Planned Parenthood movement. She never did experience a serious sex-role identity crisis. She continued to assume the major responsibilities as parent and homemaker, and this clearly gave Rogers the added mobility to advance as fast as he did in his profession.

In the summer of 1939 Bernard Covner was working as an intern in the Rochester Guidance Center. He recalled how, "having gotten an M.A. in June from Penn, I had not an ounce of *practical* experience. My first assignment from Rogers at the beginning of the summer was to do a work-up on a family of 12 children coming up for adoption. He sure was willing to take risks! . . . During that summer, I decided to forfeit my scholarship at the University of Pennsylvania and not return. I told Rogers I was considering Ohio State and Iowa. He said both choices were good. I applied to both, was accepted at both. He made no attempt to influence me. I decided on Ohio State. *Then* he told me that he would join me there in January, having been appointed full professor. . . ."

William Snyder, then a graduate student at Ohio State, remembered that "it was strongly implied that since Rogers had little academic experience, he would not threaten any of the academicians in the department." Rogers thought, "I am sure the only reason I was considered was my book on the *Clinical Treatment of the Problem Child,* which I had squeezed out of vacations and brief leaves of absence. . . . Clinical psychologists were very few in number; by writing the book, I suppose I demonstrated that here was a person with practical experience in the field who also could do a reasonably scholarly job of bringing together much of the evidence. Ohio State at that time was looking for a replacement for Henry Goddard, who was one of the first people in the clinical field, and they invited me to come there. And I came in the best mood that one can come for getting a job. I really didn't think I wanted the position. I had just finished setting up . . . the Rochester Guidance Center . . . and I felt I was obligated to stay there. So they offered me an associate professorship and could see that it was very much touch and go as to whether I would even be interested in their offer. Then they upped it to a full professorship. . . ."

"I heartily recommend starting in the academic world at the top level," he once wrote. "I have often been grateful that I have never had to live through the frequently degrading competitive process of step by step promotion in university faculties, where individuals so frequently learn only one lesson—not to stick their necks out."

Even with the full professorship offer he still wavered in his decision. Helen influenced him to accept it, saying, "Now look. You've always liked teaching, you've always thought you wanted to get into a university sometime; here's a good opportunity and you shouldn't be too bound by the Rochester situation." Rogers followed her prompting and subsequently felt that "the outcome of that has helped me to make other decisions, leaving places when everyone else would say that in the obvious light of common sense I should *not* leave."

"So," Helen wrote, "with many protests from our teenage son who was loath to leave Rochester, we moved to Columbus in a blizzard in December, 1939."

CHAPTER 5
The Ohio State Years
1940-1944

The Rogers moved into a rented house on Weisheimer Road in Columbus. David told them it was a "crummy little house" and they had ruined his life by moving from Rochester. Carl and Helen agreed with the first charge but not the second, and David quickly adjusted to Columbus. Regarding the living situation Helen recalled, "We knew we wished to build ourselves a home and we started as soon as possible. It was a great experience for me—choosing the lot and planning and supervising the house as it went up." Their large lot, with many black walnut trees, was in a rural area on Rustic Bridge Road in Beechwold, on the outskirts of Columbus. They built what they considered a very beautiful home—stone work up to the first floor, stucco above that, a slate roof, and a red brick fireplace—at a cost of fourteen thousand dollars. "It was a lovely creation, and with my art training, I had a field day choosing colors and carpeting, making drapes, and so on. We moved in in January of 1941. . . . the brunt of the moving fell on my shoulders, as both Carl and Dave were down very sick with the flu. Natalie and I did it all."

Although the Rogers lived outside the city, the children were able to attend the University's Laboratory School. This meant Carl or Helen chauffered David and Natalie to and from school each day. Carl usually was able to drive them in the morning and then go on to his office. If he left the University in the late afternoon, he could also pick them up, or they would walk over to his office and read or do their homework while their father finished up his counseling, meetings, classes, or paperwork.

Rogers' contract called for a $5,100 salary for teaching three quarters of the year. His natural predilection for work was augmented by a desire to do well at his first full-time college teaching position. So, in addition to teaching a full load of courses in each of the four quarters of 1940, he supervised counselors in training both in the schools and in the campus Psychological Clinic, gave eighteen speeches and workshops for local, state, and national organizations, had seven articles accepted for publication, served as a consultant to the Kellogg Foundation and the Rochester, New York, schools, served on several college and professional committees, carried on intensive counseling with seventeen students for a total of over one hundred interviews, and saw fifty-four additional students for one or two interviews on personal or vocational problems. After the first year the number of individuals he personally counseled decreased, although he continued to accept enough cases so that he would be working with one to three students at all times. With the decrease in counseling, however, came a rapidly growing number of graduate students working for advanced degrees under his supervision.

While he felt successful enough with the undergraduate students whom he taught in a standard course called Mental Hygiene, he derived his greatest satisfaction from his graduate seminars and supervision of counselors in training. After taking mostly laboratory and theory courses, the graduate students were extremely interested in the process of therapy with real, as opposed to textbook, human beings. This mirrored Rogers' own growing interest in that area. Because of his pragmatic bent and his minimal interest in theory at the time, his courses emphasized the actual therapeutic techniques employed in treatment interviews. This was rather unique then, as most counseling programs emphasized psychological theory and diagnostic, rather than treatment, techniques.

In the winter quarter of 1940 he taught a seminar called Techniques in Psychotherapy, covering the various direct treatment approaches he had described in the last section of *Clinical Treatment of the Problem Child*. Later, in the fall quarter that year, he set up a practicum in advanced clinical treatment. "Each student carried at least one case on intensive treatment, and many of the interviews were recorded phonographically. The two-hour session was devoted to a thorough-going analysis of the treatment procedures used in a particular case, and the ways in which they might have been improved." Rogers later wrote, "I have been told that the practicum in counseling and psychotherapy which I established in 1940 was the first instance in which supervised therapy was carried on in a university setting—that neither Freud nor any other therapist had ever managed to make supervised experience in the therapeutic relationship a part of academic training. I am not certain that this statement is true. I do know, however, that I had no such brash thought in mind when I inaugurated this practicum. It simply seemed essential that if students were to study therapy, they must also carry it on, and should have the opportunity to analyze and discuss what they were doing."

One of the students in this practicum, William Snyder, remembered that "Carl's classes were intensely popular. Harold Burtt would schedule them in the evenings and on Saturday morning and at all the most unpopular times and still they would be filled to overflowing. I remember, for instance, that there were two clinics, one on Wednesday afternoon and one on Saturday morning. Students usually took the Wednesday afternoon because no one wanted to be there at 8 A.M. on Saturday mornings. . . . But when Rogers was in charge of the Saturday morning clinic, we all gladly got there before 8 A.M. and spent the morning in the most delightful work anyone can imagine. Then, voluntarily, we would go to lunch together and come back and spend the afternoon holding case conferences with him. This was above and beyond the requirements of the course, but everyone did it because it was such a stimulating situation to be in."

It was stimulating for Rogers, too. In *Clinical Treatment of the Problem Child* he had described the major approaches to psychotherapy and had given the pros and cons of each. But he had not argued for any one point of view, although his preferences for the "expressive" and "relationship" therapies were easily discernible. But the graduate students at Ohio State wanted more than the pros and cons of the various schools. They wanted their professor to teach them to be good therapists, and that meant he would have to formulate his own concept of good therapy. Pressed by their questions and comments Rogers began to describe successful therapy in his own terms and to share that notion with his students.

The process of therapy which he began to explain and to advocate, however, seemed not very original to him. It seemed that what he was advocating was what most modern therapists were already taking for granted. It was all rather obvious, certainly not controversial. True, his students regarded his ideas as new, but he assumed this was because most of their experiences were in the classroom, and they had not had much contact with practicing clinicians.

Fortunately he soon had the opportunity to put these assumptions to the test. He had been invited to deliver a speech at the University of Minnesota, before the campus chapter of Psi Chi, the psychological honor society. Recalling this speech, he later said, "It would seem quite absurd to suppose that one could name a day on which client-centered therapy was born. Yet I feel it is possible to name that day and it was December 11, 1940."

The counseling program then at the University of Minnesota had developed under the leadership of E.G. Williamson, who had a definitely directive approach toward counseling. He believed firmly in psychological tests and the ability of the trained counselor to guide the student toward satisfying personal and vocational choices. This viewpoint tended to characterize the philosophy and practice at Minnesota, which was regarded as one of the leading centers for student personnel work at that time. It was before this group that Rogers naively went to present his paper on "Newer Concepts in Psychotherapy."

"If we can see outworn and discarded techniques as the background out of which recent therapeutic approaches have developed," he told his audience, "we shall have a deeper understanding of present points of view and an increased ability to criticize them in a constructive fashion." He went on to briefly describe and criticize the more traditional approaches to counseling and psychotherapy—ordering and forbidding, exhortation, suggestion, advice, and intellectualized interpretation. Of all the approaches he criticized, he was harshest when it came to the use of advice. To prove his point he quoted part of the record of an interview conducted by an advice-giving counselor.

My job was to dissuade him from continuing in pre-business and in having him accept a substitute program of general education. First I pointed out the standard of competition in the professional School of Business. This made no dent in his armor. He still maintained that his D+ average would come up to a C this year. Knowing his dislike of courses involving math, I showed him the courses as catalogued in the professional business curriculum: statistics, finance, money and banking, theoretical economics, insurance accounting and so on. (With silent apologies to my friends who teach these courses) I told the student that these courses were "highly theoretical and abstract" and considered "very dry." On the other hand, courses in general education were practical and interesting; no economics or math prerequisites were necessary. I described some of the interesting features of the Orientation Courses. He finally agreed to think it over. I outlined this plan of action: (1) see the counselor in the general education unit for further information (I arranged an appointment); (2) discuss the matter with his folks; (3) secure transfer blanks from the Registrar's Office.

Rogers neglected to tell his audience that the counselor in this interview was none other than the program chairman of that very meeting. Having criticized the older methods, many of which his audience were still practicing, he went on to describe the "newer practices," crediting its roots in the therapy of Rank as modified by Taft, Allen, and Robinson, in the neo-Freudian analysts—notably Karen Horney—and in the fields of play therapy and of the more recent group therapy.

"The aim of this newer therapy," he said, "is not to solve one particular problem, but to assist the individual to *grow,* so that he can cope with the present problem and with later problems in a better integrated fashion . . . it relies much more heavily on the individual drive toward growth, health, and adjustment. . . . In the second place, this newer therapy places greater stress on the emotional elements, the feeling aspects of the situation, than upon the intellectual aspects. . . . In the third place, this newer therapy places greater stress upon the immediate situation than upon the individual's past. . . . Finally this approach lays stress upon the therapeutic relationship itself as a growth experience."

Later he wrote, "I was totally unprepared for the furor the talk aroused. I was criticized, I was praised, I was attacked, I was looked on with puzzlement. By the end of my stay in Minneapolis it really struck me that perhaps I was saying something new that came from *me;* that I was not just summarizing the viewpoint of therapists in general. It was shortly after that that I decided I would work toward a book presenting my point of view—a point of view drawn in large measure from others, nourished by others, but still a point of view which was my own."

He began to write *Counseling and Psychotherapy: Newer Concepts in Practice* shortly thereafter; but given all his other responsibilities at Ohio State, he made little headway. Then after teaching a full load of courses for six consecutive quarters, he managed to take the next two quarters off-duty and so spend the summer and autumn of 1941 writing his second major book. It was soon ready for publication, but Houghton Mifflin, who had published *Clinical Treatment of the Problem Child,* was not happy with his latest achievement. They did not see what college courses would use it, and when they asked the author if he knew what courses might adopt it, he could only mention two such courses—his own and one taught by an acquaintance at another university. The publisher thought he should have written the book to fit into already existing courses. They couldn't picture it selling the two thousand copies necessary for them to break even financially. Only after Rogers threatened to take it to another publisher did they reluctantly agree to publish it.

In spite of his stubbornness about getting the book published, Rogers still had his own doubts about its likelihood of success. While still writing the manuscript, he had shown it to some of his graduate students and asked them whether they thought it was publishable and whether anyone would read it. William Snyder recalls Rogers' "deep humility about his book. . . . To us, the mere asking of such questions was almost unbelievable. I perceived the book practically as the New Testament. . . ." In addition, when Rogers heard that Frederick Allen, one of the major proponents of "relationship therapy" with children and one of his own influences, was also writing a book on therapy, he felt very discouraged. He doubted whether many people would pay attention to his own book, compared to one written by the older, more experienced, and more venerable Allen. As it turned out, Allen's book had relatively little impact, while Rogers' book has sold over 110,000 copies, an extremely high figure for a clothbound volume of highly technical interest.* It has had a major, and some would argue revolutionary, effect on the field of psychotherapy.

In his preface, both speaking for the profession and describing his own growth, Rogers set the book in its historical context: "In the period of the 1920's the interest in the adjustment of the individual was primarily analytical and diagnostic. In social work it was the period of the flowering of the case history; in psychology there was a lush tropical growth of tests; in educational guidance both records and tests grew apace; in psychiatry multisyllabled diagnostic labels blossomed

---

*None of the sales figures cited throughout this book include sales of foreign translations, which were substantial. *Counseling and Psychotherapy,* for example, has been translated into Portuguese, French, Italian, German, and Japanese. Altogether there have been over fifty foreign editions of Rogers' books.

into elaborate diagnostic formulations. Never had so much been known about the individual. As time has gone on, however, these groups, and others with similar interests, have given more consideration to the dynamic processes through which adjustment is improved. The balance has definitely shifted from diagnosis to therapy, from understanding the individual to an interest in the processes through which he may find help."

The book contained many "firsts." One of these might appear rather inconsequential on the surface; Rogers used the word "client."

For the first twelve years of his career he had never had any question about what to call the recipient of therapy. In Rochester, the recipients had been either children or parents. "Dr. Rogers, there's a parent waiting to see you," the receptionist might say. "Sorry, I have two children coming in for appointments this afternoon," the counselor could explain. At Ohio State "student" joined "child" and "parent" as an appropriate description to use in the clinic and in writing about counseling.

But once he began to generalize about the therapeutic process and to describe it in terms which would cover the various forms of counseling, he needed a broader term to describe the recipient of help. He chose the word "client," which he had first used in a 1940 article. The term became popular in the counseling field only after the publication of *Counseling and Psychotherapy* in 1942.

His choice of the term, however, was not important as the solution to a semantic problem. Rather it was important in its connotation of a newer therapeutic relationship, in which the traditional word "patient" was no longer appropriate. Since psychiatry had grown out of the medical profession, it was natural that psychiatrists and psychoanalysts would view their clients as patients. The word, however, indicates much about the two roles in the relationship. A patient is usually regarded as a "sick" person. He expects the doctor to cure him, to do something *to* him, to assume much of the responsibility for his well-being. The assumption is that the doctor, because of her training, can know, even better than the patient, what is wrong with him and can prescribe the necessary method of treatment.

Rogers had long been dissatisfied with this approach to therapy and counseling. He often called it "counselor-centered therapy", in which the therapist administers tests, asks questions, makes a diagnosis and suggests—directly or subtly—courses of action for the client to follow. He had difficulty controlling his old tendency toward sarcasm, when it came to describing this type of approach: ". . . we find these counselors deciding with assurance such diverse issues as how to study history, how to get along with one's parents, how to solve the issue of racial discrimination, and what is the proper philosophy of life. From other records we know that such counselors decide issues of marital adjustment, questions of vocational choice, problems of discipline, and, in fact, all the puzzling questions which a perplexed individual can face. Obviously a generous portion of supernatural wisdom is required of the individual who takes such an attitude toward counseling. When the goal is more modest and the aim is to help the individual to free himself so that he can decide these issues in his own way, then the necessary attributes of the counselor are reduced to a human dimension."

His experiences in Rochester had convinced him that counselor-centered therapy "may serve only to make the counselee more dependent, less able to solve new problems of adjustment," while it simultaneously creates unproductive resistance in the client. He believed that the greater the responsibility the individual could take in guiding his own life, in and out of therapy, the more effective and long-lasting the therapy would be. If, as Taft had said, the therapeutic hour was a microcosm of life itself, then as the client learned to set and achieve his own goals within the hour, he also would be learning how to do it during all the other hours of life. In this context, the name "client" implied a locus of control. One consults a professional who has some helping skills, but the locus of control remains with the client who will make his own decisions. Call a client a patient, and he is liable to act like one.

The new term also faced head-on the question of whether the person who seeks psychological help is to be regarded as being mentally ill, unfit, or sick. It was a common prejudice in the early years of therapy that individuals seeking psychological help were, at worst, crazy and, at best, inferior. Many employers, for example, would not consider hiring a person if they knew he had been or was seeing a psychiatrist. But after working intensely with hundreds of individuals, Rogers was finding less and less meaning in the traditional distinctions between sick and healthy people. Although his early work had given him the tendency to label people according to their intelligence (average, dull, superior, etc.) and their personality (neurotic, psychotic, normal, etc.), this early work in testing had also taught him that adjustment and maladjustment were arbitrary terms assigned to the distribution of test scores on a bell-shaped curve, meaning that all individuals are maladjusted to some degree. Many professionals and laymen thought (and still think) that therapy is for sick people, while counseling is for basically healthy people with one or two specific problems. After counseling so many students whose "presenting problem" of vocational choice or poor study habits were soon revealed to be the symptoms of much deeper psychological conflict, Rogers no longer accepted these superficial labels and distinctions. He wanted a client to be able to come for psychological help—counseling *or* therapy—in much the same spirit that a client comes for legal counsel or consults an accountant or architect. Rogers always sat face-to-face with his clients, conveying this same egalitarian idea.

The word "client," then, symbolized a basic attitude toward the therapeutic relationship—one which gave considerable dignity to the client, which conceived of the counselor and client as equals working together to achieve the client's goals as he sees them. To describe this approach, Rogers introduced two terms: "client-centered" and "nondirective" counseling and therapy. Probably because he used the latter term much more frequently and even devoted a whole chapter of *Counseling and Psychotherapy* to contrasting "The Directive vs. the Non-Directive Approach," beginning in 1942, the phrases "nondirective counseling" and "nondirective therapy" became associated with the name of Carl R. Rogers.

But was it really his own contribution, this nondirective therapy? Back in 1939 Frederick Allen had lectured:

We are prepared to take people as we find them—willing, resistive, skeptical—and create a situation which from the beginning gives both parent and child the feeling that here is a place which imposes nothing beyond helping them to clarify what they are ready to do in their relation to us—where they can feel the interest is in them as people, not as problems, and where if they continue they are doing so because there is some desire and not because of our decision. They become participants—not recipients of help from the very beginning.

From the beginning, our relation to parent and child is based on a respect for the integrity and capacity of that person—limited though at times it may be—and disguised as it frequently is by a sense of defeat and failure. We do not bring into our relation with them, except where our own human limitations prevent it, a preconceived conception of what they should be or how they should manage their relationships. We are anxious that this relation shall provide an opportunity for both parent and child to get a clearer understanding and acceptance of what they are, at that time, and what they are able to do, with the strengths they have, to deal more responsibly with a reality which is theirs and which no one, however well equipped, can assume for them.

So much of Rogers' thinking and practice was steeped in earlier traditions, especially that of relationship therapy, he hardly knew himself what was original and what was not. To assess his unique contribution it is necessary to go beyond general descriptions like the above and to look more closely at what many psychologists and counselors, for almost a generation, came to view as "The Method" of nondirective counseling.

To Rogers, nondirective counseling was a clearly structured process that consisted of three major phases, often overlapping: (1) release, (2) insight and (3) positive actions based on insight. In a highly condensed fashion, his account of therapy with Johnny and his mother illustrates the three phases:

> Johnny . . . in his contacts, is made to feel free to express his attitudes toward his parents, toward other persons and elements in his environment, and toward the clinic and the therapist. He is free to vent his angers by bitter talk, by shooting toy soldiers, by criticizing the clinic equipment, or in any other way which gives free expression to his feeling. The only limitation is upon destructive action which has social consequences. He can hate the therapist, if he wishes, and can destroy a doll which represents him, but he cannot attack the therapist directly: All of John's attitudes are recognized and clarified. The therapist shows his understanding, but he does not criticize, does not approve, does not try to meet the boy's needs himself. If Johnny feels unloved, the worker may recognize this ("You feel that nobody cares about you at all") but he does not try to become a parent substitute. Gradually, as Johnny begins to see himself in a certain way—for example, as a boy who feels very much unloved, and who in return hates his parents and torments them, but turns to others who will give attention—he finds that he has more control over his actions. He begins to see that there are some limited things he could do about his own situation. Perhaps he puts these into words. Perhaps he merely surprises his mother by offering to help her in her housework. A slight, but deeply significant change, takes place.
>
> In her interviews, the mother goes through a parallel experience. For the first time in her life she finds herself able to talk of hidden attitudes which she has never admitted to herself. She does not know how the therapist makes this possible, but the dropping-away of the necessity of defending all her actions is something which is vividly experienced. Gradually she can admit how much she prefers her other child to John. Suddenly it occurs to her, and she can face the thought, that this is one of the reasons why John likes to do mean things just to annoy her. Because of her new understandings, her tone of voice changes when dealing with the boy at home, her discipline loses its slightly sadistic

quality, and when John offers to help with the dishes, she is able to respond with a thoroughly sincere expression of her gratitude, and of her affection for him. Freed from the necessity of always being "right," she decides to discard some of the rigid methods she has devised for controlling him and to put their relationship on a more realistic and comfortable basis—a relationship in which each may express annoyance at the other, but in which there is also room for real affection. In her case, as in John's, a release of feeling leads to self-understanding, and this in turn leads to actions directed toward a more satisfying goal—a more genuine, more mature parent-child relationship.

In the first phase, that of "release," the client unburdens himself about his problems and concerns. This process, initially, has a cathartic value; it is psychologically, emotionally, and even physically freeing to express pent-up feelings. If rightly handled by the therapist, the release of feelings can move the therapy rapidly forward. Correct handling consists essentially of two specific techniques—"simple acceptance" and "reflection of feelings." Simple acceptance might be an "I see," "Yes," "M-hm," or anything, verbal or nonverbal, to let the client know he is being heard, followed attentively, understood, and still accepted. This helps him continue to reveal himself and explore the issues he has been discussing. Reflection of feelings is a more difficult skill for the therapist to learn. It requires a deep concentration on what the client is saying and then a restatement of, not the intellectual content, but of the essential *feeling element* in what has been said. For example there is the student who wanted Rogers to solve his problem for him—whether or not to tell his parents that he was failing in his college work.

STUDENT: Oh, I don't know if they're going to sort of condemn me. I think so, because that's what they've done in the past. They've said, "It's your fault. You don't have enough will power, you're not interested." That's the experience I've had in the past. I've been sort of telling them that I improved in this respect. I was—I was all right the first quarter. Well, I wasn't entirely all right, but I just got worse. *(Pause.)*

ROGERS: You feel that they'll be unsympathetic and they'll condemn you for your failures.

STUDENT: Well, my—I'm pretty sure my father will. My mother might not. He hasn't been—he doesn't experience these things; he just doesn't know what it's like. "Lack of ambition" is what he'd say. *(Pause.)*

ROGERS: You feel that he could never understand you? •

STUDENT: No, I don't think he is—is capable of that, because I don't get along with him, don't at all!

ROGERS: You dislike him a good deal?

STUDENT: Yes, I did feel bitter toward him for a while and I've gone out of that stage, and now I don't feel bitter against him but I—I'm sort of ashamed. I think that that's it more than anything else, an experience of shame that he is my father. . . .

Reflection of feelings communicates to the client that whatever his feelings and behavior are or have been, no matter how troubling or frightening or socially disapproved of, he is still accepted as a worthy human being by the therapist. This kind of acceptance enabled Mike, a teenage boy, to share his feelings about his stepfather, while talking to Rogers, for the first time, before a large audience of high school counselors:

ROGERS: But, uh, part of what really makes for difficulty is the fact that your relationship with your stepfather is not completely rosy.

MIKE: M-hm. Let's just put it this way: I hate him and he hates me, and it's that way.

ROGERS: You *really* hate him and you feel he *really* hates you.

MIKE: Well *(thinking about it),* I don't know if he hates me or not, but I know one thing. I don't like him whatsoever.

ROGERS: M-hm. You can't speak for sure about his feelings, cause only he knows exactly what those are; but as far as you're concerned. . . .

MIKE: He knows how I feel about him.

ROGERS: You don't have any use for him.

MIKE: Not whatsoever. . . . And that's been for about eight years now.

ROGERS: So, for about eight years, you've lived with a person whom you have no respect for and really hate.

MIKE: Oh, I respect him. . . .

ROGERS: *(simultaneously)* Oh, I got that wrong.

MIKE: . . . I don't have to but I do. But I don't love him. I hate him. I can't stand him.

ROGERS: There are certain things you respect him for, but that doesn't alter the fact that you definitely hate him and don't love him.

MIKE: That's the truth. I respect anybody if they have bravery and courage and he does. And though I respect him—I don't like him.

Rogers often used the expression "clarification" of feelings along with "reflection." The two previous examples illustrate this well, when the student says, "Well, my—I'm pretty sure my father will. My mother might not." and Mike says, "Oh, I respect him. . . . But I don't love him." In both cases, the young men, in responding to the therapist's reflection, modify more explicitly their previous expression of their feelings. In the process they become a bit clearer about and see more vividly what their own feelings are. It is just as though they are looking into a psychological mirror which the therapist holds up for them to view themselves. They might have some previous understanding of their feelings, but the mirror helps them see more clearly, and in an accepting context.

The potency of this method is apparent in a brief but moving exchange between Ernest (E) and Virginia Axline, his teacher-therapist (T), one of Rogers' students at Ohio State. Ernest is six years old, very insecure because of earlier events in his young life, and unable for psychological reasons to take food orally. He must be fed intravenously. He cannot even swallow water without regurgitating it. Ernest and his teacher, on the first day of school, are watching the other children gleefully drinking from the water fountain, the "bubbler," which obviously fascinates them all.

E. It looks like fun.
T. You think it would be fun to drink from it, too.
E. *(Nods agreement)* But *I* can't.
T. You don't think you could drink it.
E. It looks like fun.
T. You don't think you could drink it, but still you would like to.
E. I'd like to try.
T. You want to try it.
E. I used to take a drink from one of those things when I was in the hospital. I don't drink now.
T. You remember what fun it was *(E. grins and goes over to the drinking fountain.)*
E. It might not stay down.
T. You think it might not stay down, but you still want to try. *(E. nods his head. He takes the handle and turns it up too high and jumps back.)*
E. It's a lot of water.
T. It looks like a lot of water to you.
E. I'll drown myself. *(He takes a drink, glances at the teacher, grins broadly.)* It stayed down!
T. Yes. It stayed down. *(He drinks again.)*
E. It stays down. *(He seems quite delighted.)*

What was significant to Rogers in this dialogue was how the teacher showed "an accepting, non-argumentative, non-coercive attitude, being just as ready to accept his discouraged and fearful attitudes as his courageous ones. Untrained workers are prone to persuade—'I'm sure you can take a drink'—or to be supportive—'I'll help you and then it won't be so hard'—or to bring pressure to bear—'You want to be a big boy like the others, don't you.' It takes restraint and a therapeutic point of view to let the child know that he is accepted for what he is, not for what he is not."

Clients often try to express the usefulness of this approach for them. An adolescent girl once told Rogers, "You're like a balance wheel. . . . It's almost as if I were talking to myself, but with someone listening and trying to think on it. . . . What you do is let a person talk and put in comments that keep it going instead of stewing in a circle. . . . You're someone to blow off steam to and to talk to so I can make up my mind."

Not only does reflection and clarification of feelings help the client see himself more objectively, it also helps him accept himself as he is, which gives him a firmer foundation on which to grow. Implicit in the process is the growing attitude in the client of, "Well, I'm saying all these terrible things about myself and showing myself to be a deeply troubled, confused, perhaps even despicable person; yet here this other person is listening to me, understanding what I'm trying to say, doesn't seem shocked by anything I say, doesn't approve or disapprove, but gives me the feeling that I'm not so bad or abnormal or crazy. . . . Well, then maybe it's true. Maybe I'm not such a bad, unhealthy person. Maybe I have more value than I give myself credit for. Maybe I shouldn't put myself down all the time and believe all the things people tell me about myself. Maybe if I stay with this, I'll learn more about myself and more about how to solve my problems."

Thus the therapist, through her attitude of acceptance and her skill in reflecting and clarifying feelings enables the client to move naturally into the second phase of therapy, that of "insight." As he accepts himself more easily and recognizes his feelings and the facts about himself more clearly, the client soon begins to make connections between the separate feelings and facts. "To see new relationships of cause and effect, to gain new understanding of the meaning which behavior symptoms have had, to understand the patterning of one's behavior—such learnings constitute insight," wrote Rogers. For example a "graduate student says with feeling, 'I'm really just a spoiled brat, but I do want to be normal. I wouldn't let anyone else say that of me, but it's true.' A husband says, 'I know now why I feel mean toward my wife when she's sick, even though I don't want to feel that way. It's because my mother predicted when I married her that I'd always be saddled with a sick wife.' " Or in a counselor's account of a mother's gradual recognition of her own responsibility for the poor relationship with her son: "One of the things that she brought up was that he seems to want attention, but that the methods he uses get negative attention.

After we had talked a little bit about that she said, 'Perhaps what would do him most good would be for him to have some affection and love and consideration entirely apart from any correcting. Now, I guess we've been so busy correcting him that we haven't had time to do anything else.' "

How does insight develop? What does the therapist do to promote it? Rogers wrote, "The primary technique which leads to insight on the part of the client is one that demands the utmost in self-restraint on the counselor's part, rather than the utmost in action. . . . The primary technique is to encourage the expression of attitudes and feelings . . . until insightful understanding appears spontaneously. . . . To recognize that insight is an experience which is achieved, not an experience which can be imposed, is an important step in progress for the counselor."

As the client gains increasing insight into his patterns of feeling and behavior, he gradually begins to enter the third major phase of therapy, that of "positive actions resulting from insight." A small, scared boy takes a drink from a water fountain. A man brings flowers to his sick wife whom he has resented. A mother changes her way of disciplining her son. The actions may be small ones, but terribly important as symbolic, self-initiated first steps in a lifelong process of psychological growth. "In actual counseling practice," Rogers wrote, "such positive steps are almost invariable concomitants of insight."

At this point, therapy begins moving rapidly toward its conclusion. With the new positive actions the client takes outside the therapy comes further insight which, in turn, leads to still newer, more independent action. There comes a time when he begins to wonder aloud whether he isn't about ready to end the interviews. The therapist, by reflecting and clarifying these feelings, allows the client to work through his ambivalence about ending therapy. When the client feels ready, he terminates the relationship. However, "it is not expected that his problems will all be solved through counseling, nor is this assumed to be a desirable goal. Satisfying living consists, not in a life without problems, but in life with a unified purpose and a basic self-confidence which gives satisfaction in the continual attack upon problems." Rogers emphasized this point. Describing the ending of therapy with a teenage girl, he wrote, "She has not achieved complete insight into her behavior, nor has this ever been the goal of counseling. She has achieved what might be called a 'working insight,' sufficient to enable her to meet her present problems, and to make continued growth inevitable."

This was nondirective counseling. "Release," "catharsis," "acceptance," "reflection and clarification of feelings," "insight"—all these terms have become a routine part of most psychologists' vocabularies, as well as those of many laypersons. But what, if anything, was new with Rogers'? As he pointed out himself, release or catharsis had long been used as a therapeutic tool—for example, in Greek drama, for centuries in the confessional of the Catholic church, later in psychoanalysis, and still later in the field of play therapy from which he had learned a great deal. Neither did he introduce the concept of acceptance, nor the technique of recognizing, reflecting, and clarifying feelings, nor the practice of refraining from directing the client in his life. All these had been used often by the Rankian school and by other individual therapists of different schools. Insight too, was a widely used word in psychiatry and psychology, although it had many different meanings attached to it. It was not by introducing new concepts, then, that Rogers made his initial mark on the field of counseling and psychotherapy. What, then?

I would suggest that Rogers' contribution lay not in his uniqueness, but in his *extreme* and *systematic* approach to therapy. In effect he took many of the newer concepts and practices in therapy and built them into an organized system which was more extreme than any of his recent predecessors or contemporaries.

To appreciate his radical approach, one might make some comparisons between Rogers and his teachers in the Rankian school. The following is an excerpt from the third interview that Jessie Taft conducted with a child named Helen.

> Helen is drawing a picture of a lady holding an umbrella:
> "That's you," she says laughingly.
> "Helen, were you mad at me last week?"
> "No."
> "Weren't you mad—just a little? I should have been in your place—
> because I wouldn't let you take the crayons home."
> "I wasn't mad. I like to come here to draw."

Later in the same interview, Helen reiterates, "I like to come," and Taft responds, "Yes, I know you do, but you may feel differently some day."

Or, as Taft describes her fourth interview with a boy named Jackie:

> He goes over to the steam pipes which he had found hot before, and shows extreme caution and fear. Can hardly bring himself to touch the

pipe which burned him. Finally does so after much effort and finds it
cold.

"You decided to stay home on Thursday, didn't you, Jack?"

"Yes." No further comment. "It's hot here."

Again with Jackie:

He runs out quickly to see if the broom is there. When he comes back
the story has grown. "We took the broom away from her and chased her.
She was going to chase us, but we chased her."

"And that's what you'll be doing to me some day. I see I have to look
out."

Clearly Dr. Taft is trying to help the children express their feelings and is communicating that feelings of anger, of avoidance, and
of the eventual desire to end the relationship are all acceptable.
However, she is also responding to feelings which the children
probably hold but have not yet verbalized or which she expects the
children will come to hold in the future. In Rogers' view, while the
reflection of unexpressed feelings might sometimes prove helpful,
it is a highly dangerous technique which usually sidetracks the interview—either because the therapist cannot really know what the
client is feeling and might perceive it incorrectly, or because, even
when the therapist is correct in reflecting the unexpressed feeling,
the client often becomes resistant, since he is not yet ready, emotionally, to recognize the feeling on his own. In recognizing and reflecting unexpressed feelings, the therapist attempts to hasten the
process of therapy, but, in fact, often retards it by driving the client
into a stance of defensiveness. The therapist, said Rogers, should
avoid "the verbal recognition of repressed attitudes which the client has not yet been able to express."

None of Rogers' predecessors had gone to this extreme. How would
therapy move forward if the therapist refrained totally from introducing new data in the form of questions, comments, or reflections of
feeling designed to delve beyond the surface and let the client see his
previously hidden feelings? Rogers was not troubled by this. When the
client was ready to acknowledge his deeper feelings, he would. Probing
is more than likely to produce resistance. Provide total acceptance and
the accurate reflection of feelings, and the therapy will move forward
on its own. Speaking with increasing authority, he often reminded his
readers that "in this type of situation, insight and self-understanding
come bubbling through spontaneously. Unless one has thus watched

insight develop, it is difficult to believe that individuals can recognize themselves and their patterns so effectively."

But what about interpretation? Could this not hasten insight? The therapist has spent years studying the dynamics of personality. Does she throw all this knowledge out the window and merely reflect the client's feelings? Admittedly even Freud recognized that interpretation could produce resistance rather than insight, if it were ill-timed; but still he advocated interpretation, as long as it were well-timed and offered in a way likely to be accepted by the patient.

Here, again, Rogers went to the extreme, advocating that the counselor refrain entirely from any interpretation. He wrote, "The counselor will do well to refrain . . . from giving interpretations of the client's behavior, the elements of which are based, not on the client's expressed feelings, but on the counselor's judgment of the situation." Even if the interpretation were accurate and accepted, it would still be more valuable to allow the client to achieve it on his own, thought Rogers.

He did make one exception. "When the interpretation is based entirely upon statements which the client has made, and when the interpretation is merely a clarification of what the client has already perceived for himself, this type of approach can be successful." An example of this comes in an interview Rogers conducted with a teen-age girl, Barbara, who is explaining,

> "Before all this, I believed in controlling oneself, in complete mastery of my mind and feeling." Counselor discussed this, saying that what she was gradually learning was that there was no such thing as complete control of mind and feeling; that it was rather hard for her to recognize that the part she was shutting out was a part of herself. She said, "You know that motto, 'Be yourself.' I used to hear that, and I couldn't understand it. I didn't think that I wanted to be myself, or that I knew what it meant to be yourself. I guess I have acted that way so long that I don't quite know how to be myself."

The counselor's interpretation inserts no new ideas or attitudes into the therapy. In effect, it is not an interpretation at all, but a reflection and clarification of several attitudes Barbara has expressed earlier. Thus Rogers' position remains an extreme one: no interpretations, unless the client has already achieved the insight on his or her own.

In both encouraging release and furthering insight, then, Rogers' client-centered therapist was more nondirective than any other writer had ever advocated and illustrated. What about the third phase of therapy—the positive actions which result from insight? Surely the therapist takes some more active stand here—suggesting alternatives, pointing out possible consequences of certain actions, asking clarifying questions that would help the client think through his situation. Surely she does more than continue to accept, reflect and clarify feelings. On the contrary, Rogers maintained his extreme position, writing that ". . . social behavior originates in a genuine desire to be social . . . mature behavior grows out of the desire to be grown up . . . affectionate behavior can come only from feelings of affection. We cannot *make* people social, or mature, or affectionate. We can, however, help parent and child to see themselves more clearly, to explore their own purposes more deeply, and to make a more clear-cut conscious choice as to the direction they wish to take and the behavior which is in accord with their own deepest purposes."

But even when a person knows his deepest purposes, does that necessarily mean he will act on them? Just because people know what is right or know what they want does not mean they are going to act accordingly, does it? Yes, said Rogers. If the insight is real insight and not insight imposed by the therapist, then positive actions based on the insight are almost inevitable. They may not be fully mature actions, but they are first steps which are highly significant for the client.

Still, all this assumes that we operate rationally, that we can behave in more mature ways simply because we know it would be better for us. Even Rogers admitted that the neurotic person will often cling to his symptoms and, "because he is unhappy and threatened by others or by circumstance, he cannot consider clearly or objectively the alternative courses of action which may offer less in the way of immediate gratification, but more in long-term satisfactions. Like Hamlet he finds that the situation 'puzzles the will/And makes us rather bear those ills we have/Than fly to others that we know not of.' "

Why should a client give up the security and satisfactions that his neuroses have provided for so long? Why take that leap into the unknown? Again because of insight. "When the neurotic sees clearly the choice between his present satisfactions and the satisfactions of adult behavior, he tends to prefer the latter." Why? Here Rogers borrowed a concept from the Rankians, and mentioned, only in passing, a type of "creative will," which acts upon the situation in a similar way to "the choice exercised by the child who decides to forego the immediate ice-cream cone in order to save his nickels for the prized roller skates. He chooses the course which gives him the greater satisfaction, even though that satisfaction is delayed." And so the client makes his own positive choices as he more clearly sees himself and his situation.

With each chapter of *Counseling and Psychotherapy* the system in Rogers' therapy emerged with cumulative clarity. With all his ambivalences, the client wants to grow, wants to mature, wants to face his problems and work them through. Accept and clarify his initial expressions of feeling, and a fuller, deeper expression of feelings will follow. Accept and clarify these and insight will spontaneously occur. Accept and clarify these insights, and the client will begin to take positive actions in his life, based on his insight. Accept and clarify the meaning the client sees in his positive actions, and at some point, when he feels enough self-acceptance, self-understanding, and confidence in his ability to continue to deal with his own problems, he will end the relationship.

"Clinically," Rogers wrote, "we know that sometimes this process is relatively shallow, involving primarily a fresh reorientation to an immediate problem, and in other instances so deep as to involve a complete reorientation of personality. It is recognizably the same process whether it involves a girl who is unhappy in a dormitory, and is able in three interviews to see something of her childishness and dependence, and to take steps in a mature direction, or whether it involves a young man who is on the edge of a schizophrenic break, and who in thirty interviews works out deep insights in relation to his desire for his father's death, and his possessive and incestuous impulses toward his mother, and who not only takes new steps but rebuilds his whole personality in the process. Whether shallow or deep, it is basically the same."

It was incredibly simple, yet incredibly profound in its ramifications. For several years Rogers had been saying that psychotherapy was not an intuitive art, but a scientific endeavor which could be described and measured. Now he had described it in terms and with examples so concrete that any therapeutic interview could be evaluated in terms of his nondirective model. In fact he and his students began doing just that, measuring various aspects of therapy. In the chapter blatantly titled "The Directive vs. the Non-Directive Approach," he described the first pieces of data they had gathered when the two types of therapists were studied. In one chart he listed the techniques most frequently used by the directive and nondirective groups of counselors. Typical directive counselor techniques were: asking highly specific questions, explaining, discussing, giving information, indicating topics of conversation, proposing client activities, and so on. The most frequent nondirective counselor techniques were: recognizing the client's feelings or attitudes, and recognizing or interpreting feelings or attitudes expressed by general demeanor, specific behavior, or earlier statements. Although each group sometimes used techniques more typical of the other, Rogers pointed out, "the fundamental contrast is emphasis, the directive group stressing those techniques which control the interview and move the client toward a counselor chosen goal, the nondirective group stressing those means which cause the client to be more conscious of his own attitudes and feeling, with a consequent increase in insight and self-understanding."

In a sentence which undoubtedly made many therapists distinctly uncomfortable, he pointed out how, in this small study, "the directive counselors used on the average almost six times as many words as the nondirective." He also pointed out how their studies showed that "most counselors are far more directive than they suppose."

Although this initial research proved nothing about the relative effectiveness of the two types of therapy, it did serve to focus attention, more specifically than ever before, on the methods used in therapy. Vague concepts like "accepting" and "directiveness" were given concrete meaning in therapists' specific behaviors. The therapist responses could then be correlated with the subsequent client responses. The research of one student, William Snyder, enabled Rogers to write that the therapist's asking questions, giving information and advice, persuading and pointing out, neither encouraged release nor led to real insight by the client. Simple acceptance and the recognition and clarification of feelings did. By classifying almost ten thousand counselor and client responses, in thirteen interviews with six clients and four different counselors, Snyder showed how acceptance by the counselor was followed by insight by the client, with a marked degree of regularity.

Rogers had introduced a new model of therapy—new not in concepts or techniques, but in its collection of already existing ideas and practices into a clear, consistent, and extreme system of thought and practice. He had supported his new model with page after page of examples based on his own experience, with forceful polemical writing and with the smallest beginnings of empirical research. Still, I wonder whether *Counseling and Psychotherapy* would have received a small fraction of the attention it did receive were it not for its most exciting innovation of all—"The Case of Herbert Bryan."

In 1935 the Yale Institute of Human Relations had recorded a complete psychoanalysis; but though transcribed, it was never published and made widely available. Few people knew of its existence, not even Rogers. Consequently, in the *Clinical Treatment of the Problem Child,* in 1939, Rogers had written that "a verbatim record of intensive psychotherapy with one child, giving in full all the conversation of both child and therapist, would be a new and valuable contribution."

In Rochester he thought he might try to make that contribution himself. In 1938 Virginia Lewis of the Rochester Guidance Center staff was conducting some interviews in the clinic, and Rogers and the others set up some borrowed recording equipment in the office next door, concealing the microphone in the lamp by the counselor's desk. They recorded the first interview, then eagerly gathered around the phonograph to hear what they expected would be a landmark in the history of psychotherapy—the first interview of the first fully recorded therapy case. What they did hear was an excellent reproduction of streetcar rumblings, automobile traffic, and street noise, and Rogers abandoned the whole idea for the time being.

In 1940 Bernard Covner, one of Rogers' graduate students at Ohio State, reminded him of what he had written in *Problem Child* and informed him that he was a radio ham with some skills in electronics. Covner located the equipment they would need in Columbus, while Rogers managed to obtain two hundred dollars from the department chairman to buy the equipment and a year's supply of discs and styli. Covner obtained from his father's store enough old drapes and rugs to sound-treat three recording rooms, and then set up the whole operation. They were in business. The 78-rpm discs were set up on two recording machines, so while one record was being turned or removed, the other machine could begin recording, without missing a word. This had to be done about every three minutes. Meanwhile it was necessary to continue cleaning off the shavings which the stylus cut into the recording discs.

Within a few months about eight hundred record faces, or fifty hours of actual interviewing, were recorded in this manner and then laboriously transcribed. The recordings and transcripts served several valuable purposes. First, they proved to be excellent case studies for Rogers' practicum with graduate students in training. Second, the recordings and transcripts enabled Rogers and his students to study certain therapeutic concepts in much more detail than before. For example, disagreeing with classical psychoanalysts, Rogers wrote, "In fact, study of our recordings has led us to new concepts of resistance in therapy. We have come to feel that resistance to the therapist is entirely due to too much probing, or too rapid interpretation on the part of the counselor and that it is neither a desirable nor a constructive part of therapy." With their recordings he and his students could identify just when resistance first appeared, what the counselor had said to encourage it, and whether he increased or lessened the resistance in subsequent responses. Third, the recordings furnished the data for research studies on psychotherapy, including many dissertations under Rogers' sponsorship. Finally, the verbatim transcripts of interviews could be used in articles and books as concrete examples of psychotherapy as actually practiced. In this last area Rogers made an historical contribution.

From among the eight hundred record sides came the last hundred and seventy pages of *Counseling and Psychotherapy*—"The Case of Herbert Bryan"—eight full interviews with a young man, constituting the first complete series of therapeutic interviews ever to be fully recorded, transcribed, and published. Never before had the field of psychotherapy had the opportunity to follow, word for word, complete with "U-hm's" and pauses, the full course of a therapy, from the first words the client uttered to the final good-byes. Never before had any therapist been willing and able to subject himself to the minute scrutiny of the entire profession, to hold himself up as an example to be praised, ridiculed or emulated. Never before had such a valuable tool, one which could furnish the raw data for innumerable scientific studies on psychotherapy, been placed so dramatically before the psychological community.

In the transcript of the case, before each counselor response, Rogers wrote the letter C and then a number. Thus, the counselor's first statement prefixed with a C1 and his very last ("O.K. And good luck to you") with a C614. Likewise, an S, the traditional designation for the subject in an experiment, and a number preceded each client response. In this way Rogers, in commenting upon the interviews as they evolved, could refer to precise statements of the two parties.

One has to read several of these interviews—both the transcript and Rogers' running commentary on it—to appreciate fully the cumulative impact of this type of presentation upon the reader. Several of Rogers' comments on the first interview convey some of the flavor of "The Case of Herbert Bryan."

C1.   The counselor by this very broad kind of opening question makes it easy for the client to discuss his problem in any way he wishes. Note that S1, 2, and 3 are all in response to this one question.

C4.   Here is a moderately directive question limiting the client to a specified area for discussion. It might have been better for the counselor simply to recognize the material expressed, in some such statement as, "You've noticed a real change in these symptoms?"

C7.   This counselor response is definitely helpful in bringing progress. It must already be evident to the counselor that these are psychological, not organic, sufferings. The usual reaction is to question, in some way, their validity. Any such implication would have thrown the client on the defensive and made him intent on proving that his pain was real. The counselor's recognition that he is describing real pain helps Mr. Bryan to feel that he is genuinely understood, and makes it possible for him to go ahead and tell of times when he is not suffering (S8).

C11, C12.   Good instances of entirely non-directive responses which simply recognize the feeling being expressed, make conversation easy, and enable the client to continue to explore his attitudes.

C26.   Why did the counselor interrupt here? This seems to be a quite unnecessary directive question breaking into the flow of feeling. It leads to brief client responses ending in a pause (S28), which the counselor has to break with another rather directive question. This in turn leads to a repetition of the symptoms originally described (S29), and it is only following this that a fresh start in recognition of feeling is made. This is a minor example of the way in which clumsy handling by the counselor can delay progress.

C40.   This direct question is in line with the client's feeling, and in the rapid give and take of the interview we cannot expect perfection. Nevertheless, it is plain that a better response on the part of the counselor would have been, "You like to write, but this blocking keeps you from it." It often seems difficult to catch and bring into the open the ambivalent impulses.

C43, S43, C44.   Adequate recognition of attitudes brings the flow of feeling around again to the same point which was poorly recognized at C18, C19. The phonographic recordings indicate that this frequently occurs. If the client expresses some attitude which has significance for him, and this is misunderstood or inadequately recognized by the counselor, the same attitude is likely to be expressed again later. Adequate recognition, on the other hand, tends to lead to further and deeper expression.

C46.   Here the counselor makes a more complete and satisfactory attempt to define the type of help which the client can expect from counseling.

S46, S47.   Is it because the counselor's remarks sound almost as though he were bringing the interview to a close that Mr. Bryan is able to reveal this highly significant feeling? Or is it merely that having revealed his superficial symptoms, he is now ready to recognize that they are to some extent symptoms that he wants? At any rate, in this one interview, he has gone through three levels of expression of his problems. At first they are described as pain, suffering, maladjustment. Then (S35) they are described as conflicting forces within himself. Now they are recognized as symptoms to which he can cling, in spite of his desire to change. This is actually the beginning of insight, a clearer degree of self-understanding.

C48. Fortunately the counselor recognizes and states clearly the ambivalent feeling which is being expressed. This enables the client further to express his feeling in what are the most significant items of this first interview. They show clear progress in exploration at more than a superficial level.

C53. Here, again, the counselor must have been tempted to agree or disagree. He wisely does neither, but merely clarifies the attitude that is being expressed.

C57. Here is the second blunder of the hour. The counselor departs from sound recognition of feeling. Instead of some such response as "You feel that someone else must start the ball rolling," he asks a direct question which goes deep into the client's situation. If Mr. Bryan were fully aware of why his "negative" side was in power, he would have little need of help. The counselor draws nothing but a confused and somewhat defensive answer (S57), and follows it with another direct question which endeavors to tie the client down to a specific situation, that of dancing (C58). The client makes a partial response, and then definitely retreats into a long philosophical statement (S59) which has no direct relation to his problems and is as far as possible from being specific. . . . This indicates how easily the course of constructive therapy can be diverted by errors which may not be recognized as errors at the time.

C79. The first portion of this conversation is helpful in that it defines the client's responsibility for the direction of the counseling interviews. In the last portion the counselor returns to the same direct question which delayed therapy before (C57) and unwisely tries to give this problem as a "homework assignment." This would seem to be the third blunder in the interview.

S79, S80, S81, S82. The client is determined to answer the counselor's questions at once. To some extent this represents insight. To some extent it is almost certainly an attempt to prolong the interview. The counselor has definitely to call a halt (C85).

The "Case of Herbert Bryan" was a fitting summary for *Counseling and Psychotherapy*. The eight interviews with Herbert Bryan made all the preceding chapters come dramatically alive in what amounted to a "supervised internship" for all the counselors and psychologists reading along. What therapist could read these interviews, with Rogers' comments, and remain aloof? Vicariously each reader became the counselor of Herbert Bryan, wondering, "Now how would I respond at this point?" In fact Rogers advocated just that—that readers cover up the counselor's response, while reading, and formulate their own response before reading further. In critiquing the anonymous counselor in the case of Herbert Bryan, then, Rogers was critiquing all counselors; for all counselors, more or less frequently, do what this one counselor got praised or blamed by Rogers for doing.

Thus Rogers became the conscience of counselors and therapists across the country. In his nondirective approach every single statement or reaction of the therapist could be judged according to a set of criteria. Although there was hardly anything in his approach which could be described as his invention, nevertheless the extremity of his views, the clarity of his writing, and the concreteness of his examples —especially the case of Herbert Bryan—made Rogers, almost overnight, the foremost proponent of the "newer concepts in practice" in psychotherapy. Even personally he became the symbol of the nondirective counselor, for most readers soon realized that it was Rogers himself who was the counselor of Herbert Bryan. At the very end of the eighth interview, this exchange took place:

S598.   You're sort of a pioneer in this, aren't you? Is this largely your own technique?
C599.   Oh—I don't know. It seems to work, at any rate.
S599.   I haven't kept up so much with the latest psychoanalytic techniques.
C600.   Well, there certainly are many others. I think that a good many different people have been working toward somewhat the same point of view.
S600.   Well, perhaps some day I can bring you a copy of my novel.
C601.   (Laugh.) Right. I'd be delighted to get it. Well, now, you're feeling pretty confident in your ability to handle this. I would like to leave the notion of further contacts up to you. . . .

Readers of transcripts and, even more so, listeners and viewers of tapes and films where Rogers is the counselor often comment upon how deeply he seems to understand and accept the client and how sincerely and creatively he manages to communicate this understanding and acceptance to the client, as he reflects and clarifies feelings. Unfortunately not all counselors have this degree of acceptance, understanding, and skill. Consequently, while attempting to employ the deceptively simple method of reflecting feelings, many counselors unintentionally acted out a grotesque parody of the client-centered approach. Movements are often condemned because of the first people who jump on the bandwagon. One hears many anecdotes like the following:

I once went to a Rogerian counselor. I started talking about my problems and all he did was repeat back, word for word, everything I said.
I couldn't figure out who was the crazy one, him or me. I said, "I know
that; that's what I just told *you.*" So he said, "You know that. That's what
you just told me." After a while, I really started getting angry. So then
he tells me I'm getting angry. . . .

Certainly the nondirective approach is easy to satirize. The best
known satire of all, a favorite of Rogers' critics, originated some time
in the early forties and goes something like this:

It seems a client came into Dr. Rogers' office, on the thirty-fourth
floor, and said, "Dr. Rogers, I've been feeling awfully depressed lately."
"Oh, you've been feeling very depressed lately?"
"Yes, I've even seriously been considering suicide."
"You feel you might like to kill yourself."
"Yes, in fact, I'm going to walk over to the window here."
"U-hm. You're walking over to the window there."
"Yes, I'm opening up the window, Dr. Rogers."
"I see. You're opening the window."
"I'm about to jump."
"U-hm. You're about to jump."
"Here I goooo. . . ." *(He jumps.)*
"There you go."
A loud crash is heard below. Dr. Rogers walks over to the office
window, looks down, and says, "SPLAT!"

Of course, Rogers never lost any patients in this manner. His experience taught him that adequate recognition of self-destructive attitudes
mitigated a client's desire to do himself harm. He also believed that
definite limits preventing physical violence should be a part of therapy.
Nevertheless there was one passage in *Counseling and Psychotherapy*
which probably helped the suicide anecdote to spread. It was his reference to "Jessie Taft's story of a little girl who persisted in hanging
farther and farther out of the window to test out the situation to the
utmost. Dr. Taft was rightly reluctant to put a limit to this activity,
which did not directly affect the rights of others. When she made it
plain that the responsibility rested with the child and that she might
fall if she wanted to, the youngster became cautious."
Even had this paragraph not appeared, the anecdote, no doubt,
would have been created and repeated anyway. For, as in all satire, the
anecdote merely carried the reality to an absurd extreme, and the
reality here was Rogers' great emphasis on *technique* in nondirective
therapy. Technique was the thing. Just as free association was the

primary technique for the classical psychoanalyst, reflection of feelings was the primary technique to Rogers, the key to the whole process, the source of all growth in nondirective therapy. Thus, when Rogers' graduate students would meet in their practicum and listen to the phonographic recordings, Rogers would lift the needle after each client response and ask the students how they would respond at that point. Then he would offer his own response, not as the definitive answer, but as his own judgment. And so they would spend hour upon hour sharpening their technique. Likewise, the initial research he sponsored centered almost exclusively on counselor techniques.

With this kind of emphasis it should not be surprising that counselors came to think of counseling as the mere reflection of feelings. If one could learn this simple technique, he or she could be a counselor, or so it seemed. True, Rogers also wrote that the counselor "creates a bond characterized by warmth, interest, responsiveness . . . ," is "sensitive to human relationships," and has a "deep-seated respect for the child's integrity"; but these attitudinal elements were easily overlooked because of the preoccupation with technique. And the technique was not as easy as it seemed. Again, one has almost to hear tapes of Rogers counseling clients to appreciate the subtle yet profound difference between reflections of feeling which convey genuine acceptance and a sincere desire to understand as opposed to those reflections of feelings which come off as rote, distant, and superfluous responses. Rogers' comments are almost always tentative, conveying, "Have I understood you? Do I have it just the way you feel it, neither more nor less? Do you feel I'm really with you?" He is also very imaginative in the way he reflects feelings, as shown by how he put a tense young student at ease during a first interview, while also conveying understanding and acceptance:

> ROGERS: And you do feel, I take it, that this thing bothers you most in a social situation?
> STUDENT: Yes, whenever I'm with people.
> ROGERS: You wouldn't be bothered if you were a hermit?
> STUDENT: (Laugh.) No, but I don't want to be.
> ROGERS: I understand.

Or in interviewing a boy, for the first time, before a large group of counselors:

> MIKE: Well, my outlook on life isn't dim, but it's not the shiniest thing in the world either.

ROGERS: It's about 15 watt, maybe, or something? Right?
MIKE: Well, maybe 75.
ROGERS: *(Surprised.)* Oh, 75. . . .

Or in working with a woman who was describing her growing over-dependence on her mother:

> WOMAN: I accepted what she did for me and I just took it for granted, and it made me more reliant on her, really.
> ROGERS: You stood on her two feet.

He found lots of ways to convey his sincerity and humanness to clients—even sometimes by blatantly violating his own principles of good counseling, as in the fourth interview with Herbert Bryan:

> S337. I used to have the idea that there was perhaps one significant event which I had repressed to the subconscious which I needed to call up from the subconscious for my therapy. But I see now that the—no matter what the origin is, these things after all operate under present circumstances, and that it's the present operational function which is —which does have the true significance.
> C337. I'm tempted to say—you're damn right, m-hm. I think so. . . .

The publication of *Counseling and Psychotherapy* received a mixed reception. With it came increasing fame for its author, offices in several prestigious professional organizations, an increasing number of graduate students who transferred from other professors to his sponsorship or who came to Columbus to study with him, and numerous requests for speeches and workshops. The term "Rogerian" came to describe, for many, a whole new orientation toward psychotherapy and counseling. The psychological establishment, on the other hand, mostly ignored the book. It was not even reviewed in any major journal of the psychological or psychiatric profession. Two reactions to the nondirective approach that Rogers often heard, and often from the same person, were, "It would be impossible to conduct psychotherapy in this way, and besides we're doing just this already." The first part reflected the widely held belief that nondirective counseling was only surface therapy, too superficial to lead to any significant, longterm adjustment. The second part reflected the defensiveness which many therapists were then starting to feel about being directive, after Rogers had so vigorously associated directiveness with being authoritarian, outdated, and nonhelpful. As one writer described it, "Gradually psychologists began to realize that merely advising parents and children was not altogether effective. After Rogers introduced the concept and technique of client-centered counseling and demonstrated its effectiveness, direct advice giving became a bugaboo in many therapeutic circles."

The reaction to this book would prove to be rather typical in Rogers' career. His work seemed to move individuals, rather than systems or establishments. Within a few years hundreds, even thousands of students would be flocking from around the country to attend his courses and take his ideas back home with them. But psychology departments, medical schools, and professional journals did their best to ignore or minimize his contribution. Arthur Combs, one of Rogers' first graduate students at Ohio State and later a well-known psychologist-educator in his own right, recalled with some amazement the atmosphere in the established profession at that time.

"It is really very hard to believe the degree of rejection of Rogers and his concepts which dogged his steps in the early days. Here he was, advocating an approach to counseling and psychotherapy which was as American as apple pie, full of hope and belief in the democratic ideal. Here he was also, a product of American psychology operating at a period when American psychology was trying to be scientific with a capital S, and coming out foursquare for the necessity of applying research methods to psychotherapy practice to such an extent that during the '40s and '50s he and his students turned out more research on psychotherapy than had ever before existed. Despite all this, American psychologists by the thousands were completely enamored of psychoanalysis, a European product, contrary to most orthodox American psychology, based on the vaguest kinds of concepts and with almost a complete disdain for subjecting itself to the rigors of careful research. Looking at the degree of acceptance these points of view have now achieved, it is hard to believe that in those days humanists had practically to fight for their professional lives."

As Rogers explained it at the time, "One might suppose that there would be a generally favorable reaction to this discovery [that the client could take charge of his own growth], since it amounts in effect to tapping great reservoirs of hitherto little-used energy. Quite the contrary is true, however, in professional groups. There is no other aspect of client-centered therapy which comes under such vigorous attack. It seems to be genuinely disturbing to many professional people to entertain the thought that this client upon whom they have been exercising their professional skill actually knows more about his inner psychological self than they can possibly know, and that he possesses

constructive strengths which make the constructive push by the therapist seem puny indeed by comparison."

With his new book Rogers' stock among the graduate students at Ohio
State rose even higher than before, with a corresponding loss of popularity among many of his colleagues. As Combs recalled, "Rogers'
position on the campus was often one of being intensely admired,
sought out and respected outside the Psychology Department, while
in the Psychology Department he was often ignored, snubbed, or
attacked in petty ways. . . . The students who were there at Ohio State
at the time didn't help matters much. . . . I can remember we'd go
around and talk about 'the Bible.' We thought this was pretty funny,
you know, whenever we'd mention 'the Bible,' we'd raise our eyes to
the sky and bow a few times. Well, the faculty didn't think that was
particularly funny. . . . I'm sure he was cursed with his students."
    Rogers saw his graduate students quite differently. They provided
his most stimulating experiences at the University—in the formal classroom, in the clinic, or in the informal sessions and meetings. Several
became his and Helen's lifelong friends. William Snyder remembered
how "students were completely charmed and captivated by this man
who was so warm and understanding and approachable, who had
significant new, good ideas to share. Most of us saw him very much as
an older brother, possibly a father surrogate. . . . I asked to be reas-
signed from a previous advisor, whom I considered to be an old,
decrepit mossback, compared to the young, vigorous, and really brilliant Carl. The fact that twenty-five or so of us asked to make such a
transfer did not increase his popularity with the faculty. As a matter of
fact Carl was assigned a stuffy little office, and originally you had to get
into it by walking through another faculty member's office." (He insisted on a private entrance, and got it.)
    Consistent with his nondirective approach to psychotherapy he was
quite nondirective or student-centered in his teaching approach. "He
believed in things like letting students grade themselves, if you bothered grading them at all," said Snyder. As Father Charles Curran
recalled, "He seemed to permeate the atmosphere around him with a
genuine respect for graduate students as mature adults, equal to himself. He never assumed any prerogative of professional condescension
or professorial eminence; yet at no time did he lose any position of
dignity or authority. There always was about him a quiet dignity. And
when he needed to assert his authority as a professor of a class or in

the graduate school, he certainly seemed to me to do it with directness and unequivocal responsibility. At no point, however, did this clear image of himself assume tones of condescension or any indignity for the graduate student."

On one occasion, for example, Curran and several other Catholic priests had quite a confrontation with Rogers on several issues. Since they knew of Helen's involvement in Planned Parenthood, and Carl's support for it, birth control was one of the liveliest topics discussed. Curran described the scene:

"I and some other graduate students associated with me decided to invite Carl to a private dinner and to confront him on some issues where we felt he was not consistent with his own ideas, and certainly in some ways not consistent with our thinking. At some point in the evening, the confrontation got quite hot, and very open things were said that, as I thought about it then and afterward, was a great act of trust on the part of this group of graduate students toward Carl. I knew of no professor then—and I've met few since—that I believe could have taken as genuinely and as simply as Carl did the rough and somewhat impolite things that were said. And I remember afterwards thinking that he could show some kind of genuine resentment of this and even indicate it in some way by his manner toward us when we met again, or in his grading of us, in some form, in our graduate programs. The most remarkable thing about this to me is it seemed to me when Carl left, that he was pleased with the evening and in no way offended or even ruffled beyond the obvious effects of the immediate skirmishes that we had had, and that he left truly grateful, not as a full professor, but simply as a friend, for the dinner and the interesting company and the evening. And, again to my respect and admiration for him, at no point in our meetings later did any questions ever, even by remote suggestion, occur that he had been handled impolitely or roughly or in any kind of bad-mannered way. He seemed truly to understand our genuineness and openness in trusting him with our objections, our difficulties and even our feelings; and toward me personally, and I'm quite sure toward the others, he never showed the slightest negative response to what, in retrospect, could have been a somewhat impolite type of confrontation when he was the honored guest at a dinner."

Within two years of his coming to Ohio State, twenty-five of the sixty or so graduate students working for advanced degrees in psychology were doing so under his supervision; and he had rejected several others for various reasons. On one occasion, probably in 1942, Rogers invited all the graduate students who were working with him or who were interested in his work, about forty altogether, to his house and pointed out that probably, as a group, they would be having a significant impact on American psychology in the next twenty or thirty years. In many cases this prediction proved to be true. Arthur Comb's work has been very influential in the humanistic movements within psychology and education. Victor Raimy, originally under Rogers' supervision and then on his own, contributed much to modern psychology's interest in the self concept. Virginia Axline, who originally coauthored with Rogers a lengthy and moving case study of nondirective play therapy, went on to popularize play therapy in two well-known books, *Play Therapy* and *Dibs in Search of Self.* Thomas Gordon, who worked with Rogers for several more years, developed parent, teacher, youth, and leadership "effectiveness training" models which have had an enormous impact on parenting and the helping professions.

Quite commonly—David remembered it as almost weekly—the Rogers' would invite some of the graduate students to their home for informal professional meetings or for purely social occasions. David and Natalie both remembered fondly their ping-pong matches with Tom Gordon, Don Grummon, Nick Hobbs, and the others, and David later felt that his own way of relating to his own students was greatly influenced by experiencing his father's rapport with his students.

At home Helen always was Carl's partner in creating a warm and gracious setting that would facilitate comfortable interaction. Helen once wrote of herself, "I am essentially a home maker and have always felt that to make the wheels run smoothly and have an attractive home in which to bring our friends has contributed very substantially to the success and prominence to which Carl has risen." Natalie agreed with this description but saw it in a different light. "This model played some havoc for me, when it came to my own marriage. I took on that same model without questioning whether it was right for me."

Mother and daughter represented two different viewpoints. With rare exceptions Helen did not seem to feel captive or resentful in a traditional woman's role. Friends of the Rogers always described her as a strong and forceful personality in her own right. Bernard Steinzor's first impression was that she was "a very striking woman, taller than her husband and much more outgoing. One sensed she was a woman of great strength." Throughout her life she pursued her independent interests in painting and in the Planned Parenthood movement. A naturally empathic person, she often served as combination mother and counselor to many of their friends—so successfully that Carl occasionally felt, "Oh, my God. She's better than I am!" In later years, when I wrote to Helen and addressed the envelope to "Mrs. Helen Rogers" (this was just before "Ms." became popular), I was promptly rebuked and, in friendly terms told, "By the way—I really am very proud of being Mrs. Carl R. Rogers—as my letterhead suggests, and while I love you to call me Helen, I also like my mail addressed as above—so I don't feel like a divorcee." She was seventy then. She did subscribe to *Ms.* magazine two years later.

Natalie spent her years in Columbus attending the University's progressive laboratory school, one of the schools in the famous "Eight-Year Study." Her lengthy ninth-grade paper on "Progressive vs. Traditional Education in Elementary Schools" was a masterpiece of careful classroom observation and analysis. A typical paragraph read,

> Each family has its own problems and needs guidance from someone experienced in that field. Maybe John is an only child and has no chance to play with anyone so he becomes dependent upon his parents. Or Suzy is the youngest child in the family and is bossed so much she won't do anything for anyone else. . . . These are just samples of some of the family problems where the nursery or elementary school can help.

It sounded so much like her father's writing style that I asked them if he had helped her; but both father and daughter remembered her doing it entirely on her own. Her teacher sent the paper to the principal with a covering note saying, "Natalie has put her very youthful finger on some things which many adults—even students of education—frequently overlook. I wonder whether many of our observers could give a better account of what they see in our classes and the others they watch. I think you'll agree with me that Natalie has had a rich learning experience in carrying forward the study of her problem. I think this is a good case in point of the unlimited opportunity inherent in the emphasis upon self-directed learning."

At about this time she read *Counseling and Psychotherapy* and, like many readers, felt it spoke to her personally. She remembered reacting, "Hey, this is just the way I think," and being surprised her father thought that way too. Later in high school she visited Virginia Axline's classroom, was very impressed by her way of working with children, and decided that she would like to become a play therapist. Since the Rogers did not practice an organized religion, Natalie recalled, "I didn't have a Book to go by, so I spent a lot of time thinking about what was meaningful to me. I can remember going to bed at night and thinking a lot about that—religion and philosophy. I had to figure it all out for myself."

She felt they not only tolerated but also encouraged her independence. "I didn't feel I was bound to home. When I was thirteen, I went to a work camp in West Virginia for coal miners' children, sponsored by the Ethical Culture Society and the American Friends Service Committee, where we built the housing, fed the children, and so on." David felt one of the implicit messages in their family was "You're on this earth to be of service." If so, Natalie was clearly getting the message. But when she wrote home and "asked to bring a poor little miner's kid home and adopt her, they were very sympathetic, but explained very firmly that it wouldn't work and it just couldn't be done." She did return to the camp for two more summers as a counselor, however.

David, too, thrived in the Ohio State Lab School. Although his mother and Aunt Mags often told him what a good student his father had been, school had meant little to him until then. He had got away with what he could, although he'd continued to get good grades on the strength of his natural abilities. At the Lab School there were no grades and class attendance was optional, so he tested the limits of the system for the first three months. Then one day, as he recalled, while working on a project, he "realized, 'this is really fascinating.' " That was a turning point. "I feel I owe this school an enormous debt. It really turned me on toward learning—city planning, how it would be fun to be an architect, poetry, English lit., writing."

During a career week in his junior year he became interested in medicine and spent a period of time shadowing the doctor father of his girl friend, the woman he later married. Recognizing his potential, the school director encouraged him to work even harder, telling him that, when he went to college, he could not be both a good student and a playboy. Graduating from high school in 1942, David proceeded to try to prove him wrong. But after a year and a half at Ohio State (where there was no tuition because of his father's position), he realized he had no real direction. He decided to apply to Harvard and Cornell Medical Schools and was accepted at both. Although he regarded his father as a sympathetic listener at the time, he did not discuss the decision with his parents, actually choosing Cornell because he liked the pictures in the catalogue better. Later he discovered that Cornell Medical College was in New York City, not in Ithaca and in the beautiful Chenango Valley, as he had thought from the pictures.

During the Rogers' four years in Ohio the graduate students were consistently impressed with each member of the Rogers family and the relationships among them. One student, Charles Curran, saw in Carl and Helen "a genuine openness and naturalness to their own children as well as to others." He recalled that someone once asked Rogers if he used the nondirective counseling method with his children and that Rogers somewhat explosively answered, "Hell, no, I'm not a counselor to my children. I am their father." To Curran this remark seemed to characterize Rogers' relationship to his children. "Somewhat like the minister's children, we sometimes think of the psychologist's children as having some kind of special burden to bear and a certain kind of official good children's or successful children's role they have to carry out. I found none of this at all in my occasional visits to Rogers' home. On the contrary, it seemed a very ordinary, but rich and genuinely respectful relationship, as any sensitive, considerate father would have with his children. There were no tones, not even remotely, of the somewhat stiff quality that psychologists sometimes have with their children, in trying too hard to play the role of understanding parents."

Speaking of David and Natalie, Curran also recalled,

"I admired them. I felt pleased, in the way an adult is, that he is around charming and likeable, alert children who respond openly to him. . . . They were both remarkably normal, in the best sense of that term, and each, in his or her own way, obviously already outstanding and unusual. . . . While he was not a hero to his children, he had their rich and deep respect. They saw him very much as their father and also as a man of most unusual ideas and fineness of response and feeling to others."

Another graduate student recalled an event which, for him, illustrated the type of relationship Carl and Helen had with their children. As part of his supervised field work William Snyder was administering intelligence tests to several of the more gifted students at the University School and interpreting the results to them. David Rogers, near the end of his high school career, was among those Snyder tested. The boy's scores were astoundingly high, and in interpreting the results to David, Snyder explained that the tests showed he had intellectual abilities which made him capable of doing anything he wanted to do, in terms of a career. David went home and told this to his parents and, very honestly, asked if they thought this were so. To Snyder, this event indicated how relaxed the Rogers were about bringing up their children. Many parents would have been continually reminding their children of how bright they were and how they should be using their abilities. The Rogers had the easy confidence that David and Natalie would come to recognize their own abilities and find their own interests without much pushing from their parents.

This proved to be true. David received his medical degree, with highest honors, in 1948, at age twenty-two. Natalie entered Stevens College in Missouri, in 1944, just before her sixteenth birthday. As we shall see, both went on to distinguished careers.

On July 1, 1941, at Warwood, Walter and Julia Rogers celebrated their fiftieth wedding anniversary, receiving over two hundred guests who came to offer their best wishes. All the children and grandchildren made an impressive picture for the family album: Lester, head of the Bates and Rogers Construction Corporation, with his wife Lucile and their four children; Margaret, a school teacher, unmarried and living with the parents; Ross' wife Jean and their two children (Ross had died in 1933); Carl, Helen, David and Natalie; Walter, an obstetrician-gynecologist in Pasadena, with his wife Elise and their two children; and John, also an officer in Bates and Rogers, with his wife Ruth and their daughter.

Fortunately, David and Natalie were developing their own interests in Columbus, for their father's growing professional stature meant more and more commitments which competed with his family time. Even before the publication of *Counseling and Psychotherapy* in 1942, Rogers had become prominent in many professional organizations. The publication of the book only increased the momentum of his already growing reputation. He remained involved in the American Orthopsychiatric Association, serving as vice-president of the national organization in 1942. He also became deeply involved in the newly formed American Association for Applied Psychology, a group which splintered off from the American Psychological Association because of objections to the rather authoritarian structure of the parent organization and its relative lack of interest in clinical and applied psychology. Rogers' rise in that organization is somewhat indicative of his growing professional stature in the early 1940s. In 1940 he was a member of the executive committee of the Clinical Section. In 1941 he became chairman of the Clinical Section, served on the Executive Committee of the Ohio branch and on the national Committee on Professional Training, and became an associate editor of the *Journal of Consulting Psychology*. In 1942 he remained as chairman of the Clinical Section and also became a member of the national Board of Governors and associate editor of

Applied Psychology Monographs. In 1943 he was elected President of the national organization, serving the 1944–45 term.

"Meanwhile," he later wrote, "Robert Yerkes was arguing that if the parent organization, the APA, could be reorganized so as to be democratic in its structure, all of psychology might again be brought together." Serving on the Subcommittee on Survey and Planning in Psychology, with such distinguished figures as Yerkes, Ernest Hilgard and Edwin G. Boring, he expended much time and energy attempting to reunify the profession.

His rising stature was helped considerably by the many studies and articles bearing his name that were appearing in the professional journals. "At Ohio State University," he wrote in one article, ". . . we have phonographic and typescript accounts of nearly one hundred interviews"; he then went on to describe this valuable new tool, the electronically recorded interview. In another article on "The Development of Insight in a Counseling Relationship," he wrote, "In the counseling and research on counseling which is being carried forward at Ohio State, we are gradually accumulating more information about this important aspect of psychotherapy." He had a way of creating an excitement about the work he and his students were doing, of calling attention to himself and his university, but in a way that was hard to call arrogant; since the tone was always tentative about what they were learning, forward-looking in terms of new questions they were investigating, and inviting in that he always seemed to hold out the offer to others to join them in the valuable work. All told, he had about twenty articles and studies published between 1940 and 1945.

In addition, his students' work at Ohio State was soon adding to his reputation and to the growing interest in nondirective therapy. By 1945 he was able to refer in his writings to eight theses and dissertations on the nondirective approach. The students themselves, adapting and expanding on their dissertations, by 1945 had published about a dozen articles in the professional journals, all mentioning Rogers and the work going on in Columbus. This was only the beginning of Rogers' and his students' research efforts—a handful of studies compared to the deluge to come. Nevertheless it was highly noticeable, pioneering work in a field which had never before attempted serious and extensive scientific research on a therapeutic approach. In the introduction to his article "Counseling," in the April 1945 *Review of Educational Research,* Rogers was able to write: "For the first time in the history of these reviews, there is sufficient research in the *process* of counseling to justify a separate chapter. . . ."

As he had in Rochester, he became quite involved in committee work and consulting in the Columbus community, giving many speeches to groups like the Home Economics Institute, the Ohio Guidance Association, the State Welfare Conference, Columbus Psychological Society, various school faculties, parent and church groups, and many others. He conducted an extensive survey of "Mental Health Problems in the Columbus Public Schools," which, based on fifteen hundred school children studied in grades one through six, led him to conclude that there were over five thousand seriously maladjusted children in the Columbus schools. He did a statewide survey on the problems of youth in wartime. He served as consultant to several schools regarding their guidance programs and arranged for several of his graduate students to get part-time or full-time positions working as counselors in churches, schools, and youth groups in the community. In May of 1942 the *Columbus Citizen* ran a five-part newspaper series on Ohio State's Psychological Clinic, with Rogers featured prominently throughout the series. He sounded far from nondirective in these articles, when it came to advising parents.

> Says Dr. Rogers, "Tell the children the truth, when they ask about the sirens and the blackout. Be entirely realistic about it. . . . Say calmly and matter-of-factly, 'Why, yes—there is a possibility that German planes may come over Columbus some day. But it isn't a very big chance. And certainly, there's a very, very small chance that bombs will hit our house.' "
> If there is one particular factor in child training that Dr. Carl R. Rogers, clinic psychologist, is particularly emphatic about, it is this: Give your child a chance to become an independent, responsible person—a chance to grow. . . . "Managing an allowance is one of the best ways to learn responsibility," Dr. Rogers declares. "But let your child handle the money absolutely by himself. Don't dictate how it should be spent. If he wants to spend the whole quarter, or whatever it is, in one day, and be broke the rest of the week, let him do it! Let him take the consequences. . . . As your children grow older, encourage them to plan their own parties, to choose their own clothes. What if they do make rather a mess of things once in a while! They'll learn many valuable lessons from their mistakes. . . . A child must learn to take the risks of growth," says Dr. Rogers, "even though he gets some bumps in the process. It's the only way he can get the satisfaction of growing."

While Rogers' stature was growing both in the professional community and in the Columbus and Ohio area, by an interesting series of events he gradually became deeply involved in the national wartime, and then the peacetime, effort. The beginning of this involvement was described in the November 1942 *Psychological Bulletin:*

> For a number of years the Division of Program Surveys, U.S. Bureau of Agricultural Economics, under the direction of Dr. Rensis Likert, has had a staff of interviewers conducting intensive interviews with farmers to explore all aspects of rural attitudes toward farm programs. With the coming of the war, this surveywork was greatly expanded to cover urban as well as rural groups, and its scope broadened to cover topics of national significance in war time.
>
> This rapid expansion meant multiplying the staff, and created a need for training new members in interviewing techniques. The Division became interested in the "non-directive" approach to treatment interviewing which is being developed by Dr. Carl R. Rogers and his students at Ohio State University, and in the phonographic training devices which have been used there. The "non-directive" approach, in which the interviewer is trained to develop techniques which release emotionalized attitudes without directing the client or influencing the expression of such feelings, seemed particularly applicable to the survey task of getting attitudes, and reasons or factors underlying those attitudes. Dr. Likert made arrangements for his interviewers to be given an intensive period of training at Columbus. . . . In all, forty-two interviewers were sent to Ohio State for this training, each group staying for one week. . . . According to those in charge of the surveys, the training program. . . . conducted by Dr. Rogers and Mr. Charles Cannell. . . . did much to improve the field work of these interviewers.

In 1943 Nicholas Hobbs, a former graduate student of Rogers and then a major in the Psychological Branch of the Air Force, asked Rogers to conduct a new survey, later called "Adjustment After Combat: A Study of Returned Combat Gunners and Their Utilization in the Flexible Gunnery Training Program." In conducting the survey, Rogers and his staff interviewed one hundred gunners who had been returned to the United States after serving their required number of combat missions overseas. Many of them had participated in air raids in which there were terrible losses, such as those over the Ploesti oil fields in Romania where sometimes as many as twenty-five percent of the planes were lost in a single mission. They were having a difficult time adjusting to army life back in the States. Aside from suffering varying degrees of battle fatigue, the men also felt that their skills and knowledge were not being used. They had been in actual combat, in life or death situations where performance was all that counted. Now they were required to sit through gunnery classes conducted by young lieutenants who had never seen combat, forced to march up and down on parade grounds, shave every morning, shine their shoes, and otherwise play at military life. It was not long before they became disgruntled and, then, became discipline problems of major concern to their commanding officers. Rogers listened to these men, encouraged them to express their feelings, their frustrations, their fears and anxieties. Based on his findings, he made eighteen recommendations designed to help them adjust to their new situation and to use their resources more effectively so they would feel they were continuing to play a meaningful role in the war effort.

Again the government was pleased with Rogers' work. In distributing Rogers' ninety-page "restricted" report, the commanding officer of the base where the study was conducted wrote a covering letter in which he said, "The accompanying study of the adjustment of ex-combat gunners to their duties in Training Command Schools is believed to be a very important contribution towards understanding gunners with combat experience and towards their fullest utilization in the gunnery training program. The efforts of Dr. Rogers and his assistants are greatly appreciated by all who have given thought to this problem." The letter may have sounded perfunctory, but many of Rogers' recommendations were implemented.

As the war years continued, more and more men and women entered the armed forces and faced the problems of adjusting to military life. Simultaneously more and more soldiers were returning from overseas and bringing back with them problems of adjustment to civilian life and stateside military life. As Rogers described them, "There is the homesick and lonely inductee; there is the service woman who is deeply upset because her engagement has been broken; there is the man who is concerned about his wife's behavior while he is far from home; there are the returned servicemen, often bitterly resentful in regard to civilian life and confused as to their own aims and purposes; there are the wounded and handicapped individuals who, in spite of good medical care, feel deeply insecure as they endeavor to face the world; there are the psychoneurotic individuals whose conflicts and instabilities bring them often to the civilian individual in whom they feel confidence."

Once again Rogers was asked to help, and he accepted the offer of a one-year appointment as Director of Counseling Services for the United Service Organization (USO). Writing to a colleague, he explained, "My function will be to train the professional staff workers (there are about 3000 of them) in counseling techniques which will enable them to handle more skillfully the problems of personal adjustment which come to them. Consideration will also be given to the intelligent use of community resources in gaining additional help for the maladjusted serviceman. The USO is finding it necessary to modify and individualize its club program in localities where there are considerable numbers of handicapped men, wounded men, psycho-neurotics, and returned combat men. It would be part of my job function to help in adapting the USO program to the needs of these special groups."

The short appointment meant a move back to New York City, where the USO headquarters were located. Carl and Helen rented an apartment at Twenty-third Street and Seventh Avenue and enjoyed the city where they had spent Carl's graduate-school days many years before. An added job benefit was that David was attending Cornell Medical School, in New York City, at the time. Unfortunately Carl's job did not give him all that much time in New York.

One of the basic models he set up for training the USO volunteers was a short intensive training course (today it would be called a workshop) of eight to twelve hours. In a twelve-hour course, typically, the first six hours would be spent in lectures and discussions. Topics covered were: "adjustment problems and motivations," "basic counseling principles," "applying basic principles in the casual contact," "the use of resources in dealing with individuals," and "a local program for dealing with individuals in the USO." Following this period of cognitive background, four hours would normally be spent in practice and demonstrations. The client portions of a phonographically recorded interview would be played or read, and the workers would write in the responses they would make and then discuss their various responses in light of the client-centered principles they had just been taught. Then, using volunteers from the group to role-play a serviceman and a worker, several interviews would be staged before the entire group, followed by a general discussion of the worker's responses. The final two hours would be devoted to dealing with the questions, concerns, weaknesses, and interests of the particular group of workers.

Rogers repeated this course all over the country. By mid-1945 he had conducted less intensive half-day or whole-day workshops for 655 workers and had met for shorter demonstrations or talks, all told, with 4500 to 5000 USO volunteers. The repetition was too much for him. Rogers has always been a forward-looking person—either applying old ideas in new formats or settings, greatly modifying his own ideas, or moving into entirely new fields of interest. But in 1944 and 1945, week after week, with group after group, he had to muster up his energy to repeat the same ideas over and over again in the same context, trying to be as enthusiastic each time as he was the first time, hearing and responding to the same questions. Although successful throughout the year, he came to hate his job—the repetition and the pace—and to look forward to the end of his tenure with the USO. Even the amusing skits the workers would perform at the party that usually followed each course tended to get repetitive—as time after time he watched them gleefully enact the scene of the USO volunteer who dutifully repeats the words of the serviceman who threatens suicide, goes over to the window, and finally jumps!

On one occasion an intensive course had been scheduled in advance at a downtown hotel in a southern city; but when Rogers arrived he found that an unforeseen problem had arisen. The hotel, in accepting the original reservations, had not realized that blacks would also be attending the course. It was against their policy to rent rooms or serve food to "colored." When Rogers stated very clearly that black people were fighting and dying for their country alongside white people, and if the hotel wasn't willing to let them room and eat alongside each other there would be no conference, the hotel relented.

As always it came easily and naturally to Rogers to put his experience and insights down on paper. As a part of his job he wrote a series of brief articles or position papers that were distributed to all the USO branches and used in his training courses. In "A Counseling Viewpoint for the USO Worker" he summarized why the client-centered approach was especially useful in counseling servicemen. First, it works, it's effective. Second, it can be taught relatively easily, even to semi- and nonprofessionals. Third, it can be used safely, as compared with methods which intrude into the client's life or his unconscious mind. And "finally it may be stressed that it is based on a philosophy which is fully consistent with the highest development of democratic living . . . a viewpoint built upon the assumption that the individual has worth and dignity, and has the capacity to choose and live a spontaneous, independent, self-directed life."

Speaking to a wider audience, he wrote several articles on working with the returned servicemen, which were published not only in one of the major psychology journals ("Psychological Adjustments of Discharged Service Personnel," in *Psychological Bulletin*), but also in more popular magazines like the *National Parent-Teacher* ("When the Serviceman Returns to His Family") and the *Journal of Home Economics* ("Wartime Issues in Family Counseling"). Just after leaving the USO, he coauthored with John L. Wallen, a graduate student working with him at Ohio State University, another book, entitled *Counseling with Returned Servicemen*. This little book, published the following year by McGraw-Hill, was actually a simplified version of *Counseling and Psychotherapy*, applied specifically to the returned serviceman. Given its particular timing and focus, the book had a relatively short life and narrow audience; but it remains a simply written and very concise summary of Rogers' views on counseling at the end of his stay at Ohio State.

When Carl and Helen left Columbus for their year in New York, it was a permanent farewell to the Ohio city. In the summer of 1944 Carl had been Visiting Professor at the University of Chicago. Ralph Tyler, who had invited him to come and who held several important posts at the university, was very impressed with Rogers' work. At the end of the summer he invited Rogers to move to the University of Chicago permanently and to set up a counseling center there. Since he was so obviously isolated in his own department at Ohio State (he practically had to beg for increased secretarial help in the Psychological Clinic), he realized the move to the new setting would give him more freedom. Most importantly the new counseling center would be an ideal source of data for the major scientific research he was anxious to begin on the process of therapy.

In what must have been a halfhearted attempt to persuade him to stay, Rogers' department chairman at Ohio State told him, "Well, Carl, this nondirective thing you're pushing certainly won't last long; but if you stay here, you'll always have a home to come back to." Neither this dubious support nor the $5448 salary he was receiving at Ohio State was enough to persuade him to remain. However, since he was already committed to a year of working with the USO, the move to Chicago had to be delayed. They sold their house, stored their furniture, and moved to New York. Because Carl had to be in New York to begin work, Helen stayed behind to take charge of the packing and moving. When this was completed, she drove alone to New York City.

At first the thought of leaving Columbus and moving to Chicago had been very unpleasant and difficult for Helen. Hardest of all was leaving their new home, which they had planned and built to last their lifetime and into which she had put so much work. Now after three years they were selling it. As Helen later wrote, "The invitation to go to the University of Chicago was not an easy one for me to accept. I knew it meant greater freedom for Carl to explore new fields and to establish a Counseling Center of the sort that would develop and put into practice his ever-growing theories and convictions in his philosophy of therapy. I knew it was right to go. I also knew it meant leaving my beautiful rural home and finding a spot to live in the dirty, slummy area of the South Side of Chicago. Luckily, our children had departed for college. . . . So we decided that apartment living was wisest for us in the big city. This being 1945, at the end of the war, housing was almost impossible to find. But luck was with us and we found a large, airy apartment with a fine view of Lake Michigan and within walking distance of the Counseling Center. This made living in Chicago very acceptable to me."

Fortunately they had the summer to make their move from New York and Columbus to Chicago. Again Helen had to handle most of it, while Carl spent two months recuperating from another operation. It seems the surgery at the Mayo Clinic in 1926 had done some damage and new adhesions were forming on his ulcer. The new operation at the Presbyterian Medical Center in Columbus was a success, for he never had any more problems in that area. By August he was better again and ready to move on to a new chapter in his life, one that would result in a prodigious amount of innovative work and that would win him international recognition.

CHAPTER 6
The Chicago Years: Part One
1945-1951

Late in 1945 a graduate student in Massachusetts wrote to Rogers asking for his help on a paper she was writing on "Carl Ransom Rogers, 1902–". He sent her some autobiographical material, and she wrote a short, insightful analysis of his "life and work," concluding with: "This fall, Rogers moved to the University of Chicago. I suppose this means that he's still going up. It will be interesting to see whether he has created his masterpiece, or whether he can keep hold of his original scientific, hardheaded approach, and apply it to new problems. I suppose he'll have to spend some time on validation of what has been done so far. . . . Can it [his method] be applied further? To treatment of more serious cases, for instance? . . . If I have been right about the characteristic energy of Carl Rogers, I don't think that he'll stop now."

She was right. The next twelve years at Chicago turned out to be the most prolific and productive period of Rogers' life. During this time he published one minor and two major books and almost sixty articles and studies; he served as President of the American Psychological Association and as president or officer of many other prestigious groups; he won numerous awards and honors; and he saw the publication of approximately two hundred and fifty articles and studies, not including his own, on the nondirective or client-centered approach. It was for him also a time of continuing personal growth and adventure, as well as some personal turmoil.

For the first half of this twelve-year period Rogers' personal development, leadership style, and refinement of his counseling approach were the major themes. During the latter half the theoretical and research dimensions of his work received the greater emphasis.

Rogers had come to Chicago with a mandate to set up the University's first Counseling Center. With him came many students from Ohio State who valued their continued contact with Rogers enough to compensate for the problems of moving from one university to another. Among those to make the move with him was Virginia Axline, whose *Play Therapy* was about to be published. Next to Rogers she became the best-known figure in the Center.

The Center was given the south and west sides of Lexington Hall and a budget to renovate the old building and reorganize their physical setting. The space was cramped, the roof leaked, the setting never would achieve a bright or new look; nevertheless the Counseling Center staff and their families threw themselves into the restoration with enthusiasm. They created eleven small rooms for offices and counseling rooms, a play-therapy room, an observation room, and a meeting room.

As one staff member from that period, Bernard Steinzor, recalled, "The sense of being pioneers in a new adventure was very evident and very great. . . . Helen Rogers took much initiative with the wives in making curtains and selecting furniture . . . while the men did more of the physical labor. It was a sense of establishing a Center out of a community of people engaged in a variety of actions." A few years later, in September 1949, the Counseling Center was moved to another building, at 5737 Drexel Avenue. There again the staff became the interior decorators. "We had a painting party," Manuel Vargas recalled, "and I was very happy to see Carl come in with his blue jeans, as the rest of us did; and we all wielded paint and brush and scaffolding and ladders, and so forth, as we painted the walls of the three stories of the Counseling Center. There was a great deal of informality among us, so we were all able to enjoy this kind of experience together."

In these self-renovated settings the staff of the Counseling Center plunged into their work with zest, building what was soon to become one of the best-known centers for psychotherapy and psychotherapeutic research in the country and in the world. From four thousand therapeutic interviews held with clients the first year, the number grew to over eleven thousand interviews several years later. But, as Rogers wrote in 1950, in his first annual report on the Counseling Center's work, "The figures cannot begin to picture the variety of individuals who have come for help. College students of sixteen, men and women in their sixties, children four and five years of age brought by their parents, as well as all the intervening ages; students in law, theology, social work, psychology, education, medicine, as well as the College; lawyers, ministers, business executives, journalists, housewives, physicians; returned veterans and their wives; parents and their adolescent offspring,—these are some of the groups. The problems presented have represented an equal variety. Personal and social inadequacies, marital problems, fear of academic failure, inability to function efficiently, sexual conflicts, vocational perplexity and confusion—a wide range of maladjustments. . . ."

Rogers' own daily routine was similar to that which he had established at Ohio State. He walked to and from the Center each day, often returning home for lunch. Once at the Center he wore many hats—primary counselor, researcher, teacher-supervisor, and administrator. As a member of the Department of Psychology he also taught graduate courses and served as advisor to graduate students working on their advanced degrees.

Most important he was a counselor, a therapist. In the twelve years he was at Chicago, he maintained a steady number of clients—usually from seven to ten individuals, whom he saw for a total average of fifteen or more counseling hours per week. In one of his annual reports he described something of his counseling and his clients: "The largest single block of my time," he wrote, "goes to this activity. Most of my clients are students, many of them students-in-training in this field. . . . Here are a few vignettes. . . .

"A young woman from the College, an ambulatory psychotic when I first saw her, is now in for a follow-up interview. She is happily married, pregnant with her first child, very much more responsible and expressive. Not only is there this clinical satisfaction, but since she was the subject of Nunnally's thesis study, we have very complete objective evidence of the change which has occurred in the past 2 1/2 years. . . .

"A student from Psychology, one who was almost at the top in the doctoral prelims, found himself completely unable to proceed when he had to chart his own course and take initiative. He is now working on his thesis, and this is only one evidence of many constructive changes. He is one of six Ph.D. students in Psychology whom I have counseled within the year. . . .

"A physician in a very responsible post, an extremely formal, reserved person, is making great strides in his therapy and will not only be much helped personally, but will probably be a significant center of influence. The fact that he would risk his professional standing by coming to a non-medical center for personal help is of decided interest."

Throughout his career Rogers stressed the value of his experience in direct counseling. Again and again in his writings he emphasized the importance of his time spent with clients. "It is from this rich and varied and deep contact with individuals that most of my hypotheses for research and the concepts for theory arise." "It is my laboratory." "It is the laboratory which is most basic to my work, namely the laboratory of interpersonal relations." As he stated with much more feeling in the preface to his next major book, *Client-Centered Therapy,* "This prefatory note cannot be concluded without a word of thanks to the people who have really written it, who have, in the most genuine sense been its major contributors—the clients with whom we have worked. To these men, women and children who have brought themselves and their struggles to us, who have with such natural grace permitted us to learn from them, who have laid bare for us the forces which operate in the mind and spirit of man—to them goes our deepest gratitude."

In addition to his counseling, Rogers also taught graduate courses, led a practicum in counseling for advanced graduate students, and supervised the work of many of the younger staff members at the Counseling Center. In his first eight years at Chicago he chaired or served on the committees of thirty-one successful Ph.D. candidates and a large number of Masters students. The contact with his students was, as it had been at Ohio State, very stimulating for him. The case conferences, the teamwork on research projects, the open-ended discussions, the criticisms of his methods and ideas, the chance to build on each other's thinking—all this gave Rogers the occasion to reevaluate constantly his own concepts and techniques and to continue growing.

And grow he did. Just at the time that "nondirective counseling" was gaining widespread national attention, and many professionals and students were coming to Chicago to study with him and learn the "Rogerian approach," the Rogerian approach was changing. At first glance the change was rather puzzling, and seemingly contradictory: in his thinking and writing, he began to de-emphasize the nondirective technique; while in his own clinical practice he became even more extremely nondirective than before.

As has always been typical with Rogers, he did not change because after thinking things over he decided that another description of therapy would be more rational or logical. The impetus for change always resulted from his direct experiences in therapy and human interaction and from his desire to understand better the processes and phenomena involved. He has always been an inductive scientist, rather than a deductive theorist—always most inclined to experience, observe, record, look for patterns, and only much later begin to build the explanations, hypotheses, and theories to account for the observed data. Years before, in seeing what the effects of the various therapies were on clients, he had developed his nondirective approach—not because it was philosophically more defensible, but because, based on his observations, he believed it was more effective. In this way his thinking began to change when he came to Chicago. This time the changes came about not only as he observed his clients, but also as he watched other nondirective counselors.

At Ohio State, with the USO, and at Chicago, he had worked with hundreds of counselors-in-training—watching them struggle to learn "The Method," seeing the results as they applied the techniques of simple acceptance and reflection of feeling in their work with clients. What Rogers came to realize, time and time again, is vividly described by one of his students, a minister named Walter Yoder, who himself had labored to learn the method.

> Because the client-centered, nondirective counseling approach has been rather carefully defined and clearly illustrated, it gives the 'Illusion of Simplicity.' The technique seems deceptively easy to master. Then you begin to practice. A word wrong here and there. You don't quite reflect the feeling, but reflect content instead. It is difficult to handle questions. You are tempted to interpret. Nothing seems so serious that further practice won't correct it. Perhaps you are having trouble playing two roles—that of minister and that of counselor. Bring up the question in class and the matter is solved again with a deceptive ease. But these apparently minor errors and a certain woodenness of response seem exceedingly persistent.
>
> Only gradually does it dawn that if the technique is true it demands a feeling of warmth. You begin to feel that the attitude is the thing. Every

little word is not so important if you have the correct accepting and permissive attitude toward the client. So you bear down on the permissiveness and acceptance. You *will* permiss and accept and reflect the client, if it kills you.

But you still have those troublesome questions from the client. He simply doesn't know the next step. He asks you to give him a hint, some possibilities; after all you are expected to know something, else why is he here? As a minister, you ought to have some convictions about what people should believe, how they should act. As a counselor, you should know something about removing this obstacle—you ought to have the equivalent of the surgeon's knife and use it. Then you begin to wonder. The technique is good, but . . . does it go *far* enough? does it really work on clients? is it *right* to leave a person helpless, when you might show him the way out?

Here seems to me is the crucial point. 'Narrow is the gate' and hard the path from here on. No one else can give satisfying answers and even the instructors seem frustrating because they appear not to be helpful in your specific case. For here is demanded of you what no other person can do or point out—and that is to rigorously scrutinize yourself and your attitudes toward others. Do you believe that all people truly have a creative potential in them? That each person is a unique individual and that he alone can work out his own individuality? Or do you really believe that some persons are of 'negative value' and others are weak and must be led and taught by 'wiser,' 'stronger' people?

You begin to see that there is nothing compartmentalized about this method of counseling. It is not just counseling, because it demands the most exhaustive, penetrating, and comprehensive consistency. In other methods you can shape tools, pick them up for use when you will. But when genuine acceptance and permissiveness are your tools it requires nothing less than the whole complete personality. And to grow oneself is the most demanding of all.

In the latter half of the 1940s Rogers came to speak and write about this point with increasing frequency and conviction. In his own words, "It is common to find client-centered therapy spoken of as a method or a technique. No doubt this is due in part to earlier presentations which tended to overstress technique. It may more accurately be said that the counselor who is effective in client-centered therapy holds a coherent and developing set of attitudes deeply imbedded in his personal organization, a system of attitudes which is implemented by techniques and methods consistent with it. It has been our experience that the counselor who tries to use a 'method' is doomed to be unsuccessful unless this method is genuinely in line with his own attitudes. On the other hand the counselor whose attitudes are of the type which facilitate therapy may be only partially successful, because his attitudes are inadequately implemented by appropriate methods and techniques."

In a similar vein he wrote that "... to create a psychological climate in which the client feels that kind of warmth, understanding and freedom from attack in which he may drop his defensiveness, and explore and reorganize his life style, is a far more subtle and delicate process than simply 'reflecting feeling.' It calls for a total sensitivity to the client in his own perspective and the communication of this kind of acceptance and understanding. ... The overall tone of the counseling situation becomes the concern of the therapist rather than a specific kind of phrase of verbalization. ... If the counselor's feelings convey an attitude of subtle approval or disapproval, direction or guidance, etc., then all the 'reflection of feeling' in the world would still fall short of implementing a deeply client-centered orientation."

In his earlier writings the therapist's technique clearly received the major emphasis. Although the therapist's attitude always had been mentioned, it had received much less attention. Now the balance was reversed. "The primary point of importance is the attitude held by the counselor toward the worth and significance of the individual." Not only was technique de-emphasized, but Rogers began to avoid even using the word, preferring to use the term "implementation" to connote the method by which a basic attitude is conveyed.

The therapeutic attitude itself stemmed from a *basic hypothesis* about human growth. Rogers had come to believe this hypothesis while working in Rochester and Columbus. But at Chicago he began to state it more explicitly and frequently as the starting point for his whole conception of therapy. It went: "... the client-centered therapist operates primarily upon one central and basic hypothesis which has undergone relatively little change with the years. This hypothesis is that the client has within himself the capacity, latent if not evident, to understand those aspects of his life and of himself which are causing him pain, and the capacity and the tendency to reorganize himself and his relationship to life in the direction of self-actualization and maturity in such a way as to bring a greater degree of internal comfort. The function of the therapist is to create such a psychological atmosphere as will permit this capacity and this strength to become effective rather than latent or potential."

How does the therapist create this psychological atmosphere? Primarily by conveying two attitudes to the client—*acceptance* and *understanding*. "It would seem that when the individual is deeply accepted as he is, when the private world of his own reality is genuinely understood and genuinely accepted by another, without evaluation, and when this understanding and acceptance is communicated to the individual, this optimum atmosphere exists." In the late forties these two attitudes, successfully communicated to the client, became for Rogers the major ingredients in effective psychotherapy. Around the turn of the decade he began to use other terms in place of "understanding," but the essential concept remained the same.

In describing the first of these criteria, acceptance, Rogers would frequently write in this vein: "The therapeutic phenomenon seems most likely to occur when the therapist feels, very genuinely and deeply, an attitude of acceptance of and respect for the client *as he is*, with the potentialities inherent in his present state. This means a respect for the attitudes which the client now has and a continuing acceptance of the attitudes of the moment, whether they veer in the direction of despair, toward constructive courage, or toward a confused ambivalence. This acceptance is probably possible only for the therapist who has integrated into his own philosophy a deep conviction as to the right of the individual to self-direction and self-determination. . . . It may help to discuss briefly the meaning of the term 'respect,' as we have been using it. In other orientations there is also respect for the client or patient, but this is usually respect for the person as *un*revealed. It is a respect for something underneath, not respect for the person as he seems to himself at that moment. In client-centered therapy, however, the counselor attitude which we have found most fruitful is a complete acceptance of the person as he seems to himself at that moment. It is only as *he* is dissatisfied with this self that he explores further into his attitudes and feelings."

A few years earlier he had written that many therapists "will feel that they have always dealt with clients in an accepting fashion. The fact is, however, that most of the procedures actually used in counseling contacts are such as to make clients defensive. This is clearly shown by our study of recorded interviews. It is not enough for the worker to have an accepting attitude, though this is important. The techniques used must also be such that defensiveness will not be aroused."

Rogers himself seemed able to communicate this acceptance and respect. An excerpt from an interview—one which he frequently quoted—provides an extreme example. The counselor was Virginia Axline.

Miss Gil, a young woman who has, in a number of therapeutic interviews, been quite hopeless about herself, has spent the major part of an hour discussing her feelings of inadequacy and lack of personal worth.

Part of the time she has been aimlessly using the finger paints. She had just finished expressing her feelings of wanting to get away from everyone—to have nothing to do with people. After a long pause comes the following:

S (SUBJECT OR CLIENT): I've never said this before to anyone—but I've thought for such a long time—This is a terrible thing to say, but if I could just—well *(short, bitter laugh; pause)*, if I could just find some glorious cause that I could give my life for I would be happy. I cannot be the kind of a person I want to be. I guess maybe I haven't the guts —or the strength—to kill myself—and if someone else would relieve me of the responsibility—or I would be in an accident—I—I—just don't want to live.

AXLINE: At the present time things look so black to you that you can't see much point in living—

S: Yes—I wish I'd never started this therapy. I was happy when I was living in my dream world. There I could be the kind of person I wanted to be—But now—There is such a wide, wide gap—between my ideal —and what I am. I wish people hated me. I try to make them hate me. Because then I could turn away from them and could blame them— but no—It is all in my hands—Here is my life—and I either accept the fact that I am absolutely worthless—or I fight whatever it is that holds me in this terrible conflict. And I suppose if I accepted the fact that I am worthless, then I could go away someplace—and get a little room someplace—get a mechanical job someplace—and retreat clear back to the security of my dream world where I could do things, have clever friends, be a pretty wonderful sort of person—

AXLINE: It's really a tough struggle—digging into this like you are—and at times the shelter of your dream world looks more attractive and comfortable.

S: Yes. *(A long pause. Complete change of voice.)* So I don't see why I should waste your time—coming in twice a week—I'm not worth it—What do you think?

AXLINE: It's up to you, Gil—It isn't wasting my time—I'd be glad to see you—whenever you come—but it's how you feel about it—if you don't want to come twice a week—or if you do want to come twice a week? —once a week?—It's up to you. *(Long pause.)*

S: You're not going to suggest that I come in oftener? You're not alarmed and think I ought to come in every day—until I get out of this?

AXLINE: I believe you are able to make your own decision. I'll see you whenever you want to come.

S: *(Note of awe in her voice.)* I don't believe you are alarmed about—I see —I may be afraid of myself—but you aren't afraid for me—*(She stands up—a strange look on her face.)*

AXLINE: You say you may be afraid of yourself—and are wondering why I don't seem to be afraid for you?

S: *(Another short laugh.)* You have more confidence in me than I have. *(She cleans up the finger-paint mess and starts out of the room.)* I'll see you next week—*(that short laugh)* maybe. *(Her attitude seemed tense, depressed, bitter, completely beaten. She walked slowly away.)*

"I learned courage from her," Rogers said of Axline. Such a dramatic example of the therapist's complete acceptance of the client, *as she is,* calls to mind the minister's earlier questions of how far must one carry these therapeutic attitudes? The answer for Rogers goes back to the therapist's faith in the basic hypothesis, in the capacity of the client to choose wisely, given the proper psychological climate. In his words, "Is the therapist willing to give the client full freedom as to outcomes? Is he genuinely willing for the client to organize and direct his life? Is he willing for him to choose goals that are social or antisocial, moral or immoral? If not, it seems doubtful that therapy will be a profound experience for the client. Even more difficult, is he willing for the client to choose regressing rather than growth or maturity? to choose neuroticism rather than mental health? to choose to reject help rather than accept it? to choose death rather than life? To me it appears that only as the therapist is completely willing that *any* outcome, any direction may be chosen—only then does he realize the vital strength of the capacity and potentiality of the individual for constructive action. It is as he is willing for death to be the choice, that life is chosen, for neuroticism to be the choice that a healthy normality is chosen. The more completely he acts upon his central hypothesis the more convincing is the evidence that the hypothesis is correct."

Although it would be comfortable to turn the hypothesis into a "law," Rogers recognized that "it is actually a hypothesis in human relationships, and will always remain so. Even for the experienced counselor, who has observed in hundreds of cases the evidence which supports the hypothesis, it is still true that for the new client who comes in the door, the possibility of self-understanding and intelligent self-direction is still, for the client, a completely unproved hypothesis."

What happens, then, when the client's words and actions cause the therapist to doubt her basic hypothesis and tempt her to intervene in the client's therapy in a more directive fashion? Here Rogers' extremism, courage of convictions, and scientific attitude are apparent. "If the counselor feels, in the middle of an interview, that this client may not have the capacity for recognizing himself, and shifts to the hypothesis that the counselor must bear a considerable responsibility for this reorganization, he confuses the client, and defeats himself. He has shut himself off from proving or disproving either hypothesis. It is this confused eclecticism, which has been prevalent in psychotherapy, which has blocked scientific progress in the field. Actually it is only by acting consistently upon a well-selected hypothesis, that its elements of truth and untruth can become known."

More and more, for Rogers, this acceptance of the client, as he is at the moment, became a *sine qua non*, a necessary condition for effective psychotherapy. But the acceptance alone, without the therapist's deep understanding of the client, would be of little value. Most of us have experienced the doting relative or the flattering acquaintance who seems so accepting and positive toward us; yet this attitude, while it may feel good to receive, has very little lasting or significant value. Consciously or unconsciously we recognize its superficiality. This would be especially true for the client in therapy. With all of his own self-doubts and self-rejection he would be likely to respond to accept-ance-without-understanding by thinking, "If you really knew me as I know me, if you knew what I've done, if you knew the things I feel, I bet you wouldn't be so accepting then. You'd probably be shocked or offended, or you'd pity me, or you'd tell me I'm wrong or bad or abnormal." Only if the therapist really understands the client, as the client understands himself, can the therapist's acceptance of the client enable the client to be more accepting of himself.

Therefore Rogers emphasized the counselor's understanding of the client as a necessary corollary to her acceptance. By understanding, he meant "the therapist's willingness and sensitive ability to understand the client's thoughts, feelings, and struggles from the client's point of view. This ability to see completely through the client's eyes, to adopt his frame of reference, has seemed to be an important way of imple-menting the fundamental hypothesis and is the basis for the use of the term 'client-centered.' To receive completely what the client is trying to communicate of his feelings even when his communication is con-fused or incoherent or fragmentary—to be able to enter into the cli-ent's private world and see it from *his* point of view—this is what we mean by adopting the client's frame of reference."

This notion of "adopting the client's frame of reference" replaced the earlier emphasis on "the reflection of feelings." Quoting himself, Rogers wrote, "The present author, in a paper given in 1940 stated, 'As material is given by the client, it is the therapist's function to help him recognize and clarify the emotions which he feels. . . .' This has been a useful concept, and it is partially descriptive of what occurs. It is, however, too intellectualistic, and if taken too literally, may focus the process on the counselor. It can mean that only the counselor knows what the feelings are, and if it acquires this meaning it becomes a subtle lack of respect for the client."

On the contrary the therapist's attempts to adopt the client's frame of reference must be done in the most tentative, interested, and accepting manner. Rogers began to use the word "empathy" to describe the process. By no means did he invent the word; it had been popular in psychotherapy for many years. He simply appropriated it to convey his meaning and proceeded to popularize it widely. He began to use the term "understanding" less and "empathy" and "empathic" more.* He often emphasized that empathy meant seeing the world *as if* one were the client, but never so totally identifying with the client that the "as if" quality was lost.

The flavor of this "sensitive empathy," as Rogers often called it, is captured in a recorded interview with "a Mrs. Oak."

> MRS. OAK: Uh, I caught myself thinking that-that-that during these uh, sessions, uh, I've been sort of singing a song. Now that sounds uh-uh, vague, and-and-and uh-uh, not actually singing . . . sort of a song without any music. A-a, uh, probably a kind of poem coming out. (M-hm.) and uh, I like the idea, I mean it's sort of come to me with-without anything built out of-of anything. And in . . . following that, it came, it came this other kind of-of-of a uh, feeling. Well, I s-s-found myself sort o-of asking myself uh, is that the shape that cases take? (M-hm). A uh-uh, is it possible that I-I-I am just verbalizing and, and-and uh, at times kind of become intoxicated with my own-own, u-uh, verbalizations? (M-hm). And then uh, following this, came, well, am I just taking up your time? Uh . . . then a doubt, a doubt . . . (M-hm.) Then something else occurred to me. Uh, from whence it came I-I don't know, no actual logical kind of a sequence of the thinking. The thought struck me: We're (two words missing) uh, overwhelmed or uh, doubtful, or-or uh, we can show concern or, or an-a-any uh, interest when-when the, when blind people uh, learn to read with their fingers, uh, Braille. And I don't know, it-it may be just sort of-of . . . it's all mixed up . . . it may be that's something that I'm uh, uh, eg-experiencing
>
> ROGERS: M-hm. Let's see if I can get some of that "uh-uh," that sequence of feelings. First, sort of as though you're . . . and I gather that the first one is a fairly positive feeling . . . as though maybe you're kind of

---

*Other writers, after Rogers, often used the variation "empathetic." Rogers used only "empathic" and "empathically." This often created problems for the typesetter. In more than one publication, Rogers came out in favor of "emphatic listening"!

creating a poem here . . . uh, a song without music somehow but something that might be quite uh, quite creative, and then the—the feeling of a lot of skepticism about that. "Maybe I'm just saying words, uh, just being carried off by words that I, that I speak, and maybe it's all a lot of baloney, really." Uh . . . and then a feeling that uh . . . perhaps you're almost learning a—a new type of experiencing which would be just as radically new as for a blind person to try to make sense out of what he feels with his fingertips.

MRS. OAK: M-hm. M-hm.

The ability to move from one's own frame of reference to the client's internal frame of reference was a very difficult one for students of counseling to learn. As Rogers described it, "This struggle to achieve the client's . . . own perceptual field and see with him as perceiver is rather closely analagous to some of the Gestalt phenomena. Just as by active concentration, one can suddenly see the diagram in the psychology text as representing a descending rather than an ascending stairway or can perceive two faces instead of a candlestick, so, by active effort, the counselor can put himself into the client's frame of reference. But just as in the case of visual perception the figure occasionally changes, so in the case of the counselor, he may at times find himself out of the client's frame of reference, and looking at the client as an external perceiver. . . ."

To give the reader a somewhat more real and vivid experience of the attitudinal set he was describing, Rogers suggested that the reader put himself in the place of the counselor, and consider the following material, which was taken from complete counselor notes of the beginning of an interview with a man in his thirties. "When the material has been completed," wrote Rogers, "sit back and consider the sorts of attitudes and thoughts which were in your mind as you read."

CLIENT: I don't feel very normal, but I want to feel that way. . . . I thought I'd have something to talk about—then it all goes around in circles. I was trying to think what I was going to say. Then coming here it doesn't work out. . . . I tell you, it seemed that it would be much easier before I came. I tell you, I just can't make a decision; I don't know what I want. I've tried to reason this thing out logically—tried to figure out which things are important to me. I thought that there are maybe two things a man might do; he might get married and raise a family. But if he was just a bachelor, just making a living—that isn't very good. I find myself and my thoughts getting back to the days when I was a kid and I cry very easily. The dam would break through. I've been in the Army four and a half years. I had no problems then, no hopes, no wishes. My only thought was to get out when peace would come. My problems, now that I'm out, are as ever. I tell you, they go back to a long time before I was in the Army. . . . I love children. When I was in the Philippines—I tell you, when I was young I swore I'd never forget my unhappy childhood—so when I saw these children in the Philippines, I treated them very nicely. I used to give them ice cream cones and movies. It was just a period—I'd reverted back—and that awakened some emotions in me I thought I had long buried. *(A pause. He seems very near tears.)*

Rogers pointed out that, after reading this material, such thoughts as the following could represent an external frame of reference in you, the "counselor."

I wonder if I should help him get started talking.
Is this inability to get under way a type of dependence?
Why this indecisiveness? What could be its cause?
What is meant by this focus on marriage and family?
He seems to be a bachelor. I hadn't known that.
The crying, the 'dam,' sound as though there must be a great deal of repression.
He's a veteran. Could he have been a psychiatric case?
I feel sorry for anybody who spent four and one-half years in the service.
Some time we will probably need to dig into those early unhappy experiences.
What is this interest in children? Identification? Vague homosexuality?

"Note that these are all attitudes which are basically sympathetic," Rogers wrote. "There is nothing 'wrong' with them. They are even attempts to 'understand,' in the sense of 'understanding about,' rather than 'understanding with.' The locus of perceiving is, however, outside the client. . . . By way of comparison, the thoughts which might go through your mind if you were quite successful in assuming the client's internal frame of reference would tend to be of this order.

You're wanting to struggle toward normality, aren't you?
It's really hard for you to get started.
Decision-making just seems impossible to you.
You want marriage, but it doesn't seem to you to be much of a possibility.
You feel yourself brimming over with childish feelings.
To you the Army represented stagnation.
Being very nice to children has somehow had meaning for you.
But it has been—and is—a disturbing experience for you.

"If these thoughts are couched in a final and declarative form, then they shift over into becoming an evaluation from the counselor's perceptual vantage point. But to the extent that they are empathic attempts to understand, tentative in formulation, they represent the attitude we are trying to describe as adopting the client's frame of reference."

Mistakenly many people thought, and still do think, of nondirective counseling as a rather passive approach—a "laissez-faire psychology," as one writer called it. Actually, as the previous examples indicate, adopting the client's frame of reference demands the utmost in active listening, concentration, and communication on the part of the therapist. Partly for this reason Rogers, in the late forties, began to avoid the term "nondirective" and continued to use the "client-centered" label almost exclusively. It has been to his chagrin that so many individuals in psychology and psychotherapy still talk of the "nondirective method" and think of Rogers' contribution in terms of his thinking and practice in the early forties.

But now the irony. At the same time that Rogers' writings were becoming decreasingly nondirective in their reduced emphasis on technique in favor of counselor attitudes, Rogers' own clinical practice and that of his colleagues at the Counseling Center were becoming *more* nondirective. A study by Seeman, analyzing cases handled in 1947–1948, used the same method for measuring counselor techniques as Snyder had used in his study of cases from 1940–1942. The later study showed that over the six-year period, the client-centered therapists had steadily increased the frequency of their nondirective, reflection-of-feeling responses to the point where these constituted eighty-five percent of the counselor's statements! This finding seemed to emphasize a point Rogers had made—that a counselor need not fully believe the "basic hypothesis" upon beginning her work, that by testing the hypothesis with clients, she might prove or disprove it to her own satisfaction. For the group around Rogers, at least, it was apparent that their experiences with therapy led them "to depend more fully on the basic hypothesis of the approach than was true a half dozen years ago. It seems that more and more the nondirective therapist has judged understanding and acceptance to be effective, and has come to concentrate his whole effort upon achieving a deep understanding of the private world of the client."

In 1951 Houghton Mifflin published Rogers' third major book, *Client-Centered Therapy.* The world of psychology and psychotherapy at large paid little attention to it, and like its predecessor it was not reviewed in the professional journals. On the other hand it received a warm reception from those individual counselors, psychologists, and helping professionals who were either involved or interested in the client-centered movement. For them the book was challenging and controversial. In it Rogers spoke very openly about the changes in his thinking and practice which had taken place over the last several years. The first chapter was titled "The Developing Character of Client-Centered Therapy." Whereas one chapter of *Counseling and Psychotherapy* had been titled "The Directive vs. the Non-Directive Approach," the comparable chapter in *Client-Centered Therapy* was called "The Attitude and Orientation of the Counselor." In it he wrote, "As I look back upon some of our earlier published cases—the case of Herbert Bryan in my book, or Snyder's case of Mr. M—I realize that we have gradually dropped the vestiges of subtle directiveness which are all too evident in those cases. We have come to recognize that if we can provide understanding of the way the client seems to himself at this moment, he can do the rest."

In addition to describing the changes in his thinking and practice, Rogers devoted a major section of the book to applications of the client-centered approach to other fields. He wrote, ". . . The individual who comes to rely upon this hypothesis in his therapeutic work finds almost inevitably that he is driven to experiment with it in other types of activity." In this section, with the help of several colleagues, he began to explore the implications of client-centered therapy for a wide range of other helping functions. Elaine Dorfman, Nicholas Hobbs, and Thomas Gordon wrote chapters on "Play Therapy," "Group-Centered Psychotherapy" and "Group-Centered Leadership and Administration," respectively. Rogers wrote chapters on "Student-Centered Teaching" and "The Training of Counselors and Therapists." Although he had written a few articles of this nature, this section of *Client-Centered Therapy* was his first attempt to apply their insights and experiences to other fields in a consistent and organized manner. It signaled what would come in later years, when Rogers and his colleagues would continue to explore the implications of the "basic hypothesis" in various fields. The kernel for several of Rogers' later books are contained in these chapters.

Another change evident in *Client-Centered Therapy* was Rogers' developing personal style of communication. As a writer and a speaker he had always communicated his ideas in a clear, down-to-earth, nonesoteric manner, and in that sense he always came across as a sincere person. Having been trained in an academic setting, however, where it was proper to refer to oneself only in the third person, Rogers had followed the traditional mode for many years. "The author believes . . .," "the present writer has found . . . ," "explored by this investigator," would be the normal way he would insert any self-reference. Gradually he came to feel that the pronoun "I" was legitimate, even preferable in many cases. And as he began to use the first person in his speeches and writings, he became even more human to his audience. A passage from the preface to *Client-Centered Therapy* gives something of the flavor of his developing style.

> This book is about the highly personal experiences of each one of us. It is about a client in my office who sits there by the corner of the desk, struggling to be himself, yet deathly afraid of being himself—striving to see his experience as it is, wanting to *be* that experience, and yet deeply fearful of the prospect. The book is about me, as I sit there with that client, facing him, participating in that struggle as deeply and sensitively as I am able. It is about me as I try to perceive his experience, and the meaning and the feeling and the taste and the flavor that it has for him. It is about me as I bemoan my very human fallibility in understanding that client, and the occasional failures to see life as it appears to him, failures which fall like heavy objects across the intricate, delicate web of growth which is taking place. It is about me as I rejoice at the privilege of being a midwife to a new personality—as I stand by with awe at the emergence of a self, a person, as I see a birth process in which I have had an important and facilitating part. . . . The book is, I believe, about life, as life vividly reveals itself in the therapeutic process. . . .

The change in style may not seem very remarkable; but in the academic, and especially the scientific community, it was then (and to a large extent, would be now) considered an unusual, if not suspicious departure from the norm. One editor was sufficiently surprised by this that he included the following footnote on the first page of Rogers' article:

> The editor raised a question with the author regarding the frequent use of the personal pronoun in the manuscript and received a reply which deserves quoting. "The fact that it is in quite personal form is not accidental nor intended to make it a letter. In recent years I have been experimenting with a more personal form of writing for I believe that putting an article in more personal form makes it communicate more directly and, even more important, keeps us from sounding like oracles. Instead of saying, 'This is so,' one is much more inclined to say 'I believe this is so.' I just wanted you to know the reason why it is expressed in

a more personal way than is considered to be good scientific writing."
This argument appeared particularly to fit the nature of the article in
question and the original flavor of the writing is retained.—Ed.

As did Hobbs, Dorfman, and Gordon in their chapters in *Client-
Centered Therapy,* Rogers also throughout the book frequently used the
pronoun "we". "We have learned . . . ," "As we look back . . . ," "It
has been our experience . . . ," and so on. This was not the "regal we"
in which the individual projects his own viewpoint onto those around
him. Rogers was referring to a very specific "we"—his colleagues and
students at the Counseling Center at Chicago.

It was at the Counseling Center that most of Rogers' work really took
place. Aside from his fifteen or more hours per week of counseling, for
Rogers and for most of the other people connected with the Center
it was the interpersonal relationships among staff and students which
constituted the greatest satisfactions of being there.

Rogers was not the Counseling Center's Director—he was its Executive Secretary. He had chosen the title himself, and it had a special
significance for him. First, he was a counselor and scientist, not an
administrator. He had no intention of diverting the major thrust of his
life's work into details of maintaining a complex operation. Perhaps
even more important, his faith in the individual's capacity to guide his
or her own life was not confined to clients and students only. He had
a similar belief about groups. From the beginning he encouraged the
Counseling Center personnel to work together to define the purposes
and procedures of the Center. One student from that period, Norman
Brice, recalled, "I learned so much from just observing Carl. . . . One
thing I learned was a way to administer a group of professionals by
trusting them and by *delegating my authority to the entire group.* This I have
done in the fifteen years I have had administrative responsibility for
the counseling program at Chico State College."

A description of the Counseling Center, prepared in 1953 by a
"committee of the staff," explained that "over a period of seven years
the Center organization has seemed to develop in one particular direction—toward flexibility, informality, and group-centeredness. This has
been possible primarily because those who originally were given authority and leadership for the Center have been willing, perhaps even
eager, to transfer their authority to the total group and to distribute
their leadership among the members of the group."

In one of Rogers' several attempts to explain the Center's mode of operation to the dean, the latter said, "Well, I don't understand it, but I want you to know that if anything goes wrong over there I'm going to hold *you* responsible." After a moment's thought Rogers said, "That's O.K. with me, so long as you understand that I am *handling* that responsibility by giving it to us as a group."

A staff member of the Center from 1947–1953 remembered how "Carl provided a genuine, thoroughgoing climate of democracy in Center government. There was diffusion of responsibility in both day-to-day administration and in basic policy making. Staff members could exert major influence on policies in terms of their ability to persuade or influence other staff members. A concomitant of this power diffusion was the fact that Carl did not offer strong emotional support or protection to staff members. They had to make it on the power of their ideas. Carl did not play papa. This is not to say that staff members never perceived him in that way or that they did not want that kind of support. It is simply that Carl didn't behave in those terms."

This democratic structure applied not only to the permanent staff members but also to the students. Bernard Steinzor was a student at the Center in 1945, when everything was just getting underway. He remembered the "sense of colleaguality and democratic working together. The development of policies, of fee schedules, of relationships to the Dean's Office, and all the other problems that come up in a counseling center attached to a university were all worked through in as democratic a way as can be hoped for."

As Rogers described it, in his Annual Report for 1950, "This working together has not been primarily in unity or smoothness. We have been annoyed with each other; as individuals we often feel frustrated that the others do not appreciate the truth we see; as individuals we develop differing ways of carrying on therapy and of viewing therapy, and we feel disappointed that the others do not see it our way; we wrestle, often painfully, with problems which could be 'solved' very neatly and easily by a more authoritative organization; but in all of this, our feeling and our desires and our struggles are out in the open, and from this freely expressed, individualistic 'chaos' comes a deeper, organic type of unity which is very precious to us. It makes the Center *our* Center. It makes it an exciting creative spot to work where no one can predict what 1951 will bring forth, except that it can be predicted that we will push further into the unknown than we have in 1950."

There were several different "titles" for the people at the Center. Professional "staff members" were regular employees of the University who usually, as did Rogers, held joint appointments in the Department of Psychology and in the Counseling Center. They worked with clients, taught, supervised, and conducted research. Then there were the graduate students who were taking practical and supervised training at the Center. They too would work with clients and conduct research with staff members who served as consultants to them whenever they desired help. Then there were the "research fellows," "interns," and "courtesy staff members." These fell into two categories, for the most part: first, graduate students who worked at the Center doing research or counseling or both and who were paid for their work; and second, practicing professionals or post-doctoral fellows who wished to come to the Center to learn about the theories, methods and research being employed there.

One student, Leonard Hersher, said of Rogers, "When it came to hiring people for the Counseling Center, he had the idea that one should hire a good person with potential rather than one who held certain skills. And that people should try different things. He seemed to have no objection if people hired as research workers or secretaries became therapists."

Rogers told the story of how "a repairman came one Saturday afternoon to mend some damaged equipment. He found a secretary typing away, and began asking her questions about the place. Her responses were all of this sort: 'Well, we see students and others who need help.' 'We do research.' 'We. . . .' Finally the repairman said disgustedly, 'What do you mean by this "we" stuff? Don't you work for somebody here?' After a thoughtful pause, the secretary said, 'No. This is *our* outfit.'" Interestingly, after years of hard effort, this secretary went on to receive a Ph.D. degree from the University of Chicago.

The result of these several categories of personnel and the flexibility of jobs was considerable overlap in the roles everyone played. Students and staff would both be carrying on therapeutic interviews with clients and, thus, to an extent, would be colleagues, as well as supervisor and supervisee. All groups might be engaged in research, so it would not be unusual to have several of the inexperienced students studying the transcripts of interviews conducted by the experienced staff members or post-doctoral fellows, analyzing their failures and successes in fostering therapeutic change. Since the staff meetings consisted of permanent staff members, temporary staff members, and graduate students, running the Center on a democratic basis meant that no one person or group could control the direction of the Center. This was what Rogers wanted. He believed that new knowledge in psychotherapy would best be produced if the Center personnel were free to explore their own hunches, to exercise their creativity, to set their own priorities, and to make mistakes.

Compared to other pioneers in the history of psychotherapy, Rogers had no desire to achieve unanimity of thought and practice among his followers. One student, Rex Reed, recalled "a seminar which met at the Rogers' apartment near the university. The class (about 20 graduate students) met from 7:30 P.M. until all hours. Rogers, with the others in the group, was a student too. Members of his staff, counselors (Bill Kell, Ollie Bown, etc.), came and read a paper to us. All of us commented on the paper when it was finished. Then we'd divide into groups of three or four and go into separate rooms where we discussed the "meat" of the paper. After 30 or 45 minutes we would reassemble, make comments in the group again and have a supper. It was then—during these 'moments' in the seminar when I learned more definitely to assess the man's simplicity, brilliance, acceptance. . . . He always appeared to have time to listen to any of us. He never imposed his ideas. Always he joined us as . . . a learner."

Another student and teaching assistant of Rogers, Gerald Haigh, remembered him as "intellectually alive. He has always been excited about ideas whenever I have been with him. He turns me on to excitement about my own new ideas—he is an eager listener. He always seemed able to learn as much from his students as we were learning from him."

Sometimes Rogers asked his classes, at the beginning of the course, if they would all be willing to accept a grade of B, so they wouldn't have to worry all through the quarter about how they might impress him to get a good grade. They would be freer to pursue their own goals. Usually, though, he solved the grading problem by using a system of self-evaluation in which the students evaluated their own programs and helped determine their own grades.

Jim Bebout remembered, "There was no such thing as working *under* Carl Rogers—it seemed a question of 'doing your own thing' alongside him and with his considered approval. I remember staff meetings at Chicago at which all hell was breaking loose (about firings, personal relationships, or salaries). As loud as the staff screamed at each other, with a corner of all eyes on Carl, it was none of his responsibility, and if he contributed anything to the melee, it would always be a personal reaction."

One woman, Dr. Rosalind Dymond Cartwright, came to the Counseling Center in 1951 to serve as Research Coordinator. She remembered how "I was enabled in every way to do what I thought best and explore the kinds of questions and undertake the kind of work that I wanted. He provided the kind of setting and ongoing organization that had room for everybody to do their thing in a very open and communicative kind of way. Now, mind you, there were petty jealousies, troubles of all kinds at that time, but they weren't in Carl. And they infuriated him. I never saw him quite so angry as when an issue was brought up at staff meeting and people turned to him to see how he would vote, to follow his lead or his nod. He didn't want that kind of role, he didn't like that behavior on the part of other people. He wanted them to respect themselves sufficiently to speak for themselves without waiting for him."

Apparently he succeeded to a large extent. In describing the characteristics of "group-centered leadership" in 1951, Thomas Gordon used the Counseling Center as a prime example: "One of the noticable outcomes of group-centered leadership is the decreased dependence of group members upon the leader. In discussion groups this is reflected in a greater number of member-initiated problems brought before the group, in fewer requests for the opinions and judgments of the leader. In our own Counseling Center organization it has meant that members of the staff have taken the initiative to develop new areas of service to the community, they have tried out new counseling methods of their own, they effectively carry on the functions of the Center in the absence of any one person or group of persons. Instead of energies being expended in trying to figure out what the leader might want or approve, in a truly self-directing group individuals discover they can be truly creative. The conditions exist in which each member has the opportunity for real self-actualization, self-expression, and self-development. Individuals learn to assume responsibility for their own feelings, ideas, and behavior."

In one of his annual reports Rogers described this phenomenon more specifically. He wrote, "the young faculty members on the staff can satisfactorily become free and independent of my influence and my reputation. . . . Personally I find great satisfaction in the evidence that there is growing leadership among our staff members. People who are interested in psychotherapy and learning theory turn immediately to Butler, for example, rather than to me. People who are interested in groups—group therapy, group administration and so forth, turn at once to Gordon, recognizing the quality of thinking he has done in this field. People who wish to know about research methodology turn to

Seeman, Grummon or others on the staff because they have established their own reputations in these areas. I feel that the *Center* is less and less a one man show and this pleases me very much."

The genuineness of this freedom that was afforded the people at the Counseling Center turned out to be so astounding that it made a deep, lifelong impression on many of them. An anecdote recalled years later by Daniel Bergman conveys much of the flavor of the Center and how Rogers helped to foster a sense of independence there: "One of the most unusual meetings of the staff of the Counseling Center, while I was a member by courtesy appointment and as a research assistant, occurred when one of the faculty who were staff members brought a therapy case on which I was the therapist up for staff discussion. He did so for what he considered good and adequate reasons, since from people whom he knew who knew my client, he had become convinced that the client was psychotic (which in diagnostic terms he undoubtedly was) and more than possibly homicidal (and, subsequently, after the danger had passed, I learned from the client that he had experienced himself in this way for a period of several weeks during which he failed to come for appointments). He came, therefore, with the conviction that my client should be transferred to the psychiatric staff of Billings Hospital or institutionalized. He seemed to expect that he would win the consent of the staff to one of these courses of action.

"There was considerable discussion but only the member presenting the issue pressed for the action which he had proposed, and only I was positioned on the other side in equally clear-cut terms. My position was simply that I felt I had a real relationship with the client, that he was exploring himself, and that any decision of any kind was up to him. Finally in exasperation, the faculty member asked me:

" 'Well, Dan, what would you say if we as your colleagues no longer trust your judgment in this case and are unwilling to allow you to continue with it unless you also place him in the care of a psychiatrist?'

" 'That's easy to answer," I answered, 'because both you and I know that no one on this staff is going to take that position.'

"For all practical purposes that ended the discussion of the issue since my statement expressed a description of the people who made up the staff and the way in which we operated in all areas of professional work together. Shortly thereafter, the meeting ended. After the meeting, I assured the staff member that if my client ever expressed a desire to talk with one of the staff psychiatrists at Billings I would accept this desire and I would be willing to discuss the case with a psychiatrist. Beyond this I would not go. Because Carl had taken no personal position during the discussion, I felt the need to tell him this. Carl's total reaction with a slight smile was to say: 'Well, that's quite a concession, coming from you.'

"Recalling this incident after many years, I still am not sure what Carl was saying either about the merits of the concession, if any, or about his view of me as a personality. What struck me then and what strikes me now as I recall this incident is his entire willingness to receive my communication as expressing the personal meaning of the incident to me. Nothing more. Nothing less. . . .

"Rightly or wrongly, what Carl's reaction meant to me was that in his eyes I was a fully responsible person in my own right regardless of the judgment of any of his faculty colleagues. I suppose that without realizing it up to that moment I had really expected Carl to see those of us who were graduate students as 'second class citizens' in relation to the staff members who were on the faculty. Although I believe that my assurance to the faculty member who had brought up the case was motivated by a feeling of wanting him to know that I did not see him as an unreasonable person and that I sympathized with his concern even though I could not share it or act in terms of it, I think I wanted Rogers to know of it simply so that he would not think of me as a brash and inflexible member of the staff. What I wanted from him, I suppose, was his forgiveness for being the person I was. What he gave me was simply acceptance of the person that I am. That was more valuable to me than any of the times when Carl expressed his respect or admiration for things that I had done or written as a psychologist. In different ways, I think that this is one of the vital gifts which Carl made to those of us who were privileged to work with him. He helped us to realize what we really already knew: that only we could decide what was right for us and that he was completely at home with that recognition."

Rogers was a great listener. This was one of my own first impressions of him. I had driven across the country to visit him and Helen at their home in La Jolla, California, to discuss the possibility of my writing his biography. When I arrived, Helen was occupied with a friend, so Rogers and I went into his study to talk for about forty-five minutes. When we came out to join Helen, he summarized our conversation for her by reviewing all the major points I had made during those forty-five minutes. I remember my astonishment, thinking, "My God, this man *really* heard everything I said! What an incredible listener he is!" Then I laughed at myself for reacting this way, remembering why I had traveled across the country to meet him, and realizing that I really need not have been surprised to discover his ability to listen.

My reaction, in the 1970s was typical of those who knew Rogers at most any point in his adult life. Since Rogers first popularized the concept of empathic listening, or "active listening," it has come to be a well-known practice in the helping professions. But for people who have experienced this type of attention from Rogers himself, it has usually left an indelible impression. His colleague at Chicago, Rosalind Dymond Cartwright, described him as "the most acute listener I have ever known." Norman Brice, a Counseling Center student, remembered that he had "accepted an offer to join the staff of Michigan State as a counselor. I came into Carl and asked him if he might be able to work me into one or more counseling interviews, since I had never experienced him directly as a therapist. He managed to work in four. At the end of the first session with Carl, I came out to Virginia Hallman, his secretary, and practically shouted, 'Now I know the secret ingredient!' She was kind of low-key and gave me a 'What's with you?' response. I told her I have never felt so deeply and fully understood and so completely respected in all my life, and that the effect on me was electrifying."

Rogers' ability to listen empathically and his ability to encourage independent, creative work among his staff and students might be seen as two facets of one major quality: his great capacity to understand and accept another person as a separate individual, capable of self-direction and worthy of trust. I frequently have heard said of him: "Carl Rogers is the most Rogerian person I have ever met."

Therefore, in classes too, it was natural for him to respond empathically to students' comments, trying to understand the meaning the comments had for them. Joan Chodorkoff, a former student who is now a college teacher herself, wrote, "The thing I remember most vividly that has stuck with me is my initial feeling that when Carl turned to a student who asked a question and responded, that there was something ungenuine or overdone or ritual about it. Until I asked my questions, and *I* got that being accepted feeling! It *is* genuine and a student does grow on it."

Donald Tritt had originally studied psychology at Ohio State and had been warned not to come to the University of Chicago for his graduate work because he might be corrupted by Rogers. He came anyway. He remembered, "My instruction up until that time had made me pretty clever with my criticisms of Rogers and his ideas and so-called methods. Upon arriving at Chicago, the next year . . . it simply

occurred to me that, 'here I am at a good university, and I ought to
see directly about this person Carl Rogers.' So I entered one of his
beginning classes on counseling, without the prior acceptance needed,
and during that first day's meeting, gave out all of my wise criticisms.
Until sometime during that meeting it occurred to me that my questions and comments were being dealt with, for the first time I can
remember in my academic life, in a way that was honest and human
and terribly exciting. Clearly I was intrigued by this approach and the
kind of authenticity that allowed me and my questioning. . . . At that
point I think began my real education. Up to that time I had only been
an excellent memorizer and regurgitator of memorized material. Now
I clearly was being encouraged to be a critical and individual thinker.
And as it turned out, throughout all of my Chicago days and my
association with the Counseling Center, I was forever encouraged to
develop my own ideas and no longer felt any pressure to be as any
teachers asked me to be."

The combination of Counseling Center structures that encouraged
equality, freedom, and autonomy among staff and students, as well as
Rogers' own personal presence as a trusting, accepting, understanding, concerned person, seemed to have the effect of freeing students
and staff to follow their own lights and to engage in highly productive
and creative work. The experience of Manual Vargas was typical of
many students and staff who worked with him then. "During my first
two years at the Counseling Center, I felt that I had one of my most
personally creative cycles of my life. . . . I was, as usual with Carl, given
the freedom to try and do exactly as I pleased and what I liked, and
at the same time, encouraged to explore and discuss completely
openly with my peers at the Center whatever it was that I was doing.
Because of this extreme degree of freedom to try, to explore, to do my
own thing and the encouragements to share with others and to communicate from the deepest and wildest reaches of my personality, I
was, during these two years, in a constant period of deep inner
creativity, and I look back to those years as one of the most satisfying
periods of my life. And I think that the credit for that can be given very
much to the personality that Carl was, that around him could congre-
gate this aggregation of individuals."

The equality and independence that students were encouraged to
utilize carried over into the publishing area as well. Students did papers and reports, but instead of being told to write papers on subjects
about which their teachers already knew, they were encouraged to
develop new ideas and new research projects that would extend the

limits of the entire group's knowledge. Again they were called upon to act not like "graduate students," but as professionals. With this type of trust and expectation, they rose to the higher standards and produced a large number of valuable research studies and theoretical papers, many of which very much influenced Rogers' own thinking. He and the staff also initiated the "Discussion Papers" designed to encourage dialogue among staff and students over new ideas and methods. Anyone in the Center could have a paper he or she was working on mimeographed and circulated among the staff and students. This stimulated provocative discussion and thinking, which resulted, eventually, in more cogent publications.

Rogers would quote or make reference to his students' and staffs' work in most of his articles. He built much of his own reputation by reporting and synthesizing the ideas of others. But it is significant that among the dozens of former colleagues and students who shared with me their experience with Rogers, not one said that Rogers had unfairly taken credit for someone else's work. On the contrary, several pointed out how fair he tried to be and how generously they had been treated.

Elaine Dorfman, who wrote the chapter on play therapy in Rogers' *Client-Centered Therapy,* remembered, "Late on the evening of 11–3–49, I was notified of my father's death in New York. Since it was necessary for family reasons to leave town at once, I phoned my friend Lynn Rudikoff, of the Counseling Center staff, asking her to tell Rogers the next morning that I was unsure about plans to return and write."

The next day Rogers wrote her the following letter:

Dear Elaine:

   I was terribly sorry to hear this morning from Lynn that your father had passed away. I think I have some notion of the sorrow and strain and responsibilities that can be involved in such a situation. I just want you to know that we are all sorry to hear the news and hope that the situation will not make too many demands upon you.

   I had already dictated a letter telling you of your appointment to our courtesy staff and I am going to enclose it with this one, though there is nothing in it that needs your attention until you return.

   Lynn tells me that you sent a message that you would be unable to complete that chapter on play therapy. I am not quite sure how to interpret this, but I assume that you meant that you would be unable to complete it by the tentative deadline! I am not even sure that the other chapters will be completed by the first of January and in any event, as I think I mentioned to you, I want the book to be right, not just finished by some particular date. So, unless you have really concluded that you do not *wish* to write the chapter I would very much like to have you continue with that responsibility.

In this connection I have been thinking a little further about your statement that somewhat later in the year you would welcome some financial backing (I wonder if your father's death may even make this need more pressing). In any event I should think that in making a fairly modest estimate you should eventually get $1500 or so for the chapter you are writing, in royalties. (This is on the assumption that the new book will sell somewhat in the same fashion as the old.) I suspect that these royalties would mean more to you now than they would later and I would be very happy to give you an advance of $1,000 on expected royalties. This could be repaid to me as royalties come in. It could be made available to you now or at any time you would think advisable.

You do not need to give me an immediate response to these questions. I am going to send this to your home address because it seems to me that it might influence some of your plans for the current year. . . . Sincerely, . . .

The letter truly astonished her. "First, I had no idea that my contribution would mean royalties to me. Second the offer to lend me $1,000 at that time an enormous sum, was completely unheard of (and still is, some 20 years later). It was a gesture of complete faith, since neither he nor I knew whether my as yet unwritten chapter would prove acceptable for his book. . . . On the topic of this same book, you may be interested to know that royalties to all four authors were shared pro-rata. Likewise, we are all co-owners of the copyright, although it is by contract registered in Rogers' name. This egalitarian arrangement with two former students and one current student demonstrates, I think, Rogers' commitment to non-power relationships."

The cooperative, egalitarian, accepting side of Carl Rogers is the side which most people know, or assume to be there from the tone of his writings. Another quality that is often recognized by those who have known him personally, but which often surprises those who know him only through his writings, is his strength and "drive." Colleagues and friends have described him as "a very hard driving, forceful individual" and "driving, ambitious," and having a "realistic sense of his own personal importance in the contemporary world but nevertheless unassuming." This theme comes up again and again.

Fred Fiedler wrote, "Considering Rogers' concern with client-centered therapy, his permissiveness and non-directive methods, I found him to be a very hard-headed and disciplined person. He was certainly not 'cuddly.' I did not feel that anyone could put something over on him (and I don't believe that any of us tried—even if we had wanted to)."

His college debating experience served him well. Charles Ferguson "saw and heard him on a panel in a crowded ballroom in The Palace Hotel at the APA meetings in San Francisco when his work and ideas were under attack by eminent men. He waited patiently and collectedly while his several critics turned their attack on him, and then he spoke coolly, clearly, persuasively and skewered the lot . . . he was cool, collected, competitive; he was intellectually tough, he knew where he stood, he was well informed and he was extremely able."

Ferguson's picture of Rogers as a cool competitor is also borne out by several of the "battles" which he fought at the University of Chicago. The first was over a rather trivial incident but well serves the purpose of illustrating Rogers' readiness to stand up for his rights, his delight in rhetorical battle and his tendency toward witty sarcasm— usually gently wielded but sometimes with a real edge to it.

Before Rogers had come to Chicago, Robert Hutchins, the acclaimed President of the University, had instituted the "4E policy." This policy meant that the faculty would receive a relatively high pay schedule, but in return they would relinquish all monies earned from speeches, consultation, and writing to the university. This was done to foster a sense of community among the faculty and to discourage them from spending the bulk of their time seeking to enhance their own reputation or finances away from the university. On one occasion the University disallowed certain expenses Rogers claimed for Helen's accompanying him on a consulting trip, citing a rule that a Mr. Colwell had formulated that spouses could not accompany faculty on trips shorter than forty-five days. In a letter to the Assistant Comptroller, Rogers summarized the situation and concluded:

> As I puzzle over this situation, I see that I have made three mistakes in regard to it.
> In the first place, I had assumed that the relationship between the University and a faculty member was one of mutual confidence, decency and fair play. I thought that I could trust the University to be fair and equitable, and thought that they would feel the same way about me. I see now how mistaken I was. Your implicit attitude in this seems to be based on the assumption that "He's probably a chiseler unless he can prove otherwise." I realize that I should have taken the same attitude toward the University, and will now try to do so.
> In the second place, I was evidently mistaken in thinking that I needed my wife with me. I have the greatest regard for Mr. Colwell as a scholar and administrator, but I had not realized that he knew when I needed

my wife. I shall of course consult him before taking her on any other trip.

Incidentally one of the big disappointments of this whole affair is your refusal to send me the fascinating rules governing such situations. I had looked forward to receiving this Kinsey Report in Reverse. I wanted to know the evidence on which it was based. Is forty-five days the average time that faculty members can go without their wives, or is Mr. Colwell the norm which we must all try to achieve? Also how are exceptions made? What sort of evidence must one submit? Must the evidence be made public? (It seemed to me that at the very least this set of rules would be good for a skit at the Faculty Revels).

But this is a digression. The third mistake which I seem to have made was to have submitted fair expenses instead of actual expenses, with the evidence therefore . . . I shall now correct all three mistakes. . . .

He went on to reitemize his expenses, attach his receipts, and continue his letter:

> I will appreciate it if you will please send me a check for $505.38. . . . I realize that it is considerably more than the money I earned, but I hereby give you full permission to take the additional amount from the $1100 I turned in the previous month.
>
> It seems to me that as it now stands, everyone will be happy. You should feel very satisfied that you have been able to impose the rule that I cannot take my wife. I will feel very happy to receive $200 more than I had expected as reimbursement. The University should be very satisfied since, to judge by their administration of the 4E contract, their purpose seems to be to make every faculty member detest it. In this they have your very efficient help.
>
> I feel much better having gotten this off my chest. Now I suppose that I will have to give my time to worthwhile work until the next time when I try to turn money over to the University, when I am sure you can think up some new way of making the experience annoying.

Another more serious example of Rogers-as-protagonist occurred in 1951, after a year-long period when the Laboratory School of the University of Chicago had been studied by a committee of the University Council. The committee's report was very critical of the school, which was "progressive" in its educational philosophy. The report began by making it clear that "we are convinced that the chief end of education should be growth in knowledge and intellectual powers." Although the committee admitted that "as compared with the average achieved by students throughout the nation, the students in the Laboratory School are advanced by about three years in most basic intellectual skills" and "also compare favorably with other superior students who enter the College," still they felt that "dominant influences in the school clearly encourage concern for the 'happiness' and 'socialization' of the child as the ruling end of education. Consequently, 'democratic' rituals may be observed at the expense of disciplined work under legitimate authority."

When the committee's report came to Rogers' attention, he took the initiative of writing a letter to the members of the committee and to others involved in the matter. Part of his letter read:

> I realize that basic philosophies differ. I think differences are best explored when attitudes are brought out clearly, and for this I commend your report. I share with you a feeling that many of the procedures in the Laboratory School are accurately labelled as democratic rituals. But I disagree, as deeply as it is possible for a person to disagree, with the point of view you take. You feel that the solution for this situation is discipline by authority—giving up the democratic attempt. I can think of no better way of undermining the already badly shaken democratic philosophy of this country [the letter was written during the Sen. Joseph McCarthy period] than to move the elementary schools in the direction of a more authoritarian philosophy. My own experience in working with individuals and groups leads me to believe that the solution lies in a direction which is diametrically opposed to yours. I feel the solution is to work toward a *real* democracy in our schools, with each individual genuinely participating in responsible choices. I would replace "democratic rituals" with real democracy rather than with authoritarianism. I would aim for responsible *self*-discipline, not for discipline imposed by "legitimate authority."

On another occasion the disagreement struck much closer to home. Throughout his career Rogers has had frequent differences with the psychiatric profession, who often feel that psychologists are not qualified to carry on intensive psychotherapy. Years before, in Rochester, there had been the year-long battle over whether a psychiatrist or a psychologist would be appointed as the head of the Child Guidance Center which Rogers had initiated. As the psychology profession grew and as it developed a greater interest in the areas of counseling and psychotherapy, this issue arose with increasing frequency in a variety of settings throughout the country. At Chicago it had been a source of friction from the start with the University Medical School's Department of Psychiatry at Billings Hospital taking a dim view of the activities of the large and prestigious Counseling Center, which handled between eight hundred and a thousand new clients a year. There had been several open conflicts between the "Rogers group" and the "Billings group" during the late forties and early fifties, but it became particularly bitter in the middle fifties. Something of the flavor of the relationship between the two groups can be sensed from one small part of a twelve-page memorandum Rogers wrote to Lawrence Kimpton, Chancellor of the University of Chicago, in November 1956.

> I would like you to know of some of the statements which are being made about me and the Counseling Center by members of the medical group at the University. I believe you would want this situation brought to your attention. Let me give an example.
>
> Dr. Aldrich, of the Department of Psychiatry, in a conversation with me on October 24, said, "From where we sit you are practicing illegal medicine with patients for whom the medical group here is responsible. What you are doing is not only illegal but dangerous." He went on to say that in his opinion I was violating the code of ethics of the American Psychological Association regarding the obligation of psychologists to have adequate channels of medical assistance. . . .
>
> These remarks by Dr. Aldrich are similar to ones we have heard previously from Billings. My reaction can be stated by one sentence. I am tired of being maligned and slandered by members of the Billings group who know almost nothing of our work. . . .
>
> Dr. Aldrich's statements contrast so sharply with the statements and actions of physicians and scientists who *do* know something of our work, that I would like you to consider some of these contrasts.
>
> 1. Dr. Harold G. Wolff of Cornell Medical School is one of the world's leading authorities in psychosomatic medicine. He has been a serious student of my work, and knows it very well. A week ago he asked me if I would serve with him as a consultant to the Department of Defense on a top-secret matter having to do with mental health. He said, "I am asking the five top-ranking men in the country in this field to serve on this task. You are one of the five, and I hope you will serve."
>
> Now I submit that I may be one of the top-ranking men in the country in the field of mental health, or I may be an unethical law-breaker in my work. I do not believe that *both* statements can be true.
>
> 2. Dr. Seymour Kety is a leading neurologist and director of research for the National Institute of Mental Health. Dr. Merton Gill is a leading psychoanalyst. Doctors Kety and Gill studied intensely the work and program of the Counseling Center for the Ford Foundation. The result of their study and that of their committee (which included Dr. John Romano, a leading psychiatrist) was that the Counseling Center was one of 20 organizations selected out of many hundreds of applications for support in the field of research in mental health. A five year grant of $350,000 was made.
>
> I submit that we may be an outstanding organization in the field of mental health, or we may be a group working illegally, unethically and dangerously. I do not believe it possible that we are *both*. . . .

Norman Brice summed up all the comments and anecdotes cited above. "What has bothered me so through the years has been the misguided notions of some who have read bits and pieces of what he has written and have proceeded to miss the whole point of what he has to say. They so often regard Carl as a softie, a 'gentle Jesus' type of person, permissive to a fault and therefore weak and ineffectual. In contrast to this, I have never in all my life met such a strong man as Carl. He puts *first* in his writings about psychotherapy the concept of *congruence* and that means *being yourself.* Being yourself means that you express anger when you feel it or boredom when you feel it, and that you are an authentic person in your own right. So many people don't seem to get that message. Someone, somewhere who does understand Carl said of him that he has a 'whim of steel.' Carl is nobody's push-over. He is a very, very strong and controversial man."

There seems to be a considerable disparity between Rogers' associates' view of him as both accepting *and* forceful and many readers' rather one-sided impression created by his writings. J.C. Nunnally, a strong supporter of Rogers' work, wrote, "My major criticism is in terms of the failure to communicate his own theory and metaphysics to other people. Although he wrote clearly and spoke beautifully, I always felt that he was to some extent speaking in parables that were frequently not correctly perceived by the audience, e.g., giving the impression of always being highly passive in the therapeutic role."

One wonders after an explanation. How was it that this man who behaved in a confident, direct, and self-assertive manner withheld from his writings the tone or anecdotes or transcripts of interviews or whatever it would take to convey more of the person he was?

In my opinion the answer to this lies in another set of Rogers' characteristics that were frequently mentioned by his students, associates, and friends—a combination of great warmth, giving, and caring and also, paradoxically, an impression of distance and aloofness.

I have heard dozens of people describe him as "warm." It seems to be one of the first things mentioned by most people who have known him for any length of time. Arthur Combs wrote, "The love and the genuineness of the man has a way of getting through to almost everyone who sees him or hears him. He seems to be able to convey even to a very large audience the feeling that he is expressing himself honestly, genuinely and caringly to each person in the audience. The interesting thing is that he really does."

Joan Chodorkoff, a student at the Counseling Center remembered him as "a most non-threatening person, I suppose, because he is not easily threatened. I particularly noticed this (and appreciated it when I was young and shy). He really made himself available as a teacher, person and as the Director of the Center." J.C. Nunnally, now a Professor of Psychology at Vanderbilt University, agreed that Rogers' "patience, understanding, and capacity for interpersonal warmth are as much as or more than would be expected of him."

Yet many other people, and often the same ones who described him as warm, also saw him as being occasionally or frequently aloof.

Part of this impression, undoubtedly, was caused by Rogers' shyness, a boyhood quality he never quite got over. Many people expect a famous figure or a leader to be extroverted, socially self-assured, the life-of-the-party, and so on. Rogers fit none of these stereotypes. He has always been ill-at-ease at social gatherings. Even in later years when he became involved in the encounter group movement, he would often begin a group by expressing some of his own nervousness or feelings of unsureness about what would happen. One of his associates at Chicago recounted: "I remember once my wife and I visited a small get-together at Russ Becker's apartment, along with Ros Dymond, and Carl and Helen. Both Russ and Ros are great yarners. They out-did one another with different stories of their experiences and travels. Carl just sat back and thoroughly enjoyed them but never once attempted to match them in their song-and-dance. In fact, he said something, good naturedly, about not being able to come close to telling such interesting stories."

Rogers is the first to admit this. "Most individuals who have attained some status," he wrote, "tend to dominate a situation—they are brilliant in conversation, tend to be the center of attention in any group, simply cannot be ignored. I, on the contrary, am absolutely at my worst if I am expected to be a 'leading figure' or an 'exciting person.' As my wife can testify, I simply 'clam up' and seem to be the dullest person around."

At the University of Chicago he and Helen once got on an elevator heading to an upper floor where Rogers was to deliver a lecture to a large audience. Just before the door closed, a young couple entered. As the four of them ascended, the young woman asked her friend, "Have you ever met this guy Rogers?" "Oh, yes," he said impressively. "What's he like?" she asked. "Well, he's a very unprepossessing kind of person," began the young man, as the door opened and they all left the elevator.

Beyond his natural reticence, which must have occasionally been mistaken for aloofness, there was still some validity to those impressions of Rogers as somewhat withdrawn. John Levy suggested that Rogers "is blocked here, not only by his shyness, but also very strongly by his intense integrity. Carl is very strongly committed to emotional honesty, and some of his reserve is a result of his fear of conveying an emotion which he does not feel, or communicating it more intensely than is real. He has a passionate commitment to honesty, in his relationships no less than his work."

Arthur Combs saw still a different aspect of Rogers' remoteness. "He is a person of deep sensitivity and compassion. A kind of paradox which I think is common to men like him: He has the capacity for intense concentration and is capable of responding flat out to persons who have real need of him like clients and members of his encounter groups and the like. He is likely, however, to seem somewhat aloof to persons in more casual contacts. It is almost as though he did not quite know how to handle situations in which he could not operate with the kind of intense giving which he shows in his professional relationships."

John Levy again: "He has a strong need for privacy and for his own living space. He has developed an ability to say 'No,' and he says it in a way which is unmistakable. He values himself quite highly (this does not negate his shyness) and has learned to protect himself from those who would take advantage of him. Sometimes this comes out harshly, and sometimes people are offended. He doesn't play social games very well, or professional games, and often seems more interested in being sure that his position and his attitude are understood accurately than he is in protecting people's feelings or in being diplomatic."

Having read dozens of character sketches or cameos written by Rogers' former associates, I cannot help but marvel at how each not only has something in common with the others, but also manages to add an original nuance to the overall description of the man. Jim Bebout, for example, saw Rogers' need for privacy from another vantage point. "I'm afraid so many of us at Chicago and elsewhere were 'following the great man.' I'm sure he knew this. And perhaps it was because of this or perhaps it was a more general part of his nature that he was so successful at keeping his distance. It was probably not so hard for him to remain apart from the internecine quarrels around him, or to maintain non-binding friendships with former clients or current colleagues. For example, one of his most favorite 'successful clients,' a dear friend of mine, came to work at the Chicago clinic after seeing him in therapy and stayed for years. But her contact with him was kept in some kind of careful balance, both from his doing and from her shyness and appreciation of his need for privacy. Years after he left Chicago, she left Chicago and joined me in San Francisco. She hungrily wanted to write him or have him visit but would not ask. He would ask about her as often as he remembered but would not initiate a reunion. She died the month I saw her in San Francisco and I'm sure one of her fondest memories was her relationship with Carl Rogers."

Shy and private, by nature and by choice. Warm and caring or cold and aloof—according to the beholder. T.M. Tomlinson tried to put the pieces together. "What kind of person is Carl Rogers? For me he is a person of whom I can as easily say 'I hardly know him' as 'He is one of the most important people in my life.' People often say with dismay that Rogers is really a cold man whose personality and life style are at direct variance with his writings and professed beliefs. They are wrong of course, but only because they expect something different than they get. . . . I don't know where those expectations come from. . . . What Rogers gives personally is what he says, namely, acceptance. He isn't demonstrative about it and most people don't know it when it's happening; only later do they realize the nature of their experience with him. Rogers doesn't give love; he's fairly lovable but not very loving. That, I think, is what leads to the conclusion that he's cold, i.e., people approach him expecting to be loved immediately for what they are, whereas Carl simply accepts them for what they are without implications of love. It's an easy distinction to draw, but most people are hard put to do it and feel rejected because they are not embraced. At the same time, however, it is difficult to feel that one is inside Carl Rogers. There are no psychic veins and arteries which pump blood from him to us, thus there is little feeling of shared worlds. The worlds touch but they don't overlap except in rare circumstances. What this sums to is that Carl is very much like the rest of us, some things are public, some things are private, sometimes he's gentle, sometimes he's tough, etc., except that he has a vision of how it ought to be and, to the extent possible for him, he practices it, always hoping that others will benefit and even more, that others will push beyond his own limits of behavior and thought."

Julius Seeman took Tomlinson's analysis one step further and related Rogers' remoteness to his theoretical development as well as his personal style. "I worked with Carl for six years and felt that I got to know him relatively well in a professional context. But there was always a certain reserve when it came to personal self-disclosure, and I learned virtually nothing about his personal life during those six years. In retrospect I see this attribute as quite compatible with his early theoretical position and its emphasis on autonomy. However, there was also another central theme which I saw in Carl's development, both personally and professionally, and it touched also on the issue of autonomy. I think that the history of Carl's development, personal and theoretical, could fit on a continuum from insulation to involvement. His early theory emphasized the permissiveness of the therapeutic climate, and said astonishingly little about a person to person relationship with the client. Even the concept of 'reflection' was an insulating one, picturing as it did the mirroring of the client's own self as given back by the therapist. This distancing climate, however, had by 1950 come to be questioned, and alternative formulations were in the air. The reexamination took two forms. A small group at the Counseling Center talked of a more involved relationship and considered 'caring' and 'love' as ways to describe the relationship. Another dimension emphasized the congruence of the therapist, and suggested that such congruence had to involve greater self-disclosure by the therapist. . . . It seemed to me that about this time Carl's therapy was reflecting some movement toward a more internal and involved style, though I still experienced an underlying reserve. It was to take years of steadily growing involvement before Carl's personal self came through in therapy."

The Seeman statement implies that Rogers, in the middle years of his stay at Chicago, was commencing another period of change. Several previous changes had already taken place in his therapeutic style. In the early and mid-1930s, from an interest in manipulating the external conditions of a child's environment, he had become more interested in therapeutic personality change as the means for helping the individual. From the middle 1930s to the early 1940s, from the use of directive methods for psychotherapy, he had come to rely on and develop nondirective methods. From the middle to late 1940s, from an emphasis on nondirective methods, he had come to emphasize client-centered attitudes—acceptance and empathic understanding. The change now occurring was the insertion of "congruence" as the third necessary ingredient in the therapeutic relationship. As Seeman suggests, the change did not come about all at once. What he does not suggest is that this change in Rogers' conception of psychotherapy was also one of the most personally significant changes in his life.

One has to go back to Rogers' childhood to understand his evolution on this point. As described earlier, his childhood background had taught him to keep his emotions to himself. In the Rogers household, emotional displays were a sign of weakness and usually interfered with good common sense and getting one's work done. Perhaps it was this suppression of feelings which he experienced in his own upbringing that later helped Rogers be more aware of the importance of the client's accepting his feelings as a part of himself and learning to live with them, instead of denying them. Acceptance and empathy became the therapist's tools for helping the client to accept and understand his own feelings. Little or nothing was said of the therapist's feelings, other than she *should feel* accepting and understanding if she wants to be helpful. What of the therapist who doesn't feel accepting or understanding with a particular client or at a particular time? Rogers provided no transcripts or anecdotes to answer the question. Thus he provided a very unrealistic picture for readers of his books who had to assume that either Rogers and his group were "perfect"—always accepting, always understanding—or that this presentation of therapy was much oversimplified.

Apparently, even though he had come to understand the importance of the *client's* feelings in the relationship, his own personal background still held him back from giving due attention to the therapist's feelings. The turning point came during the years 1949 through 1951. This was a time when Rogers experienced "two years of intense personal distress" and almost had a serious psychological breakdown. In his own words, pieced together from several published and unpublished accounts, here is what occurred:

"There was a deeply disturbed client (she would be regarded as schizophrenic) with whom I had worked fairly extensively at Ohio State, who later moved to the Chicago area and renewed her therapeutic contacts with me. I see now that I handled her badly, vacillating between being warm and real with her, and then being more 'professional' and aloof when the depth of her psychotic disturbance threatened me. She began to take up a bigger and bigger part of my therapy time—two or three times a week. She would sometimes appear sitting on our doorstep. I felt trapped by this kind of dependence. She said she needed more warmth and more realness from me. I wanted her to like me though I didn't like her. This brought about the most intense hostility on her part (along with dependence and love), which completely pierced my defenses. I started to feel it was a real drain on me, yet I stubbornly felt that I *should* be able to help her and permitted the contacts to continue long after they had ceased to be therapeutic, and involved only suffering for me. I recognized that many of her insights were sounder than mine, and this destroyed my confidence in myself, and I got to the point where I could not separate my 'self' from hers.

I literally lost the boundaries of myself. The situation is best summarized by one of her dreams in which a cat was clawing my guts out, but
really did not wish to do so.

"The efforts of colleagues to help were of no avail, and I became
convinced (and I think with some reason) that I was going insane. One
night, we saw a movie with some very bizarre happenings on the film,
and I thought quite seriously, 'Well, when I'm locked up and start to
hallucinate and so on, they'll think it all comes from inside me and
actually a lot of it will be what I saw in this movie.' I was sure it was
going to happen. I was so raw emotionally that anything had a real
impact. Yet I continued this relationship, destructive to me, because
I recognized her desperately precarious situation, on the brink of a
psychosis, and felt I *had* to be of help.

"Gradually I realized I was on the edge of a complete breakdown
myself and then suddenly this feeling became very urgent. I had to
escape. I am everlastingly grateful to Dr. Louis Cholden, the promising
young psychiatrist, who was working in the Counseling Center at that
time, for his willingness to take over the client on an hour's notice. I
invited him to lunch at the Faculty Club. I said I needed help and
explained the situation. He said, 'All right, how about my seeing her
next week?' I must have shown something then and he must have been
fairly sharp, because he added, 'Or isn't that soon enough?' I said,
'Well, she's coming in this afternoon.' I was really in a panic state at
that time.

"I pulled a desperate trick on her. Knowing that she wouldn't want
to see anyone else of her own accord, I arranged to give some kind of
signal to the secretary, when Dr. Cholden should come into the office.
He came in, I said a few words to introduce them and quickly left. She,
within moments, burst into a full blown psychosis, with many delusions
and hallucinations. She started telling Cholden of how she was related
to me in some way, there was some uncle in Wisconsin and so on.
[Later she tried to gain entrance to Rogers' apartment and to hang a
large sign out their window saying, "Come Home!"]

"As for me, I went home and told Helen that I must get away, *at once.*
We were on the road within an hour and stayed away two or three
months on what we can now calmly refer to as our 'runaway trip.'
Shortly after leaving, I wanted to buy a couple of cans of beer. I went
into a store, got the beer, paid for it, came out and thought with
amazement, 'My God, I was able to do that!' I was fairly far gone.
Helen's quiet assurance that I would come out of this distress in time
and her willingness to listen when I was able to talk of it were of great

help. However, when we returned I was still rather deeply certain of my complete inadequacy as a therapist, my worthlessness as a person, and my lack of any future in the field of psychology or psychotherapy.

"For a time before I left, I was in therapy with one member of my staff [Nathaniel Raskin]. When I returned I felt my problems were so serious it would only be threatening to ask a staff member to help me with them. I am deeply grateful that one member of our group [Oliver Bown] simply told me that it was obvious I was in deep distress, that he was not afraid of me or my problem, and that he was offering me a therapeutic relationship. . . . He said, 'I just want you to know that I can see you're in trouble. And I also want you to know I'm not afraid of you. If you'd like to talk to me, I'd be glad to do so.' . . . I accepted in desperation and gradually worked through to a point where I could value myself, even like myself, and was much less fearful of receiving or giving love. My own therapy with my clients has become consistently and increasingly free and spontaneous ever since that time."

These last two sentences deserve a closer examination. Rogers seems to be identifying two problems he had, quite apart from the relationship with the disturbed woman. That he came to value and even like himself suggests that at some level he had not valued or liked himself. That he became much less fearful of receiving or giving love suggests that such a fear previously existed.

It is at first glance ironic, though in fact it's not ironic at all, that even Rogers should have had to deal with problems like these. If there was any one problem common to the hundreds of clients he had helped over the years, it was that they did not accept themselves. The manifestations of this self-attitude were vastly different, but the root problem was still the same: At some level, different for different people, they believed they were not "ok"—not lovable, not capable, not good enough. In his own words, Rogers felt, "Nobody could love *me*, even though they might like what I did. I was an unlovable person. I really was inferior, but putting up a big front."

This feeling was buried quite deeply. It had been years since the time when he always had to work and produce to be deemed worthy in his parents' eyes. It had been years since he last heard his mother suggest that his righteousness was "as filthy rags in Thy sight, oh Lord." It had been years since he had to keep his feelings submerged (although as an adult he frequently continued to do so). These cumulative experiences had been clouded over by time; subsequent years of professional success and a growing personal confidence had been almost enough to render that underlying, childhood remnant of nonacceptance irrelevant. Perhaps he might have gone along and never been troubled by those early "scars" and lived his life out as a satisfied and famous man. On the other hand perhaps this unfinished business from childhood —all the family's teasing, all the not-so-complimentary nicknames, all the criticism for being too absentminded or too immersed in fantasy or not religious in the proper way—perhaps this had created a wound that was very near to the surface and, had the relationship with the disturbed woman client not developed, something else would have triggered the process of distress, then therapy.

We will never know how it might have happened, only what did happen. The personal stress precipitated by the prolonged and complicated therapy with his client led to his entering into therapy with one of his staff members. The therapy, which started out by exploring specific current problems, led gradually toward deeper unresolved problems of self-attitudes and self-acceptance. Of his therapy he commented, "I have often been grateful that by the time I was in dire need of personal help, I had trained therapists who were persons in their own right, not dependent upon me, yet able to offer me the kind of help I needed. I have since become rather keenly aware that the point of view I developed in therapy is the sort of help I myself would like, and this help was available when I needed it."

He felt greatly helped by his therapy, writing in July of 1951, "I believe that during the past year the therapy I have conducted has been better than anything I have ever done before. I think that my counseling is showing increasing results from my own therapy undertaken two years ago when I was really personally disturbed by the deep hostility of a client. I think that I see in myself now more freedom in venturing into deep emotional relationships with clients, less rigidity, more ability to stand by them in their deepest emotional crises."

CHAPTER 7
The Chicago Years: Part Two
1951-1957

None of the people I interviewed or heard from who knew Rogers during the early 1950s commented on seeing any major changes in his personal or professional style during or after his therapy. Many did not even know he was in therapy. The warmth, acceptance, and understanding were still there. And people still sometimes would see him as aloof or distant, though perhaps not so frequently. The changes were more apparent in other ways. As discussed earlier one change was in his writing style.

A second change toward a more spontaneous, personally revealing style came in Rogers' increasing stress on the therapist's *congruence* in therapy. As implied earlier, this was not Rogers' idea, but one which many members of the Counseling Center were exploring at the time. In fact several of his colleagues of that period pointed out that except in the research area Rogers was less of an innovator than he was a learner and a popularizer. Manual Vargas said of him: "He was able to learn and very sincerely was willing to listen to others and learn from their experiences. He was able to learn from the viewpoints of his students and it is this ability that helped him to be in the forefront of much of the thinking and the research in psychotherapy. And even now he's still moving in the advance group. However, since he was primarily committed to research and the rational explication of psychotherapy, I do not see him as being an innovator and he was not that at the Counseling Center. It was others of us who were more willing to try out new reactions to our clients, and it was some of us who were more willing to work out our emotional reactions *in* the therapeutic relationship, as well as outside of it, and who were more willing to do a variety of new approaches—change the hours, extend the hours, be much more flexible than he seemed to be. But he was able to observe, to listen, to empathize, to learn from the rest of us."

In an interview in 1958 Rogers said, "I think I essentially picked up this idea from the Atlanta group that's working with Carl Whitaker." Nevertheless, while Rogers may not have introduced the concept of congruence, he certainly was the one who is most responsible for its widespread usage in psychotherapy and the other helping professions today. He also recalled coining the actual term, based on the geometric concept of congruent triangles. Beginning in 1956, he began to use the term with increasing frequency.

In his first written use of the word Rogers stated ". . . it appears essential that the therapist be genuine, or whole, or congruent in the relationship. What this means is that it is important for the therapist to be what he is in his contact with the client. To the extent that he presents an outward facade of one attitude or feeling, while inwardly or at an unconscious level he experiences another feeling, the likelihood of successful therapy will be diminished. It is only as he is, in this relationship, a unified person, with his experienced feeling, his awareness of his feelings, and his expression of those feelings all congruent or similar, that he is most able to facilitate therapy. It is only as the therapist provides the genuine reality which is in him, that the other person can successfully seek the reality in himself. The therapist is nondefensive about the reality in himself, and this helps the client to become nondefensive.

"The following paragraphs describe some of the attitudes [acceptance, empathy] which, if genuinely held, seem most conducive to therapy, but it seems even more important to be genuine than to hold these attitudes. Thus, if the therapist is persistently bored in the interview, or feels a persistent disbelief in what the client is saying, it is better for him to voice these genuine feelings than to pretend to a more positive attitude which he does not have. This seems especially true if he is able to express his feelings as something pertaining to himself, not as an accusation toward the client. He may be able to say, 'I feel bored in this interview,' *not* 'You are boring' or to say, 'I find myself disbelieving what you say,' *not* 'You are untruthful.' This is an area in which our point of view is changing, and this paragraph is written tentatively as an indication of the direction of some of our more recent practice and thinking. It seems likely that the more deeply the counselor can be himself in the relationship, the more certainly will therapy take place."

As Rogers further explored the concept of congruence, he modified this statement slightly. He pointed out that congruence does not mean the therapist interrupts the client to say, "I feel hungry," or "I wonder what my wife is doing right now," whenever these thoughts occur. Rather, it is when feelings in the therapist occur persistently and are relevant to the relationship that the therapist would do well to express them. Otherwise they will surely be communicated anyway and are likely to interfere with the therapist's ability to continue to accept and empathize with the client. In addition, when such a message is not communicated clearly it is likely to confuse the client, who has to guess what the therapist is feeling.

Uncharacteristically Rogers provided few examples in his writing of how a therapist might be congruent in therapy. Normally he tried to make his concepts come alive by providing excerpts from transcripts of real interviews. He did not do this with congruence. Apparently at the time he began to emphasize the therapist's congruence in the relationship, he was still finding this somewhat difficult himself. Or stated differently, although he was experiencing a growing congruence himself, the habit of many years of withholding his own feelings was still present, and this influenced his writing on the subject. One of the few fully articulated examples of his own congruence in therapy comes not from any article or book, but from the unpublished transcript of a discussion he had in 1958 with a group of students at the University of Rochester. After mentioning that the therapist's being congruent with his client "sounded like a wild and crazy idea when I first heard it," he gave an example from his own life.

> I'm sure that one of the problems that troubled me for a long time and probably still does to some degree is that I don't like to have people *cling*. I can bear it to have people have lots of feelings toward me but if I sense something that seems like clinging, I tend to get a little uneasy. One very disturbed woman that I was working with kept asking for more frequent interviews. My feeling was "She's just grabbing more and more—there is no limit to this." I don't think I was too much aware of that but I'm sure that that was what I was feeling.
>
> I would feel, "Oh—I suppose I should see her more—because she is in a pretty bad state." It is no doubt that it was a grudging agreement.

Then I realized that my attitude changed so that now when she was coming in I would feel—"Oh, here she comes again!" which is not exactly the attitude I feel towards most clients. I felt, "I'm *not* a therapist for her any more. These aren't the attitudes that will help her" and I felt really very much troubled by it because I felt, "She has trouble enough of her own. I can't burden her with my problems." This didn't seem fair.

So it was a difficult internal struggle. I was surprised to find how deeply it troubled me to stop the flow of the interview at one point and say, "There's something I've got to talk over and that is that I'm just no longer feeling comfortable with these greater and greater demands on my time. I just feel as though you're pushing me to the wall. I can't stand it." She was quite jolted by the fact that I *had* interrupted her struggling with her own problems but she listened and said, "But I've always *said* I wanted more time *if* you felt you could give it to me." I said, "Yes, I realize you always have used those words but I guess I didn't feel you meant them." So we had a good discussion about the *issues.* The amazing thing to me was that that just dissolved my feeling that I was being pushed and pushed. As a matter of fact, shortly after that I did give her additional time and just didn't feel any strain about it. I was able to *give* it to her not *feeling* that she was demanding more and more.

Another example of Rogers' congruence in therapy comes in a letter from one of his students at Chicago, who wrote, "A fellow graduate-student friend of mine was almost literally tossed out of psychotherapy with Rogers. Rogers had grown quite tired of the student's self-indulgence and refusal to accept mature responsibility, and Rogers told him so in no uncertain terms."

Significantly both of these examples are unpublished. A dearth of examples of this nature has made "congruence" one of the most ambiguous and easily misunderstood of the concepts Rogers has popularized. Bernard Covner suggested that "the non-directive approach, in retrospect, served as a convenient cop-out for people lacking in wholesome self-assertiveness." This may have been due in part to Rogers' late emphasis on the importance of the therapist's congruence.

Just as acceptance and empathy were attributes of Rogers' personal as well as professional style, there was a similar connection between his personal and professional interest in the concept of congruence. His own period of distress and therapy had made him much more aware of his feelings and how he dealt with them. His desire to be more in touch with his feelings and express them when appropriate in his personal life made him receptive to his colleagues who were arguing for the importance of the therapist's congruence in therapy. Accepting this idea and popularizing it himself made Rogers that much more convinced of the importance of congruence in all relationships, including his own. Thus each aspect of his life, the professional and personal, reinforced the growing congruence in the other.

It is not surprising that his friends and colleagues did not see a dramatic change. The process unfolded over a ten-year period—from the start of his therapy to the advocacy of congruence in his writings. Then it continued to unfold. It has been suggested that part of Rogers' motivation for later entering the encounter group movement was a desire for greater spontaneity and expression of affect in his own life. It is enough to say, for now, that the period of the late forties to late fifties was one which legitimized the expression of personal feelings— both for Rogers the person and Rogers the therapist.

Congruence was not the only concept Rogers borrowed from his colleagues and students. In the mid-fifties, influenced by a dissertation of one of his doctoral students, Stanley Standal, Rogers substituted the phrase "unconditional positive regard" for what he had up until then always called "acceptance." Again, he did not adopt the term all at once, but played with the concept for a few years, getting the feel of its meaning by using it in several articles in piecemeal form, as in 1956 when he wrote, "By acceptance is meant a warm regard for the client as a person of unconditional self-worth."

Before long he adopted Standal's own term. Its meaning was not too different from what he had always meant by acceptance, but it seemed to capture that meaning better for him. Using it himself for the first time, he explained, "To the extent that the therapist finds himself experiencing a warm acceptance of each aspect of the client's experience as being a part of that client, he is experiencing unconditional positive regard. This concept has been developed by Standal. . . . It means that there are no *conditions* of acceptance, no feeling of 'I like you only *if* you are thus and so.' It means a 'prizing' of the person, as Dewey has used that term. It is at the opposite pole from a selective evaluating attitude—'You are bad in these ways, good in those.' It involves as much feeling of acceptance for the client's expression of negative, 'bad,' painful, defensive, abnormal feelings as for his expression of 'good,' positive, mature, confident, social feelings, as much acceptance of ways in which he is inconsistent as of ways in which he is consistent. It means a caring for the client, but not in a positive way or in such a way as simply to satisfy the therapist's own needs. It means a caring for the client as a *separate* person, with permission to have his own feelings, his own experiences."

With the introduction of the term "unconditional positive regard," Rogers solidified his conception of the therapist's role. In a speech in 1946 he had said the counselor's role was "best described by the terms: "warmth, permissiveness, acceptance, understanding, and nondirectiveness." At Chicago, little by little, he augmented, abridged, and modified this description. Warmth and acceptance became acceptance and liking. Acceptance and liking became "a warm regard for the client as a person of unconditional self-worth," which became unconditional positive regard. Understanding became empathy. "A nondefensive genuineness," later called congruence, was added to the list. Though permissiveness and nondirectiveness were maintained in practice as effective ways of implementing the key attitudes, they were dropped in theory. Years of experience, hundreds of clients, years of training new therapists, hundreds of staff meetings, classes, and informal sessions, voluminous readings, the reflection that results from writing— all these provided him with the data and the occasions to continue to modify his thinking, to achieve the formulation which best expressed for him what effective therapy is all about.

In 1949 he had written: "It no longer appears impossible that we may at some foreseeable date be able to make a statement of this sort, with objective evidence for it. 'If conditions a, b, and c are met, then a process of therapy is initiated which involves changes x, y, and z in the attitudes and personality of the individual.' " In 1956 he made such a statement for the first time: "If the therapist provides a relationship in which he is (a) genuine, internally consistent; (b) acceptant, prizing the client as a person of worth; (c) empathically understanding of the client's private world; then the client becomes (a) more realistic in his self-perceptions; (b) more confident and self-directing; (c) more positively valued by himself; (d) less likely to repress elements of his experience; (e) more mature, socialized, and adaptive in his behavior; (f) more like the healthy, integrated, well-functioning person in his personality structure."

A year or so later he further developed his formulation of the a, b, and c, in one of his most important essays, "The Necessary and Sufficient Conditions of Therapeutic Personality Change."

In his introduction, he explained how for years he had been trying to understand what the essential ingredients of therapy were: "As I have considered my own clinical experience and that of my colleagues, together with the pertinent research which is available, I have drawn out several conditions which seem to me to be *necessary* to initiate constructive personality change, and which, taken together, appear to be sufficient to inaugurate the process." The first two conditions he listed were described as preconditions to therapy. First, there must be some type of psychological contact between client and therapist; in other words there must be a relationship. Second, the client must be in a state of some psychological malaise, dissatisfaction, or in Rogers' terms "in a state of incongruence, being vulnerable or anxious." Then came the three conditions which he had been developing over the previous several years. "3. The therapist is congruent or integrated in the relationship. 4. The therapist experiences unconditional positive regard for the client. 5. The therapist experiences an empathic understanding of the client's internal frame of reference and endeavors to communicate this experience to the client." Then adding a sixth condition, lest it be taken for granted: "The communication to the client of the therapist's empathic understanding and unconditional positive regard is to a minimal degree achieved." "No other conditions are necessary," he wrote. "If these six conditions exist, and continue over a period of time, this is sufficient. The process of constructive personality change will follow."

Such an extreme and specific statement had many implications, and Rogers was quick to spell out many of them: ". . . it is *not* stated that these conditions apply to one type of client, and other conditions are necessary to bring about psychotherapeutic change with other types of client. . . . It is *not* stated that these six conditions are the essential conditions for client-centered therapy, and that other conditions are essential for other types of psychotherapy. . . . It is *not* stated that psychotherapy is a special kind of relationship, different in kind from all others which occur in everyday life. . . . It is *not* stated that special intellectual professional knowledge—psychological, psychiatric, medical, or religious—is required of the therapist. . . . Intellectual training and the acquiring of information has, I believe, many valuable results —but becoming a therapist is not one of those results. . . . It is *not* stated that it is necessary for psychotherapy that the therapist have an accurate psychological diagnosis of the client. . . ."

This point in Rogers' evolution deserves a more careful examination in light of what we know of his career. Over many years the man had developed his ideas and methods and had formulated them into an approach which was called "nondirective therapy." All over the country, and in many parts of the world, counselors, therapists and other professionals were practicing his "method," many of them calling themselves "Rogerians." Then, during the late forties and early fifties, he began to change his thinking and to suggest that the methods are not nearly as important as the attitudes of the therapist. Then, in modifying these attitudes, he came to believe that, even more important than the therapist simply holding these attitudes, the attitudes must be lived and experienced by both therapist and client in a genuine, interpersonal relationship.

When one concentrates on the single steps in a long staircase, he or she may neglect to notice that whole floors are passing by. So it was with Rogers' changes during this decade. All the subtle modifications of terms and concepts and techniques could easily obscure the major changes in thinking and practice which had occurred. In the twelve years at Chicago he moved from the *method* to the *attitudes* to the *relationship* as the key ingredient in the therapeutic process. In so doing he diminished the importance of the very approach he had been building for the previous twenty years.

After all, if congruence and empathy and unconditional positive regard are the key aspects of the relationship, cannot the Freudian, or Jungian, or Alderian, or Sullivanian, or Gestalt therapist, or rational therapist, or the practitioner of almost any other school of therapy form a relationship with her patients which has these three ingredients? True, they may be expressed differently. But isn't the psychoanalyst's emphasis on free association, to some extent, a desire to understand the client from his own frame of reference? And isn't the rational therapist's belief that the patient can learn to approach his problems in a rational, systematic manner also a form of unconditional positive regard? And isn't the Gestalt therapist's refusal to be manipulated by her patients a sign of congruence? Although Rogers did not go into detail on this point, he answered affirmatively. In fact he was quite fond of quoting several studies done by one of his students, Fred Fiedler, which showed how experienced therapists of *different* schools of thought were more similar in their actual practices than experienced and inexperienced therapists of the *same* school of thought. Moreover, some of the qualities that the experienced therapists had in common were some of the very conditions Rogers was calling necessary and sufficient for therapeutic change—namely, "the therapist's ability to understand, to communicate with, and to maintain rapport with the client."

Rogers always continued to prefer his own client-centered style as the best way he knew for him to enter into a therapeutic relationship with his clients. But he remained open to other valuable approaches which contained enough of the necessary conditions to be helpful to clients. Bernard Steinzor told of how, "Even though Rogers knew of my development away from a 'Rogerian,' he would still on occasion, when people asked him about possible counselors in New York, refer people to me. This kind of real tolerance of differences, despite Rogers' own emphasis on his own mode, is one of his really great qualities, and perhaps can even be considered one of the significant contributions he's made to the development of ways of thinking about psychotherapy. He has been mistakenly considered to be a rigid technician, whereas the spirit of his work has always been open to people developing their own style."

Paul Bergman wrote to Rogers in 1959, saying, "I was very touched by your willingness to participate in my plans. You have been very good to me for many years now. Even though I now propose formulations different from yours, I consider my having encountered you and your work one of the lucky and great events of my life."

How did this openness to differences reconcile itself with Rogers' postulating such an extreme view as the "necessary and sufficient" conditions for successful psychotherapy? There was really no contradiction. These conditions, for Rogers, were and always remained *an hypothesis*. The scientist had not become a polemicist. If he stated his views in extreme and specific terms, it was only because the more categorical he was, the more he and others would be able to support or reject the hypothesis through sound research. Therefore, when he wrote his article on the necessary and sufficient conditions of the therapeutic relationship, for each condition he tried to suggest an operational way of defining and measuring it.

In 1951 Rogers wrote, "Like Maslow, the writer would confess that in the early portion of his professional life he held a theoretical view opposed at almost every point to the view he has gradually come to adopt as a result of clinical experience and clinically oriented research." Even thereafter he continued to modify his views. How was it possible for Rogers—who might have become emotionally tied to any one of his various formulations—to keep on changing his thinking, to use later writings to correct or modify earlier writings, to risk losing the large number of adherents to the client-centered method by outgrowing them? Many people as they grow older or as they achieve prominence in some field, cling to one set of ideas or practices, for in this unchanging attitude comes a type of security, a buffer against the confusion and flux of the changing conditions around them. It was not that Rogers did not need some kind of security too; he simply got that security from a different source. As he explained it, ". . . adherents of any clinically effective procedure tend to become dogmatic. If client-centered counseling does not provide sufficient examples, psychoanalysis or Rorschach will be glad to oblige. As the clinician's emotional security becomes tied up with dogma, he also becomes defensive, unable to see new and contradictory evidence. But when research is persistently undertaken, the security which all of us must have tends to become lodged, not in dogma, but in the process by which truth is discovered, in scientific method."

He really believed it, that "psychotherapy may become a science, applied with art, rather than an art which has made some pretense of being a science." It was a quality that many of his students and colleagues recalled very vividly. Fred Fiedler recalled, "My Ph.D. proposal was very controversial. It proposed that experts of different schools were more similar to each other than they were to non-experts of their own school. Rogers, probably in a rash moment, said that he wouldn't believe this study even if it came out the way I said it might. While this was not exactly a comforting comment from a member of your thesis committee, I nevertheless worked on the study and Rogers has since then quoted the study widely. In my opinion it testified to the flexibility of the man as well as to his willingness to adapt his own thinking to empirical data rather than the other way around."

This "willingness to adapt his thinking to empirical data" is found in Rogers' long monograph "A Theory of Therapy, Personality and Interpersonal Relationships, as Developed in the Client-Centered Framework." Having stated that the three major therapeutic conditions were sufficient to initiate therapy with *any* client population, he included a footnote saying, "This paragraph may have to be rewritten if a recent study by Kirtner is confirmed. Kirtner has found, in a group of 26 cases from the Counseling Center at the University of Chicago, that there are sharp differences in the client's mode of approach to the resolution of life difficulties and that these differences are related to success in therapy. Briefly, the client who sees his problem as involving his relationships, and who feels that he contributes to this problem and wants to change it, is likely to be successful. The client who externalizes his problem and feels little self-responsibility is much more likely to be a failure. Thus the implication is that different conditions of therapy may be necessary to make personality change possible in this latter group. If this is verified, then the theory will have to be revised accordingly."

LEFT: *Carl, circa 1908.*

BOTTOM LEFT: *Julia Rogers and her five children in Oak Park. Clockwise: Lester, Carl, Walter, John, Margaret.*

BOTTOM RIGHT: *Carl, circa 1911.*

Warwood

Carl at the University of Wisconsin, 1920.

Walter and Julia Rogers at Warwood, circa 1916.

The delegation to China, 1922. Top row, fourth from right: *Carl.*
Fourth from left: *traveling companion Kenneth Latourette.* Seated,
center: *delegation leader Dr. John Mott.*

Carl and Helen, honeymoon, September 1924.

RIGHT: *Helen and Carl,
summer 1929.*

*Natalie and David near Seneca
Lake, 1934.*

Carl, December 1934.

Walter and Julia Rogers' Golden Wedding Anniversary, July 1, 1941. As identified in family album, seated l. to r.: Mrs. Walter C. Rogers; Mrs. John Rogers; Miss Margaret Rogers; Mrs. Walter A. Rogers; Walter A. Rogers; Carol Rogers; Mrs. Sherman Johnson, widow of Ross W. Rogers; Mrs. Carl R. Rogers. Standing: Lucile Rogers; Mrs. Lester C. Rogers; Lester C. Rogers, Jr.; Lester C. Rogers, Sr.; Dr. Carl R. Rogers; David Rogers; John W. Rogers; Dr. Walter C. Rogers; Barbara Rogers; Natalie Rogers; Nancy Rogers. Seated in front: Janet, Diane, Marcia, and Steve. (ORLIN KOHLI)

ABOVE: *First officers of the American Psychological Association, as reorganized in 1946: Helen Peak, Recording Secretary; Donald Marquis, President-elect; Carl R. Rogers, President; Dael Wolfle, Executive Secretary.*

ABOVE: *Rogers with a client at the University of Chicago, circa 1950.*

LEFT: *Portrait, 1952.* (LOUISE BARKER)

ABOVE: *Helen and Carl in Estes Park, Colorado, summer 1960.*

LEFT: *Rogers in Japan, 1961, with Tsutomo Endo and interpreter Logan Fox.*

BOTTOM: *"I want to speak to you as Carl Rogers, in 1969, not as a medieval symbol. So I hope I will not offend you if I remove these medieval trappings ..."*

*Portrait of Carl Rogers
in the seventies: at home
in his garden, leading
a televised encounter
group, talking with
college students and
faculty.*

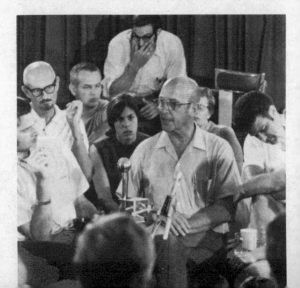

ANTHONY DI GESU

Eugene Gendlin recalled how, when the Kirtner study was completed, "most of the staff of the Counseling Center were outraged and sought to argue one loophole or another against the study. Only Rogers welcomed the findings and cited them in his next publication. Rogers sought to argue with all the rest, saying, 'Don't you see, facts are always friendly. This will lead us to some further step.' When the retort was, 'But perhaps thus-and-so would account for the findings differently . . . ,' Rogers would say, 'And perhaps you will be the person to find that in your next study.' "

When Rogers first entertained the idea of undertaking research in psychotherapy there were no precedents for him to follow. The privacy of the psychoanalyst's or psychiatrist's office had always been sacrosanct. Recording or transcribing actual interviews was unheard of. One had only the psychotherapist's word as to whether a particular method was effective or not; and so many different therapists declared that their methods were effective. It was, indeed, to use Rogers' phrase, "an art which made a pretense of being a science." Which methods really worked and which were merely "placebos" that gave the patient the illusion that he was being helped; how was one psychotherapeutic approach similar to or different from another; what constitutes real therapeutic personality change or growth or health; what happens in "successful" psychotherapy—all these questions were wanting answers as the field of psychotherapy continued to grow and spread.

Then, in the early 1940s, Rogers, with the help of his student Bernard Covner and his client "Herbert Bryan," revolutionized the field of therapy by recording, transcribing and publishing a complete verbatim series of psychotherapeutic interviews. Of course the revolution didn't happen at once. But having established the precedent, Rogers and soon others began to record interviews on a regular basis. These recordings and transcripts provided the raw data on which sound research could be conducted. Several of these recorded interviews were published in books and articles—by Rogers, William Snyder, and others. Speaking in 1947 at a panel on research in psychotherapy, Rogers was able to say, ". . . we have at the Counseling Center of the University of Chicago a half dozen unpublished complete cases with every interview recorded and transcribed, available to qualified research workers in the field." Within a few years the number had grown to nearly thirty. In addition they had scores of single interviews recorded and many of them transcribed—again, available for research and for the training of counselors. In 1956 Rogers wrote that among client-centered therapists, "thousands of therapeutic interviews had been electrically recorded and studied."

With this data on which to work, the research studies followed almost immediately. Elias Porter's dissertation, which he completed at Ohio State in 1941 and which was published in 1943, was the first of the studies in the client-centered framework. By 1950 Rogers could speak of some forty studies which had been completed. By 1952 the number had grown to sixty. In 1957, when Desmond Cartwright's "Annotated Bibliography of Research and Theory Construction in Client-Centered Therapy" was published, Cartwright was able to describe one hundred and ten separate research studies. I have found at least thirty others, most of them published, which could be added to Cartwright's pre-1957 list, bringing the total number to 140 or more. Because Cartwright's listing did not include the applications of client-centered therapy to areas such as group therapy, play therapy, education, industry and group leadership, nor did my thirty additional studies include many of these areas, there is good reason to believe that if an accurate summary were ever made of all the research done on the client-centered approach from 1943 to 1957, the number of studies would be considerably higher, perhaps as many as two hundred separate researches.*

What did all these researchers, then, spend their time discovering? And if this much was accomplished, why has the world of psychology not come to some unanimity of opinion regarding the effectiveness of the client-centered approach?

The first question is, perhaps, the easier to answer, requiring as it does only a careful observation and analysis of all the research studies, and not inferences about the motivations and directions of the psychology profession. A close look at the research trends of Rogers and his colleagues and students over this fifteen-year period reveals to me three phases which are worthy of discussion.

The first research phase would begin in the early forties and continue through 1947 or, perhaps, 1948, when many of the studies in this period reached publication. Cartwright lists thirteen studies that might be included in this phase. Almost all of them fit a pattern which I would term "exploratory and descriptive" in nature. For the most part these

---

*Research studies in the client-centered framework have continued, unabated, over the subsequent decades in the United States and abroad. In 1975, for example, Dr. Reinhard Tausch of the University of Hamburg, West Germany, reported that in the preceding six years 120 Masters theses and nine Doctoral dissertations exploring client-centered therapy had been completed at his university alone.

studies took the recordings or transcripts of interviews or cases and attempted to classify what happened during these therapies, from various points of view. Porter with his pioneering study devised a system to measure the degree of directiveness or nondirectiveness a counselor employed. The scale was then used to rate individual counselors. Curran carefully studied the changes in emotional expression and insight over one case. Snyder categorized both counselor and client statements, so he could see what type of client responses followed particular counselor responses. Raimy, in a study which was to have much significance in later years, measured the changes in self-references made by clients during the course of their therapy. Occasionally the studies in this period would distinguish between cases which the counselor regarded as successful or unsuccessful, to see if what was being measured would turn out to be different in the two types of cases.

What these researches had in common was that they attempted to find out *what happened* in nondirective counseling. In *Counseling and Psychotherapy* Rogers had said that therapy was a fairly predictable process in which expression of feeling led to insight which led to positive actions by the client. He also said that the nondirective method encouraged insight. These earlier studies attempted to put his description to the test, to see if what he said happened in therapy really did happen with any predictable degree of reliability. In general the results supported Rogers' observations; what the studies did not do to any great extent was to support his overall "Method." To show, for example, that acceptance by the therapist led to verbalized insights by the client, as Snyder's study indicated, might support Rogers' notion of what happened in therapy; but it did not show that this insight made any real difference in the client's life or that six months after therapy he was any different from when he began. Nor did it show that nondirective therapy was any more effective than any other approach.

Thus the research was exploratory only. It was a time of developing ways to measure some of the therapeutic phenomena or variables. It was a time of seeing whether, in fact, the therapeutic process was similar to what Rogers had been describing in his writings. The research raised many more questions than it answered; but this was not necessarily a weakness, in that all pioneering research in a field tends to be more suggestive than conclusive.

The second phase of the research (which ran simultaneously with the third) had several components. Many of the studies were continuations of the exploration phase. Bergman, for example, showed that

when clients asked for advice, structuring, or opinions from the therapist, if the therapist complied, the client tended to abandon self-
exploration; but if the therapist reflected back the clients' feelings at
the time, the result was further exploration and insight. Like the studies in the exploratory stage, this one stayed mainly with the concepts
Rogers originally used, found ways to measure them, and showed that
what Rogers said happened in nondirective therapy really did happen.

But this was not the major characteristic of the second phase. More
frequent was the attempt by the investigators to take some other already proven tool in psychological research and to apply that tool to
determine the *results* of the client-centered method. Thus several studies used the Rorschach ink blots to see if, after client-centered therapy,
diagnosticians would rate the client's Rorschachs as having shown
improvement. Several other "projective techniques" were used to
measure adjustment after therapy, including the Thematic Apercep-
tion Test, in which the client is shown a cartoon-type figure and asked
to tell a story connected with the picture, thereby revealing many of
his own unresolved issues. Bartlett, working in a Veterans Administration hospital, had clients' "training officers" rate their degree of improvement in adjustment six months or more after they began counseling. Haimowitz investigated whether clients' attitudes toward minority
groups changed as a result of therapy, the hypothesis being that as
hostility toward oneself decreases in therapy and self-acceptance increases, one should grow more accepting of and less hostile toward
other groups. Other researchers used the lengthy Minnesota Multi-
phasic Personality Inventory (MMPI) to assess the results of client-
centered therapy. Still others used tests of anxiety, attitudes toward
self and others, perceptual acuity, and even Galvanic Skin Response
and heart rate.

These studies were attempting to use known methods of assessing psychological health to determine the kinds of outcomes client-
centered therapy produced. The research was done in a more or
less random fashion, with each researcher following her own
hunch, using some measure she was probably familiar with, and
finding a population to work with—whether it was patients in Veterans Administration hospitals, current cases in the Counseling
Center, transcripts of previous interviews, or whoever else was
available. In general the results were positive, showing favorable
change after therapy. It was a very important phase of the research,
because by the use of known measurements of proven reliability
and validity, client-centered therapy was given an added legitimacy

in the eyes of many psychologists—not to mention the added confidence given to client-centered therapists themselves. As these accepted instruments showed that clients had changed for the better during and after therapy, then it became very difficult to dismiss the approach as ineffective or superficial.

As valuable as it was, however, this second phase of research had some serious flaws. First, the number of clients studied in most of the researches was very small, usually ranging from one to ten clients, with an occasional exception where the client population was larger. A small sample is usually characteristic of pilot studies and exploratory research and can yield many valuable results. But the expectation usually is that the researchers will repeat much of their work with larger populations in order to be sure that their results were not merely the reflection of some unusual qualities which their small groups of subjects shared. Thus, on a panel discussion on research in psychotherapy, a psychiatrist, Lawrence Kubie, criticized the lack of any larger studies and, probably referring to Rogers who was also on the panel, said, "Until these come into existence we will continue to have large numbers of publications with large claims based on a few cases, and books published which ought to be mere pamphlets or case reports—ballyhoo instead of science."

A second problem with the research was that, in almost every case, there were no experimental controls provided. For scientific purposes it is really not possible to state that therapy is effective in bringing about this or that change, unless there is another group, a control group, which is very much like the group that receives therapy, and this control group receives no therapy or receives some other type of treatment. If the experimental group changes in a way the controls do not, then, since the only thing they received that the controls did not was the therapy, it can be maintained that changes in the clients were caused by the therapy. So, while many of these studies of the second type produced clear, positive results, a common reaction was still to question: How do you know *the therapy* produced these results? Maybe once people are motivated to change enough to want to go into therapy, then even if they don't receive therapy, they still improve anyway. Or maybe the test-taking is the catalyst that encourages the client to start thinking about his situation, which then leads to positive changes. Experimental controls would be needed to find out which variables were really responsible for any changes.

A third shortcoming in the research was that, in measuring the outcomes of client-centered therapy, none of the measurements really assessed what Rogers regarded as the key ingredient in the change process, namely, the client's attitudes toward himself. It was these changing self-attitudes, self-concept, self-acceptance or self-rejection, self-esteem and self-evaluation which seemed to Rogers and others to be the main factors in the behavioral changes that often occurred during and after therapy. But in trying to assess the results of therapy, Rogers had only tests and measurements derived from other orientations. The Rorschach or TAT tests, for example, had mostly a psychoanalytic background and interpretation. The scales of ethnocentrism and prejudice were developed by the social psychologist. The job supervisor's estimation of the client's progress was given in terms of employment, not psychological criteria. These were all very important tests, insofar as they enabled the client-centered group to show the psychoanalysts, the social psychologists and the employers that there were some significant results brought about by their therapeutic approach. But in all of these tests the clients were viewed from an outside perspective. There was still the disappointment that, as yet, there were no ways to reveal the therapeutic process in scientific terms from the point of view of greatest interest to the Rogers group—from the viewpoint of the client himself.

It was these three problems which were addressed by the third phase of research undertaken by the staff and students of the Counseling Center. It began as Rogers' idea, although as usual it was modified by the inputs of his colleagues. As "principal investigator" on the original research proposal (with the help of James Miller, Psychology Department Chairman, who was increasingly supportive of Rogers' work), he was able to obtain a five-year grant of $172,000 from the Medical Division of the Rockefeller Foundation, enabling them to begin. When this funding was ending, Rogers secured another $97,000 from the United States Public Health Service, $30,000 from the Grant Foundation and $5000 from another source. Shortly thereafter the Ford Foundation awarded Rogers and the Counseling Center still another $350,-000, over five more years.

Given their initial funding, the Counseling Center was able to set up a "program design," that is, "the planning of an integrated series of research activities, focused on a central problem and involving a number of scientists for several years." The number of researchers working on the project ranged from fifteen to thirty over the several years it continued. About ten persons stayed involved in the project from beginning to end, while the rest stayed for various lengths of time. These people came to be known as the "Research Group," which was a continuation of an already existing, popular term for the Counseling Center at Chicago—the "Rogers Group."

The clients in the study were organized into two "blocks." Block I consisted of twenty-five clients (and controls) who came to the Counseling Center seeking help and who agreed to participate in several batteries of psychometric tests in conjunction with their therapy. The information collected became the data upon which the researchers conducted their different studies. Later on a second group of clients would constitute Block II, thus providing a whole new set of data upon which to base new studies.

Although Rogers was the "principal investigator" for the purposes of getting the grants, the research program was carried on in typical Counseling Center fashion. The leadership was "group-centered." Using the same body of data, each researcher explored the questions and hypotheses that were of interest to him or her. As to the nature of the research, several of the group wrote, "There are studies concerned with process and with outcomes. There are researches in which the object of the study will be the client's visual perception, his physiological reactions during the interviews, his verbal productions, his social attitudes, his concepts of himself, his values, his social behavior. Looked at from another point of view, there are represented in the program studies of the client alone, of the therapist alone, and of the relationship between client and therapist."

Because many of the members of the Counseling Center were graduate students, they participated in much of the research on the project —test administration, data analysis, counseling, generating hypotheses, and writing the actual reports. In the first three to four years of the project, nine doctoral dissertations and four Master's theses were completed, and an equal number were in process.

The first problem of the previous research, the small number of clients, was to a large extent corrected in the program design. With twenty-five clients in the first block and more in the second it was possible to have greater confidence in their conclusions than when one, five, or even ten clients constituted the entire population. This design also had the advantage that many therapists would be working with the population of clients. In this way the results would not merely reflect the unique style of one particular therapist.

The second problem of the previous research, that of controls, also was confronted. How can you get a control group for an experiment in psychotherapy? The ideal solution that comes to mind is to randomly select only fifty percent of those who come seeking help, and tell the other half that you're sorry, there is no room for them, but would they mind taking this battery of tests every now and then for the next couple of years, so you can see how they progress compared to the group that is getting therapy. While this might be desirable from a scientific viewpoint, it is untenable from a professional and ethical standpoint. How, then, does one manage to provide controls for one's experiment? The Research Group solved the problem in two ways, neither of which was perfect from a scientific point of view, but both of which were better than anything that had been done previously in research on psychotherapy.

The first method of controlling the experiment allowed for the possibility that it was not the therapy that produced the changes in clients, but perhaps other variables which might not at first be apparent. For example, maybe in simply having someone take the personality tests every few months, the very act of taking the tests and thinking about the items begins to initiate a personality change process in an individual. The only way to control for these extraneous variables would be to have another group of people who are not in therapy, but who are very similar to the people in therapy, and who take the same tests, and see what happens to them during this time period. Therefore the research design arranged to have each person in therapy "matched" with another person who took all the tests but did not receive therapy. This control group was composed of people who volunteered to serve as subjects for a "research on personality." They were paired with the therapy group on the basis of sex, student or nonstudent status, age, and socio-economic status. Clearly the matching was still far from exact; but it was hoped that combined with the second control method, most of the possible intervening variables could be accounted for, and they might say with reasonable certainty that, if any changes came about in the therapy group, the therapy was the cause of the change.

Of course, the major flaw in this type of matching was that the experimental group came to the Counseling Center in a state of incongruence, desirous of receiving help and wanting to change. The control group did not. To control for this important variable, therefore, the research design included a second method of control. What they did was to ask half of the experimental group, the therapy group, to *wait two months* before beginning their therapy. If it could be demonstrated that the "no-wait group" began to change in the beginning two months of their therapy, but that the "wait group" did not change during the waiting period, then it could be maintained that motivation for therapy, by itself, could not account for the changes, and that it was the actual therapy that produced the results. Again, while far from perfect, the design was the first large-scale, serious attempt to provide research controls for an experiment in psychotherapy.

Finally, the third problem was tackled—the lack of any instrument to measure therapeutic change from the client's own point of view. Previous attempts had been crude and unscientific. To ask the client if he felt any better or to have him fill out a questionnaire normally produced invalid or unreliable results, with clients tending to answer affirmatively so as not to hurt the therapist's feelings or to admit that they had failed at an attempt which had cost them considerable time, energy and, perhaps, money. It was not until William Stephenson, a British-trained researcher at the University of Chicago, developed a measurement tool known as the "Q-technique," that the Rogers group had a tool with which they could assess the results of counseling in the manner they had been hoping for.

The Q-technique which Rogers and his associates adapted to fit the counseling process, began with a "population of self-referent items" that were originally drawn from statements that real clients had made about themselves in counseling interviews. Some examples would be: "I am a submissive person," "I am a hard worker," "I am really disturbed," "I am afraid of a full-fledged disagreement with a person," "I am likeable," etc. The client would be presented with one hundred of these self-referent items, on cards, and be asked to sort the cards, usually into nine piles—the first pile being those self-descriptions which seemed most like him and the ninth pile being those which were most unlike him. Only a certain number of cards were allowed in each pile, so that the sorting approximated a bell-shaped curve and was, therefore, easier to work with for statistical purposes.

All the clients in the study were asked to do three different types of "Q-sorts" at different points during their therapy. The first was the Q-sort of items they regarded as most like themselves and most unlike themselves—their "self-concept." The second was a sorting of items that were most like the person they would like to be or least like the person they would like to be—their "ideal concept." The third was a sorting of which items they thought best described the "ordinary person" and which items were least like the ordinary person. By administering these three Q-sorts at different testing points before, during, and after therapy, it was possible to assess how the client's attitudes toward himself changed, if he became more like the person he wanted to be, and how his attitude toward other people was affected by therapy. The results showed, among other things, that in client-centered therapy, clients' self-ideals over therapy were reduced to more achievable proportions and their self-concepts changed to become more like the self they wanted to be, the self-concepts changing even more than the ideal selves.

"Our work," wrote Rogers, "has been similar in intent to that of Piaget, for example, rather than to that of most American psychologists. Piaget's study of the stages in the development of intelligence and reasoning in the child, based on the analysis of the way these processes *seem to the child,* is a significant instance of this sort of approach."

Having developed this final tool for their research, the group was able to proceed with their program design. The time and effort involved in gathering their data makes it obvious why so few people had previously cared to undertake any extensive research on psychotherapy.

Several *test points* were designated: just before therapy began (and before the waiting period began for the "wait group"), after therapy was completed, and after a follow-up period of six months to a year. At each of these test points, the client completed (1) an SIO (Self, Ideal, Ordinary) Q-sort, (2) a Thematic Apperception Test, (3) the Willoughby Emotional Maturity Scale, (4) the Self-Other Attitude Scale, designed to measure antidemocratic trends, ethnocentrism, political-economic conservatism, dependence upon experts, acceptance of the worth of others, and desire to change others, and (5) a role-playing situational test designed to determine how the client would react to others in certain critical impersonal situations.

In addition to these measurements which were always taken at the various test points, other data included: (6) a short personal history form filled out by the client at the beginning of the therapy, (7) a request for the names of two friends who knew the client well and whom he was willing to have contacted so that they might fill out the Emotional Maturity Scale on him during the course of the therapy, (8) recordings and transcripts of every counseling session (and these were the days before tape recorders!), (9) SIO Q-sorts after the seventh, twentieth and, if the therapy lasted that long, after each succeeding twentieth interview until the end of therapy, (10) a counselor sorting of the Q-items at the end of therapy based on how she thought the client would sort them (this was used to assess the counselor's empathy), (11) a counselor rating scale used to assess her picture of the outcomes of the therapy, the quality of the relationship between her and the client, and the nature of the therapeutic process just com-

pleted, (12) two follow-up interviews which were given after the follow-up tests were administered—one interview with the counselor and
one with a test administrator who didn't know the client—both interviews being used to determine, in detail, the client's evaluation of his
therapy and the results it did or didn't produce, and (13) a follow-up
questionnaire which was somewhat similar to the follow-up interviews.

If one wonders where those hundreds of thousands of dollars in
grant money were spent, the above listing should be an indication. A
single, forty-interview case required almost seven hundred hours of
time by the counselor, client, psychometrist, control subject, and tran-
scribers to gather all the data necessary for the research (not counting
the client's time in therapy). Considering how these seven hundred
hours were repeated twenty-five times in Block I alone, it is staggering
to contemplate the investment of time and energy in this project.

Having all that data certainly had its advantages, though. A team
could spend their lifetimes analysing the results. There were hundreds
of interrelationships that could be explored. Did clients whose self-
concepts become closer to their ideal concept also show positive
changes on the TAT tests? Were clients who were shown by the Self-
Other Scale to be more rigid and authoritarian, more likely or less
likely to change as a result of client-centered therapy? Where the
counselors were more empathic, did the clients show greater change?
How did the "wait" therapy group compare to the "no-wait" therapy
group, and how did each of these compare to their control groups? In
cases which counselors regarded as "successful," were the "objective"
tests also more likely to show positive change? Dozens of staff members and graduate students were able to use the group data to explore
numerous questions. The results were published in single studies and
in combined efforts such as the June 1949 issue of the *Journal of Consulting Psychology*. At one time Rogers had been the associate editor of this
journal, and president and multi-office-holder in the parent organization, the American Association for Applied Psychology. Consequently
the *Journal* was always a friendly forum for Rogers and his students.
The June 1949 issue was entirely devoted to the studies which the
Rogers group had been undertaking (most of them at their own expense, before the grant money was awarded). Seven research reports
were included, and Rogers wrote what he called "A Nonobjective
Introduction."

"The seven research studies in psychotherapy which follow this
introduction are all based upon the same group of cases. They are, as
research reports should be, cautious, objective, impersonal, formal,

and always mindful of the standard error in drawing their conclusions. But this introduction to them is personal, incautious and speculative and the reader is hereby warned against it. It is written to indicate that the series of projects reported are more than a cold collection of tables, charts, and correlation coefficients—they constituted a discouraging, exciting, difficult and rewarding experience for all of us who participated.

" 'The studies are based upon ten completely recorded and transcribed cases, with pre and post tests . . .' How simple that statement looks in type! No one would suspect the profanity toward all recording devices which it conceals—the tapes that split, the wires that broke, the discs that were an inaudible jumble of squeaks and hisses. To say that this is a random selection of cases is inaccurate—to call it a selection by frustration would be more sound—consisting of all those cases in which neither mechanical gremlins nor circumstances frustrated the completion of the case. The miracle is that it does seem to have a number of the characteristics of a random sample . . ."

In 1954, although the research program was still in progress, Rogers and his coeditor Rosalind Dymond [Cartwright] published an entire book of the Block I results. *Psychotherapy and Personality Change* was published by the University of Chicago Press. It was the first of Rogers' major books that Houghton Mifflin did not publish since the three titles that began with *Clinical Treatment of the Problem Child* in 1939. But Rogers felt it appropriate that the Press publish the book since the University had, in a sense, sponsored the research project through the offices of its Counseling Center. They were glad to accept. A highly technical, scholarly work, the book is still available and, in 1969, went into its sixth printing.

The first section of the book consisted of Introduction that described the project, its purposes, how it developed, its design and procedures. The second and major section was its "Findings," containing eleven studies derived from the First Block of clients. Then Rogers wrote two very lengthy analyses of individual cases—one a "success," the other a "failure"—showing how all the different research tools could be used to study the therapeutic process, in depth, with one client. He also wrote the conclusion.

Rogers' tone conveyed a feeling for the people behind the research. "In endeavoring to introduce the reader to the total investigation to be reported," he wrote, "there keeps coming to mind the oft-repeated statement of Robert Hutchins about the university of which he was chancellor: 'It isn't a good university; it's just the best that there is.'

One can perceive in this epigram nothing but pride and confidence; on the other hand, one can perceive in it a deep disappointment in falling so far short of the aim. In very much the same ambivalent spirit I am tempted to say of what follows in this book, 'It isn't a good research in psychotherapy; it's just the best that there is.' " To elaborate he proceeded with "We Point With Pride" and "We View with Disappointment" to indicate some of his and his colleagues' feelings about their work, mentioning with equal candor the study's shortcomings and its strengths.

By introducing the work of his colleagues and students in this manner, Rogers was putting himself in a position to be seen as the human figure and the moving force behind the scientific research. That he got most of the credit is interesting in light of the fact that he carried out almost none of the studies. Nor did he conduct any of the thirteen early studies included in the "exploratory phase" of research. This pattern continued into the later stages of the research. In Desmond Cartwright's bibliography of the 110 client-centered research studies mentioned above, Rogers was the author of only three. It is ironic to think that Rogers wrote more research reports *before* he came to Chicago than he did once he arrived there; yet this Chicago period was by far the most prolific time for research on client-centered therapy. During his pre-Chicago years he had been developing his own skills in the research area. Once he came to Chicago it must have seemed more exciting to be the *facilitator* of many research studies than to be the author of only a few. And, as often happens when people are free to do their own work, the group-centered method of leadership turned out to be much more productive than would have been the case if Rogers had controlled and written most of the studies himself.

Still, indirectly, the credit for the voluminous amount of research done in these years clearly goes to Rogers. First, in almost every article he had ever written he had stressed the need for further research. In 1940, for example, he not only made this point, but foreshadowed much of the work he and his colleagues would later do. He wrote, "attention might be called to the research opportunities with which the therapeutic process bristles. There is the need of adequate records—stenographic, even phonographic—upon which comprehensive studies may be based. There is the question of accessibility for therapy. Can we draw a line between those who would profit, and those who might be better helped by other treatment procedures? There is the need for both imagination and research in the field of expression. Are the same basic feelings expressed in dreams, in play materials, in dramatic constructions, in verbalizations? There is need for much more study of the give and take of the interviewing process. How is expression encouraged, how may interpretations be made, how may the therapeutic process be accelerated through the interview? There is the need for translating individual therapy into group procedures, to make it more widely helpful. There is the need for much more refined analysis of complete records and formulated in terms of known psychological facts." This was a typical example of how his writing opened doors of exploration through which he, his students, and his readers would later venture.

Because of his influence and example as a research-oriented practitioner, the Counseling Center at Chicago was set up and developed, from the beginning, with an eye toward research. The recording equipment, the permission to use the clients' time to fill out questionnaires and take tests for their studies, the added secretarial help for typing up transcripts, reports, and results—all these were signs that the Counseling Center was a research-oriented body from the start. Then, because of the atmosphere Rogers created at the Counseling Center, many staff members and students were encouraged to initiate their own research projects and also learn from their colleagues in meetings and discussions. Here Rogers was able to be very influential —suggesting research ideas, helping others improve their research designs, raising questions that stimulated the development of new studies, etc. In addition, because he was the dissertation advisor to so many graduate students, he was able to work directly with and help students prepare and execute research studies in the client-centered method. His name can be found among the acknowledgments on numerous articles which were the synopses of his students' dissertations—for example Lipkin's "The Author is indebted to Dr. Carl R. Rogers for his help in planning and carrying through the project on which this article is based, for his criticism of the manuscript and for his writing the summarizing discussion." In a lighter vein Nathaniel Raskin inscribed for his teacher a copy of one of his articles: "to Dr. Rogers . . . who thunk it up . . . Nat."

Because Rogers wrote both widely and prolifically, and because wherever possible he would refer to the research that was going on at the University—often mentioning specific studies and authors by name —the atmosphere created within the Counseling Center was one of great excitement. Students and colleagues realized that if they produced a good research study, it was very likely that their names or results would be publicized in writing and before conventions across the country. This, and the growing number of people who were visiting the Center to study, observe, or participate in its work, helped to create a sense that what they were doing was terribly important. This kind of reinforcement was an impetus to further research and publication.

Finally, Rogers helped facilitate most of the research at Chicago through the more than half million dollars in foundation support he managed to obtain. So although he did not conduct and write up the results of many studies himself, when the influence of his attitudes and ideas, the atmosphere and norms and structures he created at the Center, and his roles of publicist and fund-raiser are all combined, it can be argued that he well deserves all the credit he has received for the research from this period.

And receive credit he did. As early as 1950 the *Yearbook* of the *Encyclopaedia Britannica* wrote, "These first efforts of Rogers to subject his methods of nondirective therapy to scientific test constituted a landmark for clinical psychology." The *Library Journal* called the research project reported in *Psychotherapy and Personality Change* "the first thoroughly objective study of outcomes of psychotherapy in which adequate controls have been utilized." The American Personnel and Guidance Association selected the book as the outstanding research work in the field. In the *Journal of Consulting Psychology* Hans Strupp wrote, "The research effort by Carl Rogers and his students to describe and elucidate the process of nondirective counseling has provided objective evidence in an area in which such evidence has been sorely lacking. . . . The result of this development is a reasonably well-documented body of knowledge concerning client-centered counseling but almost a total absence of empirical data on psychoanalytically oriented therapy."

Placing the Rogers group's research efforts into historical perspective, Joseph Matarazzo wrote in 1965 that "his approach to the interview stimulated research more than the works of any single writer on the interview before or since," and that the Rogers and Dymond volume was "probably the single most important research publication on interviewing (as found in psychotherapy) of the decade." William Patterson, in 1966, maintained that Rogers' theory "is one of the more detailed, integrated and consistent theories which currently exist . . . it must be noted that the client-centered approach has led to, and is supported by, a greater amount of research than any other approach to counseling or psychotherapy." Hall and Lindzey, in their popular textbook *Theories of Personality,* paid similar tribute: "Rogers has been a pioneer investigator in the area of counseling and psychotherapy, and deserves a great deal of credit for stimulating and conducting research into the nature of the processes that occur during clinical treatment. . . . Largely through his efforts, we are beginning to learn something about the processes of psychotherapy."

But by no means were reactions to the client-centered research entirely positive. There were many psychologists and others who would have agreed with Allen Calvin's article "Some Misuses of the Experimental Method in Evaluating the Effects of Client-Centered Counseling," or with Eysenck's review of research in psychotherapy in which he said of the Rogers and Dymond book that "the faults of the experimental design are such, however, that on the grounds of merit alone it is doubtful whether it should have been included," or with Lloyd Humphreys of the National Science Foundation who thought Rogers had had "a retrogressive influence on psychology, basic and applied. . . . He has treated the 'soft' side of psychology in a 'soft' manner when it needed tough mindedness." As Rogers himself admitted in the Introduction to *Psychotherapy and Personality Change,* their research was far from perfect. But even those who were critical usually made a point to praise his dedication to the scientific method. One of his most bitter critics among clinical psychologists wrote to an editor at Houghton Mifflin in 1949: "Carl has always been willing to subject his ideas to experimental verification. One may question the superficial nature of much of the experimental design and the thinking back of it, but at least the man is willing to check his beliefs against empirical findings." Criticisms of *Psychotherapy and Personality Change* tended to share this same acknowledgment. As a reviewer in the *American Journal of Sociology* wrote: Although "I found myself irritated by the use of fluctuating criteria of significance," and although "very few hypotheses in this volume were established on the secure probability level of .01 or less," still "the present volume . . . is valuable not only because of the manifest character of its method but also because its content is of great significance for clinical and social-psychological theory."

The accolades outnumbered the criticisms by far. Respect and enthusiasm were the major reactions to the research generated by the Rogers group. So much was this the case that, in 1956, Rogers, along with two other prominent psychologists—Kenneth W. Spence and Wolfgang Kohler—was selected to receive the first Distinguished Scientific Contribution Award ever to be presented by the American Psychological Association. As chairman Dr. Arthur Melton explained to the assembly representing a great number of the fifteen thousand members of the association, "The awards have been created in an attempt to express the debt of many of us to the few of us who, in the course of a lifetime or a significant portion thereof, make distinguished contributions to the development of the science of psychology. Your Committee on Awards used two criteria in selecting the three persons to be so honored this year: (a) the contribution must have represented a major effort of the scientist's career and must have been made, or have come to its full development, in the past ten years; (b) the trio of contributions honored in any one year must reflect the broad scope of scientific psychology."

As stated in his citation, Rogers had been selected to receive the Award

> for developing an original method to objectify the description and analysis of the psychotherapeutic process, for formulating a testable theory of psychotherapy and its effects on personality and behavior, and for extensive systematic research to exhibit the value of the method and explore and test the implications of the theory. His imagination, persistence, and flexible adaptation of scientific method in his attack on the formidable problems involved in the understanding and modification of the individual person have moved this area of psychological interest within the boundaries of scientific psychology.

Twenty years later, looking back over his long career, Rogers wrote, "Never have I been so emotionally affected as I was by the scientific contribution award and its accompanying citation. When I was elected to an office it could have been partly due to my ambition—for I was ambitious to get ahead in my profession. But this award was to me, in some sense, the 'purest' recognition I had ever received. For years I had been struggling to objectify knowledge in a potential field of science that no one else seemed to be concerned about. It was not ambition nor hope of any reward that pushed me on. In the empirical research itself there was more than a little desire to prove something to others— clearly not a scientific goal. But in the basic phases of the work—the careful observation, the recorded interviews, the hunches as to hypotheses, the development of crude theories—I was as close to being a true scientist as I ever hope to be. But it was clear—I thought—that my colleagues and I were just about the only ones who knew or cared. So my voice choked, and the tears flowed, when I was called forth, at the convention in 1956, to receive, with Wolfgang Kohler and Kenneth Spence, the first of the awards for a *scientific* contribution to psychology. It was a vivid proof that psychologists were not only embarrassed by me, but were to some extent proud of me. It had a greater personal meaning than all the honors which have followed since...."

This honor, the American Psychological Association's highest award, came near the end of Rogers' tenure at the University of Chicago. But his national prominence in the field of psychology had begun much earlier. It had begun with the publication of *Counseling and Psychotherapy* in 1942 and had continued with the publication of more articles, his participation on many committees of the American Psychological Association, the honor of being elected as the first President of the American Association for Applied Psychology, and his work attempting to bring the APA and AAAP back together again. And so, when he moved to Chicago in 1945, he was a fairly well-known figure, with a growing stature in the psychological profession.

Nevertheless it did seem premature when he was elected president of the American Psychological Association in 1945 to serve the 1946–1947 term. Less than one fourth of the APA membership then indicated an interest in psychotherapy, and certainly this minority were far from unanimous in their support of the "nondirective method." Furthermore, Rogers and his students and colleagues had barely begun their research efforts, so this could not account for his election by the research-oriented association. Rogers' own explanation for why he was elected, with many other prestigious psychologists to choose from, is simple. "There were two other more august figures in contention. They couldn't decide, so rather than offend one or the other, they chose me."

At any rate his prestige in the APA continued to grow during and after his term as president. From 1946 through 1957, at nine of the twelve annual conventions, he presented one, two, or even three papers or presentations on each occasion. He continued to serve on several committees of the APA, including the Presidency of the Division of Clinical and Abnormal Psychology, from 1949 to 1950. In 1950, just before the APA convention, he was selected as one of three outstanding practitioners to conduct a post-doctoral training institute at Penn State. When the American Academy of Psychotherapists was formed in 1956, he was elected its first president, a post he held from 1956 through 1958.

Meanwhile his prolific writing was appearing in a wide variety of professional journals. Besides those published by the usual psychological journals, his words saw print in publications as varied as: *Marriage and Family Living, Teachers College Record, Pastoral Psychology,* the *American Journal of Nursing, Harvard Educational Review, Educational and Psychological Measurement, Annals of Allergy, Scientific American, Management Record, ETC.* (the journal of the Society for General Semantics) and the *Harvard Business Review,* to name a few.

As this list of publications indicates, Rogers had a diverse appeal. He never let himself get tied down to one professional identity or clique. He has moved back and forth primarily between psychology, social work, and, later, the education profession, and among many associations within these professions. "He travels fastest who travels alone" is a maxim Rogers has applied to himself, confident that if his contribution had merit, it would attract the attention it deserved.

His classes at Chicago reflected his growing reputation. Theron Alexander who, years later, wrote in an introduction to his book *Psychotherapy in Our Society,* "My orientation to psychotherapy comes from Carl R. Rogers, and his teaching is an important basis for my own work," was a student of Rogers then and recalled how "I took several courses under him and most of the time there were three or four hundred people in them that met in a large auditorium. People came from all over the world, and the University did not feel it could make any restrictions on who could come in. So they just kept getting a larger and larger auditorium until it accommodated the people. . . . He would start out to discuss some topic and maybe discuss it for ten or fifteen minutes and then open it up to discussion. People were very anxious to discuss and it was never a dragging discussion. Most of the time it was very interesting. . . . The people were so excited, either by great hostility for the ideas or enamored with the ideas; but there were enough who were either way to have arguments not only with Rogers but with each other across the auditorium. . . . In his heyday, he was probably the most talked about person in psychology. He thrived on controversy, even though he avowed strongly that he eschewed it. 'No student just goes to a professor for information.' He would like to say something like that to start a discussion. Actually, he was so controversial and so many people argued with him and got very upset with him that he must have enjoyed it or he wouldn't have engaged in so much of it."

Through Rogers' and his students' efforts, the influence of the client-centered approach began to spread to other helping professions

—education, social work, nursing, pastoral counseling, even management. In the *Journal of Pastoral Care*, for example, the Very Rev. H. Ralph Higgins wrote:

> ... the modern clergyman will welcome a type of psychotherapy whose basic assumptions are compatible with a religious view of the nature and destiny of man, and whose techniques may be readily learned and effectively applied without the necessity of a medical background or a rigid psychological training. . . . In the newer techniques of client-centered therapy the clergyman has available a method which can prove of immense significance and genuine practical benefit in his work. . . . The Christian teaching that suffering can be turned to joy, sin forgiven, and redemption attained, greatly fortifies the attitude of the pastoral counselor in undertaking parishioner-centered therapy. . . . It may also be pointed out that just as Christianity is a way of life to be lived and not a proposition to be argued instead of lived, so client-centered therapy is a method of counseling which can be proved only as it is practiced in sincere obedience to its basic hypothesis. 'By their fruits ye shall know them' applies equally to therapy and to the Christian life.

Or, as the Assistant Executive Secretary of the American Nurses' Association, Evelyn B. Ferguson, wrote in their journal, "Dr. Rogers' general hypothesis that the relationship he describes 'offers exciting possibilities for the development of creative, adaptive, inner-directed persons' has great meaning for all—not only for nurse counselors, public health nurses, educators, and administrators, but also for any nurse who is interested in helping a person with a problem."

Even *Time* magazine, in 1957, acknowledged Rogers' stature in the psychology profession by devoting three columns to him and his work—complete with full photographic portrait and the typical *Time* writing style: "Among variegated practitioners of talk-it-out treatment for emotional problems, Chicago's Psychologist Carl Ransom Rogers, 55, has long been a maverick. He calls his method 'client-centered therapy,' tries manfully to define it: 'We see therapy as an experience, not in intellectual terms. We treat the client as a person, not as an object to be manipulated or directed.' Snorts a Chicago psychoanalyst of neo-Freudian persuasion: 'Rogers' method is unsystematic, undisciplined and humanistic. Rogers doesn't analyze and doesn't diagnose. We have no common ground.' To Rogers this is fine. . . ."

All this acclaim made the Chicago years a time when he was much in demand, receiving many invitations to give speeches and workshops to various professional groups. In his annual report for 1952–1953 he noted, "During the year I have been invited to speak to three important medical groups: at the opening of the Psychiatric Institute of the University of Maryland, where I gave a short paper; at the Forum of the Menninger Foundation at Topeka, where I was the speaker at the largest forum they have ever had; and at the Department of Medicine of the University of Illinois, where I spoke to their monthly seminar. These invitations may even foreshadow the day when our own medical school might be interested in what we are doing."

In addition to the speeches and workshops he accepted offers to serve for a quarter or semester as "Visiting Professor" at five universities: the University of California at Los Angeles (1947), Harvard (1948), Occidental College (1950), the University of California at Berkeley (1953), and the University of Wisconsin (1957). He also received an honorary degree from Lawrence College in Appleton, Wisconsin (1956); and his alma mater, Columbia University, presented him with its silver Nicholas Murray Butler Medal in 1955. The latter was awarded him when he delivered an address at the inauguration of Dr. Hollis Caswell as the new President of Columbia's Teachers College.

These objective measures of success and growing influence are but one indication of Rogers' increasing stature in the psychological and other helping professions. As his fame grew, so did a mystique about him. One story is a good illustration of this. Before the APA convention in 1950 he was leading a post-doctoral institute in which he counseled a very disturbed young man for two weeks, before the group of participants. The therapy, as several members of that group recalled years later, seemed extremely skillful, moving, and successful. Arthur Combs remembered how, after each therapy session, "Carl chaired a discussion of what had happened. . . . During this time he did not particularly answer questions but acted in a sense like a counselor for the group. On the last day the group asked him to respond more directly to questions which they had and he agreed. He is a real master at this sort of thing and can often answer a question with the kind of statement that has great impact. While he was doing this a storm came up and it became darker and darker in the lounge where this session was being held. Then, at one point when Rogers had just completed a beautiful answer to a student's question somebody, somewhere pulled the switch and all the lights came on in the room. For a moment there was a kind of stunned silence in the group, then someone was heard to exclaim, 'My God! Dr. Rogers! Do you walk on the water, too?' "

Others have commented on his ability to electrify a room, to ener-
gize a group with his sincerity and quiet charisma. This would be
particularly apparent on panels whose participants were somewhat
hostile to Rogers' ideas or methods. The result was usually a lively
session that alternated between antagonism and camaraderie. The
following excerpts from a 1952 panel discussion before the American
Association of Marriage Counselors gives something of this flavor.
Rogers had given the major address.

> CHAIRMAN LAIDLAW: Thank you so much. This has been, I know, a real
> treat to all of us to hear such an outline not only of a technic but of
> a philosophy of life, a philosophy that entails continual growth, and
> it is so unlike some of our scientific friends who make some outstand-
> ing mistakes in their early years, in their early writings, and then spend
> the rest of their lives defending them. . . .
> ROBERT HARPER: I think we can take a cue from Dr. Rogers in making
> ourselves, all of us, more flexible, more willing to learn about what we
> are doing. But it seems to me, Dr. Rogers, that you carried this point
> of striving to be flexible in one's rationality, to the extreme of rejecting
> rationality, very often, in the counseling process. . . . I think this
> nebulous new discovery that neither you nor your client seemed very
> rationally to depict is essentially a religious experience and not a
> scientific contribution to the counseling field; that it is a religious
> experience, unchecked, unscientific, unvalidated, unreliable. . . .
> ROGERS: That is a very worthwhile comment. I think that you will proba-
> bly get much more enjoyment and satisfaction out of the forthcoming
> issue of the *Psychological Service Center Journal,* which contains three long
> articles on our research, with control groups and careful measurement
> and reliability, and factor analyses of the Q sort, and so on. . . . Let
> me come back, too, to your statement that I seem to be going off in
> mystical directions, and so on. Well, that doesn't frighten me as long
> as it is well rooted in solid experience. I think I can only try to interpret
> the experiences that I have in the way that seems most appropriate to
> them, and I wouldn't be honest if I said that the most appropriate way
> to interpret therapy is simply to feel here is a complex organism and
> you manipulate it this way and something constructive comes out of
> that manipulation. . . .
> ABRAHAM STONE: Now, I haven't the slightest doubt that Dr. Rogers in
> his work obtains excellent results because he has a quality of personal-
> ity, an intensity of feeling and a spiritual temper which not many of
> us, unfortunately, possess. The majority of us, I fear, could not do as
> well in our work unless we had a more realistic, a more concrete and,
> shall I say, a more directive approach to some of the problems that
> come before us. (Applause.)
> ROGERS: Thank you, Dr. Stone, especially for what I suppose was in-
> tended as a compliment, but I can assure you that at home I am not
> regarded as the spiritual type. (Laughter.) . . .

ALBERT ELLIS: I happen to be in a radically different position from that of Bob Harper. Having attacked Dr. Rogers in print several times, I can now afford to be kind to him; and to most of what Dr. Rogers said tonight I would agree, and would highly commend his manner of saying it. I would say that his errors, if you would call them such, were largely errors of omission, as Abe Stone would appraise them, rather than of commission. . . .

Dr. Ellis went on to elaborate on Rogers' "errors of omission," describing a patient of his own who exhibited extreme paranoid thinking.

> I consider it my duty as a therapist gradually to point this out to the patient; and, so far, I have apparently effectively been doing so, and have been showing him how he developed the rationale for Oneness and Goodness out of his sexual and other problems. However, if I were a philosopher myself, or if I were another kind of therapist—such as a Karen Horneyite or perhaps a Carl Rogersite—it would be the easiest thing in the world for me to accept sympathetically this paranoid thinking of my patient. If I did so, when we would finally come to the end of our therapeutic relationship, I would feel much elated about understanding and accepting his ideas, and he would feel wonderfully happy knowing I accepted him and his philosophy—and heaven knows where we would end up. I doubt whether, according to almost any criteria which we usually have of helping the patient—and that is frankly what I am in this profession for, to help the patient— I doubt if we would end up with anything like a so-called normal, or well adjusted, or effectively functioning human being. . . . If I fully appreciated and accepted his paranoid thinking, and if we both ecstatically went off to end up in some religio-mystical state of paranoia *a deux*, I am sure that his concept of himself, as objectively shown through the Q technic or any other technic, would definitely appear to be more favorable—and would, of course, agree with my own Q technic matchings of his therapeutic "progress." The question would still legitimately arise, however: Would the patient (or the therapist!) *really* then be improved? . . .

ROGERS: I think that I should like to agree with Dr. Ellis that if he treated this patient of his in the way that he described, by accepting and agreeing with his philosophical notions, I am as sure as he is that such a procedure would work out badly. This is a good example of real failure in communication, obviously, because I really have not been talking about that at all. . . . I would agree also that if the way we are using the Q technic is simply to objectify a testimonial type of statement, I would see no point in it, either.

LENA LEVINE: In the first place, I want to express my gratitude at meeting the master. Until now the only persons I heard from were the disciples. If I may predict on the basis of the development of your thinking to May, 1952—although I don't know the rapidity of your growth, that

in a few years you will have discovered the science of psychoanalysis which has a very, very excellent record, and that it will be the one to which you will find you were growing. . . . [She continued.]
ROGERS: Thank you for your first bit of information. (Laughter.) . . .

And so it went. The panel members would begin by mentioning some widely acclaimed, positive quality of Rogers and exaggerate it or use it to criticize him, often in a condescending manner. Many apparently expected "the master" to be a pushover. While others might have risen to the bait and become somewhat aggressive, he invariably responded with equanimity—with humor and sincerity. This, perhaps, explains the good personal feelings so many people have toward him, even those who disagree with much of his thinking or practice. Although he would usually respond to the substance of any criticism, the tone of his answer always contained enough agreement or humor or desire to understand the other's position that the response tended to minimize a potential argument. As a frustrated antagonist once exclaimed, "Damn it, you can't fight with Carl Rogers!"

William Archie, who in connection with evaluating a grant proposal Rogers had submitted, wrote to psychologists across the country for their reactions to the proposal, said, "not a single person to whom I wrote . . . said an unkind word about Carl Rogers. Even when they obviously disagreed with his viewpoints as a professional psychologist, they all thought he was an honest man and said so."

The Chicago years were very different for the Rogers than their previous times together. Both children were off pursuing their own careers and families, so Carl and Helen had their apartment at 5844 Stony Island Avenue all to themselves.

David was attending Cornell Medical School when his parents moved to Chicago. A year later he married Cora Jane Baxter ("Corky"). Both of them were twenty years old at the time. He went on to Johns Hopkins as an intern and assistant resident, spent several more years in postgraduate training and research, and returned to Cornell as Assistant, then Associate Professor of Medicine and Chief of the Division of Infectious Diseases at the New York Hospital. Between 1951 and 1957 he had fifteen scientific papers on infectious diseases published in the professional journals. In the years between 1950 and 1954 he and Corky had three children—Anne, Gregory ("Greg"), and Julia ("Julie").

Natalie, who was fifteen when she was graduated from high school, completed two years of undergraduate work at Stevens College in Missouri where she majored in psychology. Still planning on becoming a psychologist, she transferred to De Pauw University in Illinois, where, since she was closer to Chicago, she was able to become somewhat involved in the work of the Counseling Center. Using the data from the Center she wrote and had published two research studies which her father often cited in his writings. After De Pauw she moved to New York City to work full-time with the United World Federalists, making speeches and organizing for world government. There she met and, in 1950, married Lawrence Fuchs, who was then working on his Ph.D. in political science at Harvard. When he became a faculty member at Brandeis University, they settled in the Boston area. Natalie later finished her Masters Degree in art therapy at Brandeis, where she worked closely with Abraham Maslow. Their three daughters, Janet, Frances ("Frannie"), and Naomi, were born during the years 1952 and 1957. When she was pregnant with Janet, on her twenty-third birthday, Natalie received these two notes from her parents:

> Dear Nat, I hope this reaches you on a very happy birthday. It seems a long time back that I was pacing up and down the house at 180 Eastland Ave., wondering whether Helen should go to the hospital right away or wait a while. For some reason that part of the experience stays with me quite vividly. And to think that a whole generation has whizzed by—a short one to be sure—and that now in a few months you'll be wondering whether or not it's time to go, and Larry will be doing the pacing! . . . Dad

> Dearest Nat—Larry—Happy birthday, Nat. We will be thinking of you and remembering what a happy day it was for us 23 years ago. And it makes it doubly happy now to know you are going to be responsible for another birthday in March. Hope you have as nice a baby as we had. We have enjoyed both of your recent letters lately. They really mean very much to us and it's always a red letter day when I find mail from any of my four kids in the box. . . . We love you both very much, Mom.

Both David and Natalie felt they could talk to their father fairly openly during their earlier years; but it was during the Chicago years, as young adults, that they felt they achieved a truly comfortable and open relationship with him. "I felt I could start to talk to him openly in Chicago," said Natalie, who even used him as a therapist at times. David said, "I felt Dad was terribly consistent in his several roles. I could sit down and talk to him as a therapist, even though he was my father. I knew he was my father but I also felt he was my friend."

David also felt that he learned a lot from his father which helped him in his role as medical administrator and teacher. "Some of Dad's skills rubbed off. . . . I sometimes play the counselor's role. I'm much more comfortable with the human side of medicine. As a teacher of medicine, I will show students that I care, that I'm vulnerable, that I don't know, that I'm congruent."

With their children away from home, Carl and Helen had a freedom they had not experienced since their first year of marriage in New York City. They also had the financial means now with which to take advantage of that freedom. The University of Chicago assisted them by allowing faculty to take one of the four quarters away from the campus. Once Carl had become established at the Counseling Center, he and Helen made it their annual custom beginning in 1951 to spend the winter quarter in Mexico or the Caribbean, usually starting or ending each trip with a visit to their children and a growing number of grandchildren out East. Once headed south, they would be thankful to be away from the Chicago winters.

As had been his custom as far back as 1922 when he traveled to the Orient, Carl often recorded his observations in letters to friends and family back home. He would occasionally have the letters duplicated at the Counseling Center and sent to more friends than he could possibly have written to personally. One such letter described a scene in a church in Tecalpulco, a small Indian Village in Mexico, during a fiesta. It shows his keen eye for detail as well as his tendency to reflect upon his observations:

> While the dance goes on, another group catches our eye. Six people, an older man, and assorted women and girls are chanting. The man is the leader. He carries a candle and a cheap leaflet in his hand, on which are the words of the chant. As they sing they move slowly backward, a shuffle at a time, toward the church door, always facing the altar in front. The man's voice is cracked and frequently off key. The woman next to him peers out from under a black rebozo with a face like a dried apple. The others can't see the words too well, and fumble and halt in their singing. Yet as the droning chant is repeated over and over, in their slow retreat down the long nave, one cannot help but be impressed by this picture of simple reverence. No one told them to do this—this is their Lenten offering of hymn and supplication, and Nuestro Senor must see it, as do we, as an expression of more real worship than would be found in ten churches on city boulevards.

But traveling about as tourists did not characterize the Rogers' winter vacations. They much preferred to find a quiet spot they enjoyed and to stay there for anywhere from two to eight weeks. There they could really rest and paint and write and engage in what came to be a favorite pastime of both Carl and Helen—snorkeling. Carl described their schedule in one of his letters, written from the small British West Indies island of Bequia, where they spent two lengthy winter visits.

> Here is the way the day goes. We waken to the sound of the gentle surf, and the crowing of a rooster or two, and step out on our porch. The harbor is dotted with boats, mostly rowboats, filled with men who have been fishing since four or five o'clock. We stroll down to the beach to see what new shells have washed in. . . . As the sun comes over the ridge behind us, Carmen, the neat and smiling girl from the hotel, appears with a tray of breakfast. After breakfast, Helen paints, I daub, or we read or write letters or walk along the beach collecting shells, until we decide it is time for a swim. The water is a beautiful green, though because of a long spell of rough weather it is too cloudy for our masks and snorkels to be of maximum use. The water is warm, the sun is hot, and everything conspires to make us feel langorous. Lunch and dinner we eat at the hotel, but four-o'clock tea (at which we first turned up our noses) is brought to the cottage by Carmen. The food is excellent, and all in all we feel that we are not being overcharged when we pay $9.00 a day for the two of us, which includes all our meals (*and* afternoon tea!), our cottage, occasional use of a row boat, and a climate and view that seems as close to Paradise as mortals are permitted to come.

Carl would bring some work along to Paradise and usually spend a few hours a day reading or writing. His writings began to range far afield from the strict clinical experience and research findings to which he had confined himself. These few months each year, away from the daily cares and routines of the Counseling Center, gave him the distance with which to view his own work and to see its implications in many areas.

On one occasion he wrote, "I first became acquainted with the work of Soren Kierkegaard and that of Martin Buber at the insistence of some of the theological students at Chicago who were taking work with me. . . . Though Kierkegaard lived one hundred years ago, I cannot help but regard him as a sensitive and highly perceptive friend. I think this paper shows my indebtedness to him, mostly in the fact that reading his work loosened me up and made me more willing to trust and express my own experience. . . . Another helpful element in writing the paper was that I was far away from colleagues, wintering in

Taxco, when I wrote the major portion of it. A year later, on the Caribbean island of Grenada, I completed the paper by writing the final section."

Referring to the winter quarter of 1952, he wrote, "I made it my purpose during the Winter Quarter to get some perspective on my work and to extend my thinking into the theoretical and philosophical implications of what we are doing. I not only read, but really studied, some of the most significant recent books in psychology, such as Hebb's *Organization of Behavior* and Marx's collection of writings on Psychological Theory. I also read a couple of books on modern physics to try to learn more of the development of science and theory in a field other than my own. But much the most rewarding reading was in the field of philosophy. Kierkegaard was a most exciting discovery to me, and Buber very stimulating. Sartre and Whitehead each contributed something. Now that I have returned I am beginning to realize the impact that this reading, and the opportunity for leisurely thinking, has had on me. I know that it will sharply influence my work and my writing."

His prediction was correct. Some of his best-known essays, many of which were later published in *On Becoming a Person* in 1961, were written during winter vacations or stemmed directly from the reading and thinking he was able to do in Mexico or the Caribbean. "Personal Thoughts on Teaching and Learning" (1957), "A Note on the Nature of Man (1957), "Persons or Science: A Philosophical Question" (1955), and "A Therapist's View of the Good Life: A Fully Functioning Person" (1957) are examples of his thinking and writing during this period.

Remembering how Rogers "took time out for vacation and extensive travel" and how "he often brought back good ideas," Julius Seeman reflected that "Carl seemed to have the ability to work in a sustained way and to take distance from his work. I always felt him to be steadily productive without any indication that he was driven or compelled to produce."

Professional work, however, never characterized the major part of the Rogers' winter vacations. Excerpts from one particular letter of his, written from Bequia in 1956, gives an excellent picture of Carl and Helen's pleasure in snorkeling together and also shows how Carl's sense of adventure at age 54 had not diminished much from that of the young man of 22 who on the eve of his return from the Orient spent all night climbing Mt. Fujiyama.

Yesterday was a day of real adventure, and I guess I'll have to write about it to get it out of my system. It all begins with our snorkeling, which we find most fascinating. Every day that the water is clear we don our masks and snorkel tubes and investigate the nearby waters. We have a little private "aquarium" that we love—a big rock on the harbor floor, right out from the hotel, with a bevy of many-colored fish and two lobsters always around it. Then there are the coral heads quite far out that we swim to when feeling particularly bold, and other favorite spots. Helen and I discovered what we call our "prehistoric fish"—a strange creature with two fins forward which it uses like paws, turning over sea-urchins, and scraping for tid-bits along the bottom, and two enormous fins trailing backward which at times open out into great semi-circular wings, tinged with translucent purple edging. And then Helen spotted a fish which we are now sure was a barracuda—and watched him while she called me. When I swam over and spotted him, he politely swam away. . . .

They had met three young Americans and the next morning Carl went with them in a big rowboat, outfitted with sails, to do some snorkeling.

We sailed out into the large waves beyond the harbor and scudded down to the southern end of the island, which ends in a rocky narrow tip, with three great rocks or tiny islands on beyond. . . . The water was blue black and very deep. The waves were enormous and they went surging in to the great rocks and up and up, bursting into spray—and then falling, draining, sucking away, down and down, until twenty feet of rocks and boulders were exposed which had been covered when the wave was at its height. . . . By that time it looked too exciting to miss, and I thought of a scheme which was sufficiently safe to me. I donned my mask and snorkel and went overboard, having first fixed a trailing rope from the boat to hang on to. I was glad I had, because in the very rough sea, small amounts of water kept getting into my breathing tube and giving me trouble. But the sight was tremendous. You could see straight to the bottom in what they said was thirty to seventy feet of water, and a great fantastic landscape it was. . . . [At a new location] I decided, though I was now somewhat cold, to go overboard for a few moments. I stayed for nearly an hour. . . . And then as I turned my head I saw the shark. Four feet, six feet—I wouldn't know for sure, but the tail was unmistakable shark! He was heading away from me, down near the bottom, and because I was so close to the boat I didn't feel frightened.

By this time we knew we would already be late for lunch, so we piled aboard in a drizzle . . . the wind outside the cove was *very* strong. The mast was set, the various stays were pulled tight, the mainsail and jib unfurled and we turned out into the wind. Did it hit us, and did we move! . . . we set a northwest course (heading approximately for New York!) so that when we got far enough out into the ocean, we could come about into a northeasterly direction which would take us back into the harbor.

It was a wild ride. The waves were larger and larger as we got further out to sea, and the wind was vicious, heeling us over in sudden puffs. I've never been in a boat that shipped so much water. . . . Then all at once it happened. We were zooming along into the heavy sea, drenched with spray by every crest, with the sails as tight as drums, when a particularly angry gust hit us and crunch! the five inch mast snapped off like a broken match! . . . The moment the mast gave way the whole boat careened to the side we were sitting on and we might have capsized if we hadn't all jumped as one man to the middle of the boat. . . . It was all so sudden I can't honestly say that I was upset, but I surely would have been if I had known that Helen had been watching our progress from the hotel, miles away, with our trusty binoculars. She knew it was rough, because at times our boat would disappear in the trough of the waves and only the top of the mast and sail would be visible—then it would come into view again on the crest of the next wave. But suddenly to her complete dismay the sail disappeared while we were in a trough, and when the boat appeared it had no mast! She was really frightened then, and went tearing down the shore until she found a sailboat just coming in and persuaded them to sail out to find us.

They made it back safely. And although this day's adventure was considerably more dramatic than a typical day's itinerary, they always regarded the decade or so of yearly winter vacations as among their most memorable and pleasurable times together.

Even their unanticipated vacation—the "runaway trip" in the spring of 1949, described earlier—turned into a bit of an adventure. As Helen described it, "We finally came to roost at our hideaway on Seneca Lake [the one they had built during their years in Rochester] and spent a month roughing it in our cabin in the cold temperatures of May in New York State. There were periods of real despair which we weathered together. It never occurred to me that he could not or would not recover. We roamed the hills and I taught him all I could about painting. We spent many hours enjoying and exploring and painting the countryside." In Carl's words, ". . . throughout this whole period Helen was certain this state of mind would pass away, that I was not insane, and showed in every way how much she cared. Wow! That's the only way I can express my gratitude. That's what I mean when I say she has stood by me in critical periods."

She had stood by him another time, earlier in their stay in Chicago. "During my forties," he wrote, "there was a period of nearly a year when I felt absolutely no sexual desire—for anyone. No medical cause was found. Helen was confident that my normal urges would return, and simply 'stood with me' in my predicament. It is easy to think up possible psychological causes, but none of them 'click' as far as I'm concerned. It remains a mystery to me. But her quiet continuing love meant a great deal to me, and probably was the best therapy I could have had. At any rate, I gradually became sexually normal once more."

He was able to reciprocate this "standing by" during their years at Chicago. As he described this period, "Helen's mother suffered several strokes as she grew older. This had the unfortunate (but not rare) effect of markedly changing her personality. Where she had been a warm and kindly person with strong intellectual interests, she became a carping, suspicious, sometimes viciously hurtful person. This was terribly hard on her daughters, but particularly on Helen, who would feel terribly crushed and hurt by the psychological jabs which came from a mother with whom she had been very close. Her mother became impossible to live with, and could not live alone. Then came hard decisions—to take her from her apartment; to place her in a nursing home (the best of which is a forlorn place); to face the fact that she was no longer the person she had been. Helen felt terribly guilty about what she was doing to her mother, and her mother retained enough shrewdness to know how to heighten that guilt. Through six long and very trying years I believe I stood by Helen. She could not help but feel hurt, guilty, and upset by her twice-weekly visits to her mother. I could let her have those feelings, but also let her know that I thought the accusations false, the decisions sound, and that I believed she was doing the best anyone could in a most distressing and complex situation. I know that she was strengthened and helped by my 'standing by.' Our physician son also was of much help to her in understanding the physical and psychological deterioration which had taken place, and that her mother's complaints were not to be taken at face value."

During this period Carl's mother died, in 1954 in Florida. After her husband's death in 1944, she had eventually sold Warwood. She and Carl's sister Margaret had then moved to Daytona Beach, where, after her mother's death, Margaret continued to live alone for the next twenty-five or so years.

Aside from these problems that the Rogers had to face during these years, their personal life in Chicago was full and social. Helen was often involved in the Counseling Center in nonacademic ways, with many get-togethers at their apartment for meetings or for purely social occasions. These were times Helen enjoyed very much. She later wrote, "It was during this period in Chicago that it was brought home to me frequently that my husband was emerging as a very well-known and important person in his field of endeavor. At the most unexpected times—signing a charge-a-plate or giving my name and address for the sending of packages—the person would look at me and say, 'Are you THE Mrs. Carl Rogers?' It was a new and joyful experience to find my husband influencing so many people in so many different walks of life."

In addition to her homemaking, two major interests from earlier years still occupied her. She continued to paint and to be active in the Planned Parenthood movement.

During this period Carl developed more hobbies of his own. He had always loved to work with his hands. He began to take an interest in painting. According to several of their friends, he did *extremely* well. This seemed to threaten a private area of Helen's sense of competence, and partly for that reason and partly because he had so much else to do, he gave it up. Another of his hobbies was making mobiles. Helen remembered, "We were intrigued with Alexander Calder's new idea of art in motion. Carl, coming from an engineering family, enjoyed the combined problem of balance and composition that you are faced with when making a mobile. I remember that once I had to be in the East for two weeks, when the second of our grandchildren was born. 'Grandma' was called to take care of little Anne, so I left Carl and our daughter, Natalie, to care for themselves. I returned to find they had been having a 'ball' making mobiles, experimenting with cardboard, balsa wood, copper, aluminum. I found a mobile hanging in every room of the house, including the bathrooms! This hobby has continued to be a great source of joy through the years and Carl has made some unusual and very artistic creations."

This is not only his wife's opinion. Visitors at the Rogers' home in California often comment on the intriguing mobiles they see, and then are amazed to find that Carl is their creator. The same is true with his color photography, another hobby he loved, especially during their trips to Mexico and the Caribbean. It seems that the man had real range. Whether working with his head or his hands, he excelled. Interestingly, when fifty past presidents of the American Psychological Association were rated on the Strong Vocational Interest Blank, Rogers tied for fifth place as an artist. He also placed third for the forest service, tied for fourth as a farmer and sixth for a minister, and was down near the bottom of the list as least likely to be an office worker, accountant, and purchasing agent. In later years when his professional writings emphasized more the trusting of one's own instincts and inner voices, it is interesting to remember that this was an artist speaking as well as a scientist. That polarity between artist and scientist had always been an important tension within him, constantly moving him beyond static conceptions or routinized technique.

As Rogers began to think more philosophically and widely about the implications of his work in psychotherapy, he also began to devote more time to thinking about and developing a theoretical foundation for his previous work. In part this came from a personal desire to understand more fully the phenomena he was observing in his work. Another motivation was the pressure from others who criticized him for not having a sound theory on which to build his therapeutic approach.

He did not originally feel the need for formalized theory. Partly this stemmed from his pragmatic nature. "I was a practical clinician and held an open scorn of all psychological theory, as my early students at Ohio State can testify." Another part of his skepticism about theory was based on its role in the scientific search. As he wrote in 1951, "There is no need for theory until and unless there are phenomena to explain. Limiting our consideration to psychotherapy, there is no reason for a theory of therapy until there are observable changes which call for explanation. Then a unifying theory is of help in explaining what has happened, and in providing testable hypotheses about future experiences. Thus, in the field of therapy the first requisite is a skill which produces an effective result. Through observation of the process and the result, a parsimonious theory may be developed which is projected into new experiences in order to be tested as to its adequacy. The theory is revised and modified with the purpose—never fully attained—of providing a complete conceptual framework which can adequately contain all the observed phenomena. It is the phenomena which are basic, not the theory."

He first theorized publicly about the "self-concept" in his 1947 Presidential address at the American Psychological Association's convention in Detroit. Victor Raimy had contributed to his thinking and, at the same conference, Arthur Combs was giving a talk on the same subject. But Rogers' tentative formulation got the most attention—mostly negative. He recalled that "following the address . . . Chairman John Anderson and I went to the men's room which was crowded with psychologists, buzzing loudly with talk. When I entered, all conversation stopped. The silence was deafening. I felt I had interrupted many highly critical comments."

Nevertheless his theory did develop over the years and achieved its two fullest descriptions in a chapter entitled "A Theory of Personality and Behavior" in *Client-Centered Therapy* and in "A Theory of Therapy, Personality, and Interpersonal Relationships, as Developed in the Client-Centered Framework," written in 1957 and published in 1959 in Volume Three of Koch's massive series *Psychology: A Study of Science.*

Rogers' theory was a "phenomenological theory," that is, a theory which begins with the assumption that every individual perceives a separate world of phenomena all around him and also within himself. This "phenomenal field" governs his behavior. For example, the infant may be picked up by a friendly, caring person; but if the infant *perceives* the person as strange or frightening, he will behave accordingly, with fear, crying, pulling away—all to the adult's dismay. Thus, while many individuals' phenomenal fields may overlap as they perceive the same phenomena, it is also true that part of any individual's phenomenal field may *not* correspond to what others would agree is "reality." The extreme example is the person who is hallucinating. The hallucinations he sees are real for him in that they are part of his phenomenal field.

Rogers' theory was also a "self theory," the *self* being one very important part of a person's phenomenal field. Here he followed a recent tradition in psychology, a relatively new school of thought, which regarded the *self* as the "organizing and creative and adaptive core of personality" which was most influential in determining a person's behavior. For Rogers the self was "the organized, consistent conceptual gestalt [i.e., overall picture] composed of perceptions of the characteristics of the 'I' or 'me' and the perceptions of the relationships of the 'I' or 'me' to others and to various aspects of life, together with the values attached to these perceptions." For example, a perception of the self might be "I am six feet in height." A perception of the self in relation to others might be "I am tall." The value attached to this perception might be "I am too tall."

The concept of self grows out of the interaction between the child and his environment. Whether or not he comes to feel he is a lovable or capable person depends on the extent to which he is treated as a person worthy of love and respect by his parents, his friends, his teachers. Once this concept of self is formed it is difficult to change, and it governs a person's behavior. If a person thinks he is not very capable, he will, despite all the evidences of success to the contrary, continue to go into new situations feeling not very capable. Moreover, if he feels incapable, it is likely his behavior will reflect this. As the famous Coleman Report showed in 1966, the greatest factor affecting students' success in schools was their self-concept.

Not only is a person's self-concept difficult to change, the person also builds up "defenses" to maintain it. This often means denying or distorting new evidence which would tend to threaten the old self-concept. For example, the mother who views herself as a loving and responsible person, a "good mother," finds herself experiencing the beginnings of very resentful and rejecting feelings to her third child, whom she really did not want to have. To admit these hostile feelings would threaten her image of herself as a caring and unselfish mother. Consequently she denies the negative feelings and instead finds reasons in the child's behavior to feel justified in finding fault with him. The child feels the rejection and behaves in a way that justifies her negative opinion of him. When he behaves more positively, she becomes suspicious of his motives and wonders what he wants from her. Their relationship deteriorates. Inside she feels a growing anger toward her child and toward herself, but cannot understand it. She begins to feel she is failing as a mother and is greatly confused about herself, her actions, and her feelings. She comes to therapy for help.

This example is typical of many individuals who come for therapy. They are feeling some anxiety or conflict because their previous self-concepts are being threatened by new feelings or facts which are not consistent with their view of themselves. When this "incongruence," as Rogers sometimes called it, is small, the person may experience only minor discomfort, and the process of dropping his defenses by admitting the new data to awareness and enlarging his self-concept may be a relatively easy one. This happens to all of us at times, outside of therapy. On the other hand, if the previous self-concept is very deeply imbedded in one's personality, and the new evidence to be incorporated seems to him so inconsistent with his concept of self that he can see no way that it *can* be incorporated, the effect can be one of enormous stress. In its most extreme form the stress may be so hard to cope with that a psychotic break, such as schizophrenia or catatonia, is the only way the person finds for resolving the conflict.

In therapy, though, the goal is for the person to become more open to all of his inner and outer experiences so that he can incorporate new evidence into his concept of self, without undue stress. The mother may then acknowledge, "Yes, I basically am a loving and responsible mother, but I also felt and feel a lot of resentment toward my third child, and this has caused me to act in certain ways." This can only be done when the client can lower his defenses and experience his feelings and his relationships without distortion or denial. He is able to lower his defenses because of the therapeutic relationship, in which the therapist's congruence, empathy, and unconditional positive regard make the climate so safe that the client feels free to explore the most frightening, unchartered aspects of his experience. Gradually his self-concept changes, is enlarged by this newly discovered information. He no longer feels threat or anxiety, because he has become open to the feelings which were threatening his defenses. In the process he has not only learned to cope with the initial problems he had, but he develops a greater confidence in his organism—if he can be open to his experiences, admit his feelings, somehow he will be able to integrate these into his personality and make whatever decisions need to be made in a rational manner. Old defense patterns are no longer necessary. These have been replaced with the individual's feeling a greater confidence to deal with life as it is, people as they are, and himself as he really is.

This, in abridged form, is Rogers' theory of how the concept of self influences behavior and undergoes change in the development of a healthier personality. As usual, little in the theory was invented by Rogers. He was the first to acknowledge his influences in the formation of his theory, namely: Goldstein, Angyal, Maslow, Mowrer, Lecky, Sullivan, Masserman, Murphy, Cameron, Murray, Kluckhohn, White, Snygg, Combs, and Burrow, as well as his colleagues and students at the Counseling Center. Nevertheless, with all these other theorists to choose from, when Calvin Hall and Gardner Lindzey wrote their text on personality theories—which is perhaps the most widely read book on the subject in graduate schools across the country—they chose Rogers' theory as the prototype for their chapter on self theory. "For our specimen theory we have selected Carl Rogers' formulation because it is the most fully developed statement of self theory. Moreover, Rogers has buttressed his speculations with an imposing array of empirical supports. . . . Rogers' theory of personality represents a synthesis of phenomenology as presented by Snygg and Combs, of holistic and organismic theory as developed in the writings of Goldstein, Maslow, and Angyal, of Sullivan's interpersonal theory, and of self-theory for which Rogers himself is largely responsible, although he acknowledges a debt to Raimy and Lecky."

Reluctant to begin theorizing in the first place, Rogers was still reluctant to place too great an emphasis on his own formulation. His view of theory, in relation to science, might challenge many a psychologist. He wrote in 1959, "I believe that there is only one statement which can accurately apply to all theories—from the phlogiston theory to the theory of relativity, from the theory I will present to the one which I hope will replace it in a decade—and that is that at the time of its formulation every theory contains an unknown (and perhaps at that point an unknowable) amount of error and mistaken inference. The degree of error may be very great, as in the phlogiston theory, or small, as I imagine it may be in the theory of relativity, but unless we regard the discovery of truth as a closed and finished book, then there will be new discoveries which will contradict the best of theories which we can now construct.

"To me this attitude is very important, for I am distressed at the manner in which small-caliber minds immediately accept a theory—almost any theory—as a dogma of truth. If theory could be seen for what it is—a fallible, changing attempt to construct a network of gossamer threads which will contain the solid facts—then a theory would serve as it should, as a stimulus to further creative thinking. . . . I am sure that the stress I place on this grows in part out of my regret at the history of Freudian theory. For Freud, it seems quite clear that his highly creative theories were never more than that. He kept changing, altering, revising, giving new meaning to old terms—always with more respect for the facts he observed than for the theories he built. But at the hands of insecure disciples (so it seems to me), the gossamer threads became iron chains of dogma from which dynamic psychology is only recently beginning to free itself."

Again we see how Rogers' sincere belief in the scientific method contributed to his flexibility and willingness to change over the years. In fact, while he was writing his longest and fullest theoretical formulation for the Koch volume, another type of change was in the offing.

At the height of his career, at a time when the Counseling Center of the University of Chicago was regarded by many as the most innovative center in the country for research and new methods in psychotherapy, Rogers surprised the world of psychology by leaving Chicago to move to the University of Wisconsin.

In the spring of 1957 he had been invited to spend one semester in the Department of Education at Wisconsin as the visiting "Knapp honorary professor." Virgil Herrick, a professor of education at Wisconsin, had been most responsible for bringing this about, and the Rogers and Herricks became very close friends after that. The five months at Wisconsin were very enjoyable and productive for him.

One Wisconsin student, Charles Truax, would never forget one seminar Rogers led. He told of how "I would challenge him . . . and Carl wouldn't operate that way. . . . I'd say, 'What is your evidence?' and he'd say, 'Well, you don't feel that what I am saying is of real meaning,' and I'd say, 'That's right, now defend yourself,' and we went back and forth like this a few times, and he'd respond in the therapist role by saying something like, 'The son-of-a-bitch won't fight back,' and I'd say, *That's* right.' "

Rogers recalled, "I held a seminar for faculty members in which I was, I fear, rather rigidly 'student-centered.' I had not yet learned how to place full responsibility with the group and yet give freely of myself. Nevertheless, it was an exciting and unusual experience for most of the participants. I also held a large seminar for graduate students in counseling, psychology and education. This was highly successful and, judging from letters over the years, had a significant impact on the lives of the members. During this time, Helen and I had many warm personal and social contacts with faculty members in education, psychiatry, and with several of the psychologists."

The guest professorship also gave him considerable free time for his own thinking, research, and writing. He spent many hours listening to recorded interviews trying to better understand the process of therapy. His later paper "A Process Conception of Psychotherapy" was a direct outgrowth of this time and proved to be an important development in his thinking.

"Meanwhile Vergil Herrick was working devotedly and selflessly behind the scenes to bring me to Wisconsin. I had assured him that nothing could lure me from Chicago, and he had challenged me to write out the description of a position which would entice me. I wrote a description of an impossible position—appointments in both psychiatry and psychology, opportunity to train psychologists and psychiatrists, time for therapy and research with psychotic and normal individuals (the two extreme groups where I felt my experience was deficient), and other improbable requirements. To my amazement, he was able to bring this about, though the approval of ten separate committees, besides his persuasive talks with many individuals was necessary."

Once Rogers had made the decision to move, while still in Wisconsin he wrote to the Counseling Center staff to explain his decision fully, "so that the period of rumors and uncertainty would be as brief as possible." His explanation to his friends and colleagues conveys the meaning to him of that move far better than anything else he has written or said on the subject.

. . . You will want to know why I have accepted this position. The biggest reason is the opportunity it gives for greater impact. What influence will I have at Chicago if I remain there? As I see it I will have a continuing influence on the profession of psychology, I will have some influence on the research we are doing, though the research leadership is rightly passing to the younger people. I will have some influence through the development of new ideas. If I come to Wisconsin, I will have all of those possibilities of exerting influence plus the opportunity to have an important impact on a whole new profession. Psychologists and psychiatrists will sit in the same seminar with me, and will participate in the same research projects with me. If psychologists and psychiatrists get a feeling for what the experience of therapy means, and at the same time a feeling for the research approach to these problems, I think this could set a very significant pattern of future development in the whole mental hygiene field. There will be eleven new psychiatric residents per year, each of them planning to stay for three years. Thus there will be an opportunity to be in contact with thirty-three young psychiatrists at any one time and an equal or greater number of psychologists. This represents a really outstanding challenge. If we can turn out here, psychologists and psychiatrists who are accustomed to working together, and with twin capacities for doing effective therapy and carrying on sound research, it could start a revolutionary trend in the whole mental health field. So this matter of potential impact is the big reason why I have decided to make a move.

Other elements of the picture are the opportunity to influence the University in more general ways. For instance, I will have an opportunity to influence the program in guidance and counseling in the School of Education which is most eager to see me stay on. My influence upon the University as a whole has in a sense already begun. Some of the most interested members in my seminar are the Associate Dean of the College of Letters and Science, the Dean of Women, a member of the Department of Psychiatry, the psychiatrist in charge of the Child Guidance Center, members of the faculty of the School of Social Work, of the Department of Speech, and Sociology, as well as Psychology and Education. The atmosphere has been in general very cordial toward my ideas.

Another factor which has influenced us is the opportunity to live in a beautiful spot. Helen has not been happy with the conditions in Chicago, and I share this feeling, though I am less troubled by it than she is. We certainly would not move solely to obtain better living surroundings, but when a rare professional opportunity comes up, combined with the chance to live in a nice home in a lovely city, the combination is irresistible.

There are some other reasons, but all of them I think are minor. One of them is that I have always felt that a person does what he can do in one institution in a period of some six to ten years. I have stayed twelve years. By moving now, to a new University, I'd have the opportunity to make a significant dent in a new situation during the ten or fifteen years before I retire. If I stay much longer at Chicago it is unlikely that there would be the opportunity to move, and it is also unlikely that I would be in the new place long enough to make my influence felt. So this opportunity seems to have come at an appropriate time.

He continued for another page, discussing some of the realities of the transition—the funding at Chicago for their research project, the doctoral committees he was sitting on, the future of the Counseling Center—and suggested how he would try to help facilitate the solutions to these various problems brought about by his departure. He signed his letter "with the warmest affection for all of you," but then felt the need to add a postscript, which I think explains as much about his move to Wisconsin as all the other reasons he provides.

P.S. As I think over what I have dictated, I realize that in one respect it does not quite express my feeling. Because I fear that my decision will cause temporary pain and upset, I have soft-pedalled my own feeling of enthusiasm. I tried once to tell staff in a memo—you may remember it —what a large streak of pioneering spirit there is in me. I really am kin to the old frontiersmen, and my feeling at the present time is that I can hardly wait to throw my pack on my back and leave the settlement behind. I itch to get going! In my feelings I am already in the excitement of meeting the new problems, new challenges, and the broad horizon of new opportunities I see here. The thought of new wilderness to explore, with all that I believe it will mean to me and to others in the way of significant learnings and fresh developments, is like wine in my blood. I feel ten years younger.

So if what I am saying in this memo seems to you as if I am talking to you from a distance, halfway up the ridge on the trail of a new adventure, you are right, for that is the way it is. What I hope you will realize is that this in no way alters my affection for you, but is simply my need to keep on going.

CHAPTER 8
Freud, Skinner, and Rogers
The Growth of Humanistic Psychology

Abraham Maslow, in the 1950s, often spoke of a growing "third force" in psychology, which showed signs of becoming the most important emphasis in modern psychology. Carl Rogers, along with Maslow and several others, is often credited with being one of the pioneers or father figures of this third force, known variously as holistic, existential, or humanistic psychology. The first two forces are the psychoanalytic and behaviorist schools of psychology, most prototypically represented by the work of Sigmund Freud and B.F. Skinner.

Freud, of course, is the universally acclaimed father of modern psychotherapy. During the 1920s Rogers was exposed to Freudian thinking in New York City at a time when psychoanalysis and its jargon were gaining widespread popularity in many Eastern cities. He was not very taken with the Freudian approach, for his training in psychological testing and measurement (not to mention his earlier scientific farming background) inclined him to be somewhat scornful of the intangible and unmeasurable concepts—like id, ego, superego, Oedipus complex, and the like. He much preferred the more defined world of personality testing and tangible measures of adjustment to what seemed to him the almost mystical procedures of the psychoanalysts.

Which is not to say that he was entirely unchanged from his exposure to psychoanalytic theory and methods. Speaking of his early nondirective method that emphasized release, insight, and positive action, he wrote, in 1946, ". . . In its concepts of repression and release, in its stress upon catharsis and insight, it has many roots in Freudian thinking." But on the practical level Rogers was not much affected by his exposure to psychoanalysis and, instead, developed his own theories and methods out of his experience in working with clients in Rochester, Columbus, and Chicago. As his approach developed a coherence of its own, contrasts to the psychoanalytic approach became clearer. But at no time did he work out his thinking as a reaction to Freud, as an antithesis to the psychoanalytic thesis. It always grew out of its own soil of experience.

One of the most apparent contrasts in the thinking of Rogers and Freud is in their basic evaluation of human nature. Freud was very clear on this point. The human being, at his core, is wild, unsocialized, selfish, and destructive. If a person's "id" were to govern his behavior, the results would be disastrous. Fortunately the "superego" develops to serve as a conscience for the individual, and the "ego" develops to negotiate the demands of the id and superego and to relate to the outside world in a realistic fashion. But at best the healthy individual is a person who has managed to "sublimate" the libidinal energy of the id toward more creative, socialized channels. Underneath lurks the untamed beast, glimpses of whom can be caught in dreams, fantasies, and free associations. "Our mind," wrote Freud, "is no peacefully self-contained unity. It is rather to be compared with a modern State in which a mob, eager for enjoyment and destruction, has to be held down forcibly by a prudent superior class."

Rogers has said it took years for him to get over both his religious and his Freudian training with their view of humans as being fundamentally evil. He gradually adopted a more positive view, maintaining that at his core, the human being is basically socialized, constructive, and trustworthy. For this view he was greatly criticized by psychoanalysts and nonpsychoanalysts alike. It has been said that this opinion of human nature is unsound for it is based on Rogers' work with only mildly neurotic people, not those whose profound conflicts show the deeper, darker, demonic, side of human nature. He has been accused of being naively optimistic. To this type of charge he once replied, "It disturbs me to be thought of as an optimist. My whole professional experience has been with the dark and often sordid side of life, and I know, better than most, the incredibly destructive behavior of which man is capable." Although most of his psychotherapy was conducted in university clinics, this did not mean his work with clients was confined simply to vocational counseling and mild problems of adjustment, as the following excerpts from an interview with a woman client illustrate.

> CLIENT: *(. . . begins to talk in hard flat voice, quite unlike her usual tone. Does not look at counselor. There was much repetition, but the following excerpts give the major thoughts.)* You feel I want to come, but I don't! I'm not coming any more. It doesn't do any good. I don't like you. I hate you! I wish you never were born.
>
> ROGERS: You just hate me very bitterly.*
>
> CLIENT: I think I'll throw you in the lake. I'll cut you up! You think people like you, but they don't. . . . You think you can attract women but you can't. . . . I wish you were *dead.*
>
> ROGERS: You detest me and you'd really like to get rid of me.
>
> CLIENT: You think my father did bad things with me, but he didn't! You think he wasn't a good man, but he *was.* You think I want intercourse but I *don't.*
>
> ROGERS: You feel I *absolutely misrepresent* all your thoughts.
>
> CLIENT: . . . You think you can get people to come in and tell you everything, and they'll think they're being helped, but they're *not!* You just like to make 'em suffer. You think you can hypnotize them, but you *can't!* You think you're good, but you ain't. I hate you. I *hate* you!
>
> ROGERS: You feel I really like to make 'em suffer, but I *don't* help them.
>
> CLIENT: You think I haven't been straight, but I have. I *hate* you. All I've had is pain, pain, pain. You think I can't direct my own life, but I can. You think I can't get well, but I can. You think I had hallucinations, but I didn't. I hate you. *(Long pause. Leans on desk in strained, exhausted pose.)* You think I'm crazy, but I'm not.
>
> ROGERS: You're sure I think you're crazy.
>
> CLIENT: *(Pause.)* I'm tired, and I just can't get loose! *(Despairing tone of voice, and tears. Pause.)* I had a hallucination and I've got to get it out! . . . (Goes on about her own deep conflicts, and tells of the hallucination she has experienced, with terrific tension in her voice, but with an attitude very different from that at the beginning of the interview.) *(Later in interview)*
>
> CLIENT: I knew at the office I had to get rid of this somewhere. I felt I

*[Rogers' footnote] Just as it is impossible to convey on paper the venom and hatred in the client's voice, so it is utterly impossible to convey the depth of empathy in the counselor's [Rogers'] responses. The counselor states, "I tried to enter into and to express in my voice the full degree of the soul-consuming anger which she was pouring out. The written words look incredibly pale, but in the situation they were full of the same feeling she was so coldly and deeply expressing."

could come down and tell you. I knew you'd understand. I couldn't say I hated myself. That's true but I couldn't say it. So I just thought of all the ugly things I could say to you instead.

ROGERS: The things you felt about yourself you couldn't say, but you could say them to me.

CLIENT: I know we're getting to rock bottom. . . .

By the time he left Chicago, Rogers had been a psychotherapist for over thirty years. Interviews of the type portrayed above, while not exactly typical for him, occurred often enough over the years. He had many opportunities to observe and interact with the many levels of the human personality. And always he came back to a positive view of human nature. "Professional experience has forced upon me the realization that man, when you know him deeply, in his worst and most troubled states, is not evil or demonic."

Was it that humankind was "basically good"? Although people often attribute such a sentiment to Rogers, he never quite put it in those terms. He often explained his viewpoint through the use of metaphor or analogy with the world of plants and animals. In 1977 he wrote, "I remember that in my boyhood the potato bin in which we stored our winter supply of potatoes was in the basement, several feet below a small basement window. The conditions were unfavorable, but the potatoes would begin to sprout—pale white sprouts, so unlike the healthy green shoots they sent up when planted in the soil in the spring. But these sad, spindly sprouts would grow two or three feet in length as they reached toward the distant light of the window. They were, in their bizarre, futile growth, a sort of desperate expression of the directional tendency I have been describing. They would never become a plant, never mature, never fulfill their real potentiality. But under the most adverse circumstances they were striving to become. Life would not give up, even if it could not flourish. In dealing with clients whose lives have been terribly warped, in working with men and women on the back wards of state hospitals, I often think of those potato sprouts. So unfavorable have been the conditions in which these people have developed that their lives often seem abnormal, twisted, scarcely human. Yet the directional tendency in them is to be trusted. The clue to understanding their behavior is that they are striving, in the only way available to them, to move toward growth, toward becoming. To us the results may seem bizarre and futile, but they are life's desperate attempt to become itself. It is this potent tendency which is the underlying basis of client-centered therapy and all that has grown out of it."

Many years earlier, in the fullest discussion he ever gave to the subject, an article called "A Note on the Nature of Man," he had approached the topic from a different angle.

"Let me see if I can take the discussion of these points of view into a fresh area where perhaps we have somewhat fewer preconceived biases. Suppose we turn to the animal world and ask ourselves what is the basic nature of the lion, or the sheep, or the dog, or the mouse. To say that any one or all of these are basically hostile or antisocial or carnal seems to be ridiculous. To say that we view their nature as neutral means either that it is neutral in terms of some unspecified set of values, or that their natures are all alike, all putty waiting to receive a shape. This view seems to me equally ridiculous. I maintain that each has a basic nature, a common set of attributes generally characteristic of the species. Thus the sheep is by far the most gregarious or group-minded, the mouse the most generally timorous. No amount of training—therapeutic or otherwise—will make a lion out of a mouse, or vice versa, even though a wide degree of change is possible. There is a basic substratum of species characteristics which we will do well to accept.

"We might take a closer look at some of those characteristics. Since the lion has the most pronounced reputation for being a 'ravening beast' let us choose him. What are the characteristics of his common nature, his basic nature? He kills an antelope when he is hungry, but he does not go on a wild rampage of killing. He eats his fill after the killing, but there are no obese lions on the veldt. He is helpless and dependent in his puppyhood, but he does not cling to the dependent relationship. He becomes increasingly independent and autonomous. In the infant state he is completely selfish and self-centered, but as he matures he shows, in addition to such impulses, a reasonable degree of cooperativeness in the hunt. The lioness feeds, cares for, protects, and seems to enjoy her young. Lions satisfy their sexual needs, but this does not mean they go on wild and lustful orgies. His various tendencies and urges come to a continually changing balance in himself, and in that sense he is very satisfactorily self-controlled and self-regulated. He is in basic ways a constructive, a trustworthy member of the species *Felis leo*. His fundamental tendencies are in the direction of development, differentiation, independence, self-responsibility, cooperation, maturity. In general the expression of his basic nature makes for the continuation and enhancement of himself and his species.

"With the appropriate variations, the same sort of statements could be made about the dog, the sheep, the mouse. To be sure each behaves in ways which from some specific point of view are destructive. We wince to see the lion kill the antelope; we are annoyed when the sheep eats our garden, we complain when the mouse eats the cheese we are saving for our picnic; I regard the dog as destructive when he bites me, a stranger; but surely none of these behaviors justifies us in thinking of any of these animals as basically evil. If I endeavored to explain to you that if the 'lion-ness' of the lion were to be released, or the 'sheep-ness' of the sheep, that these animals would then be impelled by insatiable lusts, uncontrollable aggressions, wild and excessive sexual behaviors, and tendencies of innate destructiveness, you would quite properly laugh at me. Obviously, such a view is pure nonsense.

"I would like now to consider again the nature of man in the light of this discussion of the nature of animals. I have come to know men most deeply in a relationship which is characterized by all that I can give of safety, absence of threat, and complete freedom to be and to choose. In such a relationship men express all kinds of bitter and murderous feelings, abnormal impulses, bizarre and anti-social desires. But as they live in such a relationship, expressing and being more of themselves, I find that man, like the lion, has a nature. My experience is that he is a basically trustworthy member of the human species, whose deepest characteristics tend toward development, differentiation, cooperative relationships; whose life tends fundamentally to move from dependence to independence; whose impulses tend naturally to harmonize into a complex and changing pattern of self-regulation; whose total character is such as to tend to preserve and enhance himself and his species, and perhaps to move it toward its further evolution. In my experience, to discover that an individual is truly and deeply a unique member of the human species is not a discovery to excite horror. Rather I am inclined to believe that fully to be a human being is to enter into the complex process of being one of the most widely sensitive, responsive, creative, and adaptive creatures on this planet.

"So when a Freudian such as Karl Menninger tells me (as he has, in a discussion of this issue) that he perceives man as 'innately evil' or more precisely, 'innately destructive,' I can only shake my head in wonderment. It leads me to all kinds of perplexing questions. How could it be that Menninger and I, working with such a similar purpose in such intimate relationships with individuals in distress, experience people so differently?"

Later in the same article he asked this last question again, thinking of Freud himself. Freud, too, was a keen observer of the therapeutic process and the human personality. How was it that the two of them ended with such different views of human nature? Rogers offered an interesting hypothesis—an untestable one, unfortunately—to answer the question: "It has been my experience that though clients can, to some degree, independently discover some of their denied or repressed feelings, they cannot on their own achieve full emotional acceptance of these feelings. It is only in a caring relationship that these 'awful' feelings are first fully accepted by the therapist and can then be accepted by the client. Freud in his self-analysis was deprived of this warmly acceptant relationship. Hence, though he might come to know and to some extent to understand the hidden and denied aspects of himself, I question whether he could ever come to accept them fully, to embrace them as a meaningful, acceptable, and constructive part of himself. More likely he continued to perceive them as unacceptable aspects of himself—enemies, whom knowing he could control—rather than as impulses which, when existing freely in balance with his other impulses, were constructive. At any rate I regard this as a hypothesis worthy of consideration."

The client, in other words, internalizes the therapist's attitude toward him. If the therapist regards the client with unconditional positive regard, the client will develop that same attitude toward himself, valuing all parts of his inner experience, without labeling some impulses good and others bad. If the therapist regards that total organism of the client as trustworthy, the client, too, can develop this attitude toward himself. Freud, though he developed much self-understanding (the "empathy"), did not develop the sense of basic self-trust which Rogers described. Not having found it in himself, neither did he find it in his patients and, he therefore continued to hold the view that humans, in their most inner selves, are destructive and antisocial.

Ironically the two men were not so far apart. Although he did not use the terminology, Rogers would be the first to admit the presence of id-type and superego-type impulses in humans and the ego-type mechanism or function which weighed all of the person's impulses and arrived at the behavior meant to maximize all his needs. Both Freud and Rogers saw the psychology of the person function in this similar way. The point of difference arose in the primacy Freud gave and the equality which Rogers gave to the id functions. For Freud the id was basic; for Rogers it existed simultaneously and equally with the superego.

From this difference stemmed a difference in psychotherapeutic approach. The Freudian, who was accustomed to thinking of the darker reality behind the more superficial, civilized superstructure, would use interpretation of the patient's free association to attempt to discover and help the patient discover: What's behind this? What really happened? What are the real, deeper feelings he's not saying? Where did this all begin? What is the real meaning of this memory, or slip, or figure of speech, or behavior? One analyst might do this in an accepting way, so that the patient would come to feel a real safety to say whatever came into his mind, a freedom from evaluation, an atmosphere of trying to understand himself and his experiences. Another psychoanalyst might create an opposite tone of suspicion and mistrust which the client would come to feel toward himself. In the latter case, the result of years of analysis could be a person who is greatly self-conscious and continues to view his own words and deeds with suspicion, analysis, and lack of acceptance. In the first case, an accepting, genuine, and empathic analyst might be building the same attitudinal ingredients into the relationship that Rogers advocated. As the previously mentioned Fiedler studies showed, the results achieved by the experienced Freudian and experienced Rogerian would often be surprisingly similar.

While most of Rogers' statements about psychoanalytic thinking and practice were quite negative, his references to Freud personally were usually respectful and often seemed to indicate that Rogers identified with the earlier pioneer, as when he said, "I feel more and more sympathy with a statement that I understand Freud made—that he 'was not a Freudian himself.' I certainly feel and know very well that I'm not a non-directivist myself."

At the same time that Freudian thinking was becoming popular in many parts of the country, another movement in psychology was emerging and taking hold. This movement took place, not in the doctor's office or the hospital, but mostly in the scientist's laboratory. It began with E.L. Thorndike, just before the turn of the century in the United States, and with Pavlov in Russia in the early twentieth century. Working with animals to discover the principles of human learning, both these men used the concepts of "stimulus" and "response" to understand how learning took place. Pavlov's famous experiments with dogs showed how, by pairing an unnatural or "conditioned" stimulus (like ringing a bell) with a natural or "unconditioned" stimulus (like a piece of meat), the dogs' natural, unconditioned response (salivation) could eventually be induced by ringing the bell, even when no meat was present. His approach came to be called "classical conditioning." Thorndike, Pavlov, and other, later scientists, were called "behaviorists," because their main interest was in the subject's behavior, as opposed to his (or its) feelings, goals, and so on.

B.F. Skinner, in the 1930s, began working in the behaviorist tradition. His focus was on the fact that if a particular response was rewarded or "reinforced," it was more likely to occur again. It did not matter what stimulus produced the original response. Most of Skinner's experimental work was done with pigeons. By reinforcing with food certain behaviors of pigeons, Skinner was able to teach pigeons to dance, play ping-pong, and even keep guided missiles on their proper course. By varying the timing and consistency of the reinforcement, Skinner showed how the animals' learning could be either strengthened or "extinguished."

This appealed to American psychology. Like the testing and measurement emphasis that had preceded it, the behaviorist's work was concrete. The results could be measured. The principles could be readily demonstrated in the laboratory. Moreover, Skinner's basic work could be easily understood by laypersons and academics alike. We have all been reinforced by parents or teachers for "good" behavior, or punished for the opposite, and most of us have rewarded some pet for fetching or eating or purring; so that we readily accept the correctness of Skinner's learning principles. His school of "operant conditioning" soon became, and still is, the most widely taught learning theory in colleges across the country.

Like Rogers, who when he became confident in his understanding of the principles of psychotherapeutic learning began to apply these insights to other related fields, Skinner also began to apply his principles of learning to spheres other than the laboratory. In a widely read novel, *Walden Two,* Skinner described his ideal society, built upon the principles of operant conditioning. By rewarding certain behaviors, the architects of *Walden Two* were able to "grow" people who were happy, productive, secure, and able to deal with frustrations. Neither democracy nor capitalism was necessary in this utopia, yet the citizens felt free, had as many if not more choices than they presently do in almost every facet of life, and all lived in material comfort and security. The book is fascinating to me in the way it takes one set of traditional American values i.e., the use of technology and science in solving problems and in furthering "progress," and shows how these values render other traditional values—like democracy and capitalism—obsolete. Yet the motives of Frazier, the chief mover in the book, and Skinner, the author, are scientific, not political. As of this writing,

Walden Two has sold well over a million copies—a testimony to its unique insight into a culture whose contrasting values often result in conflict.

Another area into which Skinner extended his influence was that of education. "Programmed learning" and many of the teaching machines are direct outgrowths of Skinner's work. In a programmed textbook, for example, the learner is asked to fill in the blank correctly. When he turns the page, he sees he has the right answer—for the texts are written in such a way as to allow the learner almost always to answer correctly. This "success" is its own reward and encourages the student to continue working through the book, at his own pace. Proponents of programmed learning have claimed that students can usually cover a course of study in half the normal time and with greater than normal comprehension. In the sixties, for a while, it seemed to some as though programmed learning and teaching machines would revolutionize education. After a few years, though, it became apparent that it would be a long time before enough good educational programs could be developed and that programmed learning had certain drawbacks and was not applicable to all educational situations. It will probably be years before we know just how important this educational technology will be. At any rate it was Skinner's pioneering work that made these developments possible.

His impact even extended into the field of therapy. Although there are different types of "behavior therapy," a good deal of it is based on operant conditioning techniques. In one study, for example, a behaviorist worked with three hospitalized, chronic, paranoid schizophrenics. She instructed all the hospital personnel who came into contact with the patients to ignore—i.e., not reinforce—their bizarre or paranoid verbalizations. When working with them herself, she would, if they began to say bizarre things, turn the other way or change the subject. On the other hand, normal comments and behaviors were reacted to by therapist and hospital personnel with nods, pats on the shoulder, full attention, and the like. By not reinforcing abnormal behavior and reinforcing normal behavior, the normal behavior increased to the point where all three patients were able to leave the hospital in three months. Behavior therapy has spread very quickly, and the number of studies that support this approach has now begun to challenge the record held by the client-centered model.

Of course, Rogers didn't read Skinner in college, nor Skinner Rogers. The two men were contemporaries, with an age difference of only two years, Rogers the elder. They grew out of the same native soil, each working on different, though related problems—Skinner in learning principles, Rogers in psychotherapy—each building a school of thought from his own scientific endeavors. Skinner had an established and concrete behaviorist tradition upon which to build his work. Rogers, though he had some predecessors, had no such clearly defined tradition.

Although he went off in his own direction, he could have found a more congenial tradition in Gestalt psychology, as developed by the German psychologists Max Wertheimer, Wolfgang Kohler, and Kurt Koffka, before and after the First World War.

As Hall and Linzey explained, "The chief tenet of Gestalt psychology is that the way in which an object is perceived is determined by the total context or configuration in which the object is embedded. Relationships among components of a perceptual field rather than the fixed characteristics of the individual components determine perception." The significance of this movement for the development of psychology was that it was the first time that credence and major importance were given to the individual's perception of reality. The Freudians attempted to go beyond what they regarded as the patient's distorted perception of reality and eventually discover the truth. In a sense, they were outsiders looking into the person, trying to discover what was really there. The Gestalt psychologist—who worked primarily with monkeys and other laboratory animals and attempted to generalize their findings to human beings—could be described as trying to get inside the individual in order to look out, to see the perceptual field as the person himself saw it. The behaviorists, like the Freudians, viewed the individual from an external frame of reference, but unlike the Freudians they showed little or no interest in the person's internal frame of reference, faulty or otherwise. Their interest was in behavior, and as they usually explained it, an animal learned to solve a problem by behaving randomly, until one of its random behaviors paid off with a reward, thus causing it to repeat the desired behaviors to receive another reinforcement. This change in the animal's behavior was synonymous with learning. Koffka, however, showed how a monkey could sit in his cage and look over sticks he had played with before, and get the "insight" to attach two sticks together to reach the banana which lay more than a stick's length out of reach. Putting the sticks together and reaching through the cage bars for the banana was not a random behavior but a clearly goal-oriented, reasoned, problem-solving attempt. Here was an approach to psychology which seemed very consistent with Rogers' evolving thinking.

At the time that Rogers began developing his ideas, however, he was working with problem children in a clinic in Rochester. The theories and laboratory experiments of the Gestalt psychologists were foreign to the practical problems he encountered daily. Although he did acknowledge the influence of Gestalt Psychology on his thinking, this influence came much later, once he had developed the client-centered approach and sought a theoretical foundation for it.

Rogers was not alone in trying to build a psychology and psychotherapy based on different assumptions from the Freudians and behaviorists. A growing number of psychologists, therapists, and other helping professionals were working daily with thousands of clients, in clinics, schools, consulting rooms, minister's offices, homes, and agencies. Psychoanalysis was clearly inappropriate in most of these situations. The learning principles derived from studying rats and pigeons seemed equally irrelevant. Work in behavior therapy had not yet begun. Psychological tests and diagnoses were only a small part of the answer for most of the problems encountered. Where were all these nonanalytic, nonlaboratory-oriented professionals to turn?

Many turned to the American Association for Applied Psychology, the offshoot of the American Psychological Association that had been formed in the late thirties as an antidote to the laboratory-oriented parent organization. Their attitude toward the APA could be characterized as, "You're not asking the most important questions—questions of human values, growth, and helping relationships." Many turned to Rogers' 1942 book *Counseling and Psychotherapy* as the most detailed, practical description and rationale for a new style of helping yet written. And many turned to Rogers' contemporaries who were moving in similar directions. The work of Rank, Taft, and Allen has been mentioned earlier as an influence on Rogers' development. More widely known is the work of Kurt Goldstein, Abraham Maslow, and Gordon Allport.

What these individuals and others were doing was building a body of theory, method, case studies, and research which gradually came to be known, most popularly, as "humanistic psychology." Through the forties, fifties, and especially in the sixties, this movement gathered more and more followers. Eventually, in 1961, the Association of Humanistic Psychology and its *Journal of Humanistic Psychology* would be formed, with Rogers as one of its founding sponsors. He had been approached about becoming president of the new group, but felt that after serving as president of the American Association for Applied Psychology, the American Psychological Association, and the American Academy of Psychotherapists, he had had enough of that kind of responsibility.

Because the word "humanistic" is used by so many people in so many different contexts, it is difficult to define humanistic psychology in a descriptive way. The tendency of many proponents is to regard "humanistic" as standing for all the good things one might be or do, which unfortunately leaves other approaches as appearing, by contrast, to be *non*humanistic. Clearly any responsible therapist in the Freudian or behaviorist tradition is a humane person with humane goals for the client, and moral and ethical procedures for reaching these goals. On the other hand the detractors from humanistic psychology often take an opposite, yet comparable stance—associating "humanistic" with all that is negative in psychology.

Attempting to avoid the debate between the humanists and the other schools, I would describe three major, distinctive characteristics of humanistic psychology. The first is its *phenomenological* emphasis, i.e., an emphasis on the individual's perception of reality (phenomena) and of his relationship to it. The humanists, in general, seem to share this orientation. They tend to show a greater interest in the client's picture of his world or to attach a greater importance and validity to it. For Rogers, adopting the client's frame of reference in an empathic way was the client-centered therapists' primary approach. Other humanistic therapists demonstrated their phenomenological emphasis in other ways. Victor Frankl's "logo-therapy" emphasized the importance of the patient's finding a *meaning* for his existence. Rollo May's "existential" psychology and psychotherapy emphasized meaning and "will," the patient's act of courage to choose a course of his own after understanding his history and his present situation. These approaches and others take seriously and work with the client's conscious view of the world. While this often comes up in classical psychoanalysis, the Freudians attach less significance to the patient's conscious phenomenal field, often trying to bypass it through free associations and dreams or deal only with one small part of it, that is, the patient's attitudes toward the therapist and therapy (and even these attitudes are viewed primarily as a transference from earlier relationships). Similarly, the early behaviorists obviously had no interest in the inner world of the rats in their laboratory. Some behavior therapists entirely ignore the patient's inner world and confine their efforts to reinforcing or extinguishing particular behaviors. Other behavior therapists who attempt to change the client's perceptions (e.g., "I'm a failure" or "Everyone's against me") focus on only certain aspects of the client's frame of reference and reinforce these, while inhibiting others. In short, the humanists tend more than the others to accept and work with the whole person which the client perceives himself to be. This first distinction is a matter of emphasis; the second and third show a qualitative difference between the humanist and other schools.

The humanists have shown a decided interest in developing our understanding of psychological *health* and in working with so-called "normal" or even "above average" populations. Freud built his entire system on his experiences with disturbed patients and on his self-analysis. The behavior therapists work specifically with that which is malfunctioning or producing anxiety in a person. Their concept of health, implicitly, is the absence of the undesired behavior. The humanists began to reverse this trend. Goldstein described a "self-actualizing" tendency he saw in his patients. Maslow used this concept and built a "hierarchy of human needs," showing how people begin with physiological and emotional needs which, if not met, cause illness but, if met, allow the person to move on to meet his need for self-actualization, that is, for creativity, meaning, and "vocation" in life. He noted that self-actualizing people sometimes had "peak experiences"—moments of ecstacy, beauty, and understanding—and he spent many years studying the characteristics of peak experiences and of the self-actualizing person. Rogers, in the late 1950s, began to write of the "fully functioning person," and attempted to describe what "the Good Life" would be for the psychologically healthy and self-actualizing person.

Early work of this type gave courage and ammunition to those professionals moving in similar directions. Combined with the influence of Gestalt-trained Kurt Lewin in social psychology, the humanistic thrust led to the group dynamics work of the late forties and fifties and the "human potential movement"—human relations and sensitivity training, encounter groups, body awareness, meditation, and so on —of the sixties. All these approaches tended to expand our conception of human potential and to explore questions like: What are human beings capable of? How can normally functioning individuals most fully realize their capacities? To what extent can daily living become a peak experience? This meaning of the term "humanistic" stands in marked contrast to the other forces in psychology which have focused on helping people solve their problems so they can make an "adjustment" to living. The humanists have said, "We don't even know yet what real living is."

Finally, the humanists have shown a major concern in discovering and working with that which is uniquely human about human beings, especially the ability to make choices. For years the practice in psychology was to study the learning process in laboratory animals and then extrapolate these understandings to human beings. Thus, when Thorndike demonstrated that rats learned certain tasks through repetition, many psychologists and educators eagerly used this to justify classroom learning by repetitive drill. The humanists believed that working with people, not animals, was the best way to build a body of data upon which a full and accurate understanding of human beings could emerge. They wanted to consider values, goals, choices and feelings, as well as behavior. Likewise, the Freudian approach was built upon a medical model which was not unique to human beings. The model maintained that every illness—physical or mental—had a cause. If the expert can accurately diagnose the cause and, with the patient's cooperation, take appropriate remedial measures, the problem can be eliminated. In classical psychoanalysis, if the patient could be helped to understand the proper interpretation as to the source of his difficulties, the difficulties would go away. The patient didn't have to do anything, other than cooperate with the analyst. But this reduced the patient to an object, not the subject or the author of his own destiny. Just as things have been done to him which once caused his problems, so now things were being done to him which would remove his problems. The humanists insisted that this explanation was not sufficient, that human beings *choose* and, in this way, are different from other creatures or natural objects upon which external forces operate. They both choose to give in to the emotional pressures which surround them and choose to behave differently or think differently about themselves. Surely the environment provides many stimuli, many hurts, many pressures and rewards; but ultimately the person chooses his response. Rollo May, for example, accepted the importance of the patient's understanding the sources of his problems, but said that unless he acted upon this understanding with a willful act in the direction of health, he would not get better. In this emphasis on free choice, humanistic psychology has also been known as existential psychology. The human being's ability to choose is an assertion ignored by the Freudians, who stress understanding, and denied by the behaviorists, who see cause and effect as the entire explanation for animal or human behavior.

This description of three distinguishing characteristics of the humanist movement does not include the social context from which it emerged. In 1942 Rogers wrote, "What a picture that is of our world situation! We have conquered space, and go from coast to coast in one daylight. We have defeated time, and the ironic result is that we can hear tomorrow's bombing of London tonight. We have learned in incredible fashion to control the physical universe. We can bend to our will and our purpose the strength of steel, the power of liquid oxygen, the penetrating force of radium and the infrared rays. We control with a flip of the switch complex resources which yesterday we could not even have dreamed about. We have achieved amazing technical control over the physical universe—yet we cannot live together." At a time when the world was becoming increasingly impersonal and alienating, at a time when technology seemed to be spreading into almost every area of life and threatening humanity's control over its own world, and at a time when totalitarianism, in several forms, was sweeping over many parts of the globe, the humanist's message had great potential social significance. Thirty years later, looking back over his life's work, Rogers tried to describe its social significance. What he said of his own contribution could be generalized to include the whole humanist movement as a way of understanding its historical importance.

". . . it seems that without knowing it I had expressed an idea whose time had come. It is as though a pond had become utterly still, so that a pebble dropped into it sent ripples out further and further and further, having an influence which could not be understood by looking at the pebble. Or, to use a chemical analogy, as though a liquid solution had become supersaturated, so that the addition of one tiny crystal initiated the formation of crystals throughout the whole mass.

"What was that idea, that pebble, that crystal? It was the gradually formed and tested hypothesis that the individual has within himself vast resources for self-understanding, for altering his self-concept, his attitudes, and his self-directed behavior—and that these resources can be tapped if only a definable climate of facilitative psychological attitudes can be provided . . . it was discovered that they had wide applicability. . . . Situations involving persons, change in the behavior of persons and the effects of different qualities of interpersonal relationships, exist in almost every human undertaking. Hence others began realizing that perhaps the testable hypothesis of this approach might have almost universal application, or might be retested or reformulated for use in an almost infinite variety of human situations."

With the behaviorist and humanist movements in psychology developing simultaneously, it was inevitable that the leaders in both movements would eventually come to know of each other's work. Especially so, since Rogers and Skinner were tending to generalize the findings from their own laboratories to a wider variety of situations. Had they remained focused on the specific scientific problems presented by their separate work, they might never have clashed publicly. But as they began to write with conviction about such fields as child rearing, education, and society, the contrast between their viewpoints became increasingly evident. And when they finally spoke directly to one another on the issues of their disagreement, the "Rogers-Skinner debate" soon became the most widely popularized discussion of the differences between behaviorist and humanistic psychology.

Actually Rogers began the Rogers-Skinner debate much earlier than 1956, when the two men first spoke from the same platform. A decade earlier he had written, "The clinical experience could be summarized by saying that the behavior of the human organism may be determined by the influences to which it has been exposed; *but it may also be determined by the creative and integrative insight of the organism itself.*" He did not want to deny Skinner's truth, but as his own emphases indicate, he insisted that this was not the only truth. While Skinner devoted his life's work to the first half of the statement, Rogers devoted his to the second part. Yet he was concerned with the implications of the different emphases. Referring to the first trend—understanding behavior as determined entirely by its antecedents—he wrote humorously, though pointedly: "If we are happy about its application to students, then we will be happy when it is applied to us. But I doubt this. Do we really believe that we will be better, more effective faculty members when the dean has the complete record of our lives, our abilities, our personalities—the same type of record we are striving to build up in regard to students? When your request for curriculum changes, for better teaching facilities, your request for promotion, your difficulties with the Buildings and Grounds department, your tension with your wife, are all understood by a benevolent dean in the light of your test results and your Rorschach pattern, will you be more effective, will your university be a better place? Certainly much wiser guidance can be given you.

You can be helped to see that promotion is hardly justified in view of your ability on the College Faculty aptitude test, which has enabled us to select such a homogeneous faculty. It can be gently hinted to you that the dissension in your home and your truculence in faculty meetings as well as your disputes with the janitor, grow out of your unresolved conflict in regard to authority, and that psychiatric guidance would assist you in all three respects. When you leave for another university, your cumulative record can be forwarded to your new dean, who can also evaluate you and your behavior in the light of all this knowledge."

Of course, Skinner and the operant conditioners would not go in for all this personality testing either; but Rogers saw the attempt to control people with psychological information and the tendency to control them through the selective reinforcement of their behavior as part of the same basic direction. "It is the direction in which an increasing portion of the world is moving. Life seems too complex. We should surrender the responsibility for our lives into the hands of someone wiser—a dean, or a psychiatrist, or eventually of course, into the hands of the state."

In another article, written only a few years after the fall of Hitler, Mussolini and Hirohito, and now moving into the Senator Joseph McCarthy period, he continued the argument, pointing out that, "This cultural direction would have much weight behind it. Man's need for dependence runs very deep. To leave individual guidance primarily in the hands of the master, the ruler, the priest, has a long history, and it would not be too surprising if it were followed by a tendency to leave the basic guidance of individual lives in the hands of the doctors of mental health. The wave of the future appears to contain in it a strong tendency toward admitting our own incapacity to deal with our problems in this complex world and laying our destiny in the hands of a few who seem stronger. If this is the direction which we are taking, then the major trend in clinical psychology and psychiatry is serving a useful purpose in laying an effective technological groundwork for eventual control by the state, or by a small group which regards itself as the state."

Thus Rogers laid the groundwork for their debate before he ever mentioned Skinner by name. That first occurred in a 1949 article in the *Harvard Educational Review* (Skinner had just moved to Harvard the year before), in which he wrote, ". . . it is my concern that this major trend in clinical work [counselor-centered therapy] leads gradually and subtly to some loss of confidence in the ability of the self to evaluate, to a basic dependence growing out of that loss of self-confidence, to a lesser degree of personhood, to a subtle and sincerely well-meaning control of persons by a group which, without realizing it, has selected itself to exercise control. . . . From the broader social point of view I have also come to view this development with concern. Does it not lead to a philosophy of social control by the few? Not many psychologists or psychiatrists have voiced the possibility. Skinner, a psychologist not himself in the clinical field, is one of the few to do so, and to advocate such control. In regard to 'extending the practices of an experimental science to the world at large,' he says, 'We can do this as soon as we wish to do it.' "

It was at a symposium at the American Psychological Association's annual convention, on September 4, 1956, that Skinner and Rogers both spoke on "Some Issues Concerning the Control of Human Behavior." Two days earlier Rogers had received the Distinguished Scientific Contribution Award from the APA. Skinner's work also was very familiar to the APA members, and the hall was filled to overflowing. Each man had prepared a paper and had had a chance to read the other's paper before the convention and revise his own. Otherwise, the meeting followed a standard debating formula. Skinner read his paper first. Rogers then had a somewhat longer time in which to read his paper and react to what Skinner had said. Finally, Skinner had another, smaller amount of time for a final rebuttal.

They were excellent antagonists. Each is skillful with words, logical, humorous, widely read, an expert and leader in his own field, and deeply committed to his point of view. Even though they did little actual debating, the mere fact that the two of them would stand on the same platform to offer divergent positions on an issue that concerned a large part of the psychological community marked the occasion as an historic confrontation.

Rogers did not object so much to Skinner's desire to more effectively predict and control human behavior, but he argued that he and Skinner differed over the questions of: Who will be controlled? Who will exercise control? What type of control will be exercised? Most important of all, toward what end or what purpose, or in the pursuit of what value, will control be exercised? On the last question, of ends and values, he characterized Skinner's utopia as a static one in which people were "happy and well-behaved" and maintained that "at a deep philosophic level" *Walden Two* and *1984* are "indistinguishable." Rogers would have humans become "self-directing, self-actualizing, creative, and adaptive." Toward these ends and values he would enlist the help of science. Near his conclusion, he stated, "It is my hope that we have helped to clarify the range of choice which will lie before us and our children in regard to the behavioral sciences. We can choose to use our growing knowledge to enslave people in ways never dreamed of before, depersonalizing them, controlling them by means so carefully selected that they will perhaps never be aware of their loss of personhood. We can choose to utilize our scientific knowledge to make men happy, well-behaved, and productive, as Skinner earlier suggested. Or we can insure that each person learns all the syllabus which we select and set before him, as Skinner now suggests. Or at the other end of the spectrum of choice we can choose to use the behavioral sciences in ways which will free, not control; which will develop creativity, not contentment; which will facilitate each person in his self-directed process of becoming; which will aid individuals, groups, and even the concept of science to become self-transcending in freshly adaptive ways of meeting life and its problems."

Skinner did not see his ideal society in static terms at all. After quoting many of his critics who had characterized *Walden Two* as combining the worst aspects of the Dark Ages and dictatorship, he responded by saying, "One would scarcely guess that the authors are talking about a world in which there is food, clothing, and shelter for all, where everyone chooses his own work and works on the average only 4 hours a day, where music and the arts flourish, where personal relationships develop under the most favorable circumstances, where education prepares every child for the social and intellectual life which lies before him, where—in short—people are truly happy, secure, creative, and forward-looking. What is wrong with it? Only one thing: someone 'planned it that way.' If these critics had come upon a society in some remote corner of the world which boasted similar advantages, they would undoubtedly have hailed it as providing a pattern we all might well follow—provided that it was clearly the result of a natural process of cultural evolution. Any evidence that intelligence had been used in arriving at this version of the good life would, in their eyes, be a serious flaw. No matter if the planner of *Walden Two* diverts none of the proceeds of the community to his own use, no matter if he has no current control or is, indeed, unknown to most of the other members of the community (he planned that, too), somewhere back of it all he occupies the position of prime mover. And this, to the child of the democratic tradition, spoils it all.

"It saddens me to hear Rogers say that 'at a deep philosophic level' *Walden Two* and George Orwell's *1984* 'seem indistinguishable.' They could scarcely be more unlike—at any level. The book *1984* is a picture of immediate aversive control for vicious selfish purposes. The founder of *Walden Two,* on the other hand, has built a community in which neither he nor any other person exerts any *current* control. His achievement lay in his original *plan,* and when he boasts of this ('It is enough to satisfy the thirstiest tyrant') we do not fear him but only pity him for his weakness."

But for Rogers, ". . . in Skinner's presentation here and in his previous writings, there is a serious underestimation of the problem of power. . . . To hope that the power which is being made available by the behavioral sciences will be exercised by the scientists, or by a benevolent group, seems to me a hope little supported by either recent or distant history. It seems far more likely that behavioral scientists, holding their present attitudes, will be in the position of the German rocket scientists specializing in guided missiles. First they worked devotedly for Hitler to destroy the U.S.S.R. and the United States. Now, depending on who captured them, they work devotedly for the U.S.S.R. in the interest of destroying the United States, or devotedly for the United States in the interest of destroying the U.S.S.R. If behavioral scientists are concerned solely with advancing their science, it seems most probable that they will serve the purposes of whatever individual or group has the power."

Richard Evans wrote a short biography of B.F. Skinner and gave a copy of it to Carl Rogers. In the cover he wrote, "To Carl Rogers, without whom Fred Skinner would be at a loss for a protagonist-antagonist whom he really respects." That respect grew not only out of the 1956 symposium, but out of two subsequent meetings they had early in the 1960s. The APA debate was published in *Science* magazine shortly after it took place and has received wide attention, with many requests to reprint it elsewhere. The two subsequent meetings have received very little publicity and many interested people are not aware of their occurrence.

The December 1960, meeting was arranged by the American Academy of Arts and Sciences. They invited twenty-nine outstanding figures in psychology to a closed conference to discuss issues relating to science and society. Skinner delivered one of the papers on "the design of cultures," and Rogers participated in the discussion. Rogers, having penned this note while Skinner spoke, "He avoids, like the plague, the dual questions of choice and values," asked Skinner this question during the discussion period: "From what I understood Dr. Skinner to say, it is his understanding that though he might have thought he chose to come to this meeting, and might have thought he had a purpose in giving this speech, such thoughts are really illusory. He actually made certain marks on paper and emitted certain sounds here, simply because his genetic make-up and his past environment had operantly conditioned his behavior in such a way that it was rewarding to make these sounds, and that he as a person doesn't enter into this. In fact, if I get his thinking correctly, from his strictly scientific point of view, he as a person doesn't exist."

In replying, Skinner said that he would not go into the question of whether he had any choice in the matter, but stated, "I do accept your characterization of my own presence here." (Rogers has said that he admired Skinner's consistency.) Later in the meeting, Rogers proposed that they get a person skilled in operant conditioning to shape the behavior of the individuals in that group, toward the direction of producing a blueprint for a model society. Of course, all irrelevant behaviors toward that end would have to be extinguished, including the humorous stories that had been told at the meeting and Maslow's going to sleep in a comfortable chair. Their personal contact at this meeting was actually minimal, and not for another year and a half would they get a chance to engage in an extended discussion.

This came about in 1962 on June 11 and 12, when B.F. Skinner was in Wisconsin to receive an honorary degree from Ripon College. Students at the University of Minnesota's Duluth campus who learned of this got the idea to invite Skinner and Rogers to come together for two days of meetings. They felt that with the longer time to talk, with a smaller audience, and with an informal, spontaneous agenda, the two men would be much more likely to have a dialogue instead of a debate. Skinner accepted. Rogers was at the University of Wisconsin in Madison when he received the invitation. He wasn't enthusiastic about the idea, but he figured that Minneapolis was only about four hours away from Madison and that since Skinner had to travel all the way from Harvard, he would probably say no. When he found out that Skinner already *had* accepted and that the invitation had come not from the Minneapolis campus but from the Duluth Campus, then another three hours north, he had no choice but to follow through on his commitment.

The format allowed for fifteen minutes of opening remarks by each of the principals, a break, then an hour and fifteen minutes of discussion between them. That evening an invited panel would discuss the issues raised, and the audience would then break into small groups to continue the discussion themselves. The next morning Rogers and

Skinner would have another hour and a quarter of discussion, a question-and-answer period with the audience for an hour, and then a final opportunity for brief closing remarks. After the program chairman introduced Rogers and Skinner, and pointed out that this would be a dialogue, with no debating or speechmaking, he called upon Rogers to begin with his short summary of the issues which separated the two of them. Rogers proceeded to give a fifteen-minute speech on the importance of the humanist movement in psychology, philosophy, religion, and politics. Next came Skinner's turn.

"Thank you very much, Dr. Gladstein. . . . I always make the same mistake! When debating with Carl Rogers I always assume that he will make no effort to influence the audience. [Laughter.] And then I have to follow him and speak as I am speaking now to a group of people who are very far from free to accept my views. [Laughter.]

"In fact, I was just reminded of a story that I once heard about Carl Rogers, and I'll tell it now hoping to confirm or have him deny it. I suppose it is apocryphal; at least I'm sure it has grown in its dimensions. The story as I heard it is as follows: Carl Rogers was never much of a duck hunter, but he was persuaded upon one occasion to go duck hunting. He and some friends went into a blind and sat on a dreary, cold early dawn, and no ducks arrived, until the very end of the time when shooting was possible. Finally, one lone duck came in and his friends allowed him to shoot, and he did. At the same time, along the shore a few hundred yards away, another man shot at the same duck. The duck fell—plop. Dr. Rogers got out of the blind and started toward the duck. The other man got out of his blind and started toward the same duck. They arrived at the same moment. Dr. Rogers turned to him and said, 'You feel that this is your duck.' [Much laughter.] The reason I was reminded of that story was that the end of it is that Dr. Rogers brought the duck home. [Laughter.] I shall do my best to prevent a similar . . . [Laughter]."

From that point on, the dialogue became friendly, often personal, filled with humor, and punctuated with laughter by both speakers and the audience. Rogers, of course, was compelled to reply to the duck hunting story, which had some basis in truth. He once *had* been duck hunting with his brother in Wyoming, had shot a duck which had fallen, and did wade out in the shallow lake only to find another duck hunter who also claimed the bird as his. (Later he wondered: "It's a story I thought only our two families knew. I don't know where the hell he picked that up.") The only difference was in how the story ended. As he explained to the audience, "I'm sure I don't know how word of that got to Harvard; but there's a great deal of truth in that story, except for the punch line. Instead of saying, 'You feel that you shot the duck,' we resorted instead to a procedure very highly regarded in scientific circles—we flipped a coin, and that proved that I had shot the duck [Much laughter]."

The next morning the roles were reversed, with Skinner now using his opening remarks to give a long speech with an emphatic ending. This time it was Rogers' turn to comment, "Dr. Skinner told me he got up early this morning. I didn't know he got up *that* early [Much laughter]."

They covered a good deal of ground in their several hours together. Their topics included utopias, the role of the behavioral sciences, the nature of freedom, the importance of feelings and the subjective life, education, child rearing, the nature of verbal behavior, creativity, and science. Rogers was very pleased to hear some of the things Skinner had to say, for they seemed to speak directly to some of the points he had raised in their first debate and in the December 1960 meeting.

At one point, for example, Skinner said he was "very much concerned about the possible misuse of the behavioral technology." At another point he said he would choose creativity as one of the traits of citizens in his ideal society. Previously Rogers had criticized Skinner's utopia as characterized by only "static" values, that is, a "happy, productive, and well-behaved" citizenry. On the subject of feelings and subjective experience, Skinner spoke very eloquently of his own inner life—his love of music, his angry feelings which occasionally surprised and dismayed him—but denied that these emotions had any "causal efficacy" in influencing his behavior. His statements about feelings and subjective experience left Rogers somewhat uncertain as to where Skinner stood on that issue. Rogers quipped, "At one point yesterday, he said with real conviction, 'I believe. . . .' I was so shaken by this, I've forgotten just what it was he believed [Laughter]."

One subject that came up frequently was the both ancient and modern dilemma between free will and determinism. To a questioner who asked, "Is a subjective feeling of freedom sufficient evidence that this freedom is real and that man is not subject to the control of his genetic and environmental conditions?" Rogers summed up this position by saying, "I think that that indicates some misunderstanding of the point of view I've presented, because as I've said, I feel in thorough agreement with Dr. Skinner—that, viewed from the external scientific, objective perspective, man is determined by his genetic and cultural influences. I've also said that, in an entirely different dimension, such things as freedom and choice are extremely real. . . . I would remind you of the example I gave you of Victor Frankl in the concentration camp. It would be very interesting to try to tell him that the freedom of choice which remained to himself was completely unreal. He knew it was real, because he saw people who did not exercise that, who felt that they were completely controlled, die like flies. For the ones who had the best chance of survival were the ones who still retained the concept that 'I am a person. I choose.' And so for me, this is an entirely different dimension which is not easily reconcilable to the deterministic point of view. I look at it as being similar to the situation in physics, where you can prove that the wave theory of light is supported by evidence; so is the corpuscular theory. The two of them are contradictory. They're not at the present state of knowledge reconcilable; but I think one would only be narrowing his perception of physics to deny one of these and accept only the other. And it is in this same sense— that's why I keep using the term paradox—that I regard these two dimensions as *both* real, although they exist in a paradoxical relationship."

Sometimes their communication was not very effective, as when Rogers said of Skinner, "I'm not quite sure who it is he's talking to, but somehow he's not talking to *me,*" and later Skinner spoke of how "you and I ought to be able to analyze verbal behavior better than that." On the other hand there were several times when real understanding did occur between the two, as when a questioner referred to an article Skinner had written and Rogers answered:

"I welcome being reminded of that article of Dr. Skinner's in the *American Psychologist,* which was a very inspiring article on the processes of science as he had experienced them in his own career. . . . I hadn't quite thought of that in relation to this discussion. As I remember that article, Dr. Skinner there gives a very vivid picture of the scientific life as process, and this is exactly the kind of thing which I've been trying to describe as the "Good Life" from any angle—that far from knowing where he was going to come out, he had to live in process and had to let learnings emerge as they emerged, and they shaped his behavior, and so on. Now, somehow this makes me feel a great deal better about Dr. Skinner [Laughter]—to realize that in his own life he values that emerging unpredictable process, and I guess what I've been trying to say about the kind of culture I would want to design and the kind of outcomes I see in therapy when therapy is successful, is it leads to exactly that kind of thing—that the individual becomes an ongoing process of life in which the outcome is not set. There are *not* static goals. You don't even know whether you will come out happy. You are living this on a day-by-day basis, endeavoring to be open to all your experience—this was another aspect of that article, of endeavoring to be open to all aspects of what had occurred in order to learn from them. . . . On this we would really get together, because this sense of life as a process which can only be existentially lived if it is to be meaningful—that makes all kinds of sense—makes to me much more sense than saying, 'Here is where we should come out, and we must plan it that way.' "

To which Skinner replied: "This may be an historic moment. I think I have been changed by that argument. The point of that article was actually to criticize the codification of science by methodologists, statisticians, design of experiment people, who having very little experience with science as it is practiced, try to tell you how the scientist works. I think it's a great mistake to teach our young psychologists science in the form of statistics, because this has very little to do with actual scientific practice. However, I'm not going to concede everything, because I am interested in teaching scientific practice as such, and I should suppose that with skillful planning one could make sure that more people would be the product of lucky histories of this sort than is now the case. I'm sure I've had a great deal of luck which has not only directed me in profitable directions, but has kept me going by the very lucky schedule of reinforcement which I've experienced. But I think this ought to be viewed as a very important factor in building scientific dedication, and some of it can be arranged. Although I quite agree that you cannot foresee all of the courses it's going to take, and I'm now beginning to understand what you mean by 'becoming.' " [Applause.]

Some of Rogers' closing remarks aptly captured the tone and context of the memorable dialogue.

"I would like to say, I've acquired an increasing respect for Dr. Skinner, the person—his sincerity, gentleness, his wit, his wide scholarly interests, the honesty with which he is trying to face the implications of the directions in which the behavioral sciences are taking us. I certainly have learned deeply from him, both in the past and during these meetings. I have often felt and would like to say that I think he is the one person in the behavioral stream of psychology who has really had a highly significant impact on our society and our culture, and I respect his work.

"I think that there do remain some profound differences between us, though I think definitely less than when these discussions commenced.

But I suspect that the deeper differences will not be reconciled by us. They will be reconciled by you [the audience] and by other people. One thing that I thought might come up for mention in this discussion, but it hasn't so far, is that—I don't know whether Dr. Skinner is aware of this—but a former student of his and a former student of mine are working together on developing a programmed instruction for the improvement of interpersonal relationships. . . . [Laughter.]

"There's one helpful, hopeful and ironic thing that I'd like to mention: For a man who believes that value and choice and purpose really retain very little of their ordinary meaning in a scientific world, there is just no question but what Dr. Skinner's work has stirred up, will continue to stir up, enormous controversy over choice, of values and purpose and the directions that we choose to go. And in this sense I feel he's really on *my* side because that's exactly what I would like to do, too. That's the way I see the purpose of this meeting, that we have tried to expose various points of view, various possible purposes, various values in regard to education, in regard to the design of a future culture—and that the choice of those values is something that we all will be working on over the years to come."

Rogers had the impression that all the sessions, which had been taped, would be made available to the public, on tape or transcripts. On several occasions he indicated that "the only thing I've ever regretted about any of our meetings is that Skinner has never been willing to release the full transcript, nor even the full tape recordings, of our nine hours [sic] of encounter in Duluth in 1962." They both did give permission to the American Academy of Psychotherapists to condense the entire dialogue into one tape and make this available to the public. (Apparently Skinner eventually agreed to the release of the entire dialogue, as these were finally made available in 1975.)

Of course, the debate did not end in 1962, although Rogers and Skinner did not confront each other publicly after this. The bigger debate continues to this day. In 1947 Rogers had written, "Significant problems of social philosophy are also involved in these diverging attitudes regarding therapy. If objective study supports the conclusion that dependence, guidance, and expert direction of the client's therapy and life are necessary . . . , then a social philosophy of expert control is clearly implied. If further research indicates that the client has at least the latent capacity to understand and guide himself, then a psychological basis for democracy would have been demonstrated. It is therefore an issue in which sound research is vital."

If, for example, the behaviorists or humanists could clearly demonstrate a solution to the problem of drug addiction, it might influence a great deal of legislation, funding, and social action. On the other hand, the changes that take place in society at large could also help determine the fate of the behaviorist and humanist models. If crime, drug abuse, alcoholism, racial tensions, alienation, energy shortages, corruption in government, deterioration in the educational system, inability to set social goals and priorities, and other similar human and value problems continue or grow, people will eventually grasp at any solutions which seem capable of solving the problems. Some individuals will see the behaviorists as having the best answers, others will see the humanists. Then it will be in state and national legislatures, not in laboratories and classrooms, where the future of psychology will be discussed. There are many complex political, economic, and social forces which influence funding, legislation, and mass opinion, which in turn influence the evolution of the physical and social sciences. The issues of political power, values, ends and means, which Rogers and Skinner raised in their various discussions and writings, might ultimately decide how their work will be used by future generations.

I would be remiss in closing this chapter without acknowledging the important recent advances in drug therapy, developmental psychology, and other areas that bear upon these issues but are beyond the scope of this biography, or without questioning the dichotomy between behaviorism and humanism that has been assumed throughout this discussion.

Rogers hinted about a possible reconciliation in his closing remarks with Skinner in 1962, but as Carl Pitts wrote in 1973, "There is an argument going on today in psychology which, like most arguments, dichotomizes into bipolar, antagonistic points what are assumed to be two different 'schools' of thought, humanism and behaviorism. Crudely put, the humanists seem to view the behaviorists as manipulative, depersonalizing, and controlling slaves to scientism, concerned with forcing men into submission, conformity, and docility. The behaviorists view humanists as soft-headed, non-scientific, vague, sentimental, and hopelessly caught up in nonoperational, meaningless values. The charges have been made public and the battle lines set, particularly since the now famous Rogers and Skinner debate."

Rogers, in the symposium with Skinner and on other occasions, acknowledged that the client-centered therapist is engaged in the reinforcement and control of the client's behavior. To a group of graduate students at the University of Rochester, he said, ". . . if you think of therapy as operant conditioning and certainly there is enough evidence in that field to make us think very seriously about the meaning of that—then I've come to feel that perhaps my hypothesis would be that effective therapy consists in the reinforcing of all experienced feelings. So then when you have reinforced *all* the feelings of the individual, then he can *be* all of those and he can be himself." To Skinner and the APA he said, "As therapists, we institute certain attitudinal conditions, and the client has relatively little voice in the establishment of these conditions. We predict that if these conditions are instituted, certain behavior consequences will ensue in the client. Up to this point this is largely external control, no different from what Skinner has described. . . . But here any similarity ceases."

The main difference, in his opinion, was that of ends. While the humanists were attempting to help clients become more self-directing, Rogers feared that the behavior techniques would be used increasingly to externally control individuals' behavior. Commenting on a 1961 article by Rogers in which he had voiced this concern, Pitts wrote that "recent work in behavioral psychology . . . has not fulfilled the warning of 12 years ago. Behaviorists have been and are increasingly concerned about teaching self-direction."

At the University of Minnesota, for example, Drs. Ann Duncan and Wells Hively have taught behavior modification techniques to teenagers in therapy and their parents. The teenagers and parents set their own goals. One wants to control his temper more effectively, another wants to be more accepting of her child, a third wants to pick at her face less often, a fourth wants to lose weight, and so on. Each person is given a "wrist counter," an attractive leather bracelet with moveable beads. Once the desired behaviors are clearly identified for each person (each compliment the mother gives; each time the desire to pick at her face is resisted; etc.), they begin to count on their wrist counters how often the desired behavior occurs each day. They learn to chart and graph the data they are gathering about themselves. Their own satisfaction in noticing their own positive behavior is reinforcing, and the desired behaviors increase in frequency. In group sessions they report on their progress, receive further information from the group, discuss problems and identify new goals. Had the term not already been appropriated by the humanists, these behavior therapists might well be called "facilitators."

Pitts gave other examples of behaviorists who were teaching their clients to be independent and self-directing. Rogers, responding to the

Pitts article with appreciation, concluded by saying, "In my estimation, behaviorists have come a long way in admitting the human being with his capacity for choice and decision and subjective appraisal back into the realm of psychology. In other words, they are rapidly becoming humanistic in their approach, and now the only discussion is what methods can the individual choose to most effectively change his behavior."

Continuing to observe this new trend in behaviorism, Rogers wrote in 1977, "In fairness to behaviorists it should be said that many of them have come to adopt a greatly changed view of the politics of relationships. In the commune Twin Oaks, patterned initially after Walden II, the residents often choose for themselves which behaviors they wish to change, and select the rewards which will be most reinforcing. Clearly this is completely opposed to the politics of the strict behaviorist, since it is self-initiated, self-evaluated change. It is not the environment shaping the individual's behavior, but the individual choosing to shape the environment for her own personal development."

CHAPTER 9
The Wisconsin Years
1957-1963

Many people are familiar with Carl Rogers' work as founder of client-centered therapy and researcher at the University of Chicago and are also familiar with his later role in the encounter group movement and education. But the seven-year interim is a time of which little is known, even by Rogers' followers, and a time which Rogers himself often wished he could forget. He once called it "the most painful and anguished episode in my whole professional life."

His dream in moving to the University of Wisconsin was never fulfilled. The hope of having psychologists and psychiatrists working together on joint training and research projects never materialized to any great degree. No great precedents were set in the education and training of psychologists and psychiatrists. His joint appointment in Psychology and Psychiatry enabled him to work in both realms, but helped little in bringing the two together.

Which is not to say he didn't make a valiant effort. After having worked most of his professional life with relatively mildly disturbed individuals, "neurotics" as they would often be classified, he was eager to see if his hypotheses about the necessary and sufficient condition of personality change worked also with seriously disturbed and with normal populations. His occasional experience with more seriously disturbed individuals told him it did. The joint appointment at Wisconsin gave him the opportunity to test this question through more careful research. Using much of the $561,035 in funding he had obtained from sources outside the University, and working under the auspices of the Psychiatric Institute in the Department of Psychiatry of the University, he set up a pioneering research project on the treatment of schizophrenics and normals through the therapeutic relationship.

A group of forty-eight subjects, comprised of patients at the Mendota State Hospital and of normal, volunteer adults from the community, was selected for the study. Sixteen "more chronic" schizophrenics (those who had been hospitalized for more than eight months), sixteen "more acute" schizophrenics (those who had been hospitalized for less than eight months), and sixteen "normals" comprised the total of forty-eight. Each group of sixteen was composed of eight matched pairs, that is, individuals who were similar to each other on the basis of sex, age, socio-educational status and degree of psychological disturbance. By the flip of a coin, one member of each pair was selected for therapy. The other would serve as the "control." If the patients who received therapy changed during and after the therapy, and if their matched control did not change, then it could be said that the change was due to the therapy and not to some other factor. Eight therapists, Rogers one of them, worked with three clients each. The clients took a battery of research instruments at three- and six-month intervals. In addition, one independent interviewer, who had nothing else to do with the research, held a "sampling interview" with each of the forty-eight subjects early in the study and every three months thereafter.

Actually, Rogers and his colleagues were putting their theories to a hard test. This was not a simple case where half of the group received therapy and the other half did not. Every patient in Mendota State Hospital received a great deal of attention normally—recreational programs, group therapy, occupational therapy, and so on. The question really was: Would the group that received all the treatment offered by a modern, efficient hospital *plus* individual psychotherapy do any better than the group which received all the treatment offered by a modern, efficient hospital? If the experimental group did improve more than the controls, it would indicate that the individual therapy was powerful indeed. Another problem for the therapists in the research project was that establishing a therapeutic relationship with schizophrenics and with normals was a very different thing from conducting therapy with individuals who came voluntarily to a clinic seeking help. The normals in the study often felt that they did not need therapy, and although they had volunteered to participate in a psychological study and to spend time doing it, they were reluctant to go into their personal lives in great depth and tended to stay on a rather superficial level of discussion. The schizophrenics, on the other hand, were often extremely reluctant even to talk to the therapists. When they found out that the therapists could not get them discharged from the hospital, they were reluctant to spend time with a "talking doctor." They often felt they did not need help, or they were very fearful, withdrawn persons who cringed at any physical or emotional closeness the therapist offered. These and other problems made it very difficult for the therapists even to begin their therapeutic contacts with their prospective clients.

To make it more difficult, Rogers and most of his colleagues in the research had little or no experience working with such seriously disturbed individuals. They had hoped to have several therapists from the hospital staff and from other than a client-centered orientation participate in the research; but when these other therapists heard that every interview was to be recorded, they declined to participate in the study. Consequently, Rogers and the others had to develop their own methods of reaching the patients and, eventually, came up with several creative means of making contact, building trust, and offering and starting a therapeutic relationship with the schizophrenic subjects.

One thing Rogers and his colleagues learned was that they needed to be much more active in the interviews and to use their own feelings more to demonstrate their congruence, understanding, and caring. One of Rogers' patients, for example, had remained silent and withdrawn for thirteen minutes; so Rogers said, softly and slowly, "I kind of feel like saying that 'If it would be of any help at all I'd like to come in'. On the other hand, if it's something you'd rather . . . if you just feel more like being within yourself, why that's ok, too. . . . I guess another thing I'm saying, really, in saying that is, 'I do care. I'm not just sitting here like a stick.' " Then, after another minute, he added, "And I guess your silence is saying to me that either you don't want to or can't come out right now, and that's ok. So I won't pester you, but I just want you to know I'm here."

On another occasion, Charles Truax recalled, one of Rogers' patients "was about ready to be discharged from the hospital, and some aide on the ward said something about he wasn't going to get discharged or something like that, and he just blew his lid, flipped out, and got very upset. When Carl came out to the hospital and met him, he talked to him like a Dutch uncle. 'What do you mean getting upset? Who is he to listen to? To hell with him!' And so on. He was mad because he had put in a lot of time with this patient and here he was blowing it, stupidly. And I think he communicated very well to that man, 'I care. I care very much what happens to you.' "

To measure the process of the therapy, Rogers and his colleagues developed several new instruments. These were based on other instruments which had just been used in some shorter studies. Halkides and Barrett-Lennard, for example, had just tested Rogers' hypothesis about the necessary and sufficient conditions of therapeutic personality change. They found that therapist congruence, empathy, and unconditional positive regard were, in fact, correlated with positive outcomes in therapy. For this major new research program, discrete scales for congruence, developed by Donald Kiesler, and for accurate empathy and unconditional positive regard, developed by Charles Truax, were employed.

Another scale which was being used measured *the process of psychotherapy.* Over the years, Rogers had changed from describing therapy as a nondirective technique to a client-centered attitude to a person-to-person relationship. In this person-to-person relationship where the therapeutic conditions are present, Rogers said, a process of therapeutic personality change would be initiated. It was Rogers' student Eugene Gendlin who began to explore and who helped Rogers to understand in greater depth what this therapeutic process is which the client undergoes. It centered around Gendlin's theory of experiencing.

In Gendlin's view, the individual has within him a continually changing process of experiencing going on at all times. This experiencing includes the person's perceptions, his thoughts, his memories, his feelings, but also the meanings he attaches to all these in the present moment. Some of his experiencing, hunger for example, may be readily accessible to his awareness. Other parts of his experiencing, some feelings of fear perhaps, may be less accessible. The defensively organized person, to varying degrees, is not aware of his experiencing or constructs it in a rigid manner. He denies that he is angry when really he is. He might always experience black people in a rigid, stereotyped way. He might believe he is unlovable, when almost everyone who knows him well expresses their affection and caring for him. In the latter case he clings rigidly to one of his "personal constructs," thus denying a major part of his experiencing. In therapy the client becomes more aware of his inner experiencing, becomes less defensively organized as he admits more of his experiencing into his awareness, and develops more flexible and realistic constructs about the world and about himself. Since his experiencing is always changing, he lives flexibly, continually open to and consulting his experiencing as a guide to his behavior.

Rogers gave much thought to Gendlin's concept of experiencing. When, in 1957, he was at Wisconsin for a semester as Knapp Honorary Professor, he spent many long hours listening to tape recordings of interviews, trying to discover what patterns could be discerned in the client's changing manner of experiencing over the course of therapy. His address to the American Psychological Association in 1957, as the previous year's recipient of the Distinguished Scientific Contribution Award, described his emerging "process conception of psychotherapy." In later articles he developed this conception further. He formulated a seven-point scale to indicate where a person is in his manner of experiencing. On the lower ends of the scale, the individual's feelings and personal meanings are unrecognized and unexpressed; he is remote from or unaware of his inner experiencing; where there is incongruence between what the person is experiencing and what he is expressing, he is unaware of the incongruence; there is a lack of communication of self; experience is construed rigidly, and the person sees his constructions not as his own perception or generalization but as fact; he does not recognize his problems or his responsibility in relation to his problems or there is no desire to change; he avoids close relationships as being dangerous.

For an example of someone at the extreme low end of this scale, one might picture the paranoid schizophrenic. He is sure "they" are out to get him. His failures are never his own; "they" are responsible. Sometimes he has these strange feelings inside him, but they are not "his own." They are being sent into him through the people on the television. He does not want to get close to anyone on the ward or even the therapist, for such exposure would make him vulnerable and be very dangerous.

On the other end of the process scale, at stages six and seven, the individual fully experiences his feelings and personal meanings; he frequently tunes into his inner experiencing and uses it as a major referent to understand himself; any incongruence is temporary only because he is constantly referring to his inner experiencing; because he is so in touch with his inner experience his communication of self is rich and varied; his constructs and generalization about himself and his world are tentative, flexible, subject to change as new data emerge in his experiencing; he accepts responsibility for his problems; he relates to others openly and freely on the basis of his immediate experiencing.

What Rogers was doing was exemplifying the thrust of humanistic psychology by describing "mental health" in concrete terms, by moving from a conception of sickness or disturbance or maladjustment to its implied opposite—what he shortly came to call the "fully functioning person." This was the last major stage in his developing theory of personality change; his later years were spent exploring new applications of theory and methods to other fields.

Rogers and his colleagues developed ways to measure the subtle differences among stages. What the process scale could do was demonstrate at what point the client was when he entered therapy and where he was at any particular time during or after the therapy. In fact Rogers and his associates found this was possible even by taking only four-minute samples of the therapy dialogue and having these rated by independent judges. In the research on schizophrenics they went so far as to train undergraduates who had absolutely no relationship to the research project to rate these four-minute samples. Their reasoning was that if these novices who had practically no prior understanding of the process of therapy could be trained to identify accurately where individual clients were on the process continua (they could), and if these independent judges' ratings would correlate highly with one another (they did), then it could be demonstrated that this was a reliable way of measuring an individual's degree of psychological maturity.

Armed with these new tools for research on psychotherapy, plus many of those which had been longer established in the field, the Psychotherapy Research Group or the "Schiz Project," as it was often called, was able to proceed, gathering the data which would support or negate their hypotheses. Although there were several hypotheses stated by the research group, these narrowed down to the interrelationships among three variables: therapist conditions (congruence, empathy, and unconditional positive regard), process level and movement (on the seven-stage scale), and outcomes of therapy. The latter was determined on the basis of traditional psychological tests, evaluations by ward personnel, release from the hospital, and the like. The overall direction of the hypotheses was to suggest that: The greater the therapist conditions in therapy, the greater would be the client's movement along the process scale, and the greater would be the positive outcomes of therapy; and these differences would be greater with the therapy group than with the control group.

Were the hypotheses confirmed by the mountains of data gathered —the storeroom bulging with hundreds of taped interviews, the volumes of transcribed interviews, test results and analyses, the scores of research reports written? As early as 1958, when Rogers began to describe their research study at professional meetings, many segments of the psychotherapeutic community eagerly awaited the results. Their curiosity, however, was not to be settled fully for nine more years, in 1967, when *The Therapeutic Relationship and Its Impact: A Study of Psychotherapy with Schizophrenics,* "edited by Carl R. Rogers with the collaboration of Eugene T. Gendlin, Donald J. Kiesler and Charles B. Truax," was published by the University of Wisconsin Press. The long interim was a time of frequent stress, conflict, and crisis, at times so serious that the research project was almost terminated, numerous legal suits were threatened, and the book's publication was jeopardized.

Some of the major protagonists in the long, agonizing story were presented by Rogers in his introduction to their 625-page volume: "Though the many individuals who shared in this enterprise are named in a separate section, I would like to mention several whose leadership was especially significant in making the program what it is. Dr. Eugene T. Gendlin initiated the program, with all of the detailed arrangements which that implies, and has contributed a basic theoretical formulation upon which a number of our process measures have been built. Dr. Charles B. Truax organized the initial data collection and analysis. The ratings on which his studies were based mysteriously disappeared and have not been recovered. This unfortunate fact made Dr. Traux' preliminary reports unusable in this book. Dr. Donald J. Kiesler gave leadership to the rerating and re-analysis of all the data, and has shown a high degree of determination, efficiency, and research competence in carrying through this task."

In Rogers' own opinion, the problem began when he failed to take the time and care needed to allow the Psychotherapy Research Group to become a truly group-centered, self-directing group. He had accomplished this at Chicago, but, being occupied with many other projects, long speaking trips and visiting professorships, did not give it the necessary attention at Wisconsin. The trouble surfaced during his long absence from Wisconsin in the summer of 1962 through the spring of 1963, when Rogers spent a year as a Fellow at the Center for Advanced

Study in the Behavioral Sciences at Stanford. Rogers began to receive letters from many different members of the project that one person in the research group, Charles (Charlie) Truax, was attempting to subvert the project toward his own ends. First they claimed that he had refused to give them access to the project data on which they could do their studies. Then it was said that someone had discovered in Truax's office a pile of manuscripts based on project data that contained Truax's individual copyright. Their conclusion was that he intended to use the entire project data to publish a work under his own name. To add insult to injury, they said, he even had used the title that everyone expected would appear on their joint publication.*

As it turned out, Truax was scheduled to be in California shortly, and Rogers arranged a meeting with him. He assured Rogers that the rumors were false, that several misunderstandings had contributed to them, and that it could all be worked out when Rogers returned to Madison. Meanwhile most of the Project staff in Madison was clamoring for his dismissal for unethical behavior. Rogers took the slower course of trying to go through channels to bring pressure to bear upon him to release the data that was in his control, which he had by now removed to his own home. When pressure by the University finally was put upon him to release the data, the boom fell. He called the police to declare that the project data had been stolen. To this day it has not been found, nor has any clear evidence been uncovered as to what happened to it.

When Rogers heard the latest episode, he decided to act, but again chose a slower course than many of the Project staff were urging him to do. In a letter to Donald Kiesler and Philippa Mathieu he admitted, "Yes, I am probably slow in taking such actions. It takes a long time to convince me that a person is intentionally unethical, and intentionally destructive. . . ."

Some readers might be inclined to react, "Aha, that's where his optimistic picture of human nature gets him." Another student close to Rogers saw it somewhat differently. "Sure, Rogers' trusting nature gets him into trouble sometimes. But hundreds of times it's worked,

*These and subsequent events were corroborated by several independent sources. I had written to Truax for general information on Rogers, but also specifically asked for his perspective on "the troubles at Wisconsin." Although Truax sent me a lengthy tape, with a great deal of information about his relationship with Rogers over the years, there was a fifteen minute or so gap in the tape (this was just about the time of Watergate!) just when he would have been discussing this period. I intended to write him again, but later learned from several sources that he had committed suicide, following what appeared to be a long history of psychological difficulties.

and think of the added benefits he's gotten from all those relationships."

At any rate, the time lapse had given Truax the chance to contact other forces in the University who disliked Rogers and to build his own support base. He also threatened the University with a lawsuit if they attempted to dismiss him from the project. The Rogers group could not muster the support it needed to take the action they wanted. Moreover, Rogers didn't want their scientific endeavor to be associated with scandal and controversy. He resigned himself to Truax's remaining with the project. Later he wrote that "one of my serious mistakes was not firing Charlie immediately. By the time that I was really convinced that he was a scoundrel and presented the case against him through the Psychiatric Institute and stated my determination to fire him, they not only would not concur in the action but would not even permit me to take the action, which was a very humiliating situation."

Then began the long period of painstaking reanalysis of all the data upon which scores of studies had already been based. New judges had to be trained to listen to the recorded interviews, new data had to be obtained from the hundreds of test instruments the patients and therapists had taken, new statistical operations were required to analyze all this data. Donald Kiesler and Philippa Mathieu, with the help of Marjorie Klein, eventually completed the task and wrote up the results in several chapters in the "Schiz book."

But this solution to the stolen data presented still a new set of problems. Having to redo a major part of the research created an entirely new staffing hierarchy in the leadership of the project. It also meant that the original contributions anticipated from the various project leaders would not be fulfilled and other individuals would be making contributions which were much greater than had been expected. Therefore the question of credit and authorship for the book increasingly became a major issue. Rogers, Gendlin, and Kiesler felt that Truax should no longer be one of the major editors. Rogers, however, believed that they were bound by a prior written agreement which said that Rogers, Gendlin, Kiesler, *and* Truax would be the editors, and that they would be likely to have a lawsuit on their hands if they attempted to do otherwise. This created bad feelings from Gendlin and Kiesler, who believed that Rogers should take a stand on having only three editors anyway, lawsuit or not. To further complicate matters, Gendlin felt strongly that Philippa Mathieu should be added to the list of editors because of all the work she had done in redoing the data collection and analysis. Mathieu agreed, but did not feel strongly about this and never complained to Rogers; but Gendlin thought she was being taken advantage of. Kiesler, on the other hand, was equally adamant that Mathieu should *not* be an editor, that she was given ample credit throughout the book, and that four editors was one too many already, and he was very certain he did not want a fifth. By this time Rogers had left Wisconsin and was living in California permanently, Kiesler had moved to the University of Iowa, Gendlin was at the University of Chicago, and the publisher, the University of Wisconsin Press, was in Madison. Resolving the problem through letters proved to be an impossible task. Letters would cross in the mail; misunderstandings occurred; a long silence by Gendlin was interpreted by Rogers as agreement, only to be followed months later by Gendlin's informing them that he was still not satisfied and they could not use his chapters in the book until he was satisfied. Instead of improving, the situation deteriorated. Dozens of letters and many angry words went back and forth.

In 1966, in August, Kiesler wrote to Rogers and Gendlin:

> Our basic problem, as I see it, is that good men sometimes castrate themselves by not acting at the proper time. I don't think Carl acted (he should have immediately fired Charlie, and denounced him to NIMH): Gene had a lawyer, but didn't use him. Now, Gene has to stand for something, so he is backing us toward the precipice. But his stand is at the wrong time and for the wrong reason. But it makes him feel better, because he knows he didn't act when he should have. [Then, after another two pages of analysis:] So my proposed strategy: If this letter leaves Gene unshaken then nothing will budge him. But neither will I budge, because *my* appropriate time to act is now. This is my moment —and unlike both of you I will not compromise a position I feel is just. If I did, I would later, like Gene, have to do something impulsive to prove that I'm still in possession of integrity. And, like Gene, it would probably involve the wrong target and certainly the wrong time. . . . So I say, if Gene does not budge, then we're finished—unless you Carl, agree to remove his name and chapters from the book.

The same month, on the very official-looking legal stationery of Kirkland, Ellis, Hodson, Chaffetz and Masters of Prudential Plaza in Chicago, Gendlin's lawyer wrote Rogers a strong letter indicating that "our client may be irreparably damaged (1) if the work is published without identification of Dr. Gendlin's role, or (2) if the work is published with an identification of Dr. Gendlin's role that has not been approved by him." But "in an effort to bring the current dispute to a quick and amicable settlement," the addition of Mathieu's name as editor, and a few related, minor changes, would suffice.

Rogers immediately wrote Kiesler, asking for his reaction to Gendlin's lawyer, and Kiesler quickly replied,

> You're squirming, sliding, and slipping again . . . your letter of August 29 is completely inappropriate. . . . I gave you my decision. . . . If the authorship is changed from its present format without my approval, then I'll have to get in this legal act. . . . I've completed my job for you, and in case you've forgotten, very efficiently and competently with much sweat. . . . Don't look to me for any more creative solutions. This is your baby. And realize that I want this book to come out since I think it's a good contribution. But I will not let it come out, *ever*, if you change your stand on the *four* major authors.

This was one of the most "unsuccessful" episodes in Rogers' career. His successes were so frequent and varied that one is inclined to view him as some kind of archetypal, benign father figure, all-knowing and wholly consistent. To view him at a time when he was most fallible presents a different perspective. His final letter in this exchange shows a very real human being, with strengths and weaknesses combined.

September 12, 1966

Dear Gene and Don:

> . . . Now that the deadlock between the two of you is absolute and complete, I will wait a while until I have cooled off and then I will make my decision as to what the spine, the cover, the title page, and the author list will be. I am in no hurry to make that decision but I will let you know when I do make it. I can assure you that I will try to take into account every factor and will make the fairest decision I can, but I will make it.
>
> I probably would be able to make the decision in such a way that I would then be sued by all of you—Gene, Don, and Charlie. This will give me all the joys of triple litigation to which, of course, I look forward with enormous pleasure and anticipation. I can't quite wait to see the judge's face when he realizes that you have been irreparably damaged in your personal lives and professional careers by: having had included in the book all of the chapters which you have submitted for it and having been given full opportunity for editing those chapters in the way that you see fit; when your names are prominently displayed as major authors and full and explicit credit has been given you, not only on the author's page but in the acknowledgements and introduction; when the important parts you have played in the research have been fully explicated and commended. He may be a bit baffled to realize that the damage you have suffered is because the name of one person, whom we all sincerely agree should be given special credit, appears in type which is either too large

or too small, which is either above or below a certain line, which either appears on one page or two or on the cover also. I am sure he will be sympathetic in realizing that this has cast a black shadow over your total career.

I am also sure that the judge can do nothing but rule in your favor when he realizes how righteous you both are. It makes me regret that one of the scales we never developed was one for self-righteousness. The correspondence we have had on this topic of authorship could then be submitted to a group of bright undergraduates for a "blind" rating as to who is the most righteous of the three—Charlie, Gene, or Don. I had always thought Charlie would win hands down, but I have had increasing doubts. I seem to be the only one who has made mistakes, but since those are glaringly evident to both of you I do not need to go into them.

I guess the above gets rid of some of the bitterness that I feel about all of this. I have tried to hold it back in recent months, hoping against hope that some amicable decision could be reached. I feel I have failed at this for the same reason that I have failed with Charlie. I really don't know how to deal with people who never in their lives have made a mistake, and whose every action and impulse has been perfectly right. It must be very pleasant to live in such a world. Some people feel that this is a very childish and immature world but, of course, you two know that it is not.

I also think of, and this is not intended as a criticism, but just as a fact of life, my enormous depression when I first read some of Don's chapters. They were so dull! Some people here who had been reading the manuscript with interest waded part way into Don's chapters and then quit in despair. I know Gene has never read them, because he made suggestions about Chapter 5, which were absolutely contradicted by Don's chapters. My own optimistic estimate is that out of every million people who might hear of the book, possibly 500 might buy it or start to read it, and five would complete the reading of Don's chapters. I hope I am wrong but only time can tell.

Well, I see the bitterness is still coming out. Let me try to express some of the other feelings which are mingled with it. I think back to the day when I felt so gleeful because Gene had agreed to come and initiate the project and I knew he had the skills and aptitudes which would make that possible where I did not. I felt then and feel now enormous gratitude that he was willing to undertake that task and for all that he has done since to carry the project through. I think of the great satisfaction I felt when Don agreed to take the responsibility for trying to redo the research which Charlie had made such a mess of, a mess which I handled rather poorly at 2500 miles distance. In spite of what I have said above about the dullness, I do appreciate the incredible amount of effort which Don, Philippa, and Marge put into the production of those chapters and I sincerely hope that some readers will appreciate their dedicated thoroughness.

I guess that lets you know where I stand as of this moment. Sincerely, Carl.

Rogers, recognizing the strength of his feelings and giving expression to them, drew an instant reaction from Kiesler, who wrote:

Dear Leader:

   Congratulations! For the first time I've known you you've decided explicitly to make a decision despite the group! Usually, you've been able to seduce the group to your decision anyway. It's beautiful to see the group process in action—when the individual Experiencings are merged into one big, absolute Experiencing in the sky, with the great White Father presiding. Congratulations, again! For the first time you are being congruent in our interaction. That dull, righteous Kiesler! In the moment of truth, the great White Father is able to say to himself: "Piss on Unconditional Positive Regard! That Kiesler is a pain in the ass!"

   At last, you are talking like a Leader. And rightly so! It really is your baby, Carl. You have to resolve this mess all by yourself. I'm so excited by the newly emergent Rogers that I am willing to say: "OK, Carl. I'll go along with whatever you decide! I withdraw all threats of legal counteraction. You have my proxy!" I say this fully aware that it is likely you will now take the course of least resistance and simply do whatever Gene wants. But, that's up to you. I'll sit back and watch what ensues. I support your stand fully. It's the only way out of the predicament. But I wanted, for once, to hear you admit that that's what has to be done. Righteously and dully, Don. . . . P.S. Would you add a simple sentence in the Introduction asking the five people who read Kiesler's chapter to contact him so he can send 'Thank you' cards?

The final solution seems anticlimactic compared to the agonizing three-and-a-half year process which preceded it. The editorship-authorship was listed as Rogers, Gendlin, Kiesler, and Truax, as originally agreed, and special credit and recognition was given to Philippa Mathieu in several ways and places throughout the book. Unfortunately the book's publication was anticlimactic also. If the psychological-psychiatric community had once been waiting expectantly for the results of the Psychotherapy Research Project, by now most people had forgotten about it. The book eventually sold out its first printing, and the publisher decided not to reprint it since the demand was so small.

The final anticlimax was the results of the research. These were mixed, with some of the hypotheses supported and many of them unsupported by the data, and with some new insights emerging that were not directly connected to the hypotheses.

On the whole there were no significant differences between the therapy group and the control group as to process movement in therapy, and only some small differences as to outcomes of therapy. This, of course, could be explained in several ways: The control group in the hospital was getting excellent therapeutic treatment also; the number of patients in the study was too small to show statistical significance; some of the data could not be used—for example, one of the most successful patients (one of Rogers') was released from the hospital and refused to come back to take the final test battery, so his data could not be used in the research; and so on. Nevertheless Rogers and the others were disappointed not to see a greater difference between the therapy and control groups.

When the overall data was examined more closely, however, some positive findings were apparent. For the most part, high therapist conditions of congruence and empathy *did* correlate with successful outcomes of therapy. The results even showed that where these conditions were low, patients deteriorated—a new and sobering finding, indeed. These results gave solid support to Rogers' basic theory (and were confirmed by a follow-up study by Truax and Mitchell conducted nine years later).

The results having to do with the scale of process in therapy were also mixed. The findings showed that therapist conditions did not correlate with movement along the process scale, but that movement along the process scale did correlate with successful outcomes in therapy. There was also a correlation between therapist conditions and process *level,* rather than movement. Although it could not be interpreted with certainty whether the therapist conditions allowed the client to begin therapy at a higher level of process or whether the clients who began at a higher process level tended to elicit higher conditions from their therapist, the concept of process level seemed to offer new possibilities for research.

In many ways the "Schiz book" was a significant contribution. Both the positive and negative findings added something to the body of knowledge about therapy with schizophrenics. But perhaps more importantly, the book suggested many new avenues of research. The explication of the research design, along with appendices which included several of the new scales developed by Truax, Kiesler, and others, would enable other researchers to build upon their techniques and findings. Excellent chapters by Gendlin on clinical techniques for working with schizophrenics and by Rogers on the significance of this research provided very informative, unesoteric reading. Nevertheless the long delay in publication and the lack of consistent, dramatic results gave this book a very different reception from that which Rogers and Dymond's earlier research volume *Psychotherapy and Personality Change* had received in 1954. While the excitement over the earlier work was widespread, the "Schiz book" made a relatively small impression in the psychological-psychiatric community. To a large extent this explains why this period of Rogers' career is not very well known to the interested public. His major endeavor of the six-year period turned out to be a mixed success, fraught with major disappointments and conflicts. It reached publication years later than intended, and then, as he had predicted, was read by only a handful of individuals.

As usual Rogers' relationship with his graduate students was very satisfying during his stay at Wisconsin. He also was often asked to speak to or meet with various student groups. Doug Schoeninger once invited him to visit a seminar of students who were meeting at the Lutheran Center to discuss philosophy, science, religion, and values. Schoeninger hemmed and hawed and, in effect, said, "I want you to come but I really hesitate to ask you because I know you're busy." He remembered Rogers breaking in and saying, "Well, damn it. I can make up my own mind. If you want me to come, you ask me, and if I don't have the time, I'll tell you I don't have the time. Don't protect me." He accepted.

Although Rogers also enjoyed many positive relationships with colleagues and administrators, once again, his conflicts with certain members of the faculty and University administration proved to be a source of tension and disappointment. This had been true at Ohio State and at the University of Chicago. Now Rogers was locking horns with some of his colleagues at the University of Wisconsin. Was this a coincidence, or was this a pattern that reveals another side of the personal and professional Carl Rogers?

A person with new ideas will always threaten others who have older, different ideas, especially when the innovative person is attracting people away from the old intrenched positions. This explains much of the resistance Rogers and his work met throughout his career. But the person with new ideas has many options as to how he or she will behave within a given institution. In a university, some innovative professors are intimidated by the others in their department or by the administration and give up some of their more controversial ideas or projects. Gradually they drift toward the norms within their group and refrain from making or suggesting changes which would be likely to incur disfavor from the rest of the group. Rogers clearly was not of this type. He has always acted on his beliefs, often quite stubbornly and tenaciously. If anything, this quality intensified rather than mellowed with age. The greater his reputation, the more he could afford to go his own way, either because he had more power or, as at Wisconsin, he was tolerated more readily. Settling for less than his goals was hardly his way.

Other innovative professors go about their business, influencing their classes, graduate students, and whichever colleagues are interested, but do not attempt to change things throughout the department or college or university. This was not Rogers' way either. Partly because he always has been rebellious against procedures that seemed self-defeating and partly because he resented some of the things being done to his own graduate students, he would make it his business to try and change student selection procedures, curricula and course requirements, examination and grading systems, and practicum and supervision procedures.

Given the desire to change things on a larger scale, others would go through channels or would use planned, organizational change methods to restructure their institutions. They would proceed carefully, fully cognizant of where the power in the institution resided and what consequences each of their actions would have throughout the structure. Again, Rogers did not proceed in this manner. If he did, he probably would never have come to Wisconsin in the first place, realizing that just because several faculty and administrators were urging him strongly to come, this did not mean he would automatically have the flexibility he wanted when he got there. He was a scientist and a therapist and, increasingly, a thinker and writer about many issues, including interpersonal communication. But he was not an organizational man or a politician. Years later, when he was connected with the Center for Studies of the Person in California, he would proudly call it a "non-organization." He had neither the patience nor the interest to follow the steps necessary to effect long term institutional change in Ohio, Chicago, or Wisconsin.

I would call Rogers' style of organizational change that of "direct communication," with his favorite tool being the letter or memorandum. When he was displeased (or pleased) about something, he wrote a letter to the particular individual or group and said just what was on his mind. The following lengthy memorandum is an example of his direct communication mode and gives a very good picture of the situation he saw himself in in Madison, as of January 1, 1963.

MEMORANDUM

TO: The Executive Committee and the Faculty of the Department of Psychology, University of Wisconsin

FROM: Carl R. Rogers

RE: The possibility of dissociating myself from the Department

As a number of you know, I have become increasingly doubtful during the past couple of years that it would ever be possible for me to work out a suitable pattern for my own activities within the Department, in view of the Department's fixed policies and philosophy. For this reason, I am seriously considering separating myself from the Department. I would like the Executive Committee and the faculty to know this and to know something of my views before I make any definite decision.

I think that my past history shows that I can tolerate a large degree of difference between my own views and the views of the department or organization with which I work. I have gradually realized, however, that there is a limit in the degree to which differences can be tolerated. I would like to set down some of the aspects of the Department and its policies with which I feel myself in great and deep disagreement.

1. *The Policy and Philosophy of Graduate Education*

The Department is deeply dedicated to what seems to me to be a self-defeating philosophy and policy of graduate education. Most of you know my views on this, but I would like to give the picture of the situation as I see it, outlining very briefly the policies which are current.

a. We devote considerable time and energy to selecting the best possible graduate students out of the many who apply.

b. In a variety of ways we manage to create a climate which tends to keep them threatened from the day that they arrive. This climate, which tends to persist, is composed largely of ambiguous threats which cannot be clearly faced by the student.

c. We devise an examination system which for several years keeps students continually thinking of the possibility of failure rather than innovating ideas for their own research.

d. In the training of these graduate students, we spend an inordinate amount of time on the statistics and methodology of research and on inculcating a mind set of hypercritical attitudes, both of which constitute further insurance that no significantly original ideas will develop.

e. During their graduate years we threaten our students enough, fail them enough, discourage them enough, so that only about one out of five or six of these carefully selected students obtains a Ph.D. Not all of those who leave are flunked out. Some of them leave in protest against the sterility of the curriculum, others because they cannot stand the general Departmental climate, which they feel is characterized by such phrases as "the student be damned," "shape up or ship out," "education consists of threats and punishment."

f. We congratulate ourselves that, since only one out of five or six achieves a doctoral degree, this proves that we have high standards. By this same token, Harvard Medical School, which only fails 1% per year, is obviously a school of low standards.

g. We ignore the fact that our educational policies with our graduate students run directly counter to the best research on learning and creativity. We ignore the fact that our policies also run counter to the ideal program of graduate education proposed by a carefully selected committee of scholars, of which one of our own group (Harlow) was a member.

h. The few Ph.D's we turn out are so orthodox and conventional that they are acceptable to any other equally orthodox department. We look upon this as further evidence that we are doing a good job.

i. We seem quite satisfied with our graduate program and, with few exceptions, have little desire to re-examine what we are doing. That students regard the program as punitive, as lacking in venturesome honesty and intellectual excitement, and deficient in good faculty-student relationships, gives us almost no concern. The fact that many other psychologists regard the Department as one of the most tradition-bound in the country is likewise of little or no concern. We are, it seems to me, very comfortably smug.

. . . I am also deeply impressed by the fact that the more small changes we painfully achieve, the more the situation remains fundamentally the same, because the *attitudes* seem to be unchanged. I want to speak of this a bit more fully. . . .

And he did, for three-and-a-half more single-spaced pages. Unfortunately such direct communication rarely elicits much of a response, especially when written from a distance of over two thousand miles, from California. On another occasion, when he sent a memorandum to several members of the Psychiatry Department, inviting them to meet to discuss policy matters, one department member replied, "I am not aware that the Department has empowered you to call committee meetings." At any rate his memoranda did serve to make his positions clear. When he saw that his latest attempts were having little or no impact, he wrote, on May 8, 1963, another memorandum, this time, "Re: My resignation from the Department." Although he resigned from the Psychology Department, he continued to work with the Wisconsin Psychiatric Institute, pursuing his research interests there and helping young staff members plan research and obtain funding.

For all the negative experiences Rogers was having in connection with the research project and the University during his stay in Wisconsin, his extracurricular life was entirely different, with many professional successes and personal pleasures.

A major joy to the Rogers was their new home. Helen wrote of it, "When we moved to Madison, Wisconsin, in 1957, and found a beautiful home on Lake Monona I felt my 'cup runneth over.' This was surely a spot in which I could spend the rest of my days." It was a spacious home, set on an acre of land with a large lawn running down to the lake. Although only about a five-minute drive from the University, it was definitely a country setting. Here the Rogers did a considerable amount of entertaining. A former colleague of Rogers' from his Rochester years, Louise Johnson, remembered spending the weekend at the Rogers' home. "I was impressed with the telephone calls from former students and the dropping in for a social call by two former students who were passing through on vacation, one bringing his wife and children. From the conversations I could sense the warmth of the friendly relationship which existed between the man and those whose lives he had touched and the high regard and affection felt for him."

Helen liked the life in Madison much more than in Chicago. She developed more of her own friends and found social norms much more relaxed and free of strict protocol. For both, their home on the lake was their favorite of all the houses and settings they had lived in, and for a while it seemed likely that this is where they *would* spend the rest of their lives. They liked it so much that when a developer threatened to buy some adjoining acres and squeeze as many houses as possible onto the land, Carl and Helen were so threatened that their quiet setting would become noisy and cluttered, that they bought the adjoining property themselves and resold it in larger lots, at some financial loss.

Another of Carl and Helen's continuing pleasures was their winter vacations to warmer climes. In previous years they had often stopped at David's and Natalie's homes in New York and Boston on their way to or from their destination. Now they began to plan their vacation trips together with the family. During the 1956–57 winter vacation David and Corky and their children accompanied Carl and Helen on a six-week trip to Bequia in the British West Indies. In the summer of

1958 they spent some time with David and Corky at Seneca Lake, New York, at the cabin Carl had built some twenty years earlier and which they still owned. During the 1959–60 winter vacation, Natalie, Larry, and their children, and Carl and Helen went to Beef Island, in the Virgin Islands. For their 1958–59 and 1962–63 Christmas vacation Carl and Helen flew to Hawaii and to the Philippines to visit Natalie, Larry, and the children. Larry was active in Peace Corps work in Hawaii and was head of the Peace Corps in the Philippines, where all the Fuchs spent two years. Over the 1960–61 vacation they went with David, Corky, and the children to Runaway Bay, Jamaica. The next year they spent their Christmas in Nashville, where David was now a Professor and Chairman of the Department of Medicine at Vanderbilt University. During this period David had another forty or so scientific papers published in the medical journals and became a nationally recognized leader in the field of bacterial diseases, especially staphylococci. For his community service work he received the Nashville Junior Chamber of Commerce's 1960 Distinguished Service Award, and in 1961 was voted one of the Ten Outstanding Young Men of the Year by the United States Junior Chamber of Commerce.

Having those one or two special and extended times a year with at least one of their children's family was a high priority for Carl and Helen, and they rarely missed an opportunity. Occasionally they even had a vacation with the entire family. Carl described a 1963 holiday gathering in a letter to his colleagues: "We had a fine Thanksgiving family reunion with Dave and Corky, Nat and Larry, and our six active grandchildren. Because of the youngsters it was a very active weekend. We played touch football. There was a continuous ping-pong tournament going on in which fortunes waxed and waned. We went on a moderately successful search for Indian arrowheads. We enjoyed a delightful Thanksgiving and good conversation with all our family. My sister from Florida was also present and we enjoyed having her there."

Natalie remembered that when the family would get together, Carl and Helen would "focus more on the adults than on the kids. With the chaos and a lot going on at once, they get confused and don't know how to relate to it." When they would be with one grandchild at a time, however, they were able to communicate and relate much more effectively. Carl also liked doing active sports and projects with his grandchildren. Living right on Lake Monona, the Rogers had a speedboat, and Carl liked to tow the grandchildren on water skis. Natalie's daughters remembered how he would take them snorkeling. They also remembered with delight the bar and refrigerator Rogers had in their basement, which the girls would play with, on, and around, whenever they came to visit.

In addition to their winter vacations the Rogers spent a great deal of time away from home on various professional trips. A look at some of the major addresses and workshops he gave from January to August, 1958 gives a good indication of the range of topics and travel resulting from his stature in the helping professions. In January he spoke to the Minnesota Counselors Association. In February he was a leader in a three-day conference for educators at Goddard College in Vermont and a participant in a three-day symposium on psychotherapy with schizophrenics in Louisiana (Carl and Helen enjoyed Mardi Gras in New Orleans that year). In March he spoke to the psychology staff at Manteno State Hospital in Illinois on research in psychotherapy. In April, in St. Louis, he lectured to the American Personnel and Guidance Association on "The Characteristics of a Helping Relationship" and, in Washington, D.C., to the American Psychological Association on "Research in Psychotherapy." In May, on the topic of psychotherapy, he conducted a two-day seminar for the Department of Psychology at the University of Rochester in New York and gave two lectures at the University of Chicago. In the summer he gave a four-week seminar at Brandeis University in Massachusetts, and in August was a coleader of a five-day workshop on therapy, in Ojai Valley, California. This list does not include several minor addresses or any of the lectures or consulting he did during that period in his own state of Wisconsin or in the University community.

Rogers' reputation was such that he received, in addition, a good many invitations for visiting professorships or other commitments that required a major period of time away from home. During his stay at Wisconsin he accepted two of these invitations.

The first spanned the summer of 1961. It resulted from the efforts of Logan Fox, a former student of Rogers' who had been instrumental in spreading client-centered therapy in Japan, where he was a professor at Ibaraki Christian College. Since 1955 Fox and several Japanese colleagues had been conducting workshops in client-centered therapy in several parts of that country. In a culture that had traditionally suppressed feelings in favor of outward form, Rogers' ideas and methods had been gaining surprising interest and acceptance. The incredible cultural revolution that Japan underwent after the war apparently had created enormous tensions, with many people caught in the transition from the traditional to the modern culture and life style. As one Japanese counselor summed up Rogers' importance to him, it was "to teach me the basic way of becoming to be democratic and not authoritative." By 1961 Fox and his colleagues thought that the counseling movement in their country had a sufficient foundation that a visit from Rogers would be particularly timely and would spur the movement on considerably. After obtaining his agreement, they began setting up an extremely full schedule of speeches and workshops for Rogers, both to give him as much impact as possible and to raise the money for the trip.

With barely a few days rest during the entire trip, Rogers did everything from presenting forty-five minute speeches to conducting five-day workshops with groups as varied as: one hundred fifty clinical psychologists and educators in Kyoto; a conference of school and college counselors in Kyoto; the Osaka Mental Health Association; the Japan Industrial Training Association in Tokyo; the Tokyo University Child Guidance Group; a conference of the Christian Education Association in Gotemba; a group of parole, probation, and institutional workers and psychiatrists sponsored by the Ministry of Justice of the Japanese government; the Social Psychologists' Association in Tokyo; and other comparable groups. It was hard for Fox to say no to groups who wanted to hear Rogers. Consequently the pace was really too much for Carl and Helen and it took a great deal of the enjoyment out of the trip. On one occasion, when Rogers was complaining about having to give another presentation, he said to Fox, "Logan, the only thing that keeps me from complaining more is that you are working harder than I am."

Fox served as Rogers' interpreter throughout the trip, and was often with Carl and Helen ten and twelve hours a day. There were two incidents that stood out most vividly in his mind which he described several years later in an introduction to the Japanese collection of Rogers' writings. "One experience drew me especially close to Rogers. For years I had idolized him and had tried so hard to be like him in my interpersonal relations. But I so often failed to be accepting of people and had often felt real guilt over my failures. But after about three days of the Kyoto workshop, one evening after a particularly trying day which had been dominated by some particularly irksome behavior from one of the leaders of the workshop, Rogers and I stood in the hotel lobby expressing our opinions about this man. I couldn't resist kidding Rogers about the unfriendly remarks we were both making, and said, 'But, Carl, we're not being very accepting of this man, are we?' He responded, 'What the hell, he's no client of mine.' And in that moment my god became human, years of guilty feelings dropped away, and I said to myself, 'It's going to be a good six weeks.'

"There was another memorable experience in Kyoto. Rogers had expressed an interest in Zen Buddhism, so a meeting with a well-known Zen Master [Hisamatsu] was arranged. A small group was present for the occasion and interest ran high. Zen Masters are noted for their ability to get straight to the heart of any matter and Rogers was eager for a real person-to-person encounter. So he opened the discussion by saying, 'I have read the transcript of the discussion you had with Jung and I must say that I found myself disappointed, particularly with the rather abstract quality of the discussion.' At this the Master began an apology for the transcript, suggested that it was a poor translation, and stayed on the defensive for the rest of the discussion. We were never quite sure why it turned out as it did, but it certainly did not produce the kind of encounter we had hoped for."

Helen had her own problems with their whirlwind tour of Japan. Traditionally women have been explicitly subservient to men in the Orient. When Carl was occasionally invited to a dinner or reception, but she was not, this hurt her. Even more unpleasant were the Japanese reactions to her height. A tall, white-haired woman in a country of short, dark-haired people, she seemed to be an object of curiosity, comment, and even ridicule throughout the trip. People would stop, stare, point their fingers, make comments, giggle—all this right to her face. On one particularly painful occasion she had to wait forty-five minutes for a subway, and each time another train would empty its passengers on her platform all the passengers streaming out would see her, stop, and register their amazement. And all she could do was stand there, hoping her train would come soon. Needless to say, her impression and, to some extent, Carl's impression of Japan was colored quite negatively by these experiences. Nevertheless Rogers' influence in that country continued to spread, and within a few years, a Japanese publisher, Iwasaki Gakujyutsu Syuppansya (in English, Academic Press), had brought out a seventeen-volume collection of Rogers' work, including numerous journal articles and unpublished writings that are relatively unknown in the United States.

The second occasion on which Carl and Helen spent an extended time away from Madison for professional reasons was during a nine-month period from August 1962 to June 1963, when Carl was a Fellow at the Center for Advanced Study in the Behavioral Sciences in Stanford, California. This privately funded group was well known for their practice of bringing together small groups of some of the best minds in the world and giving them a liberal living allowance and the freedom to spend a year doing anything they wished. The hope was that a cross-fertilization of ideas would take place that would enrich the work of each individual and the behavioral sciences as a whole. During Rogers' year in Stanford he came in contact with some outstanding individuals whose thinking he found stimulating and whose acquaintance he valued highly. Two, in particular, were Michael Polyani and Erik Erikson.

Polyani, the noted British philosopher of science, was several years older than Rogers and seemed to have an encyclopedic knowledge of the history of philosophy and science and an ability to integrate his technical and philosophic knowledge in ways which greatly impressed Rogers, who later recalled, "I do stand somewhat in awe of a real scholar like that, even though on the other hand, I'm damned if I think that's the most productive approach to life. Michael is all intellect. . . . He devours ideas, and he's absolutely single track. If he was to talk to you, in three minutes he'd be around to your view of philosophy of science, and he'd be pumping you for whatever you might know . . . or whatever his latest specific topic was. . . . But I do have a lot of respect for him. And I realize he sends us a Christmas card and I don't reciprocate. And I haven't sent him either of my last two books. I was thinking about this the other day. And it's because I think, 'Oh, hell, they're not scholarly enough for Michael to appreciate.' But I realize that why I was good for him was because I wasn't scholarly. I brought something else to it. He respected the fact that I brought to him practical experience in the world that sort of bolstered some of his views but was different from anything he could offer. . . . I really *should* send him copies of my books."

He was right in his assessment of Polyani's attitude toward him. When I wrote the philosopher in 1971, asking for his personal reaction to and recollections of Rogers, he wrote of ". . . my internal struggle between my deep friendship curiously combined with a slight personal knowledge. The fact is I love Carl Rogers, but really know very little about his many years of decisively effective work. I love his temper, so beneficent with the overhacked domain of modern mental efforts, but I really know only the way he thinks and helps by his purity. I think I disagree with its particulars, but this does not affect my joy of his person. . . . If you can find a place for a page, or half a page, which smilingly tells this affection for Rogers, I could try to say something of this kind. I would be embarrassed in trying this, but my affection for him might overcome this."

I never wrote back for that page or half page, for I thought this paragraph summed up Polyani's feelings eloquently enough. Rogers, in turn, was very much influenced by Polyani's thinking and, as a result, over the next several years, did much more thinking, speaking, and writing himself on the nature of science.

Erik Erikson was a noted psychoanalyst whose writings have been read widely by both professionals and laypeople. Rogers felt "his very appearance is therapeutic. . . . He just does have an aura of being a good therapist. Both Helen and I liked him very much." Erikson was also impressed by his contact with Rogers. After attending several sessions in which some of Rogers' tapes of therapy were played and discussed, Erikson commented, "Gosh, after listening to that, I feel like I'd like to go back to doing analyses." Rogers was quite certain the comment was meant favorably. Through contact with Erikson, Polyani, and other distinguished intellectuals and scientists, Rogers had a very stimulating year at the Center for Advanced Studies.

Another source of satisfaction for Rogers, which was some compensation for the unpleasant experiences at the University, was his writing. He continued to be prolific throughout the entire period, with many new articles appearing in the journals or in book chapters each year. But by far the most significant publication of this period came in 1961 with his seventh book, *On Becoming a Person*.

For several years he had contemplated pulling together many of his essays in book form. At one time this was to be a collection of essays on creativity. At another time he thought about a collection of more philosophical writings, applying insights from psychotherapy to many traditional philosophical questions. The book turned out to be both of these things and more. Over the years he had written a large number of essays both directly and indirectly related to psychotherapy. In collecting various articles, he found enough material for a substantial volume, including twenty-one essays—much more than the short collection of essays on creativity he had contemplated a few years earlier. Rogers has said on several occasions that *On Becoming a Person* is his favorite book. There are two reasons for this.

First is that the book practically wrote itself, taking about three weeks' work on Rogers' part, and this under the most ideal conditions. Since it was a collection of essays, it required little original writing.

What was required was choosing the essays, organizing them under appropriate headings, writing introductions to them, and doing whatever rewriting was needed to eliminate much of the repetition. The bulk of this was done on a three-week retreat Carl and Helen took near Estes Park, Colorado, from August 19 to September 5, 1960. In a rustic cottage they rented, they enjoyed a simple life with few distractions. Deer grazed within sight of the front door. Carl wrote every morning and some of the evenings; in the afternoons they explored the magnificent countryside and mountains. At the end of three weeks the book was just about completed. The idyllic setting and the ease of writing were always for him a most enjoyable memory.

The second reason that *On Becoming a Person* is Rogers' favorite is that it synthesized the work of the major part of his career. It is not just a book on psychotherapy, although the first sections of the book are on that subject; it is a book on the process of becoming a person, a process which takes place not only in psychotherapy, but potentially in every facet of daily living. Logan Fox once wrote of his studies with Rogers, "It had never been my intention to be a psychotherapist. I was a minister and a college teacher. But this was not unusual among those who were attracted to Rogers. In the group at Chicago there were ministers, teachers, social workers, writers, and many other specialists besides the clinical psychologists. And so as a disciple of Rogers in Japan, it was not my intention to launch a counseling movement. I was interested in applying his ideas in religion, in education, in school administration, and in the home. I think I was not unique in those interests. Somehow, each person who studied under Rogers became interested, not in becoming a professional counselor, but in trying to improve human relations wherever he might find himself."

Any reader of *On Becoming a Person* knows just what Fox is talking about. The book is rich and varied in its applications of client-centered therapeutic principles to many different types of human relationships. It represents the growing variety of Rogers' interests and of the areas in which his work was becoming influential. From the first introductory chapter to the long impressive list of Rogers' publications, 1931–1961, the book is a statement of the person Carl Rogers had been becoming and continued to become throughout his life.

The introductory chapter is a good illustration of this. Entitled "This is Me," the chapter is a composite of two talks he had given. One had been at the University of Wisconsin, the other in a lecture series at Brandeis, in which Archibald MacLeish, Margaret Mead, Robert Frost, Eleanor Roosevelt, Norman Thomas, Walter White, and many other noted figures had been previous speakers. "The response to each of these talks," Rogers wrote, "has made me realize how hungry people are to know something of the person who is speaking to them or teaching them. Consequently, I have set this chapter first in the book in the hope that it will convey something of me, and thus give more context and meaning to the chapters which follow."

This was a continuation of his tendency of the previous years to become increasingly personal in his writing style. More and more often phrases like, "It has been my experience that . . ." and "From what I have seen . . ." would appear in his writing. Beyond the phrases, he began to elaborate on the same theme in most of his essays.

> I would like to make it very plain that these are learnings which have significance for *me*. I do not know whether they would hold meaning for you. I have no desire to present them as a guide for anyone else. Yet I have found that when another person has been willing to tell me something of his inner directions this has been of value to me, if only in sharpening my realization that my directions are different.

> I have stated the preceding section as strongly as I am able because it represents a deep conviction growing out of many years of experience. I am quite aware, however, of the difference between conviction and truth. I do not ask anyone to agree with my experience, but only to consider whether the formulation given here agrees with his own experience.

> Out of my experience with my clients, and out of my own self-searching, I find myself arriving at views which would have been very foreign to me ten or fifteen years ago. So I trust you will look at these views with critical scepticism, and accept them only in so far as they ring true in your own experience.

Under "experience" Rogers sometimes included his experience in research and at other times referred only to his more subjective experiences. Not only did he follow this stylistic model more consistently, he even began to include in some of his writings paragraphs in which he would describe his own personal and professional background. In "This is Me" he shared his history at greater length than he had ever before done in writing. Of all his autobiographical writings, this first chapter of *On Becoming a Person* is perhaps the best known. It symbolizes his growing desire to be seen and known as an individual, to achieve a more personal encounter in his relationships, even with his readers.

He devoted the next two sections of the book to his ideas on therapy, giving many excerpts from therapeutic interviews to illustrate his points. One of his best-known essays was included here—"The Characteristics of a Helping Relationship." In one part of the essay he adapted the principles of client-centered therapy into a series of questions he would ask himself as a person in a helping relationship. As he elaborated on each question raised, he made it clear that he was not only speaking of the therapist-to-client relationship but of all helping relationships. This is one reason why the essay has been reprinted in the journals of so many professions.

"1. Can I *be* in some way which will be perceived by the other person as trustworthy, as dependable or consistent in some deep sense . . . ? 2. Can I be expressive enough as a person that what I am will be communicated unambiguously . . . ? 3. Can I let myself experience positive attitudes toward this other person—attitudes of warmth, caring, liking, interest, respect . . . ? 4. Can I be strong enough as a person to be separate from the other . . . ? 5. Am I secure enough within myself to permit him his separateness . . . ? 6. Can I let myself enter fully into the world of his feelings and personal meanings and see these as he does . . . ? 7. Can I be acceptant of each facet of this other person which he presents to me? Can I receive him as he is? Can I communicate this attitude? Or can I only receive him conditionally, acceptant of some aspects of his feelings and silently or openly disapproving of other aspects . . . ? 8. Can I act with sufficient sensitivity in the relationship that my behavior will not be perceived as a threat . . . ? 9. Can I free him from the threat of external evaluation . . . ? 10. Can I meet this other individual as a person who is in process of *becoming* or will I be bound by his past and by my past . . . ?"

Rogers was frequently asked what his picture of the healthy person was —the product of a lifetime of ideal helping relationships, or successful psychotherapy? This was a variation of one of the oldest philosophical questions humans have grappled with through recorded history—to what end does a person live, what is the purpose of life, what gives it meaning? In Part IV of *On Becoming a Person* he included two essays dealing with this question—" 'To Be That Self Which One Truly Is': A Therapist's View of Personal Goals" and "A Therapist's View of the Good Life: The Fully Functioning Person." In these and other essays he described the optimum in human functioning as he had seen it evidenced in the growth of the individuals he encountered in therapy. For him this optimum in functioning was not a fixed state, with a fixed or ultimate set of values to which one aspired. Rather, "the good life is a *process,* not a state of being. It is a direction, not a destination. The direction which constitutes the good life is that which is selected by the total organism, when there is a psychological freedom to move in *any* direction."

Where this psychological freedom does exist or where it increases in degree, Rogers saw certain common directions in people's style of living. First, the "more fully functioning person" is "open to his experience," that is, aware and acceptant of his feelings, perceptions, and thoughts. He has a "trust in his organism," a confidence that when he is open to *all* of his inner and outer experience and not blocking out certain parts of his experiencing, then his inner directions and promptings are a trustworthy guide to action. He has an "internal locus of evaluation"; that is, although he is aware of and sensitive to the "oughts" and "shoulds" and expectations of others, he trusts his own judgment as the most important guide to right and wrong, desirable and undesirable, in a given situation. There is an "increasingly existential living," in which "the self and personality emerge *from* experience, rather than experience being translated or twisted to fit preconceived self structure." Such a person, thought Rogers, seems to move away from facades and toward congruence in his daily living. There is an increase in spontaneity and creativity.

This line of thought was consistent with many humanistic psychologists' views of basic human nature. As usual, Rogers explained it more clearly and in greater detail. To those who said an openness to experience, a trust in one's organism, and an internal locus of evaluation would inevitably lead the person to run amuck, Rogers answered, "The person who is fully open to his experience would have access to all of the available data in the situation, on which to base his behavior; the social demands, his own complex and possibly conflicting needs, his memories of similar situations, his perception of the uniqueness of this situation, etc., etc. The data would be very complex indeed. But he could permit his total organism, his consciousness participating, to consider each stimulus, need, and demand, its relative intensity and importance, and out of this complex weighing and balancing, discover that course of action which would come close to satisfying all his needs in the situation. An analogy which might come close to a description would be to compare this person to a giant electronic computing machine. Since he is open to his experience, all of the data from his sense impressions, from his memory, from previous learning, from his visceral and internal states, is fed into the machine. The machine takes all of these multitudinous pulls and forces which are fed in as data, and quickly computes the course of action which would be the most economical vector of need satisfaction in this existential situation. This is the behavior of our hypothetical person.

"The defects which in most of us make this process untrustworthy are the inclusion of information which does *not* belong to this present situation, or the exclusion of information which *does*. It is when memories and previous learnings are fed into the computations as if they were *this* reality, and not memories and learnings, that erroneous behavioral answers arise. Or when certain threatening experiences are inhibited from awareness, and hence are withheld from the computation or fed into it in distorted form, this too produces error. But our hypothetical person would find his organism thoroughly trustworthy, because all of the available data would be used, and it would be present in accurate rather than distorted form. Hence his behavior would come as close as possible to satisfying all his needs—for enhancement, for affiliation with others, and the like."

Surely the organism will make mistakes, whenever crucial data are missing, or when there is not enough time to compute all the data thoroughly; but if the individual remains open to his experience, then new data will come in, and new decisions can correct the old ones.

As others have commented, Rogers himself is one of the prime examples of such a fully functioning person—open to new data, altering his thinking based on his experiences, continually changing and growing, outgrowing himself into new ideas and professional emphases. To use an oft-quoted Rogers passage, "This whole train of experiencing, and the meanings that I have thus far discovered in it, seem to have launched me on a process which is both fascinating and at times a little frightening. *It seems to mean letting my experience carry me on, in a direction which appears to be forward, toward goals that I can but dimly define, as I try to understand at least the current meaning of that experience.* The sensation is that of floating with a complex stream of experience, with the fascinating possibility of trying to comprehend its ever changing complexity."

Whether one's idea of success is a home in the suburbs, a tenured position on a faculty, or an idyllic farm in the country, Rogers' picture of the fully functioning person is in striking contrast to the typical western notion of success in life. It suggests that we never arrive at a final goal, that life is a continual state of change, that we remain open to our experiences and flow with them, that when we stop growing we commence dying. People may live happily ever after in fairy tales and

Hollywood movies, but to Rogers fully functioning success is a continual process of growth and change.

Closely tied to his concept of the fully functioning person was his view of the creative process, discussed in a chapter which appeared near the end of *On Becoming a Person*. To Rogers, creativity is not a personality quality which some people have and others do not, but a process which all people go through to one degree or another. One part of the creative process is an openness to experience. The artist is open to the sensory world around him and to the feelings within him. The creative scientist or inventor is a keen observer of the phenomena she is studying and, like the artist, is open to the unformed, the vague, the sometimes preposterous ideas, hunches and hypotheses which well up within her. Then there is a trusting of one's organism, a kind of confidence that allows a person to follow a hunch, to try out an idea or solution, to create something new. Along with this self-trust is a locus of evaluation which is mostly within the person rather than without. This enables the artist to say, "I know that no one has ever painted this way before, but *I* think my approach has merit, and I will keep doing it this way," or the scientist to say, "I know this line of thinking goes against the present theories in my field, but *I* think this would be a valuable direction to pursue." Such qualities of personality —openness to experience, trust in oneself, an internal locus of evaluation—lead to creative living. Creative living leads to creative products, which may be anything from artistic and scientific contributions, to good storytelling, to a sense of design and decoration, to a new and different life style. Just as the psychological safety in being oneself helps a person become more fully functioning, so does psychological safety nurture creativity. Psychological threat, on the other hand, nurtures rigidity of thought and psychological defensiveness. The fully functioning person, then, is creative. To the extent that each of us becomes more fully functioning, we also increase our capacity for creative living.

In the fifth section of *On Becoming a Person* Rogers included three chapters on "Getting at the Facts: The Place of Research in Psychotherapy." Here he reviewed much of the research he and others had done in the field, but also included a lengthy exploration of his personal struggle with two points of view about therapy. One viewpoint was that therapy is an intensely personal experience, that it is lived fully and subjectively in a person-to-person encounter with the client, that the therapist is not a scientist applying this or that technique but a congruent human being endeavoring to enter into a deeply personal helping relationship with another human being. The second point of view was that of a scientist. Therapy must be studied rigorously with the tried and true methods of science. All vague concepts like congruence, unconditional positive regard, and empathy must be operationalized and measurable. An individual's subjective impressions may be anything from biased to psychotic; therefore objectivity and detachment are crucial to the scientist. To sum up the dilemma: the person's goal is to live fully in the relationship, the scientist's goal is to remain detached and understand it.

Not only did he see this as a conflict he personally felt between two sides of himself, he also saw it as a tension between two points of view in psychology—between those who were interested primarily in understanding the person as he experiences himself and the world subjectively and those who were interested only in the person's behavior, as viewed from the outside. Since science views its subject objectively, when people are the subject of science they therefore become objects. Rogers asked, "If we project ourselves into the future, and suppose that we had the answers to most of the questions which psychology investigates today, what then? Then we would find ourselves increasingly impelled to treat all others, and even ourselves, as objects. The knowledge of all human relationships would be so great that we would know it rather than live the relationships unreflectively. We see some foretaste of this in the attitude of sophisticated parents who know that affection 'is good for the child.' This knowledge frequently stands in the way of their being themselves, freely, unreflectively—affectionate or not."

His way out of the dilemma was to go back to viewing the human purposes of scientific investigation. "Science," he wrote, "has its inception in a particular person who is pursuing aims, values, purposes, which have personal and subjective meaning for him." These purposes may be a burning desire to discover truth, the hope of getting a degree or tenure, the wish to solve an important problem, or any number of other human goals. In pursuit of some particular solution to a problem, there is a *creative phase*, where the person thinks he has come up with an invention, a new technique, a newly observed relationship, a hypothesis which will move him closer to achieving the goal of his research. But is it true? Does the new invention really work, or what are its side effects? Is the newly observed relationship due only to chance, or is it a consistent relationship which will appear again and again under similar conditions? Does the new technique work only because of the person using it or the person receiving it or will it work for different clients and with different practitioners? "Experience has shown each one of us that it is very easy to deceive ourselves, to believe something which later experience shows is not so." It is here that science comes in, not as an end in itself, a god to be worshipped above all other human endeavors, but as a tool—a tool which helps us check our observations and conclusions against a more objective reality to see just how good our solution, our invention, our technique, our generalization, our hypothesis really is.

For Rogers, then, both realities—the subjective and the objective— were crucially important. His goal, based on past experience, was to enter into a subjective human relationship with his clients. His belief, based on past experience, was that this would most likely lead to a therapeutic relationship and psychological growth. But how could he be sure? Maybe he was kidding himself, remembering only the successful cases upon which he built his generalizations. Scientific research allowed him to check himself, to discover blind spots, to improve and modify his techniques—in short, to achieve his goal more successfully. Without science he was akin to a faith healer. With science only, there could be no client-centered therapy. A warm human being was needed for that. The continuing struggle between the subjective and objective was, for him, a desirable tension, one which would keep him growing and changing. It was when he denied one side or the other that he was no longer the person or the effective therapist he wished to be.

The same held true for the tension between the subjective and the objective in the behavioral sciences. As long as science gave credence and importance to individuals' goals, feelings, values, and other inner experiences, objective scientists could help people. As long as the "experientialists" included a scientific method in their operations, they would remain professionals and not cultists. Both were necessary for the behavioral sciences to be of significant help to society and individuals. " 'Science' will never depersonalize, or manipulate, or control individuals," he wrote. "It is only persons who can or will do that. . . . What I will do with the knowledge gained through scientific method—whether I will use it to understand, enhance, enrich, or use it to control, manipulate and destroy—is a matter of subjective choice dependent upon the values which have personal meaning for me. If, out of fright and defensiveness, I block out from my awareness large areas of experience—if I can see only those facts which support my present beliefs, and am blind to all others—if I can see only the objective aspects of life, and cannot perceive the subjective—if, in any way, I cut off my perception from the full range of its actual sensitivity— then I am likely to be socially destructive, whether I use as tool the knowledge and instruments of science, or the power and emotional strength of a subjective relationship."

In *On Becoming a Person* Rogers pulled together his thoughts on this subject to a greater degree than ever before. In addition to the three chapters in the research section he included two more at the end of the book on "The Behavioral Sciences and the Person." After years of experience as a behavioral scientist he was becoming more and more interested in and concerned about the part the behavioral sciences would play in dealing with the world's human problems. A few years later Rogers' interest in the uses and methods of science would again occupy a good deal of thought and another volume.

The sixth and largest section of his collection of essays applied the insights of client-centered therapy to several other areas of daily living. One was education. In a short essay, "Personal Thoughts on Teaching and Learning," he wrote an extreme statement of his educational views, including such italicized statements as: *"It seems to me that anything that can be taught to another is relatively inconsequential, and has little or no significant influence on behavior." "I have come to feel that the only learning which significantly influences behavior is self-appropriated learning." "I realize that I have lost interest in being a teacher."*

In another, longer essay, "Significant Learning: In Therapy and in Education," he discussed how the same principles of learning in therapy apply to the teacher-student relationship in the classroom. Here he was generalizing on the basis of his own teaching experience in therapy, developing some of his basic premises about education. This was the beginning of an important process. Over the next few years he would continue to extend his thinking in this area and would have a significant influence on the education profession.

Essentially, his major points in the several essays in this section were, first, that the conditions of congruence, unconditional positive regard, and empathy not only foster growth and significant learning in therapy, but they do the same in every helping relationship; and second, that the benefits of living as a more fully functioning person—congruent, in process of becoming, trusting oneself, open to experience, etc. —can be seen in *all* human relationships. In education this is probably easier to recognize than in some other areas of application, for in education the teacher's role lends itself to adopting the therapist's conditions, and the student's role traditionally has been supposed to be that of openness, growth, becoming. But what about in the family, for example? Here, too, Rogers believed that the parents' congruence, unconditional positive regard, and empathy can be enormously growth-facilitating for the children. In "The Implications of Client-Centered Therapy for Family Life" he illustrated how family relationships frequently changed after one member had been involved in therapy and this one person's growth began to influence the rest of the family. First, there tends to be more expression of feeling in the family, a richer emotional life. Relationships tend to move away from facades, pretense, and defensiveness; there is an improvement in two-way communication. ". . . the individual learns to recognize and express his feelings *as* his own feelings, not as a fact about another person. Thus, to say to one's spouse, 'What you are doing is all wrong,' is likely to lead only to debate. But to say 'I feel very much annoyed by what you're doing,' is to state one fact about the speaker's feelings, a fact which no one can deny." With this type of communication developing, there tends to be a greater willingness for the individuals to be separate, to have feelings and values of their own, which can be respected or at least tolerated, even if these are different from the others.

Not content to confine the application of his ideas to education and the family, Rogers argued that the same principles of effective helping and psychologically healthy living could be used to improve communication between disputing groups and even nations. As early as 1951 he told an audience, "Some of you may be feeling that you listen well to people, and that you have never seen such results. The chances are very great indeed that your listening has not been of the type I have described. Fortunately I can suggest a little laboratory experiment which you can try to test the quality of your understanding. The next time you get into an argument with your wife, or your friend, or with a small group of friends, just stop the discussion for a moment and for an experiment, institute this rule. 'Each person can speak up for himself only *after* he has first restated the ideas and feelings of the previous speaker accurately, and to that speaker's satisfaction.' You see what this would mean. It would simply mean that before presenting your own point of view, it would be necessary for you to really achieve the other speaker's frame of reference—to understand his thoughts and feelings so well that you could summarize them for him. Sounds simple doesn't it? But if you try it you will discover it is one of the most difficult things you have ever tried to do. However, once you have been able to see the other's point of view, your own comments will have to be drastically revised. You will also find the emotion going out of the discussion, the differences being reduced, and those differences which remain being of a rational and understandable sort. . . .

"I am indebted to Dr. S.I. Hayakawa, the semanticist, for pointing out that to carry on psychotherapy in this fashion is to take a very real risk, and that courage is required. If you really understand another person in this way, if you are willing to enter his private world and see the way life appears to him, without any attempt to make evaluative judgments, you run the risk of being changed yourself. You might see it his way, you might find yourself influenced in your attitudes or your personality. This risk of being changed is one of the most frightening prospects most of us can face. If I enter as fully as I am able, into the private world of a neurotic or psychotic individual, isn't there a risk that I might become lost in that world? Most of us are afraid to take that risk. Or if we had a Russian communist speaker here tonight, or Senator Joseph McCarthy, how many of us would dare to try to see the world from each of these points of view? The great majority of us could not *listen;* we would find ourselves compelled to *evaluate,* because listening would seem too dangerous. So the first requirement is courage, and we do not always have it."

Many people have tried Rogers' laboratory experiment in listening. In fact, with all the new approaches toward teaching communication skills and interpersonal sensitivity, it has become one of the most popular communication exercises used in human relations training. "Rogerian listening" is a term which is used widely to describe empathic listening, in which the listener shares with the speaker his own understanding of the feelings and meanings the speaker has shared. Thomas Gordon, Rogers' former student and then colleague, has popularized the phrase "active listening" to describe the same process.

In attempting to apply his theories and methods to interpersonal and intergroup conflict resolution, Rogers was advocating more than good listening. Honest, open communication was another part of it. As he wrote in 1960, "Let us take a look, for example, at the conduct of our country, in its foreign affairs. By and large we find, if we listen to the statements of our leaders during the past several years, and read their documents, that our diplomacy is always based upon high moral purposes; that it is always consistent with the policies we have followed previously; that it involves no selfish desires; and that it has never been mistaken in its judgments and choices. I think perhaps you will agree with me that if we heard an individual speaking in these terms we would recognize at once that this must be a facade, that such statements could not possibly represent the real process going on within himself. Suppose we speculate for a moment as to how we, as a nation, might present ourselves in our foreign diplomacy if we were openly, knowingly, and acceptingly being what we truly are. . . . What would be the results? To me, the results would be similar to the experiences of a client when he is more truly that which he is. . . .

"We would be much more comfortable, because we would have nothing to hide. We could focus on the problem at hand, rather than spending our energies to prove that we are moral or consistent. We could use all of our creative imagination in solving the problem, rather than in defending ourselves. We could openly advance both our selfish interests, and our sympathetic concern for others, and let these conflicting desires find the balance which is acceptable to us as a people. We could freely change and grow in our leadership position, because we would not be bound by rigid concepts of what we have been, must be, ought to be. We would find that we were much less feared, because others would be less inclined to suspect what lies behind the facade. We would, by our own openness, tend to bring forth openness and realism on the part of others. We would tend to work out the solutions of world problems on the basis of the real issues involved, rather than in terms of the facades being worn by the negotiating parties.

"In short what I am suggesting by this fantasied example is that nations and organizations might discover, as have individuals, that it is a richly rewarding experience to be what one deeply is. I am suggesting that this view contains the seeds of a philosophical approach to all of life, that it is more than a trend observed in the experience of clients."

In his introduction to *On Becoming a Person* Rogers had written, "Stated in the simplest way, the purpose of this book is to share with you something of my experience—something of me. Here is what I have experienced in the jungles of modern life, in the largely unmapped territory of personal relationships. Here is what I have seen. Here is what I have come to believe. Here are some of the perplexities, questions, concerns and uncertainties which I face. I hope that out of this sharing you may find something which speaks to you."

A great number of people did. As soon as the book was published, personal letters began coming to Rogers, forwarded by the publisher, in numbers much greater than any of his previous books had elicited. They were from professionals and laypeople alike.

A young woman from Connecticut began her letter in a way which Rogers would see repeated hundreds of times: "Dear Carl, I do not want to write to you as Dr. Rogers, for although we have never met, I feel a personal closeness to you through reading many of your thoughts and feelings. At times, for me, it feels as if you are here with me or I am with you, helping me face the reality of life as a growing adult."

A Wisconsin pastor wrote,

> Dear Mr. Rogers:
>
>   When a recent blurb about your book came from the Pastoral Psychology Book Club, it seemed worth the investment and I sent for it. Your opening Part I on "This is Me" is one of the most appealing things that has yet come to my attention from our many American psychologists. The all-present mood of acceptance has such a healing power about it that it has clung to me and I cannot, though I would not, rid myself of it. As the Quakers say, "The Lord willing, I hope to finish your book." In the meantime the breath of fresh air that it has thrown into my experience makes me your debtor. This is one of the few books which does not seem to scoop up the harsh judgments of the author to indicate the trash in all the rest of us. Spiritually, sir, you are a biped and I am glad to see you standing so tall—nor does it make the rest of us seem shorter; we're about ready to reach up there, too.

A dramatic example of how the book seemed to touch people for different reasons, in many walks of life, is this excerpt of a letter from Seattle, Washington, written more than ten years after *On Becoming a Person* was published. Unsolicited letters like these have continued to come to Rogers, at the rate of two or three per week.

>   A teacher friend who was losing the struggle against alcoholism—(this was over a year ago)—accepted my suggestion that he read "On Becoming a Person." And since Rogers, he *has* become again, probably more so than before his booze era. . . . This really intelligent, good man appeared to be on the way out; and his wife and two sons are so wrapped up in him that their future seemed a useless prospect. Although you may not really need it, one more bouquet won't hurt: your thinking and its wording rang the right bell, and saved a whole family. We're truly glad you're here.

It was ironic. Houghton Mifflin had shown little enthusiasm for the book. Again their worry was, who would buy it? It was too technical and narrowly focused for the layperson, the teacher or the parent, they thought, and not technical or focused enough for the therapist, counselor, or researcher. Yet its sales were excellent from the start, and by 1971, ten years after publication, it had sold more copies than any of Rogers' other books, all of which had been available for many years more. What the publisher had not counted on, but what Rogers had sensed, was that humanistic psychology had come into its own. In the forties and fifties, interest in this third force in psychology had been growing, but only among a small number of professionals in various fields. In the sixties, just as various other movements were gaining public attention—civil rights, peace, students, women—so was humanistic psychology making its force felt in professions from counseling and psychotherapy to education to social work. It was seen in the growing interest in sensitivity training and encounter groups; in the church's explosion into new styles of worship and dress; in the use of psychedelic and other consciousness expanding drugs. Sometimes it was difficult to tell where politics left off and psychology began. Was the spread of rural and urban communes in the sixties, for example, more of a political phenomenon or a social-psychological one? The point is that people in all walks of life were attempting to guide their lives toward goals of their own choosing, which was precisely the goal of most humanistic psychologists and the gist of most of their writings. To help individuals achieve their full potential, to become self-actualizing or fully functioning, to clarify their values, to relate more effectively to those around them—this was the language of humanistic psychology, and it meshed very comfortably with the other political and social movements of the sixties. The idea whose time had come was accepted readily by thousands, if not millions, of professionals, laypeople, and students. *On Becoming a Person* appeared exactly at the right time. Rogers, while always well known in the psychology profession and by a significant minority in other helping professions, was now catapulted into even greater fame among the professional communities and the interested public.

But Rogers had publisher problems. Houghton Mifflin had been an appropriate publisher for his earlier books. Aimed at specialized professional readers, published in cloth, priced fairly expensively, the books sold well. The publisher and author were pleased. For a book of this type, five or ten thousand copies sold over the years was successful. By the late fifties and early sixties, however, the publishing world had changed in two ways. First there was a much wider audience of readers now interested in psychology, sociology, and other areas in the behavioral sciences. A good writer like Erich Fromm, a social psychologist, could make the best-seller list and reach well over a hundred thousand readers in the very first year of publication. Popular psychology books like *Games People Play* could sell well over a million copies. Second, the rise of the paperback book had revolutionized the publishing industry. A volume that previously would have cost $4.95 to $7.95, for example, could now be available in paper from $.95 to $1.95 (no longer, alas). There were smaller profits for the publisher and fewer royalties for the author on each book sold; but at such low prices, sales might increase five- or ten-fold—the net result being greater profits and royalties and five or ten times more people reading an author's work.

Rogers realized all this too late. Had he worked with another publisher on the book it might have done far better than it did, even though in traditional publishing terms it did very well. After a few years he began to have some sense of this and asked the publisher to put out a paperback edition of *On Becoming a Person* to make it more easily available to a wider audience. The publisher thought the book was doing well as it was and rejected the idea. This began a long and often angry correspondence between Rogers and Houghton Mifflin. He did everything he could to convince them to put out a paperbound volume. Rogers said the correspondence "shows me at my snottiest." When they said, "Do you realize we'd have to sell three times as many copies in paperback as we now do in hardback," Rogers wrote back that he would guarantee they'd sell at least three times as many and would repay them the difference in profits if he was wrong. Still they said no. Finally they relented and published a Sentry paperback edition at a quality paperback price of $2.95. During the first year after publication it sold four times as many copies as the cloth had sold the year before. Sales have been excellent ever since, with well over 600,000 copies in print as of this writing.

Other honors continued to add to Rogers' esteem and reputation. Just at the beginning of his time in Wisconsin he was serving a two-year term as the first president of the American Academy of Psychotherapists, formed in 1956 by professionals interested primarily in psychotherapy who wanted to form an organization in which both psychologists and psychiatrists could work together legitimately and equally. One of the things the AAP did was to begin building a catalogue of taped therapeutic interviews, conducted by some of the leading figures in the different therapeutic schools. These were duplicated and sold to the members and the general public. Rogers contributed some of the first tapes to this series and altogether made a half dozen or more. It is through these AAP tapes that many people have heard Rogers for the first time and have gotten some insight into the active and caring involvement of the client-centered therapist—a sense which isn't always conveyed in the written form.

He continued to serve during 1957 both as a member of the Policy and Planning Board of the American Psychological Association and as a Consulting Editor to *Psychological Monographs* and until he resigned in 1958, on the Editorial Advisory Board of the *Journal of Consulting Psychology.* Thereafter he quickly diminished his involvement with the professional organizations, serving only again in 1960 as Chairman of the Nominations and Elections Committee of the AAP.

In 1961 he was elected Fellow of the American Academy of Arts and Sciences, a group comparable to the French Academy but not nearly as well known or influential in the United States as its counterpart is in France. In 1962, after a committee of the American Personnel and Guidance Association reviewed fifty-six journals and several monographs and books published between September 1960 and August 1961, he was awarded that organization's "Certificate for Outstanding Research." Again in 1962 he was one of two individuals honored by the Division of Clinical Psychology of the American Psychological Association. In presenting to him the award for the Distinguished Contribution to the Science and Profession of Clinical Psychology, the chairperson read:

> Clinical Psychology has suffered a long time from anxiety neurosis reactive to the problems of psychotherapy; Dr. Carl Rogers has provided us with a defense mechanism against this anxiety. He, more than anyone else, initiated effective research in psychotherapy by opening the office to let us observe the therapist in action. Carl Rogers accustomed us to having complete records of what goes on. These records have become so common in research that we do not readily recall the times before Rogers when detailed study of the course of psychotherapy was nearly impossible. Methods from him and his students gave us our first objective studies of the progress and effectiveness of psychotherapy. Not least in this contribution was the first clear delineation of one way to do psychotherapy—client-centered therapy. . . .
>
> Dr. Rogers has become an international representative of American clinical psychology and in that role has contributed to the concept of scientific psychology as vigorous and healthy by his willingness to debate and experiment and change rather than rest upon authority and fixed opinion. We must, in justice to his contributions, emphasize the qualities of personality that have drawn to him hundreds of students, attracted not only by his achievements but by his persistent devotion to an ideal.

If we cannot add much to his public honor, we do at least express our collective recognition of the value of his contributions to clinical psychology and of the scientific qualities that have influenced so many of us.

The net impact of his experiences in the early sixties was becoming increasingly clear to Rogers. His successes, and the influence his work was having, were earned outside the university—through his writing, speeches, workshops and professional activities. The university setting at Wisconsin had proved not only less productive than he had expected, but also produced a series of continual frustrations, offset by only occasional high points. In the summer of 1963, at the age of sixty-one, he announced his decision to resign from the University of Wisconsin, and to move to California at the end of the year. As he explained the move:

"Quite unwittingly I had had a part in the formation of an adventurous new organization on the cutting edge of the behavioral sciences. Richard Farson, Thomas Gordon, and I had conducted a workshop in human relations in California in the summer of 1958. Dr. Paul Lloyd, a California Institute of Technology physicist who had become increasingly interested in the field of interpersonal relationships, was one of the participants. As a result of many discussions following that workshop, Farson and Lloyd founded the Western Behavioral Sciences Institute, a non-profit organization devoted to humanistically oriented research in interpersonal relationships, with a particular focus on the manner in which constructive change in interpersonal relationships comes about. At the time of its establishment in 1959, I accepted their invitation to serve on its board of directors. My motive was to encourage what seemed to me a pioneering venture in an area in which pioneering is often unwelcomed by established institutions.

"From the first, Farson, whom I had known for many years, urged me to come out as a Visiting Fellow, or to join the staff, or in any other way I chose to affiliate more closely than as a remote board member. I had never accepted any of these invitations, partly because of other obligations, partly because I felt that my contribution could certainly best be made through a university. While I was at the Center in Stanford in 1963, he repeated over the phone this invitation to join their staff. I gave my stock response, but later began to mull over the question. What was a university, at this stage of my career, offering me? I realized that in my research it offered no particular help; in anything educational, I was forced to fit my beliefs into a totally alien mold; in stimulation, there was little from my colleagues because we were so far apart in thinking and in goals. On the other hand, WBSI offered complete freedom with no bureaucratic entanglements; the stimulation of a thoroughly congenial interdisciplinary group; the opportunity to facilitate learning without becoming entrapped in the anti-educational jungle of credits, requirements, examinations, more examinations, and grudgingly granted degrees. As Helen and I talked it over, we were very reluctant to leave our Madison friends and our lovely home, but I recognized that professionally I could now leave university life without too much regret and that from a realistic point of view, I would have a much deeper membership in a 'community of scholars' at WBSI than at any university I knew. So we decided to make the move."

While there were many in the Department of Psychology (although he had already resigned from Psychology, he was still teaching an interdisciplinary seminar) and a few in Psychiatry who probably felt their lives would be considerably easier without Rogers, the sentiments of many other faculty and students throughout the University were well stated by University President Harrington, who wrote to Rogers upon hearing of his resignation, "Although I understand your decision to leave Madison, it distresses me very deeply. . . . In a very real sense your decision shows our failure to provide for you the opportunities and atmosphere you deserve. This is our fault, not yours; and I hope that in the years to come we will measure up better, and be able to keep men like you." Nine years later Harrington recalled how Carl Rogers "was very important to us. He was one of those most responsible for the renaissance of the Sixties, which restored the University of Wisconsin to a position of national leadership in the social sciences. He was one of the first stars who came; and I can remember clearly how elated we all were. We were on the way; we were getting somewhere. And so we did; much followed that would not have happened if Carl and a few others had not come."

To his colleagues in the Psychotherapy Research Group, just before his and Helen's departure from Madison, Rogers wrote, "One reason for writing this memo well in advance is that I want you to know that neither my wife nor I like farewell parties, going away gifts, or anything of that sort. We have had enough of those in our lifetime and we do not want any more. Consequently, I am seriously requesting that no plans of this sort be made." He also invited them all to stop by for individual farewells where they could talk personally. He said that he had packed and unpacked his books enough times in their many moves and had no desire to do so again. Therefore, aside from the relatively few books he would take with him, if they wished to look through his library and help themselves to any titles they wanted, they should feel free to do so. The rest would go to Goodwill Industries.

So in January 1964 the Rogers left Wisconsin and the midwest where they had lived most of their lives, and drove to California. From New York to Ohio, Ohio to Chicago, and Chicago to Wisconsin, each of his previous westward moves had taken him further into new territory in his profession. Where was there to go? Even Rogers, in 1964, would never have imagined how much more pioneering work was still before him.

CHAPTER 10
The California Years
1964-

Helen Rogers had doubted that they would ever find a home she could love as much as the Monona Lake home they were leaving. Once again, though, they found an ideal location. After a few weeks' looking, they discovered their new home in La Jolla, California.

La Jolla is a unique community in Southern California. Though technically a part of San Diego, it is separated from the city by a large hill, to the top of which tourists and residents often come to look down upon the lights of San Diego to the southeast and Mission Bay to the south. There, sheltered from the San Diego smog and the hot desert winds and cooled by the breezes from the Pacific, sits La Jolla, with its beautiful coastline and ocean view and its year-round temperate weather—rarely colder than forty-five degrees on winter days nor warmer than eighty degrees in the summer.

Houses, mostly expensive ones, start across the oceanside boulevard and continue all the way up the hill which divides La Jolla from San Diego. If one turns off Torrey Pines Road, La Jolla's main thoroughfare near the ocean, and starts up Hidden Valley Road, the road twists and turns higher and higher as one gets closer to the top of the hill. Near the top the view is magnificent, with long miles of coastline visible to the north and the blue Pacific on the western horizon. Up there, on a little side road, sits the Rogers' home, a modern dwelling, with floor-to-ceiling glass walls, looking out over that vista and also surrounding a bright inner courtyard. Birds used often to fly in through an open glass door, so Rogers eventually rigged up a net to catch them and release them outside. One visitor, duly impressed both by the physical openness of the home and by the personal openness of the Rogers, commented, "At the end of the evening I distinctly recalled musing that if anyone could afford to live in a glass house it would be Carl."

At first the house appears large and expansive, but there are actually only five rooms—a large living room-dining room area, a kitchen, a guest room-study, the master bedroom and, across the courtyard, a simple workshop. In the guest room-study Rogers made his office. There he wrote in the morning and had his small collection of books and several files of articles, journals, and papers (he had another office at the Western Behavioral Sciences Institute). In later years, mostly to get a bit farther from the phone, he would do his writing out in the workshop; so this room gradually became another small study. There, also, Helen would paint and Carl would work on his mobiles or fix things that needed repair.

Occasionally in a speech or publication Rogers has mentioned his hobbies—his mobiles, photography or gardening—sometimes comparing the conditions he provides for his plants and the therapeutic conditions which help clients grow. Such brief references barely indicate his real dedication to these pastimes—in fact, with respect to gardening, one would say his passion. In the courtyard, all around the house, and in an enclosed ten-foot-square walled garden adjoining their bedroom, Rogers spends many hours a week, sometimes several hours a day, caring for his plants and flowers—seeding, watering, weeding, fertilizing, transplanting, pruning. Tuberous begonias are among his favorites, and when visitors set eyes upon these bright red, white, or flame-colored flowers, sometimes as large as eight inches across, they often exclaim that they hardly can believe the flowers are real. Even the lemons that the Rogers squeeze for the drinks they enjoy serving themselves or their guests come right off the little tree growing year round outside their kitchen window. His involvement in gardening can be appreciated from a letter he wrote to a South African friend: "I enjoyed very much hearing about your garden. I wish it were possible to send me some of the aloes. I grow several South African plants and have two succulent gardens. Aloes grow very well in this climate but I expect shipping them is out of the question. . . . Gardening is like anything else—one comes to specialize more and more in the rare things. I now have three bushes of the protea family growing. . . . They produce incredible blooms but are very difficult to grow. Mine are still thriving and I hope some day they may even have blooms. . . ."

The Rogers quickly came to love their new home, with its airy expansiveness, simplicity, view, garden, and climate. High above the ocean they had the privacy and leisure to enjoy their time alone and the friends who visited them. When they entertained, Carl typically would do the barbecuing, and afterward would clean up the patio and living room while Helen did the dishes. These were special times, both with the company and in their feeling like partners while tidying up after the others had left. The home and atmosphere they created were consistent with their picture of themselves. A friend wrote to them, after a visit in California, "Dearest Helen and Carl, It almost seems as if the world's alright when we're with you." A colleague commented of Carl and Helen, "Why marriage is so powerful an institution I'll never know, except that there must have been a time when there were a lot of marriages like that."

Aside from living in a beautiful setting, they were also near enough to the city and its resources for their work and avocations. For Helen, San Diego provided the opportunity to resume her work with Planned Parenthood. Madison was a small town that Helen had found cool to the family-planning concept. Here the climate seemed more receptive; in fact, at the time they arrived, a branch of Planned Parenthood was just getting started. It was difficult to raise the funds to get the program launched, and for a few years it was uncertain as to whether they would succeed. Then came the opportunity for some substantial federal funding *if* they could raise enough money locally to match a small part of the bigger grant. For many years Helen had intended to donate a significant sum to this cause when she died. She now concluded that as long as the money could be used effectively at this point, she might as well do it sooner than later. Her ten thousand dollar gift established the San Diego County Planned Parenthood firmly on its feet, and she remained active in the branch for several years until health problems required her to stop.

For Rogers it was less than a ten-minute drive down the hill and along Torrey Pines Road to number 1121, the offices of the Western Behavioral Sciences Institute. As mentioned earlier, the story of how he came to be making that ten-minute drive dated back six years, to 1958. It was then that Rogers was invited by Thomas Gordon and Richard Farson to serve with them on the staff of an intensive workshop on group leadership, which they had organized in Ojai, California. Both Gordon and Farson had been doctoral students of Rogers and were now working together in a private consulting firm.

One of the workshop participants was Dr. Paul Lloyd, a wealthy California Institute of Technology physicist. Lloyd had retired years before and was spending most of his time on his extensive ranch near Rancho Santa Fe, part of a family inheritance derived from the Ventura oil fields. He was extremely impressed with Rogers and Farson and much of the work going on in the behavioral sciences. "The Ojai conference was a hell of a good experience for me," he recalled. "Carl Rogers elevates the individual; he made me feel worthwhile. I looked up Dick when I got back to San Diego because I thought I might set up a foundation to provide scholarship funds for people who otherwise might not be able to attend such workshops." But Farson had been trying for some time unsuccessfully to establish a humanistically oriented research center. Working with Lloyd, they soon came up with the plan for the Western Behavioral Sciences Institute, WBSI. Starting then, and continuing over several years, Lloyd began selling off $760,000-worth of Rancho Santa Fe land, which enabled the Institute to get started and survive during difficult periods. Rogers accepted an offer to serve on the Board of Trustees, a position he continued to hold when he finally moved to California to become a "Resident Fellow" at WBSI as well.

He had told his friends in Wisconsin that one minor advantage of moving to WBSI was "a very generous increase in salary." What he did not tell them was that he was going to take his $25,000 annual salary and return it to WBSI each year. He and Helen made enough money each year from his writing royalties, speeches, workshops, and consultations, and their combined investment income to enable him to do this. That he *did* do it, however, was a good indication of how excited he was about the organization and its goals. Here was a group of men and women dedicated to furthering research about human learning and growth and to applying their present and emerging knowledge to the solution of real human and societal problems. Dr. Wayman "Bud" Crow and several other WBSI psychologists, for example, were working with the United States Joint Chiefs of Staff War Games agency, using 384 Navy recruits to simulate how tensions and problems can lead to war and how better communication could reduce tensions and lessen the probability of war. Farson and Dr. Lawrence Solomon, a

California Western University psychologist, had a $23,000 grant from the office of Naval Research to study how to better predict leadership ability. They produced some interesting results showing how much leadership potential there is in the average person. This led to another project in which Solomon and Betty Berzon showed that leaderless groups could often be as effective as those with trained leaders. This, in turn, led to Ms. (now Dr.) Berzon's getting a research grant from the San Diego Vocational Rehabilitation Administration to use the leaderless groups to help Department of Rehabilitation clients get back on their feet, helping one another to overcome the physical or emotional handicaps that interfered with their employment.

Much of the funding of WBSI projects came from government sources where the "big money" was. Later this would create a problem for the Institute; but this was the type of work in which fifty or so active researchers on the staff of WBSI were engaged—trying to learn more about helping people by working with people, trying to change the traditional model of the detached researcher to one of the involved, committed researcher, learning from her own experiences in the real world.

It was this role for the behavioral sciences that truly excited Rogers. Although he had written about it several times before coming to California, his most extensive contribution on the subject came during his tenure at WBSI, in collaboration with another staff member, William Coulson. For six months, beginning in 1966, Rogers, Coulson, and others at WBSI had been working on a program of investigating the philosophy of the behavioral sciences. Dissatisfied with the notion that the logical positivist tradition in science, with its rigid objectification of one subject of scientific study, was sufficient for the study of human beings, the program had as its four goals: "to examine the current assumptions on which the behavioral sciences are built, and the model of science currently held in this field; to consider the various points of view which bear on this problem, and the contributions each has made; to hold small conferences—in which the individuals would be from different sciences, and would hold different orientations in the philosophy of science; to assist in formulating a philosophy of science and a model of science more appropriate for present-day behavioral sciences."

When project members learned that Michael Polyani, the British scientist and scholar whose book *Personal Knowledge* and other writings had contributed much to the understanding of the investigator's personal role in the pursuit of science, was in the United States as Senior Fellow at the Center for Advanced Studies at Wesleyan University, they invited him to come to WBSI for a small conference with a dozen or so people, mostly WBSI staff. He accepted, but soon one idea led to another and the conference got bigger and bigger. It was eventually held in cooperation with the Philosophy Department of the University of California at San Diego, where Dr. Polyani delivered an all-university lecture, and with the Salk Institute, which contributed the physical site for the conference and whose Drs. Jacob Bronowski and Jonas Salk participated in the conference. Other philosophers and scientists from England, France, Israel, and the United States also participated.

The format generally consisted of a speech followed by discussion, the two major exceptions being Dr. Polyani's all-university address and a televised dialogue between Rogers and Polyani. Rogers and Polyani's respect and affection for one another failed to set the tone for the conference. Rather the conference was characterized by a decided lack of communication among the representatives of the various disciplines and even among those of the same disciplines. There was, in Rogers' words, "feeling and passion in the encounters which occurred so freely. . . . There was the very rationalistically minded member of the conference who came out repeatedly with such passionate statements as 'This is nonsense,' 'You are completely wrong.' There was the representative of the hard sciences who felt that the sciences of man should 'put off mathematics as long as possible, and put off philosophy indefinitely!' There was the prominent psychologist who, stung by sharp criticism of present-day psychology, made the remark (only partly facetious) that future conferences should be limited to only psychologists, who could consequently understand one another."

Rogers, as much as anyone, was in the thick of the discussion, not only as a clarifier and facilitator, but usually as an opinionated participant, as the following exchange illustrates.

ROGERS: Now wait a minute. I take a strong dislike, I will admit, to the academic one-upsmanship that seems to me to be your hallmark. I accept most of the criticisms which you just made of what I said—but they don't apply at all to the example that Farson gave . . . [*later*] . . . I want to ask you before you leave, something of where *you* stand. You always tear down other people, but what the hell do you stand *for*?

BAR-HILLEL: I'm not a sociologist or a psychologist. Why do I have to stand for anything . . . ? But I *can* say that *methodologically* many of the remarks that I heard today are methodologically quite wrong.

ROGERS: I'm sure that whatever anyone said would to you be quite wrong.

BAR-HILLEL: No, I disagree quite strongly. Many things which you said in your talk three days ago, I found perfectly acceptable. But today, this particular formulation and this pseudo-intrusion of responsibility and so on—these I regard as pseudo-formulations.

MORRISON: We want to know where you stand in philosophy. I would like to know very much.

BAR-HILLEL: I stand 12 1/2 per cent to the right of Carnap. What kind of a question is that: "Where do I stand in philosophy . . . ?" I'm a philosopher of science, a philosopher of language, a philosopher of mathematics, an analytic philosopher, an algebraic linguist. What other information. . . .

If the previous example shows Rogers' impatience and sarcasm, which often arise when he is frustrated, what follows, as the discussion continued a bit later, is his old tenacious college debater's side.

ROGERS: Let me ask just one question. You must probably, in your own lifetime, have changed from some enthusiasms for operationism and logical positivism to enthusiasm for a different view. Is that a choice that you made? Or was that the result of scientific findings?

BAR-HILLEL: Of the scientific findings of other people, sure. It was a development introduced by the fact that we had, in addition, a better understanding of methodology of science.

ROGERS: So it was not a *choice* on your part. It was simply that the facts moved you in that direction.

BAR-HILLEL: Oh, but they moved *me*, they didn't move *others*. So obviously some choice elements were involved, because the same facts as I see them were available to everybody. And since not everybody went in this direction. . . .

ROGERS: This is what we're saying here, that the *choice* we make as to what science is and what science means and what the appropriate methods of science are, are *choices* that *we* make, and those choices make a sharp difference.

CROW: And they're not to be answered solely by scientific knowledge.

BAR-HILLEL: But the fact that so-and-so made this choice and so-and-so did not make this choice is a fact that has to be investigated, and can be investigated by science. That *A* did make this move and *B* did not, this is obviously part and parcel of purely scientific investigations. . . . [*Later*] . . . Very often—I am afraid I will again offend people— very often scientists when they philosophize (and they do it, for instance, today), very often they go quite wrong, and a good knowledge of a good methodology of science might help them not to philosophize wrongly. So the philosophy of science, the methodology of science, may help scientists not to philosophize in the wrong direction.

CROW: Is what Polyani is saying—is that right or wrong? And is that a scientific question?

BAR-HILLEL: On Sunday I made my point very clear. I don't want to repeat it. I definitely think that Polyani is *wrong* in most of what he said, as I understand it, but I don't want to repeat my arguments.

CROW: Is it on the basis of scientific evidence that he is wrong?

BAR-HILLEL: Of methodology of science. On the basis of methodology of science.

ROGERS: That's not science, that's a creed.

BAR-HILLEL: What kind of a dichotomy is this? Is science a creed?

ROGERS: Methodology of science is something that scientists themselves have dreamed up and believe in.

FAIRCHILD: It's an invention.

BAR-HILLEL: I don't *believe* in any methodology of science. I don't even understand this strange mode of speech—I'm not a fideist.

ROGERS: You just said your judgment about Polyani's statement was based on methodology of science.

BAR-HILLEL: Yes, he's using the wrong methodology. What is so strange about it?

ROGERS: Well, you believed in one methodology.

BAR-HILLEL: What do you mean by "believe it"? What do you mean, I have to *believe* it?

POLYANI: No you don't *believe* it, you *know* it.

Coulson and Rogers edited the proceedings of the conference— four papers, many excerpts from the discussions, the televised Polyani-Rogers dialogue—added some introductory and summary comments, and through the Charles E. Merrill Publishing Company of Columbus, Ohio, had a small volume published entitled *Man and the Science of Man.* Rogers hoped the book would demonstrate "the growth of a new view of behavioral science . . . a view so radically different from the current view that it will be shocking to many." He did not want to minimize the enormous accomplishments of the traditional scientific methodology, but believed that "the whole enterprise of science can be seen as but one portion of a larger field of knowledge in which truth is pursued in many equally meaningful ways, science being one of those ways."

As of June 1973, five years after publication, the book had sold a grand total of 2,100 copies, by far the least successful major publication in Rogers' career. As I have not come across any reviews of the volume, I can offer only my own speculation on the reasons for its negligible impact. Throughout his career Rogers has frequently been critical of previous conceptions, sometimes even his own. But always, in addition to his criticisms, he gave very concrete examples to show the alternative he was advocating. But here, in criticising the traditional mode of scientific inquiry in the behavioral sciences, he provided practically no concrete alternatives or examples. Most of the discussion is quite intellectualized and abstract. One might have expected Rogers to find a way to include case studies of scientists who employed this new philosophy and methodology of the behavioral sciences. Or we might have expected to hear discussed many research studies in the mode he was advocating. Such specific examples had always characterized his writing. Here they were lacking; though to be fair, it was a collaborative effort on Rogers' part, and the authors may have consciously chosen simply to report the conference, rather than write an extensive treatise themselves on the subject. Still, Rogers was stating that this new approach to science "would lead to choices of different problems as worthy of investigation; to hypotheses of a sharply different sort; to methods sharply different from those in use today." From reading this volume alone it is hard to tell just what problems, hypotheses, and methods those would be. Rogers wrote, "I regard this as a prophetic book" which "gives us a glimpse of the science of man as it will be perceived in the future." That may be; but—although the discussion is quite stimulating—if the book is meant to be a sign post pointing toward the future, it is a sign whose letters are hard to read, and the traveler will have much difficulty getting under way.

Again, to be fair to Rogers and Coulson, the book had another purpose. It was the first in a series called *Studies of the Person* which they would edit for the Charles E. Merrill Publishing Company. The series was designed to explore the many issues that would contribute to our understanding of the human being as the subject, not the object, of science. If the first book in the series lacked specific examples, the later volumes would attempt to fill the gap. Within a few years a dozen or so books—mostly in psychology and education—would be published by Merrill, many of these receiving much more attention than the keynote book of the series.

When the series began in 1968, Rogers thought he would enjoy his coeditor's role. It seemed a good way to relax, keep up with new ideas through reading manuscripts, and help to sponsor younger men and women whose work deserved wider attention. As it turned out the role proved tedious. Although he helped some good manuscripts reach publication, the pile of unread manuscripts in his study became less of a pleasurable prospect and more of an unwelcome intrusion which kept him from his own work. Allowing the publisher to continue using his name on the book covers ("Studies of the Person—a series originated by Carl R. Rogers and William R. Coulson"), Rogers resigned from the coeditorship in 1973. For several years thereafter the series continued under Coulson's direction.

While WBSI members worked on many different types of projects, the activity that undoubtedly got the most publicity was its use of "encounter groups." In this Rogers was the leading figure at WBSI, with Dr. Jack Gibb running a close second. For a period of several years, starting in 1964, Rogers became intensely involved in the encounter-group "movement" and became known nationally as a leader in the field. The magazine *Psychology Today* called him the "grand master". An article in *Look* magazine referred to him as "an elder statesman of encounter groups." Some people even believed that Rogers invented encounter groups, which is untrue, but it suggests that a brief historical look might be in order.

In 1946 and 1947 the famous Gestalt psychologist Kurt Lewin and his colleagues were developing a type of leadership training that utilized the intensive, small group as the vehicle for learning. They were discovering how, in the absence of a formal agenda, a group could study its own development—the communication and leadership patterns within the group, the development of group "norms," the reactions of members to one another—and how this type of learning could have enormous impact on the attitudes and leadership styles of group members. After Lewin's death in 1947 his colleagues continued to develop this learning model. The initial purpose of the groups was to "train" individuals to be more effective leaders. This was done by helping them to better understand group dynamics and to be more "sensitive" to the reactions of others in the group, especially to how their own behavior affected other group members. Because of this emphasis on training and sensitivity to others, the small groups became widely known as T-Groups (T for training) and the overall approach as "human relations training" and "sensitivity training."

For many summers in Bethel, Maine, the initial group of investigators and their colleagues continued to hold workshops under their organizational name, the National Training Laboratories. Affiliated with the National Education Association, the group later changed its name to the Institute for Applied Behavioral Science, with headquarters in Washington, D.C. NTL, as it is popularly called, has been more responsible than any other organization for spreading human-relations training. As Rogers readily admitted, "NTL did the real pioneering in the encounter-group movement, and really have been the prime moving force in the whole thing." For many years they had a network of certified "trainers"; they and their members sponsored a good deal of research in the group dynamics area; they further developed their training approaches into the areas of organizational and community development; and they performed contracted services for hundreds of large and small industrial, religious, and educational organizations.

Also in 1946 and 1947, Rogers and his colleagues at the Counseling Center of the University of Chicago were themselves experimenting with the small, intensive group. Rogers himself had developed a teaching style which had much in common with the later encounter group. He didn't teach. He provided resources, but let the class decide what it wanted to do, attempting to clarify the thoughts and feelings of students as these emerged. In this leadership vacuum, conflict was not uncommon nor was closeness, as members finally began taking the responsibility for the group on their own shoulders and started sharing resources and helping one another. Thus, quite naturally, Rogers began developing his own style as group "facilitator," as he came to call it.

At the same time, he and his colleagues were confronted with a task which took them in a similar direction. The Veterans Administration asked the Counseling Center to run short training programs for personal counselors who could work with the many returning GIs who needed psychological help. Realizing that experiential, not only cognitive, learning was necessary to do this training, they wondered how they could provide a large number of people with actual experience in counseling in a short period of time. Their solution was to create small groups in which the Center staff members would serve as "counselors" to the whole group. It was hoped that this would help the members to "better understand themselves, to become aware of attitudes which might be self-defeating in the counseling relationship, and to relate to each other in ways that would be helpful and could carry over into their counseling work." What they found was that the group members became extremely close, that members began counseling and helping one another, and that the experience seemed to have an enormous impact upon the participants.

The key difference between the NTL groups and the Chicago groups was that the former had as their major focus the professional training of leaders, with the personal growth of the participants being a secondary gain; while the latter had the personal growth of the participants as its major focus, with the expectation that this personal growth would enable the individuals to be more effective in their helping relation-ships. Rogers recalled, "It was probably in 1947 that Tom Gordon went to Bethel to visit the NTL lab there. I remember that he came back quite critical and sure that we were doing a better job. They were, at that time, very much focused on the skill training where our ap-proach was much more closely allied to the therapeutic and the differ-ences are quite sharp. I guess as a result of that we didn't pay much attention to NTL for some years."

Still, Rogers did not attach much importance to their experience with intensive small groups at Chicago. He was just getting his major research under way at the time, and had enough trouble designing the research to measure the phenomena of individual psychotherapy; mea-suring the "group therapy" process seemed to him an insurmountable task.

A few years later, though, he had another experience along these lines, as he told an interviewer in 1967. "The next time I was involved in a group experience was in the autumn of 1950 when I conducted a postgraduate seminar type of therapy held just before the A.P.A. meetings. I remember that for one hour each day I counseled a client in front of a group of twelve. The discussion periods started off on a somewhat academic basis, but as we got into it, sharing more and more deeply of our personal experiences, our failures, and our difficulties, it became a moving personal experience. All of us left there feeling we had gained deeply. What amazed me was the long lasting effect from the experience. It was then that I began to realize the potency of group experience."

After that his classes and training workshops and an annual summer workshop at the Counseling Center given throughout the early and mid-fifties often took on the intensity of these prior experiences. But he wrote and said little on the subject, occupied as he was with his major research effort at the time. Then in the summer of 1958 he was invited by Gordon and Farson to be with them on the staff of the two-week workshop in Ojai, California (which indirectly led to the formation of WBSI). He recalled, "I suspect it was the first one in which I had participated in which it was clear that the main focus was on our interpersonal relationships and that this was a group of people who came for that purpose and not because they felt serious prob-lems."

He began to do an increasing number of workshops of this type, with his focus shifting more toward the intensive group experience and away from a cognitive focus on a particular topic such as therapy or leadership. At the same time "sensitivity training," as it was being called more often, was gaining increasing popularity throughout the country. Esalen Institute, on the Big Sur coastline in California, gained wide publicity for its work with groups, often geared more toward the personal growth of participants and including more nonverbal and sensory awareness activities than the NTL network tended to use. By now the "trainer," "group leader," or "facilitator" was becoming an accepted role in the helping professions, and many individuals were earning most or all of their livelihood by going from group to group helping people grow personally and/or learn new skills in group participation and leadership. It was a modern version of the traveling Chautauqua meetings, except the focus was on the horizontal not the vertical, and the behavioral sciences not the scriptures was the gospel being experienced, not preached.

People often ask, "Well, what is it exactly that happens in an encounter group? What do people do?" This is difficult to answer, partly because it is a different experience from the type most people have had, and partly because there are many different types of groups, with various participant compositions and various styles of leadership. One description of Rogers', though, tried to encompass most of the groups he was a part of: "The basic encounter group is relatively unstructured, which provides a climate of maximum freedom for personal expression, exploration of feelings, and interpersonal communication. Emphasis is on interaction among the group members, in an atmosphere which encourages each to drop his defenses and facades and thus enables him to relate directly and openly to other members of the group. Individuals come to know themselves and each other more fully than is possible in the usual social or working relationships; the climate of openness, risk-taking and honesty generates trust which enables the participant to recognize and change self-defeating attitudes, to test out and adopt more innovative and constructive behaviors and subsequently relate more adequately and effectively to others in his everyday life situation."

What attracted Carl Rogers to all this? When he left Wisconsin in 1963, here was a sixty-two-year-old man who had made an enormous contribution to his field and, following most conventional patterns, should be getting ready to settle into semiretirement to enjoy his autumn years working around his garden, keeping up on his profession through reading and occasionally writing an article, making a speech, or helping some younger colleague get started. Moreover, here was a rather levelheaded individualist, a conservative when it came to fads and movements, a product of midwestern reserve and inhibition, a husband for almost forty years, grandfather of six, wealthy enough not to need the money which helped attract many others to the group-work field—in short, here was one of the least likely candidates to start a whole new phase of his career by entering the young, energetic, and erratic "human-potential movement" which seemed to be growing so fast in popularity across the nation. On the other hand, it was all very logical. Rogers' style from the beginning was that of a maverick and a pioneer. Whether moving from job to job or theory to theory, he had left comfortable places before. On leaving Chicago he had said he was eager to go to Wisconsin to work with "psychotics and normals," two populations he had had little contact with up until then. For six years he worked with schizophrenics, but the research component which dealt with a normal population did not work out. Normals did not seem to want to enter into psychotherapy. So he was unable to test his general hypothesis that congruence, unconditional positive regard, and empathic understanding would help even normals grow toward greater psychological maturity and openness. The small-group experience seemed an ideal occasion to extend the application of his theories and methods. Thousands of "normals" were flocking to these groups. In fact, in most advertising it was stressed that the groups were not designed to be a substitute for therapy but were designed for well-functioning individuals who desired to increase their personal satisfaction and effectiveness in life. Here was the perfect occasion for Rogers to be Rogers—accepting and understanding—and to see how this would help normal individuals in their own quest for growth.

Accepting, understanding . . . and congruent; and herein lies another reason for his entering the encounter-group field. As a former student wrote, "I'm not surprised he went into Encounter eventually. It could easily be a natural outgrowth from his original ideas of neurosis, but it might also reflect his own need to be closer, and to touch." Earlier chapters of this book described Rogers as a shy boy, sensitive, liking people, but awkward in social settings. When he was a young man, it was primarily through church-related work that he made contact with others his age. Previously quoted comments by his associates described a man who seemed to appear aloof but who entered readily into deep emotional contact with people when he had the occasion. Even his own professional approach indicated a gradual recognition of the importance of the congruent therapist, a whole person in the relationship. This recognition coincided with his own therapy, in which he came to trust his own feelings more and to value himself more. The composite is a picture of a man striving in different ways throughout his life to give more of himself, to come into closer contact with people around him. Where the setting encouraged this, as in therapy, he was capable of extremely close relationships and delighted in them. But in most other situations it was rarely easy. There was always the reserve to overcome. As many colleagues have commented, he lacked a natural spontaneity, although he strove always to be genuine and usually inspired great trust in those who knew him. Thus, for Rogers, encounter groups provided not only a realm of further professional interest, but a vehicle for his own personal growth, a chance to move along the same process continuum which his clients did, toward a greater trust in and openness to his feelings and a greater willingness to risk himself in relationships.

One of the major reasons he put forward for the widespread growth of intensive groups was the loneliness people feel when cut off from each other or when they feel that the deepest parts of themselves are not acceptable to others. "I can speak very personally about this," he wrote, "because I feel that risk-taking is one of the many things I myself have learned from experience in encounter groups. Though I do not always live up to it, I have learned that there is basically nothing to be afraid of. When I present myself as I *am,* when I can come forth nondefensively, without armor, just me—when I can accept the fact that I have many deficiencies and faults, make many mistakes, and am often ignorant where I should be knowledgeable, often prejudiced when I should be open-minded, often have feelings which are not justified by the circumstances—then I can be much more real. And when I can come out wearing no armor, making no effort to be different from what I am, I learn much more—even from criticism and hostility—and am much more relaxed and get much closer to people. Besides, my willingness to be vulnerable brings forth so much more real feeling from other people in relation to me that it is very rewarding. So I enjoy life very much more when I am not defensive, not hiding behind a facade, but just trying to be and express the real me."

For example, "I am often slow to sense and express my own anger. Consequently, I may only become aware of it and express it later. In a recent encounter group I was at different times very angry with two individuals. With one I was not conscious of it until the middle of the night and had to wait until the next morning to express it. With the other, I was able to realize and express it in the session in which it occurred. In both instances it led to real communication—to a strengthening of the relationship and gradually to the feeling of genuine liking for each other. But I am a slow learner in this area and consequently have a real appreciation of what others go through as they try to relax their defenses sufficiently to let immediate feelings of the moment seep through into awareness."

The incident he was describing may have been this one, told in more detail by group member Bill Laughlin: "One of the participants had been cynical about life, had been withdrawn from the group for the entire week and was, in fact, a very unpleasant fellow. Carl was determined he was going to open this person up. He tried about every concept, every approach that he had. . . . It simply didn't work. On the very last morning (we were to leave at noon) he came in completely haggard after a sleepless night. With tears in his eyes (I have often thought he was a tremendous actor) he told of how much empathy and love he had for this individual and how his complete inability to get through to him caused him to turn and toss all night. He told us of his immense anguish, and that he would never again be involved in a T-Group for executives because of his tremendous weaknesses and inability to cope with the situation. 'I'm just not any good at this kind of thing with the executives.' Of course, this set the whole group up to an immediate high. The result was vicious attacks on the withdrawn participant, which, to make a long story short, opened him up. By twelve o'clock, our departure time, Carl and the poor fellow were in each others arms weeping copiously. It was a peak experience for all —beautiful, satisfying and very helpful to the individual."

Friends and family frequently commented on the changes they saw in him resulting from his encounter-group experiences. Natalie said, "I've seen a tremendous change in him. I just can't get over it. He was very private through my high school days, and I grew up very private —not revealing myself at all, but I could help other people talk. He was that way; he could help other people open up about themselves but not say anything about himself. The group experiences he has had have changed him into being much more self-revealing, much more open about his needs for affection and being affectionate or demonstrative." For example, "being physical—the way he gives me a hug or a kiss or the way he will come sit down and put his arm around me, particularly if I may be in some emotional pain, or the way I see him in groups talk about himself or move—take himself out of a place and move toward somebody. I don't think it ever would have occurred to him to get up and move physically closer to somebody before he'd been in encounter groups, that that would matter, that that feels good to him as well as to the other person."

David felt his father was always able to be himself, even before his involvement with encounter groups. "He can tell somebody 'You bore me' in ways that aren't terribly offensive. When he's decided to go to bed, he'll leave or say 'I'm going to bed.' He's quite comfortable being himself. Once I called him and he said, 'It bothers me that you only call me when you want something.' He's totally consistent. When he says you should listen and ought to care, he listens and cares."

Whatever his motives for becoming involved with encounter groups, he certainly became deeply involved. During the five-year period from 1964 through 1968 he served as facilitator in dozens of groups lasting from one day to eight days, not including the shorter groups and the brief demonstrations of encounter groups he did before live audiences. Each year NTL invited him to lead a group in their "Presidents Lab," a week-long training experience for the presidents and executive officers of large corporations. For three years he had an ongoing relationship with the California Institute of Technology, where he spent two days a month working with the "Honker Group" of faculty and administrators. Also over a two-year period, he and his colleagues conducted numerous groups for administrators, faculty, and students in the Immaculate Heart College and School System in Southern California. He had two-to five-day experiences with the administrators and faculty of the six Claremont Colleges; with a number of trustees, administrators, faculty, and students of Columbia University just after that University's famous student uprising in the spring of 1968; with the faculty and students of thirteen junior colleges; with the counseling staff of several colleges; with business executives at various levels; with nurses—administrative, teaching, and supervisory; with religious workers of many denominations; with ghetto black and brown "consumers" of health services and health agency "providers" of medical services; with mental health workers in all categories; with couples; with adolescents; with many teachers; and with many university classes taught in an encounter-group fashion.

Rogers' role was that of facilitator. He preferred this term to "trainer," maintaining that he was not training anyone toward a specific goal, but facilitating or helping each individual achieve his or her own goals during the course of the group's life. As in individual therapy, the conditions of congruence, unconditional positive regard, and empathic understanding were the most essential ingredients in his facilitative role. One might wonder, how can a person be congruent if he is playing a role? For Rogers there was no conflict. He viewed himself in the group first and primarily as a person, a real person with many different goals—to grow himself, to learn more about groups, to achieve meaningful contact and communication with others, *and* to be helpful to others when he could. The facilitator was but one dimension of the person he was. If he tried to act "like a facilitator" in a group, that would undoubtedly be incongruent and group members would be likely to sense this before long. But simply *being facilitative* was a natural part of his personal behavior, one which he prized, one which he demonstrated frequently in or out of encounter groups.

Sitting in the circle of a dozen or so strangers, he would often begin a group by saying something like, "Well, here we are, I feel a little nervous right now. I don't know how this will turn out. It's really up to us to make of this group what we wish to. And I'm also a bit excited right now and eager to get to know you." And much to everyone's dismay, he might stop right there. Filling this unusual leadership vacuum would come several reactions: typical introductions that one of the members might initiate; small talk; one or two expressions of personal feelings—"I'm a bit confused at what's happening here," "I hope this group will help me to understand myself better," expressions that would often go unnoticed or be ignored, as the group would not yet be ready to move to more intimate communication; and talk about outside-the-group situations or past feelings they have had, as this, too, is easier to discuss than what they are feeling or experiencing in the "here and now." Throughout all this Rogers probably would be relatively passive, chuckling along with a joke but not encouraging a partying atmosphere, nodding and letting people know he was hearing them, conveying an attitude which implied, "That's OK. I know you're a little nervous. It *is* an unusual situation, I admit. But I'm confident. You're doing fine. We're doing all right as a group. It will all work out." Throughout this "milling-around" period, however, Rogers would be conveying, nonverbally and verbally, a strong attitude of acceptance to the group members. As he once described it, "I wish very much to make the climate psychologically safe for the individual. I want him to feel from the first that if he risks saying something highly personal, or absurd, or hostile, or cynical, there will be at least one person in the circle who respects him enough to hear him clearly and listen to that statement as an authentic expression of himself."

Somehow this attitude of acceptance would reach the participants, and they would experience the freedom to express more personally the feelings, thoughts, experiences, and hurts within them. This would not happen all at once, but gradually and tentatively. As people would begin to share more of themselves, Rogers would tend to become more active in his empathic responses. To a husband who had just uttered a very complicated and somewhat incoherent statement, Rogers would say, "And so, little by little, you have come to hold back things that previously you would have communicated to your wife? Is that it?" To two individuals disagreeing with one another on the subject of marriage, he would say, "There is a real difference between the two of you, because you Jerry are saying, 'I like smoothness in a relationship. I like it to be nice and tranquil,' and Winnie is saying, 'To hell with that! I like communication.' "

As these earlier expressions of feeling are understood and accepted, the level of group trust deepens, and people feel safe enough to share even more of themselves. In one of Rogers' groups, for example, there was a government executive, a man with high responsibility and excellent technical training as an engineer. Rogers recalled how "at the first meeting of the group he impressed me, and I think others, as being cold, aloof, somewhat bitter, resentful, cynical. When he spoke of how he ran his office he appeared to administer it 'by the book' without warmth or human feeling entering in. In one of the early sessions, when he spoke of his wife, a group member asked him, 'Do you love your wife?' He paused for a long time, and the questioner said, 'OK, that's answer enough.' The executive said, 'No, wait a minute! The reason I didn't respond was that I was wondering if I ever loved anyone. I don't think I have *ever* really *loved* anyone.' It seemed quite dramatically clear to those of us in the group that he had come to accept himself as an unloving person . . . before the week was over he had thought through new ways of handling his growing son, on whom he had been placing extremely rigorous demands. He had also begun genuinely to appreciate his wife's love for him which he now felt he could in some measure reciprocate."

These deeper expressions of feeling often involved members sharing their feelings toward one another, positive and negative. This often led to what Rogers called a "basic encounter," a moment of real and accepting contact between individuals, a meeting without facades, an "I-Thou" relationship. One woman described such an incident in a letter to Rogers, following their experience together in an encounter group. After describing herself as a "loud, prickly, hyperactive individual," whose marriage was in serious trouble and who had felt that life was just not worth living, she wrote, "I had really buried under a layer of concrete many feelings I was afraid people were going to laugh at or stomp on which, needless to say, was working all kinds of hell on my family and on me. I had been looking forward to the workshop with my last few crumbs of hope. It was really a needle of trust in a huge haystack of despair . . . the real turning point for me was a simple gesture on your part of putting your arm around my shoulder one afternoon when I had made some crack about you not being a member of the group—that no one could cry on your shoulder. In my notes I had written the night before, 'There is no man in the world who loves me!' You seemed so genuinely concerned that day that I was over-whelmed. . . . I *received* the gesture as one of the first feelings of acceptance—of me, just the dumb way I am, prickles and all—that I had ever experienced. I have felt needed, loving, competent, furious, frantic, anything and everything but just plain *loved.* You can imagine the flood of gratitude, humility, release that swept over me. I wrote with considerable joy, 'I actually felt *loved.'* I doubt that I shall soon forget it."

Rogers was certainly no stranger to the phenomenon of seeing peo-ple grow by experiencing previously denied or distorted feelings and incorporating these into a somewhat altered self-concept. What *was* new for Rogers was the extent to which he began operating himself in terms of his feelings. This had several dimensions.

First, he came to trust himself more than ever before. One particular occasion is a good illustration of this, when his head would have told him to do one thing, but his total inner experiencing told him some-thing else. Sue was a high school girl, shy, serious, trusted by her peers. "The next day some very moving feelings were expressed, and the group paused for quite a time in silence. Sue finally broke into it with some highly intellectual questions—perfectly reasonable but somehow not at all appropriate to what was going on. I felt, at some intuitive level, that she was not saying what she wanted to say, but she gave no clue as to what her real message might be. I found myself wanting to go over and sit next to her, but it seemed a crazy impulse, since she was not in any obvious way asking for help. The impulse was so strong, however, that I took the risk, crossed the room, and asked if I could sit by her on the couch, feeling that there was a large chance I would be rebuffed. She made room for me, and as soon as I sat down she leaped into my lap, threw her head over my shoulder, and burst into sobs. 'How long have you been crying?' I asked her. 'I haven't been crying,' she responded. 'No, I mean how long have you been crying inside?' 'Eight months.' I simply held her like a child until the sobbing gradually subsided. Little by little she was able to tell what was troubling her. . . ."

His learning to trust his feelings more also applied to making physi-cal contact with group members, as Natalie remarked. Achieving physical closeness with men and women other than Helen was a long way from his midwestern upbringing, and he wrote, "I admire the younger people who are looser and freer in this respect." Still he learned. "When a young woman was weeping because she had a dream that no one in the group loved her, I embraced her and kissed and comforted her. When a person is suffering, and I feel like going over and putting my arms around him, I do just that."

His greater self-trust also involved being more aware of his fantasizing and a willingness to use his fantasies as an effective communication tool. He wrote, "For example, 'I suddenly had the fantasy that you are a princess, and that you would love it if we were all your subjects.' Or, 'I sense that you are the judge as well as the accused, and that you are saying sternly to yourself, "You are *guilty* on every count.' Or the intuition may be a bit more complex. While a responsible business executive is speaking, I may suddenly have the fantasy of the small boy he is carrying around within himself—the small boy that he was, shy, inadequate, fearful—a child he endeavors to deny, of whom he is ashamed. And I am wishing that he would love and cherish this youngster. So I may voice this fantasy—not as something true, but as a fantasy in me. Often this brings a surprising depth of reaction and profound insights."

The previous examples show Rogers being increasingly expressive of the impulses, fantasies, and dimly formed feelings he experienced. What about the more definite feelings to which he could clearly attach words, which were much more comprehensible to him and verbally communicable to others? Here, as in other cases, his learning came slowly. "In one particular group of educators there had been much superficial and intellectual talk, but gradually they moved to a deeper level. Then in an evening session the talk became more and more trivial. One person asked, 'Are we doing what we *want* to do?' And the answer was an almost unanimous 'No.' But within moments the talk again became social chatter about matters in which I had no interest. I was in a quandary. In order to allay a considerable early anxiety in the group, I had stressed in the first session that they could make of it exactly what they wished, and operationally they seemed to be saying very loudly, 'We want to spend expensive, hard-won weekend time talking of trivia.' Had I said in the first meeting, *'We* can make of this what we wish,' which would have been preferable and probably more honest, I would have felt free to say, 'I don't like what we are making of it.' But I was quite certain that in my attempt at reassurance I had said, 'You can make of it what you wish.' We always pay for our blunders. To express my feelings of boredom and annoyance seemed contradictory to the freedom I had given them.

"After wrestling within myself for a few moments, I decided that they had a perfect right to talk trivia, and I had a perfect right not to endure it. So I walked quietly out of the room and went to bed. After I left, and the next morning, the reactions were as varied as the participants. One felt rebuked and punished, another felt I had played a trick on them, a third felt ashamed of their time-wasting, others felt as disgusted as I at their trivial interchanges. I told them that, to the best of my awareness, I was simply trying to make my behavior match my contradictory feelings, but that they were entitled to their own perceptions. At any rate, after that the interactions were far more meaningful."

Gradually, through many emotional experiences, he developed definite guidelines for how he wished to deal with his own feelings. "I endeavor to voice any *persisting* feelings which I am experiencing toward an individual or toward the group, in any significant or continuing relationship. Obviously such expressions will not come at the very beginning, since feelings are not yet persistent ones. I might, for example, take a dislike to someone's behavior during the first ten minutes the group is together, but would be unlikely to voice it at that time. If the feeling persists, however, I would express it.

"I tend to confront individuals on specifics of their behavior. 'I don't like the way you chatter on. Seems to me you give each message three or four times. I wish you would stop when you've completed your message.'

"I like to confront another person only with feelings I am willing to claim as my own. These may at times be very strong. 'Never in my life have I been so pissed off at a group as I am at this one.' Or, to one man in the group, 'I woke up this morning feeling, I never want to see you again.'

"To attack a person's defenses seems to me judgmental. If one says, 'You're hiding a lot of hostility,' or 'You are being highly intellectual, probably because you are afraid of your own feelings,' I believe such judgments and diagnoses are the opposite of facilitative. If, however, what I perceive as the person's coldness frustrates me or his intellectualizing irritates me, or his brutality to another person angers me, then I would like to face him with the frustration or the irritation or the anger that exists in *me*. To me this is very important."

Rogers tried to share his feelings not only during the group, but afterwards as well. Although it was not expected of him, he almost always followed up with some kind of group letter to the participants:

I am dictating this on Monday. . . . I am a little surprised at the sharpness of the memories that I have regarding each one of you. . . . I have various images of Dick but the one with the most meaning to me is when we were all moving about with our eyes closed and he twice pushed me vigorously out of his space and then our fingers touched and we tentatively explored the boundaries of the space between us and then with ever greater hesitancy he crooked the finger to indicate that he was inviting me—perhaps—into his life space. . . . When we came home, both Helen and I felt very much drained. We slept for 12 hours and now I ask myself sort of gently, not compulsively, "What meaning did it have for me?". . . . Perhaps by the time this letter reaches you the experience will have cooled off and you may not be willing really to accept the final phrase of this letter but I want to state it as I feel it right now. With sincere love and affection for each of you—Carl.

After one session of his ongoing group at the California Institute for Technology, he wrote the members a memo with a different flavor from that of the previous one.

I *was* angry. The thought flitted through my mind at one moment that it would feel good to just walk out of the group and out of Caltech forever. Why was I so angry . . . ?

As nearly as I can catch it, it just struck me, rather suddenly, with great force, that Caltech was a *lousy* place for infants—human infants, infant ideas, infant interpersonal relationships, and infant science. It seems like a lousy place to *grow*.

Before I try to explain myself, let me remind you of what an infant is. An infant is an ungainly, poorly proportioned, messy, smelly being. He can't communicate well, can't understand well, is exceedingly imprecise and inaccurate in everything he fumblingly does. Besides this, he is demanding. The only things which draw us to him are his helpless fragility, which evokes a warm response in some of us, and his enormous potential, which evokes a favorable response in almost all of us.

Now what would (does) happen to an infant at Caltech? If anyone were fool enough to entrust a human infant to our care, the baby would be dissected within the hour to see what was making him tick. After all, that's the only scientific attitude. . . .

This Carl Rogers is a far cry from the nondirective therapist who nods acceptingly as his client jumps out the window. While it was an exaggeration and distortion in the first place, the old characterization of Rogers seems doubly unfair for not having taken into account his significant movement toward a genuine person-to-person relationship, both in individual therapy and later in group work. It is interesting to speculate whether, if he were now to go back to individual therapy after having worked with encounter groups, Rogers' style as a counselor-therapist would be any different. Just before moving to Wisconsin, and afterwards while working with schizophrenics there, he had already recognized and written about the importance of the congruent therapist. But, as discussed earlier, his writing on the subject had been rather vague, with an uncharacteristic dearth of illustrative examples. Working with encounter groups, he seemed to come really to understand and experience the meaning of congruence in a helping relationship. It seems to me inevitable that this experience would markedly affect his individual therapy were he to return to that type of work. Such a change toward greater congruence would not be a contradiction of his previous practice, but a fuller, more sophisticated elaboration of a direction in which he had always been moving.

It is also interesting to note that the spontaneous use of his own feelings that he cultivated in encounter groups was a skill which Helen Rogers had possessed all along. Many friends of theirs have commented on this. As one said, "Helen is a very warm, supportive, direct, strong individual. When I talk with both of them, Helen is the one who's more apt to come out and 'give it to me,' if that's what I need —either really call my bluff or tell me exactly how she sees what's going on. And at times she's done this with such clarity and simplicity and directness, I've really been thankful to her."

Still it was not surprising, with her husband becoming so involved with encounter groups, that she would try it herself. Her first experience was rather disastrous. She had considered using a different name in the group so she would not be associated with her famous husband and therefore could be treated just like any individual group member. But this went against her own sense of honesty; it didn't feel right to her to lie about her name. So during a round of introductions at the beginning of the group, she identified herself and asked everybody to please forget it and just treat her as "Helen." Unfortunately it didn't work. People couldn't seem to disassociate her from their images of Carl, and she never really felt accepted for being herself. This left a sour taste in her mouth for encounter groups. She tried it a couple of times more, though, and these latter experiences were more positive. But in the end she decided that encounter groups were not her cup of tea. She understood their value and appreciated Carl's work in this area; but as she approached seventy, this just didn't seem to be the way she wished to spend her time.

Rogers stayed involved in group work for many years, believing that the intensive group was "the most rapidly spreading *social* invention of the century, and probably the most potent." In addition simply to leading many groups, he also tried to popularize them as much as he could. He made a series of twenty-six half-hour tapes for Instructional Dynamics, Incorporated, in which he talked about all aspects of encounter groups, sometimes in dialogue with others who had expertise in particular applications of the intensive group. He also used the mass media, particularly film and television. He was interviewed several times on educational television stations. On one occasion the TV camera focused on an encounter group for several minutes; then Rogers, who had been sitting in the circle with his back to the camera, turned out of the group, walked toward the camera and began sharing his thinking about encounter groups. Probably the most widely viewed television group was one led by Rogers and his colleague Tony Rose in 1970. In addition to Rogers and Rose there were eight participants each with a different perspective on drugs: Randy, black, a former addict who had grown up among crime and drugs; Amy, white, a nineteen-year-old from a small private college; Joe, white, seventeen, curious about drugs; Paul, white, a middle-aged narcotics officer; Mac, a black woman who had lost a son to a heroin overdose and who ran a rehabilitation home in the Pittsburgh black ghetto; George, a white graduate student who said he was a revolutionary; Russ, white, a nineteen-year-old who was a heavy drug user; Diane, black, a middle-class graduate student whose brother was an addict.

The action on this film could hardly have been staged to produce more drama. On one morning, for example, Diane and George launched a strenuous attack on Rogers. Diane said, "I have seen a lot about Rogers in magazine articles and everywhere. He is a big name and shit! What has he given to us?" George accused Rogers of taking all the credit for the discoveries of others; then saying "This is stupid and superficial and I am going to go out into the real world," he walked out of the group. Amy began crying after witnessing such hostility. Tony, Rogers' cofacilitator, crossed the circle to hug and comfort her. After George left, Russ said, "My mother reached out but my dad has no compassion whatsoever. He never held me, nor cried with me." (By now Russ, Amy and Joe were crying.) "You need at least one person to hold you. I couldn't talk when George was here. He's like my dad —so sure he's right. I could never be violent. I know how it feels to get kicked and hit." Rogers put his arm around Russ's shoulder and told him he had heard very clearly his deep need for a father. Russ put his head on Rogers' shoulder and said, "If my father had held me for just one minute. . . ." He sobbed as he said this, feeling it very deeply. A little later Randy said that he would rather die than go to prison again (he was scheduled to be sentenced a few days after the group. Later Rogers tried to intervene with the judge on his behalf), and Russ said, "That's why kids take drugs—because they can die to get away from the horrors of life. We have to be ashamed of feelings in our culture. We can't express them." Later he said, "My grandmother gives me love. Sometimes we sit for hours and talk. She really listens to me. And now I have this group too. I talked with Amy till after 1:00 this morning. You know, I'm really afraid of girls and it was good to be able to talk with her without being afraid." Paul, the narcotics officer, was visibly moved. He showed an increasing understanding of Russ, Randy, and the others. When the group ended, he shook hands with some, hugged Amy very warmly and, wiping the tears from his eyes he said, "How am I going to make an arrest now?"

As powerful a group as this one was, it did not receive the fame which another Rogers encounter group did. "Journey Into Self" was an hour-long documentary film of a group led by Rogers and Dick Farson, produced and directed by Bill McGaw, and distributed by WBSI. One particular sequence featured Jerry, a competent business executive. Rogers described how, "somewhat puzzled by the statements of others in the group, he said in an early session: 'I look at myself with some strangeness because I have no friends, for example, and I don't seem to require friends.' In a later session when he heard Beth, a married woman, talking of a remoteness she felt between herself and her husband and how much she craved a deeper and more communicative relationship, his face began to work and his jaw to quiver. Roz, another member of the group, seeing this, went over and put her arm around him and he broke into literally uncontrollable sobs. He had discovered a loneliness in himself of which he had been completely unaware and from which he had been well defended by an armor-plated shell of self-sufficiency."

Stanley Kramer, the well-known Hollywood producer and director, took an interest in this film, even appearing in a brief introduction to it. Between his help, and Rogers and Farson's appearing at several California theatres for the film's premier showings, the documentary received a considerable amount of attention. To the delight of Rogers, Farson, McGaw, and WBSI, "Journey Into Self" was nominated in 1968 for an Academy Award in the Feature Length Documentary category and eventually won the prestigious "Oscar."

In addition to the tapes and films, Rogers' major means of explaining encounter groups to the general public was through his book *On Encounter Groups*, published in 1970. At about the time when he was putting together the manuscript of this book, which included expansions of several former essays and speeches as well as some new material, an editor at Harper & Row named Donald Cutler showed up at Rogers' door to see if he was working on any books. When Cutler heard that Rogers was writing a book on encounter groups, he showed considerable interest and asked if he could take a copy back to New York with him to read and show the publisher. Rogers explained that he only had one copy and didn't want to lend that out, but that after he had finished the draft he would send a copy to Cutler. Not to be put off, Cutler asked if he could borrow the manuscript and take it down to a drug store in La Jolla to duplicate on their ten-cents-a-copy photostat machine. In a typically trusting manner, Rogers let him take the manuscript, and that began a relationship which proved to be gratifying to them both. Cutler obtained the contract with Harper & Row, Publishers, one of the oldest and biggest publishing houses in the country. *Carl Rogers on Encounter Groups,* as it was called, was Rogers first "trade book," aimed at a wide audience of general readers. To publicize the book, Harper & Row got Rogers an invitation to appear on Dick Cavett's nationally televised interview show. They were amazed when Rogers declined. "But one show will lead to another," they said incredulously. "That's what I'm afraid of," he answered, not relishing the idea of making frequent cross-country trips to sell books. Still by January, 1978, the book had sold 237,000 copies, and helped associate the name of Rogers and encounter groups even more closely for professionals and laypeople alike.

In his first chapter he traced the history of the encounter-group movement. In the second he described the "process of the encounter group," outlining fifteen overlapping stages of development he saw most groups going through and giving specific examples of each to make the process vivid for the reader. In a unique third chapter, "Can I Be a Facilitative Person in a Group?", he described his own behavior and attitudes as a group facilitator and behaviors he regarded as non-facilitative. In a field where very few individuals have been willing to risk describing what it is they do in leading intensive groups, where a mystique has grown up around the role of the charismatic or enigmatic group "trainer" or "facilitator," Rogers' chapter provides a real challenge and a reference point. He wrote, "I sincerely hope that this presentation will encourage others to speak for their own styles of group facilitation."

In a fourth chapter, and in a seventh chapter on research on encounter groups, he discussed the crucial question of, What happens after the group is over? Is it only a weekend love affair which members go through with their groups, or are there lasting positive or negative behavior changes that show up in participants' relationships with their families, their friends, or at work? Here Rogers cited evidence both anecdotal and scientific. Some of Rogers' participants described enormous changes for themselves, when questioned weeks or months after the group. "I am more open, spontaneous. I express myself more freely. I am more sympathetic, empathic, and tolerant. I am more confident. I am more religious in my own way. My relations with my family, friends, and co-workers are more honest and I express my likes and dislikes and true feelings more openly. I admit ignorance more readily. I am more cheerful. I want to help others more."

Others were more specific and less grandiose about the changes they observed.

"I was bothered about the squabbling between Marie and Alice. I was bothered about Marie's bedwetting. I was bothered that I couldn't give them a lot of affection. I was bothered because they never really talked to me. I was bothered by some of the hurtful things Pete and I could say to them. So, when I came floating home Sunday with this new real self, I was anticipating a response of sorts. What I didn't anticipate was the quickness and the intensity of the response." Shortly after she got home, it was bedtime for Marie, the ten-year-old daughter. Her mother asked Marie if she could scrub her. "Within the space of an hour we talked about menstruation, God, the Devil, Heaven, Hell, hating someone so much you wanted them dead, stealing candy from the kitchen, nightmares, monsters in the window. Of course we had talked about these things before, but never with such completeness. Alice, who is fifteen months older than Marie, came wandering into the bathroom and shared this experience with us. I ended up scrubbing her also. This surprised me—that she wanted me to bathe her—as her body is becoming adolescent and she is very self-conscious about this. Marie said, 'What did you do at that meeting—learn how to be nice to kids?' I said, 'No, I learned how to be myself, which is really pretty nice.'"

Others described its effect on their work. Robert Edgar wrote,

In some sense he [Rogers] was the founder of Kresge College. I first started on a personal growth journey and an educational journey as a consequence of the faculty seminar with him [run as an encounter group] where I first learned about student-centered learning. The concept excited me intellectually—I tried it in my classes immediately with disastrous results. I learned from this for the first time that the students were frightened of me and this then began a process of self-confrontation and change. . . . This led me to take the job as Provost of a new college at Santa Cruz which is now in existence. The underlying philosophy of the college is largely influenced by the contact that I've had with Carl Rogers. My ideas about education grew from his but are not his. . . . I can thank him for being the catalyst in my life and in the life of Kresge College. Up until that seminar at Caltech I never heard of him, I never heard of student-centered education. . . .

Still other participants saw no behavior changes, only an image of what life might be. "The group experience is not a way of life but a reference point. My images of our group, even though I am unsure of some of their meanings, give me a comforting and useful perspective of my normal routine. They are like a mountain which I have climbed and enjoyed and to which I hope occasionally to return."

Then, heavily quoting and drawing upon a book chapter written by his colleague Dr. Jack Gibb, Rogers summarized the research evidence in support of the anecdotal assertions by participants. Gibb had "analyzed 106 studies, including seven earlier reviews of such research. He had also examined 123 additional studies which did not measure up to his criteria for inclusion, as well as 24 recent doctoral dissertations from thirteen universities." His analysis indicated,

> The evidence is strong that intensive group training experiences have therapeutic effects. . . . Changes do occur in sensitivity, ability to manage feelings, directionality of motivation, attitudes toward the self, attitudes toward others, and interdependence. . . . The research evidence clearly indicates no basis for making any restrictions as to group membership. . . . Groups without leaders are effective as training media. . . . To be optimally effective the group training must be relevant to the organizational, family, and life environment of the person. . . . Effective consulting relationships on a continuing basis are at least as important as what occurs in the group sessions in determining impact upon the participants. . . . Training experiences to be optimally effective . . . should be concentrated in uninterrupted and continuous sessions. . . . There is little basis for the widespread concern among lay groups about the traumatic effects of group training.

Many professionals, as well as laypeople, have been concerned about the possible harmful effects of intensive groups. The research just cited seems very important, but I think it should be noted, and Rogers would often brush over this point, that any group leader known to researchers like Gibb and others and willing to have his or her group observed, recorded, transcribed, or analyzed would most probably be a fairly responsible, fairly competent practitioner. As encounter groups and sensitivity training burgeoned and spread dramatically during the 1960s and early '70s, many less responsible and less competent individuals billed themselves as "trainers" or "facilitators" and got many people to participate in their groups. If an equal amount of research were done on these groups, I think the results would be less positive than the studies Gibb reviewed.

A responsible and competent group leader like Rogers, though, was caught in a difficult position on this issue of risk and damage in intensive groups. If he glossed over the problem and said there are no risks, he would lose credibility with laypeople and professionals alike. If he dwelt on the risks, he would scare people away from an experience he believed in strongly. And if he took the middle road of saying "choose your leader wisely," he would have to answer: Choose by what criteria? Unfortunately it is difficult to tell a good leader by his or her paper credentials. For years in individual therapy Rogers maintained that naturally accepting and understanding persons could be trained in a short time to be better counselors than a randomly selected group of licensed psychologists. His belief was similar with respect to group work. In fact Chapter Nine of *On Encounter Groups* described the "La Jolla Program," a summer program designed to train professionals *and* laypeople to become facilitators. Caught in this dilemma of how to react publicly to charges of psychological damage in encounter groups, Rogers more often than not defended the intensive group, and mentioned only in passing the possible dangers resulting from unqualified leaders. Later on, as the encounter-group phenomenon continued to spread in popularity, he began more frequently to acknowledge this problem of the unqualified or harmful leader. A good example of his advocacy of encounter groups can be seen in a letter he wrote to the Editor of *The New York Times Magazine*, after it had published a scathing attack on encounter groups, written by a psychiatrist. Rogers wrote:

> I read with interest the article by Dr. Maliver in your issue of January 3, 1971 ("Encounter Groups Up Against the Wall"). There are many good things about the article and in many respects I find myself in agreement with Dr. Maliver. However, there is one omission in his analysis which is so glaring and so important that I think it needs to be corrected.
>
> First I would like to stress some of my points of agreement. Like him, I deplore the growing commercialism of the whole encounter group movement. Like him, I believe that highly interventive, interpretive, and attacking methods in the group may cause personal damage and there is now research to back up this point. Like him, I deplore the games and

gimmicks that have come to play such a large part in many groups and the manipulation which often accompanies their use. I too am concerned about the over rapid development of growth centers, the use of untested approaches like bioenergetics, Rolfing, and the like.

The enormous deficiency in the article is Dr. Maliver's seeming unawareness of a totally different approach to groups than the one he describes. It is quite true that on the one hand there is the manipulative, aggressive, interpretive, interventive leader, or "trainer," with a background usually in group dynamics, psychoanalysis, Gestalt therapy, bioenergetics and the like. On the other hand, there are an enormous number of groups conducted by facilitators who put their trust in the individual and in the group, who are genuinely trying to facilitate the emergence of insight and personal growth, who are nonmanipulative, who permit the natural group process to emerge. The facilitators of these groups usually have a background in client-centered or existential psychotherapy, student counseling, or forward-looking and innovative education. Such an approach does not tend to cause personal damage.

A number of years ago I made a survey of nearly 500 people who had been in groups I had conducted or had supervised. The follow-up was made a number of months after the group experience. Two out of nearly 500 said that they thought the experience had been more damaging than helpful. For all of the others it ranged from neutral or moderately helpful to the great majority who found it a highly positive and meaningful experience still affecting their behavior. Dr. Jack Gibb has made an excellent summary of well over 100 research studies on the outcomes of encounter groups and sensitivity training and discovers that the findings are generally positive. ". . . The evidence is strong that intensive group training experiences have therapeutic effects."

He also concludes that there is very little basis for the widespread concern among lay groups that group experiences are traumatic for individuals. The most careful study along this line was done by Batchelder and Hardy. Twelve hundred YMCA secretaries had been through encounter groups conducted by or supervised by Dr. Gibb, who belongs in the group entirely overlooked by Dr. Maliver and who places heavy emphasis on the development of trust within the group. Dr. Batchelder and Dr. Hardy decided to make a thorough investigation of this since here was a homogeneous group that could be reached. They collected the names of more than forty individuals who were reported to have been damaged by the group experience. When these individuals were contacted, all but four of them reported that this was a gross misunderstanding, that they had not been damaged, and that the group experience had been a profitable one. Four felt that the experience in the group had been negative for them when it occurred but by the time they were interviewed they had concluded that the experience had been positive. One man out of the twelve hundred felt that the experience was damaging at the time and still was hurtful to him. Nevertheless, he was working very effectively in his job.

This confirms absolutely my own experience in working with a staff of colleagues with the Immaculate Heart College, high school, and grammar schools in the Los Angeles area. We heard many reports that people had been damaged by their group experience and when tracked down these always melted into second and third hand rumors about nameless individuals. So I will stoutly maintain that when the facilitator of a group has a trustful belief in the capacity of the individual and of the group to develop a richer and more insightful life and better interpersonal communication, the risk to the individual is so slight as to be almost nonexistent.

Another bit of evidence is contained in the work of the La Jolla Program, conducted each summer by a number of my colleagues. Over a four-year period they have helped build facilitative skills in more than 600 people involved with groups. In addition, weekend groups have been held for more than 8,000 individuals in order to give the 600 potential group leaders a chance to utilize themselves as facilitative persons. Out of these more than 8500 individuals, four psychic breakdowns are known to have occurred. I and my colleagues regard this as unfortunate but probably no more than would occur statistically in any group of that size over the same period of time.

On the other hand, the kind of approach described by Dr. Maliver does produce "casualties." A recent study reported by Dr. Irving Yalom of some 210 students who had had encounter group experience showed a "nine per cent casualty rate," but some of the casualties were minor. The outstanding finding is that when the group is led by an aggressive, charismatic, intrusive, challenging person, with a sense of mission and endeavoring to convey a feeling of confidence, the members of such groups show little lasting effect and a high casualty rate, quite contrary to the experience in the less structured groups where leaders endeavor to let the group process develop of its own accord.

I do not know whether Dr. Maliver purposely ignored this whole side of the encounter group movement or whether he is genuinely unaware of it. If the latter, he could certainly learn much about it by reading my book, *Carl Rogers On Encounter Groups*, Harper and Row, 1970. I feel he has done a disservice by giving a reasonably accurate but one-sided presentation.

Another chapter in *On Encounter Groups* described "The Lonely Person—and His Experiences in Encounter Groups." Rogers spent one paragraph of this chapter discussing the "existential" aloneness which is a part of the human condition—the reality that all of us are alone, will die alone—and the need to come to grips with this reality instead of denying and trying to escape from it. Others in the humanistic psychology movement, like Victor Frankl, Rollo May, or J.T. Bugental have written extensively on this topic, but Rogers referred to it as "an important issue but one on which I shall not dwell." In this connection he once told an interviewer that his friend Rollo May "told the story that I once questioned the existence of tragedy by saying that Romeo and Juliet might have been all right with just a little counseling. I probably did say that. I'm more optimistic than Rollo. He is an existentialist—so am I, but my philosophy has more room for hope."

It was a different kind of loneliness Rogers was writing about. "I wish to speak more of the loneliness that exists when the person feels that he has no real contact with other persons. Many factors contribute —the general impersonality of our culture, its transient quality, its anomie—all elements of loneliness which grow more marked when we are crowded together. Then there is the fear, which resides in a great many people, of any close personal relationship. . . . But I believe there is a still deeper and more common cause of loneliness. To put it briefly, a person is most lonely when he has dropped something of his outer shell or facade—the face with which he has been meeting the world—and feels sure that no one can understand, accept, or care for the part of his inner self that lies revealed."

Again and again in the encounter groups he conducted, he noted how many individuals expressed that they had gotten closer to people in their group than they had felt to most of the people in their daily lives, even family. He noted also how much people seemed to value this contact, how validated and affirmed they seemed to feel by having others know them well and still accept them. He concluded, "It is, I believe, one of our most successful modern inventions for dealing with the feeling of unreality, of impersonality, and of distance and separation that exists in so many people in our culture. What the future of this trend will be I do not know. It may be taken over by faddists and manipulators. It may be superseded by something even more effective. At the present time it is the best instrument I know for healing the loneliness that prevails in so many human beings. It holds forth a real hope that isolation need not be the keynote of our individual lives."

Other chapters of the book dealt with the subjective experience of change during and after an encounter group, as experienced by the participant; the applications of encounter groups to all kinds of individuals and institutions; and the training of group facilitators. In his closing chapter he gazed into his "cloudy crystal ball" and tried to see the future of the encounter-group movement. When this was published he was sixty-eight years old and had devoted the previous six years to studying, experiencing, and, if I may, coleading the encounter-group movement. To some extent his predictions already have come true. To some extent the history of the intensive group experience is still unfolding.

"What are some of the directions it may take? In the first place, I must acknowledge that it may all too easily fall more into the hands of the exploiters, those who have come onto the group scene primarily for their own personal benefit, financial or psychological. The faddists, the cultists, the nudists, the manipulators, those whose needs are for power or recognition, may come to dominate the encounter group horizon. In this case I feel it is headed for a disaster. It will gradually be seen by the public for what it would then be; a somewhat fraudulent game operating not primarily for growth, health, and constructive change, but for the benefit of its leaders. . . .

"To the extent that this development takes precedence, 'encounter group' may come to be a dirty word, just as 'progressive education' did years ago. It may be worth our while to look at the parallel. Because progressive education became ultrapopular and was carried on more and more by extremists and by those with little or no understanding of its basic principles, it became anathema to the public, and educators were careful to deny that their schools were examples of it. I know of no educator today who would state publicly that he stands for progressive education. Therefore it *seems* to have died out. Meanwhile, the roots of almost every innovative change in education in the last several decades can be traced back to the thinking of John Dewey and to the principles which were in fact the underlying guides for the best of progressive education.

"I can envision the same thing happening to encounter groups, sensitivity training, T-groups, and all the rest. They would become objects of condemnation and die out. Meanwhile, all the essential elements—the building of trust in small groups, the sharing of self, the feedback, the sense of community—would continue to find labels and guises by which they could operate to bring about the changes and communication we so desperately need."

On the positive side, he wrote, encounter groups might grow and spread in their use and their applications. For the individual this could offer the prospect of a life in which continual growth and real closeness with others become the norm, not the exception. For the culture, this could mean a better approach to intergroup tensions and conflict, a creative means for organizational renewal and growth, a way to help citizens readjust to "future shock" and the rapid pace of technological change. For science, encounter groups could offer a new laboratory for the study of human growth, with the opportunity for each group member to become a self-scientist and to participate actively in the data gathering process. For philosophy, encounter groups might offer a new perspective on the Good Life and the purpose for living. In short,

"These changes may occur in persons, in institutions, in our urban and cultural alienation, in racial tensions, in our international frictions, in our philosophies, our values, our image of man himself. It is a profoundly significant movement, and the course of its future will, for better or for worse, have a profound impact on all of us."

Rogers' most intense period of involvement in encounter groups spanned the years 1964 through 1969, although he continued to facilitate groups after that. Near the end of this period came a series of what he called "events which have given me more agony than anything else I can recall in my professional life," even surpassing the unhappiness of his problems at Wisconsin. These events led shortly to the extreme factionalization of the Western Behavioral Sciences Institute and the eventual resignation of Rogers and about twenty-five staff members who formed a new and separate organization.

When WBSI had been formed in 1959 there had been a commitment to have it be a uniquely democratic organization, with power in the hands of the staff and delegated upward to the administration and Board of Trustees as the need arose. It was understood that to satisfy the laws of the State of California, it was necessary to have a fictional autocracy, that is, a Chairman of the Board, a President, an Executive Director, and a set of administrative procedures; but in reality the organization would operate in a democratic fashion. Initially it worked this way. Different staff members initiated different projects, either alone or with other staff members. Decisions about how WBSI monies would be spent were made by the persons involved in the various projects. Individuals felt a great deal of autonomy to develop their own programs, seek funding, and carry out their ideas. Rogers was not the only one who returned some or all of his salary to the organization. The weekly staff newsletter was always an open forum.

Then, after a few years of successful operation, WBSI began experiencing some of the problems that success brings to any organization. As more government funding poured in, there were pressures for different accounting procedures and tighter controls over spending and record keeping. As Rogers and other staff members began gaining wide publicity for their work in encounter groups, some staff and Board members became uncomfortable about WBSI's image getting too closely tied to "sensitivity training" and the possible losses of funding that might result. The various projects or "Centers" no longer felt that they had complete autonomy, as they were asked to adjust their programs for the benefit of the entire organization. As these trends continued, there was much internal disagreement, negotiation, and problem-solving intended to keep the organization together and working toward its goals. As long as Richard Farson was director, he was able to keep the different groupings functioning in some harmony. It was when he left to take another job, and Paul Lloyd was made director (supposedly temporarily) that the factional problems again became serious. Still, Rogers thought they had found reasonable solutions to their problems at the June 1968 Board meeting. Apparently they had not. A month later he wrote a long and sad letter to the Trustees, excerpts of which follow.

> I thought we had really found a workable solution at our Board meeting and I helped to sell the notion to the staff. . . . I felt that the most important decision of our Trustees' meeting was that the Centers were to be as autonomous as it is humanly possible to make them. This fact released untold energies in the Center for Studies of the Person, as we called our group. New projects, new ways of raising money, the idea of all of us turning in our fees so our full energies would go to the Center—dozens of new ideas were sprouting all over the place. It was an exciting period like the first days of WBSI. . . . Within a week I was more depressed than I have ever been before. [He was feeling so sick about it physically that he saw a doctor.] The reason was that although I deeply love WBSI and have worried about it during various previous crises, this was the first time that the dream had ever been strangled from within.
>
> Paul was in office only a week or ten days before he left on a three week vacation which he certainly needed and deserved. I learned of most of the actions he had taken after he was gone and found such actions to be absolutely incredible. I fully believed at that time that he simply did not understand what he was doing and the effects his actions were having.

He went on to describe how the leadership of WBSI, without informing anyone, had been making plans to hire and had begun hiring a Business Manager, bookkeepers and other help whose cost-accounting functions ironically would themselves "cost in salary and office space $120,000 per year."

> One other very minor thing, but one that proved to be fearfully indicative. Paul doesn't remember exactly what he told Vern except to ask him to review the WBSI Bulletin, our weekly staff news sheet. . . . Vern interpreted his instructions as a right to censor the Bulletin and acted on that belief. To me, this was so utterly incredible in this "free organiza-

tion" that I thought I must be imagining things. It also made me certain that Paul had no recognition of the significance of his actions.

When Paul returned, I found the exact opposite to be true—that he was acting consistently with his beliefs. He has completely reversed his philosophy of 1958–59. . . . Paul now believes that all power should be at the top, should flow down. He believes in a benevolent, paternalistic autocracy. Because he loves WBSI and the people associated with it, it seems certain to him that anything he decides to do will surely be for the welfare of WBSI . . .

The thing that cuts deepest for me is that every ideal for which I thought WBSI stood is being demolished with incredible speed. We will now be run by cost accountants just like any reactionary business firm, with the staff not even mentioned in the newly drawn by-laws drafted by Raoul. I have not yet had a chance to talk with Raoul, but these by-laws are the most Hitlerian I have ever seen. They make the Divine Right of Kings look like a weak-kneed sissified theory. I know that reportedly the State of California forbids the formation of a democratic corporation but that is no excuse for glorifying absolute power. . . .

Since drafting the above, I have talked with a very knowledgeable lawyer who says that it is absolutely untrue that a corporation has to be an autocracy to satisfy state laws. He says we could set up a corporation in as democratic a fashion as we please. If we wanted every staff member to be a member of the corporation, or all Trustees elected to serve only at the pleasure of the membership, even this extreme democracy would be entirely feasible. In fact, he says that Sobieski, the former head of this state division, authored several articles and lectures stressing the great importance of the *democratic* corporation. . . .

To some it may seem a relatively unimportant thing that a small, obscure organization lose all of its idealism. . . . But this would over-look the tremendous concern which outsiders feel. Everywhere I go I am being asked, what has happened and what is happening to WBSI? Bell and Howell heard some inklings and called to offer their legal counsel *free* if it would help us set up different divisions or centers in which some are operated under Government regulations because of Government contracts and others wish to operate more freely. 2000, Inc. has offered its consultant services free, offering the same kind of complete look at the whole system which they are giving to such companies as Midas Muffler, a Los Angeles T.V. station, etc. When I thought they were being facetious, one of the younger men associated with 2000, Inc. said to me, "We owe almost everything we are to WBSI It would be a pleasure to be of some help to that organization." When I met Jonas Salk the other day he told me of the tremendous progress they have made in democratizing the Salk Institute where now a group composed of the younger scientists, the Senior Fellows, and repre-sentatives from every group involved in the Institute, work with the President in an Operating Committee. Knowing the mess that they had been in a year ago, I congratulated Jonas very sincerely on the obvious progress they have made. His response was, "But we learned it all from WBSI."

He then suggested that he might be forced to resign from WBSI and requested thirty minutes at the next Board meeting to present his case and his suggestions for averting a crisis in the organization. These included:

> That we give consideration to every means by which we can honor Paul for all that he has done for WBSI—the giving of his fortune, the giving of his time, his energy, his interest, his affection. I would like to honor him in every way possible. . . . That we retire Paul from the presidency which he neither sought nor desired and which now involves him in bitter controversy which he detests. . . . I love Paul, and I know he loves WBSI, but in spite of his good will and his desire to be the best father possible I believe he is ruining the organization we all love. Hence, this letter. . . . Sadly, Carl.

A colleague of Rogers, reflecting on these events, said, "He will not accept being a second-class citizen—not even a little bit. . . . I think that he felt he wasn't being appreciated. Other people felt like they weren't being appreciated and would kind of go along with it. But he would not go along with it. In that situation, I don't think of him as being warm and loving at all. I think that he was mad and I think that was right. And he was hurt."

That hurt is apparent. Along with his letter to the Board of Directors, Rogers included another few pages that were in a very different style and written "when I was in the depths of my despair." I have read some ten thousand or more pages of Rogers' published and unpublished writings; yet the following part of "Camelot—A Fable Retold" moves me most of all.

> I want to tell you cats something about a flick I seen a while ago—*Camelot.* They tell me some of the eggheads thought it was strictly from Dullsville. But not me. I thought it was groovy. I dig all this stuff about knights in armor and a king who is scared of getting hitched to some broad he's never seen, and fellows and their chicks tumbling in the flowers and having some fun doin' it—and a lot of other stuff. But I'm not going to try to tell you the whole story—I'm not *that* square!
> But there's one bit—the last part of the flick—which stays with me and stays with me, and *I don't* know *why.* There's this screwy old dope Arthur, see, and he's just about to lose his last battle. Course there's a lot before that, because he was *really* nuts—an idealist I guess is what the squares would call him.
> Anyway, he's had this cockeyed idea that if a gang of guys were all sworn to be loyal to each other—like the Rangers or any other gang—and if they had a "common purpose" like "trying to make the world a better place to live"—yeah, that's how square he was, then they could

trust each other and live together as friends. He didn't even want to be the boss, the top dog! He even built a round table, so that every guy was just as good as the next guy, see, and nobody even tried to tell anybody else what to do. If a knight wanted to rescue some dame in distress (how's that for kookiness!) or kill some friggin' dragon, O.K., he just went ahead and did it—maybe alone, or with some buddies. And the king's treasure belonged to everybody, see, and if you needed a new suit of armor you just looked in the treasure house to see if there was enough, and if there was, you took some. Well, as I say, you can see that Arthur was strictly from the loony bin!

Crazy thing was, it *worked!* For a long time at least, 'bout ten years, I think. Then one day a cat came along who was smart, see? And he knew that the name of the game was *power,* not this crummy "cooperation" and "love" and "trust" and all that crap. So as soon as he sold this idea to some of the guys, the whole thing cracked up, as any dope would expect. So the knights got to fighting and killing each other, and mistreating the peasants. Arthur's best pal stole his chick. He was so badly clobbered he had to skip the country, and in this last scene he's sitting there in a darkening field, knowing that the other army, led by his best friends—well, his *ex*-pals really—were going to attack in the morning and he would certainly be defeated, and either get his head chopped off or he'd be stuck in the hoosegow—dungeon, they call it—for good and always. So he's not exactly feeling bright and cheery, see?

And then this squirt, this young kid, comes out of the darkness and starts to talk with him. And Arthur finds that for this kid the Round Table, and the stories about it, were just all he *lived* for! For him, Arthur and his knights were the greatest! He knew everything they'd done, the names of all the guys, and the adventures they'd had. He knew 'em like a kid knows the batting average of every Yankee on the squad. He was willing to do *anything* for Arthur, see, even *die* for him.

So Arthur—this gets *to* him, see—so he sends the kid away, and he sings a song to him telling him how to spread the news. Kinda touching, really, though 'course it didn't *really* get to me.

Crazy thing is that I've heard the song later, on records, and you know what—they've got it wrong! I didn't quite catch the lingo, but I *remember* it, and they got it *wrong* on every single record.

What Arthur really sang, sorta choked up and all, when he told the brat what to do, went like this—

> "Ask every person if he's heard the story,
> And tell him loud and clear if he has not.
> Don't let the memory die—
> That *once*—this ain't no lie—
> For one brief shining moment
> There was *double* you *be* ess *eye!*"

For some reason, I sorta got a lump in my throat, even though I don't dig the last line—some sorta code, maybe. But when I think of that song when I'm alone, sometimes—gosh you'll think I'm nuts—a tear or two runs down my cheek. I guess it's because Arthur—kook that he was— seemed so damned disappointed.

The Board, which included the future Senator from California, S.I. Hayakawa, was not responsive. He did resign, and along with about twenty-five other staff members from WBSI, formed a new group, using their former name "Center for Studies of the Person." In goals, "CSP" had a similar sound to WBSI; in organizational structure, the two groups were entirely different. Though legally organized as a corporation, they proudly thought of themselves as a "non-organization" headed by a "non-director." That is, the director had no power to direct anyone, but was empowered to speak for the organization publicly and to raise support for its various projects. It was a revolving position, one which Rogers never held. Not too far from WBSI they rented office space at 1125 Torrey Pines Road in La Jolla. There was a reception and secretarial area, several small offices or consulting rooms, and a large meeting room, thickly carpeted and brightly colored. Each member contributed a small sum to pay the rent and office expenses. They would all get together for weekly staff meetings, at which both personal and professional agendas were likely to be raised.

From this base, members organized themselves into various "projects," many of them carryovers from WBSI, many of them new ones. By 1970, with the membership up to around forty-five, the following projects were listed in CSP's brochure: Educational Innovation Project (using encounter groups to change a large school system, headed by Doug Land and Carl Rogers), the Adolescent Drug Abuse Project, the La Jolla Program (for training group-facilitators), the Conference Planning Service, the Research Design Center, the Project on Community, the Workshop Project, the Project for Developing Awareness Through Interracial Encounters, the Institute for Drug Education, Psycreation (for developing humanizing products for the general public), the Collegiate Development Project, and the Entry Training Project (to facilitate the entry of unskilled people into the world of work).

Other than the secretarial staff, no one received a salary from CSP. Members were responsible for setting up and carrying out their own projects, and whether the funding came from granting institutions or in payment for services provided, each project had to support itself. Thus most of the members had other jobs or sources of income in addition to their work with CSP. In 1969, for example, twenty members were full-time or part-time teachers at nearby colleges or universities. Membership was selective but fluid. By becoming involved with some Center members and working on their project, a person could participate in the life of the Center and gradually come to know many of the other members. If that person then desired to join, the members would vote on this. Any member could choose his or her own title, except for "director." Rogers called himself a "Resident Fellow," the same title he had had at WBSI.

Because WBSI had been formed to do action research, to help people, and improve society, it was natural that, in its early phases, CSP would also see itself as a group designed to reach out to the world around them through many and diverse projects. As the early CSP projects that were continuations of those begun at WBSI ended, however, or as funding sources ceased funding, it became apparent that the basic "outreach" premise upon which WBSI had operated might not apply to the new organization. With most of the members involved in jobs and careers outside of CSP, and with their devoting a large portion of their time to teaching, counseling, group work, or research in the community, many members began having a different expectation as to what they wanted from CSP. Many, like Rogers, still wanted CSP to be a group of close colleagues and friends working together for a common cause, that of helping people around them and, by setting an example, making a significant difference in the conduct of the behavioral sciences throughout the country. Many others wished CSP might be primarily a "support group," an association of like-minded people who could learn from each other, have fun together, and derive emotional and intellectual support from one another. They were already reaching out on their own jobs, helping others, improving conditions around them. This second group wanted more personal benefits from CSP. Of course, few individuals were totally at one or the other end of the continuum. Rogers, for example, believed that by working together they would naturally develop close personal ties and there would still be time left over for comradeship and mutual support. Others responded that that was all right for him, because he didn't have a full-time job elsewhere. They had only several hours a week for CSP and had to choose whether they wanted to spend that time primarily on professional projects or on mutually supportive discussions and activities.

Neither side of the continuum ever gained clear precedence. For many years there remained sometimes a mild, sometimes a forceful tension between these two viewpoints. Nevertheless the organization remained alive, well, and active, with members speaking highly of the personal benefits they derived from it. It never did gain the national reputation that WBSI had gained, which stands to reason given the mixed commitment of the members to the kind of activities which might have resulted in national prominence.

In moving to WBSI in California, Carl and Helen had distanced themselves geographically from their children and grandchildren. Emotionally, however, they all grew closer during this period. David and Natalie both went through divorces, and their parents provided love and support throughout the most trying periods—to the spouses, as well as to David and Natalie. David then made a much happier second marriage, and Natalie learned how to be a single woman who greatly cherished her independent life and many diverse relationships.

David grew to appreciate his father more and more, and vice versa. He felt, "He's one of the most fantastic human beings I've ever met. He's not afraid of new things. I learn something from him each time. There is almost nothing that frightens him in human experience."

During this period father and son had a chance to work together on an interesting and important project. David had left Vanderbilt University in 1968 to become Dean of Medicine of The Johns Hopkins University School of Medicine and Medical Director of the Johns Hopkins Hospital, in Baltimore, Maryland. He continued his research work —publishing over fifty articles in the next ten years—and his work with the prestigious *Year Book of Medicine,* which he has edited from 1966 until the present. After three years at Johns Hopkins, one of the most famous medical institutions in the country, he moved to Princeton, New Jersey, to assume the Presidency of the Robert Wood Johnson Foundation, the second largest private foundation in the United States (after Ford) sponsoring medical research.

Orienne Strode, who had been the secretary and administrator at the Center for Studies of the Person for several years, had been married to a physician and was alarmed at the inability of many doctors to handle the considerable stress associated with their work. She noted the strain on family relationships that doctors often experienced, the surprisingly high rate of drug addiction among doctors, and other signs of a real need for help in dealing with the pressures associated with long and erratic hours, the dealing continually with disease and death, the carrying of such a heavy responsibility, and so on. In 1971 she invited Carl Rogers and, through him, David Rogers, to work with her on a daring new project.

They designed a series of workshops for medical educators, believing that if they could influence the teachers of medicine, they would have the greatest long-range impact on the field. Eventually the participants included medical administrators, medical foundation people, medical students, internists, residents, and spouses of the physicians. Carl lent twelve thousand dollars to get the project started; David signed the initial invitations and participated in the first two workshops. Originally intended to provide a combination of personal growth and organizational development strategies, the workshops quickly came to utilize the encounter-group mode almost totally. Carl led groups in the first four workshops and occasionally presented a paper or came for a dialogue with the participants in later workshops. This is what the physicians seemed to want and need—an opportunity to be themselves and to express and explore the many personal and human relations issues connected with their work. "Human Dimensions in Medical Education" became an ongoing program of the Center for Studies of the Person. As of this writing, about one thousand medical educators—many of them in very high positions of influence —not counting the students, spouses, and others, have participated in the program. Its influence is already being felt in medical institutions across the country. As more and more people go through the workshops each year, its creators hope to see a continuing and widening impact on the medical profession. Many of David's professional writings in the last few years have supported this direction, such as "The Doctor Himself Must Become the Treatment," "Medicine and Change," and "Illness Must Be Understood Not in Scientific but in Human Terms."

Natalie Rogers, having completed her Master of Arts degree in 1960, went on to become an art therapist. She also became very involved in intensive small-group work. Just as her father was learning through encounter groups to express his own feelings more, Natalie was learning to do the same; although, as most of the family agree, she had always been their most volatile member to begin with. A letter she wrote to her parents in 1965, about her daughter Frannie, says a lot about Natalie, but also reveals much about the relationship, past and present, between Natalie and her parents.

> About Frannie: I give up on trying to communicate with you two about her, except to say that when I am a grandmother and see one of my grandchildren acting out in ways which seem to be saying, "I want attention and love, I feel unwanted," that I'll make a special effort to do

the things for *that* child and take the time and mental effort to ask myself "Why does she behave that way? What am I doing to make her behave that way?"

I feel that I have a right to point out to you, although this may be dirty words in your language, since I'm your daughter and have grown up under your parentage, that both as parents and grandparents, you *say* you want people, including children I surmise, to express their feelings; but you reward with love those who keep their angry feelings to themselves. I didn't hear either one of you say one word about Janet the night she got what *she* wanted by walking out of the house and hiding and not saying anything. I assume that all kids try very hard to get what they want when they want it. Janet told me she didn't want to go someplace and you insisted (you're right, I feel). And so she hid. This brings no wrath upon her, apparently. Fran, in the same situation would have argued til she was blue in the face. This brings your wrath. I fall into the same trap, sometimes, as a parent; but let's face it: when we do this, we're tacitly saying to children: the best way to get what you want is not by saying it, but by manipulating us someway, so as not to be troublesome.

Well, I said I wouldn't communicate about Frannie, but I still am. Both of your comments about Frannie anger me beyond words. I guess it's that I'm so damn disappointed that a very mothering mother and great psychologist father would take such a simple way out as to say, "Look, this kid is selfish." I had hoped for more. . . . If you've got to the end of this letter you're pretty good sports. . . .

The three of them argued about this issue for some time, but both Carl and Helen were glad that Natalie did confront them. Their relationship became increasingly close in later years, in part because they were able to share such feelings more openly among themselves.

This letter, incidentally, by no means characterizes the relationship between Carl and Helen and their grandchildren. On the contrary, whenever the opportunity arose, the Rogers would make a real effort to have time alone with each of the six grandchildren, both Carl and Helen together and each one with each grandchild. Carl once described how "one of the most flattering things that has happened to me in this past year is to have my 18-year-old granddaughter—whom I don't see very often, so I couldn't expect her to trust me too much —come to me one evening and simply begin to talk. Soon she was talking about all the things that concern 18 year olds—personal, interpersonal, sexual, philosophical. To find that she could talk so freely and honestly and openly with me, many, many years her senior, was an exceedingly flattering thing. I felt very much honored. When she asked me about some things she was uncertain about, and what she should do, I said, 'Don't expect me to give you any advice. You are already so much further beyond where I was at your age that I couldn't possibly offer any advice, but I will help you think about these things if that's what you would like to do'—and so we talked until far into the night."

Helen, too, felt close to her grandchildren, and was able to understand and accept much about their behavior which others her age would not be able to understand or accept. On one occasion she happened to make a passing reference to "one of my granddaughters and the boy she is living with." This so impressed me that a woman in her seventies could be so casual about this behavior in one of her grandchildren, not yet twenty, that a few years later I mentioned it to her. Her response was: "Hell, if we were born into their generation we would probably be doing the same thing. Besides, by now, five out of my six grandchildren are living with or have lived with someone, without being married. I'd better be able to accept it."

The grandchildren, in turn, felt particularly appreciative about Carl and Helen's acceptance and interest in them. One said, "He's a really nice man who you can talk to." Another said, "I've always felt like myself with him." Another talked of how she had invited Helen to the apartment where she and her boyfriend were living, and how they talked of many different topics, including Helen's growing up, her attitudes about sex, and her work in Planned Parenthood. The granddaughter cherished this time of getting to know her grandmother, woman to woman.

One of the granddaughters remembered a scene with her grandparents which she found particularly amusing. "From the other side of the wall, I overheard this snatch of conversation, and I didn't want to hear it, but. . . . Nana was commenting. And they started getting into this argument about saying 'I think that. . . .' Like saying, 'I think that this painting is ugly' instead of just saying, 'This painting is ugly,' without prefacing it by 'I think.' Obviously Granddaddy was on the 'I think' side, Nana was on the 'non-I think' side. And they went on for an hour, until I was going bananas. He would say, 'You should say "I think" before making a statement of opinion, to qualify it.' And she disagreed with him. 'You shouldn't have to say that; it's obvious.' The point was not whether I agreed with one or the other—they both seemed to have their points—but that they spent an hour doing it. Absurd. I'm sure they must have had this discussion *many* times."

More typical was an incident recalled by one of the grandchildren, when "I was talking with Granddaddy and Nana was there too. I was telling them about [a particular topic]. They were really receptive. There was no flak. There might have been a lot of things they objected to about the way I was living, but they didn't *at all.* It wasn't a personal threat to them in any way. . . . I remember that whole scene and the genuine feeling about them I have. I have a calm feeling when I think of them."

During his time at WBSI and CSP, along with his major commitment to the encounter-group movement, Rogers spent an equally great amount of attention applying his insights to the field of education. This was not something which began for him in the 1960s. Ever since his course at Teachers College with William Heard Kilpatrick, forty years earlier, he had appreciated the basic premise of John Dewey's educational philosophy—that the primary avenue for education is and should be *experience.* His own experiences—boyhood agricultural experiments, the trip to China, his marriage to Helen, the self-initiated discussion group at Union Theological Seminary, his work in the Rochester clinic—had provided many of his most significant learnings. As a psychotherapist he came to believe that reexperiencing previously denied or distorted feelings or experiences changes a person's self-concept, which in turn changes one's behavior.

Therefore, from the beginning of his teaching career at Ohio State, he endeavored to make education a process of experiential learning for his students. His practicum in counseling, one of the first, if not *the* first in this country, was such an attempt to have students learn by doing. Not just talking about research but having his students actually do important research was another type of learning experience he provided. As his nondirective approach to counseling developed, he quite naturally began to use the same approach in conducting classes and workshops. One student, Samuel Tenenbaum, in a four-week course Rogers conducted, gave a detailed account of Rogers' "nondirective teaching."

"In a friendly, relaxed way, he sat down with the students (about 25 in number) around a large table and said it would be nice if we stated our purpose and introduced ourselves. There ensued a strained silence; no one spoke up. Finally, to break it, one student timidly raised his hand and spoke his piece. Another uncomfortable silence, and then another upraised hand. Thereafter, the hands rose more rapidly. At no time did the instructor urge any student to speak.

"Afterwards, he informed the class that he had brought with him quantities of materials—reprints, brochures, articles, books; he handed out a bibliography of recommended reading. At no time did he indicate that he expected students to read or do anything else. As I recall, he made only one request. Would some student volunteer to set up this material in a special room which had been reserved for students of the course? Two students promptly volunteered. He also said he had with him recorded tapes of therapeutic sessions and also reels of motion pictures. This created a flurry of excitement and students asked whether they could be heard and seen and Dr. Rogers answered yes. The class then decided how it could be done best. Students volunteered to run tape recorders, find a movie projector; for the most part this too was student initiated and arranged.

"Thereafter followed four hard, frustrating sessions. During this period, the class didn't seem to get anywhere. Students spoke at random, saying whatever came into their heads. It all seemed chaotic, aimless, a waste of time. A student would bring up some aspect of Rogers' philosophy; and the next student completely disregarded the first . . . would start fresh on something else altogether. At times there were some faint efforts at a cohesive discussion, but for the most part the classroom proceeding seemed to lack continuity and direction. The instructor received every contribution with attention and regard. He did not find any student's contribution in order or out of order. . . . Dr. Rogers neither agreed or disagreed. It was not his habit to respond to students' contributions unless a remark was directed specifically to him; and even then he might choose not to answer. His main object, it seemed to me, was to follow students' contributions intelligently and sympathetically.

"The class was not prepared for such a totally unstructured approach. They did not know how to proceed. In their perplexity and frustration, they demanded that the teacher play the role assigned to him by custom and tradition; that he set forth for us in authoritative language what was right and wrong, what was good and bad. Had they not come from far distances to learn from the oracle himself? Were they not fortunate? Were they not about to be initiated in the right rituals and practices by the great man himself, the founder of the movement that bears his name? The notebooks were poised for the climatic moment when the oracle would give forth, but mostly they remained untouched.

"Queerly enough, from the onset, even in their anger, the members of the group felt joined together, and outside the classroom there was an excitement and a ferment, for even in their frustration, they had communicated as never before in any classroom. In the Rogers class, they had spoken their minds; the words did not come from a book, nor that of any other authority. The ideas, emotions and feelings came from themselves; and this was the releasing and the exciting process.

"In this atmosphere of freedom, something for which they had not bargained and for which they were not prepared, the students spoke up as students seldom do. During this period, the instructor took many blows; and it seemed to me that many times he appeared to be shaken; and although he was the source of our irritation, we had, strange as it may seem, a great affection for him, for it did not seem right to be angry with a man who was so sympathetic, so sensitive to the feelings and ideas of others. We all felt that what was involved was some slight misunderstanding, which once understood and remedied would make everything right again. But our instructor, gentle enough on the surface, had a 'whim of steel.' He didn't seem to understand; and if he did, he was obstinate and obdurate; he refused to come around. Thus did this tug-of-war continue. We all looked to Rogers and Rogers looked to us. . . .

". . . they began to demand more insistently that Rogers assume the traditional role of a teacher. At this point, the blows were coming Rogers' way rather frequently and strongly and I thought I saw him bend somewhat before them. (Privately, he denied he was so affected.) During one session, a student made the suggestion that he lecture one hour and that we have a class discussion the next. This one suggestion seemed to fit into his plans. He said he had with him an unpublished paper. He warned us that it was available and we could read it by ourselves. But the student said it would not be the same. The person, the author, would be out of it, the stress, the inflection, the emotion, those nuances which give value and meaning to words. Rogers then asked the students if that was what they wanted. They said yes. He read for over an hour. After the vivid and acrimonious exchanges to which we had become accustomed, this was certainly a letdown, dull and soporific to the extreme. This experience squelched all further demands for lecturing. In one of the moments when he apologized for this episode . . . he said: 'You asked me to lecture. It is true I am a resource, but what sense would there be in my lecturing? I have brought a great quantity of material, reprints of any number of lectures, articles, books, tape recordings, movies.'

"By the fifth session, something definite had happened; there was no mistaking that. Students spoke to one another; they by-passed Rogers. Students asked to be heard and wanted to be heard, and what before was a halting, stammering, self-conscious group became an interactive group, a brand new cohesive unit, carrying on in a unique way; and from them came discussion and thinking such as no other group but this could repeat or duplicate. The instructor also joined in, but his role, more important than any in the group, somehow became merged with the group; the group was important, the center, the base of operation, not the instructor."

This description of what the students experienced sounds very much like the client who gradually comes to realize that the therapist is not going to solve his problem for him, that he has got to do the work himself. But this was a college course. Was therapy or an intensive group experience all that resulted from this kind of "teaching"? Tenenbaum mentioned another student in this course who raised this very question. " 'Should we be concerned,' he asked, 'only with the emotions? Has the intellect no play?' It was my turn to ask, 'Is there any student who has read as much or thought as much for any other course?' The answer was obvious. We had spent hours and hours reading; the room reserved for us had occupants until 10 o'clock at night, and then many left only because the university guards wanted to close the building. Students listened to recordings; they saw motion pictures; but best of all, they talked and talked and talked."

The student was no impressionable youth, but an educational scholar, Dr. Samuel Tenenbaum, who had written and had published a biography of William Heard Kilpatrick. He summed up his experience with Rogers by saying, "If we accept Dewey's definition of education as the reconstruction of experience, what better way can a person learn than by becoming involved with his whole self, his very person, his root drives, emotions, attitudes and values? No series of facts or arguments, no matter how logically or brilliantly arranged, can even faintly compare with that sort of thing."

As Rogers developed his style as a "nondirective teacher," he was also reading other writers (like Nathaniel Cantor, Earl Kelley, Donald Snygg, and Arthur Combs) whose educational views seemed consistent with his own. Gradually he began to formulate his own educational philosophy, drawing upon these sources, but as usual, primarily upon his own experience. The basis of his philosophy could be summarized in one sentence, which he wrote in 1951: "We cannot teach another person directly, we can only facilitate his learning." The first lengthy exposition of his ideas on education was his chapter on "Student-Centered Teaching," in *Client-Centered Therapy*. Here he described how he and his colleagues' thinking on education had gone through a similar evolution as had their thinking on therapy. He had moved from being what he later called "rather rigidly student-centered," practically refusing to share anything of himself directly with students, confining his role solely to that of the nondirective counselor, to being more flexible in his behavior and placing greater stress on the teacher's attitudes than on his techniques. As he wrote in 1951: "We may state briefly our present concept of the role of the leader in an educational situation when the aim is to center the process in the developing aims of the students. . . . Initially the leader has much to do with setting the mood or climate of the group experience by his own basic philosophy of trust in the group, which is communicated in many subtle ways. . . . The leader helps to elicit and clarify the purposes of the members of the class, accepting all aims. . . . He relies upon the student desire to implement these purposes as the motivational force behind learning. . . . He endeavors to organize and make easily available all resources which the students may wish to use for their own learning. . . . He regards himself as a flexible resource to be utilized by the group in the ways which seem most meaningful to them, in so far as he can be comfortable in operating in these ways. . . . In responding to expressions from the group, he accepts both the intellectual content and the emotionalized attitudes, endeavoring to give each aspect the approximate degree of emphasis which it has for the individual and the group. . . . As the acceptant classroom climate becomes established, the leader is able to change his role and become a participant, a member of the group, expressing his views as those of one individual only. . . . He remains alert to expressions indicative of deep feeling and when these are voiced, he endeavors to understand these from the speaker's point of view, and to communicate this type of understanding. . . . Likewise when group interaction becomes charged with emotion, he tends to maintain a neutral and understanding role, in order to give acceptance to the varied feelings which exist. . . . He recognizes that the extent to which he can behave in these differing fashions is limited by the genuineness of his own attitudes. To pretend an acceptant understanding of a viewpoint when he does not feel this acceptance, will not further, and will probably hinder, the dynamic process of the class."

Though filled with pages of support, examples and elaboration, this chapter in *Client-Centered Therapy* was never very influential in the educational field because the book was read primarily by psychologists and therapists. It was another article, actually a speech, presented a year after the publication of *Client-Centered Therapy*, which became one of Rogers' best known, most widely quoted and reprinted treatises on education. In April 1952 he had been invited to address a conference at the Harvard Business School, to present a demonstration of "student-centered teaching." That winter, on their quarter vacation in Mexico, he read a good deal of the Danish philosopher Soren Kierkegaard and was impressed by that nineteenth-century man's "honest willingness to call a spade a spade." He decided he would try to state in simple terms his convictions about the teaching-learning process and then invite the audience to react, "endeavoring to understand and accept the often very divergent reactions and feelings" of the group. He later wrote, "I may have been naive, but I did not consider the material inflammatory." He simply figured it would provide a good discussion starter and, since this was a group of sophisticated educators interested in the discussion method, they would also keep in mind that the point of his presentation was to provide an example of student-centered teaching, not to make a definitive statement about education.

So Rogers came before the Harvard group, explained that he wished to "present some very brief remarks, in the hope that if they bring forth any reaction from you, I may get some new light on my own ideas," and proceeded to give one of the shortest speeches he ever made, barely over a thousand words, taking about five minutes to deliver. Essentially, the points he made were: "My experience has been that I cannot teach another person how to teach. . . . It seems to me that anything that can be taught to another is relatively inconsequential, and has little or no significant influence on behavior. . . . I realize increasingly that I am only interested in learnings which significantly influence behavior. . . . I have come to feel that the only learning which significantly influences behavior is self-discovered, self-appropriated learning. . . . Such self-discovered learning, truth that has been personally appropriated and assimilated in experience, cannot be directly communicated to another. . . . As a consequence of the above, I realize that I have lost interest in being a teacher. . . . When I try to teach, as I sometimes do . . . It seems to cause the individual to distrust his own experience, and to stifle significant learning. Hence I have come to feel that the outcomes of teaching are either unimportant or hurtful. . . .

"As a consequence, I realize that I am only interested in being a learner, preferably learning things that matter, that have some significant influence on my own behavior. . . . I find it very rewarding to learn, in groups, in relationships with one person as in therapy, or by myself. . . . I find that one of the best, but most difficult ways for me to learn is to drop my own defensiveness, at least temporarily, and to try to understand the way in which his experience seems and feels to the other person. . . . I find that another way of learning for me is to state my own uncertainties, to try to clarify my puzzlements, and thus get closer to the meaning that my experience actually seems to have. . . . It seems to mean letting my experience carry me on, in a direction which appears to be forward, toward goals that I can but dimly define, as I try to understand at least the current meaning of that experience. . . ."

Then he took up the consequences and implications his views would have, if others shared his thinking. ". . . we would do away with teaching. People would get together if they wished to learn. . . . We would do away with examinations. They measure only the inconsequential type of learning . . . we would do away with grades and credits for the same reason. . . . We would do away with degrees as a measure of competence partly for the same reason. Another reason is that a degree marks an end or a conclusion of something, and a learner is only interested in the continuing process of learning. . . . It would imply doing away with the exposition of conclusions, for we would realize that no one learns significantly from conclusions.

"I think I had better stop there. I do not want to become too fantastic. I want to know primarily whether anything in my inward thinking as I have tried to describe it, speaks to anything in your experience of the classroom as you have lived it, and if so, what the meanings are that exist for you in your experience."

He had hoped for some response from the audience, but was amazed with the tumultuous reception his remarks engendered. People reacted very strongly, mostly negatively. Surely he didn't mean what he said. He was exaggerating to get a reaction from them. What he was saying threatened every one of their jobs. And, occasionally, a quiet voice would echo experiences similar to Rogers'. Whatever the speaker's attitude, Rogers tried to understand and accept it. He refused to defend himself, occasionally reminding them that he was only describing his own experience, not asking them to agree. The discussion went on and on, with participants (they were no longer an audience) exploring more and more deeply their own thoughts and feelings about teaching, disagreeing with one another now as often as with the speaker. Ironically, they got so caught up in the content of the discussion that few of them seemed to realize that they were participating in a demonstration of student-centered teaching, which was the main point of the presentation. The next morning one conference member told Rogers, "You kept more people awake last night!"

His "Personal Thoughts on Teaching and Learning" did not reach publication for five more years. As he later wrote, "My views on psychotherapy had already made me a 'controversial figure' among psychologists and psychiatrists. I had no desire to add educators to the list."

Meanwhile, as his views on the therapeutic process continued to evolve, so did his views on education. In another well-known article, written in 1959, he expanded upon the comparison between "Significant Learning: In Therapy and In Education." In therapy he saw five conditions which led to significant learning—learning which makes a difference in the client's behavior, attitudes, or personality. First, he must perceive a problem he wants to work on; there must be a desire to change, to grow, to cope more effectively. Second through fourth, the therapist must provide the conditions of congruence, empathic understanding, and unconditional positive regard. Fifth, the client must perceive to some degree these conditions offered by the therapist. Speaking of education, Rogers identified a similar set of conditions. First, significant learning can be encouraged to the extent the student is working on problems and issues which are real and important to him. Second, significant learning can be facilitated to the extent the teacher is genuine and congruent. ". . . he becomes a real person in the relationship with his students. He can be enthusiastic about subjects he likes, and bored by topics he does not like. He can be angry, but he can also be sensitive or sympathetic. Because he accepts his feelings as *his* feelings, he has no need to impose them on his students, or to insist that they feel the same way. He is a *person*, not a faceless embodiment of a curricular requirement, or a sterile pipe through which knowledge is passed from one generation to the next."

Third and fourth are acceptance and understanding. The "teacher who can warmly accept, who can provide unconditional positive regard, and can empathize with the feelings of fear, anticipation, and discouragement which are involved in meeting new materials, will have done a great deal toward setting the conditions for learning." The accepting, trusting teacher creates a set of expectations that students tend to live up to, just as the nontrusting, suspicious teacher creates a self-fulfilling prophecy in which students produce all the evidence to justify the teacher's negative preconceptions. This trust, acceptance, and understanding are especially important when students are taking risks, exploring ideas and feelings which are new to them, attempting projects at which they are not sure they will succeed. To foster significant learnings the teacher is greatly helped by a genuine belief in "the self-actualizing tendency in students. The hypothesis upon which he would build is that students who are in real contact with life problems wish to learn, want to grow, seek to find out, hope to master, desire to create."

Finally, and here the condition is somewhat different in education than in therapy, the teacher endeavors to *provide resources* to assist the students in their self-directed learning. These resources include not only the traditional resources of books, materials, audio-visuals and the like, but the teacher herself as a resource—a person who has had considerable experience with life and learning and who knows of other resources which could help the student.

As in his shorter presentation, he commented on his view of what education *is not*, and again he emphasized the importance of self-evaluation. "I believe that the testing of the student's achievements in order to see if he meets some criterion held by the teacher, is directly contrary to the implications of therapy for significant learning. In therapy, the examinations are set by life. The client meets them, sometimes passing, sometimes failing. He finds that he can use the resources of the therapeutic relationship and his experience in it to organize himself so that he can meet life's tests more satisfyingly next time. I see this as the paradigm for education also."

All of Rogers' thinking on the subject of education reported thus far predates the 1960s and certainly predates 1964, the year with which this chapter begins to concern itself. It might seem more logical to some to have included this discussion in an earlier chapter. I have delayed it, however, for two reasons. First, education did not become a major focus or interest of Rogers until the 1960s. Although he wrote an occasional article or made an occasional speech on the subject, he really was most interested in psychotherapy during those years and, other than with respect to his own teaching, spent very little time thinking about education. The second reason is that, although he had developed most of his educational thinking before the 1960s, it was not until then that his ideas caught on. His first writings on therapy, in the early 1940s, had catapulted him into becoming a known and controversial figure among psychologists. Except among some guidance counselors and school psychologists, he remained little known as an educator until relatively late in life.

The "progressive" movement in American education had, for the most part, gone under by the end of the Second World War. During the fifties, when he was developing and occasionally writing about his views on teaching and learning, American education was responding to Russia's Sputnik, placing a renewed emphasis on math and science. There was little time for such sentiments as eliminating teaching, grading, and so on. Then, in the sixties, two new influences became significant on the educational scene. First, through the efforts of groups like the National Training Laboratories, and growth centers like Esalen Institute, and books like Rogers' *On Becoming a Person* and Maslow's *Toward a Psychology of Being,* by the early and mid-sixties the "human potential movement" began to be felt in many areas of American life. Businesspeople, religious leaders, school administrators, teachers, and others would attend workshops, encounter groups, human-relations laboratories and the like and come away feeling, "Why can't I bring this type of learning and growing experience back to my own system?" Many educators began thinking, "If only our students could experience learning which is as involving and exciting as what I have just gone through!" But how does one accomplish that, short of turning every classroom into an encounter group?

Another influence, occurring simultaneously in the United States with the human-potential phenomenon, provided a partial answer for this question. In 1967 the *New Republic* magazine published a series of three articles by Joseph Featherstone on the "primary schools in Britain." These articles heralded the beginning of the widespread interest in the United States in what has come to be known variously as "open education," "open classroom," "open schools," "free schools," "alternative schools," and many other terms, all of which have some common meaning with the others and each of which means something different from the others. What the British primary school was all about, though, was an attempt to build upon the natural desire of young children to explore their world, to act on their curiosity, and to grow. Its major vehicles were a classroom rich in learning materials—books, arts and crafts supplies, typewriters, Cuisinaire rods and balance scales (gamelike materials that help children learn mathematical and scientific concepts), and so on—plus human beings (teachers, aides, older students) available to help the youngsters set goals and carry out learning activities. Much of the thinking behind the open classroom approach derived from the work of the Swiss developmental psychologist Jean Piaget, who helped demonstrate the importance of a child's active interaction with his environment as an aid to concept formation. In the United States the learning approaches used in the British primary school were soon adapted and generalized to fit primary, elementary, junior high, senior high, and college learning situations. At these upper levels of education the concept of learning by doing and students' choosing their learning goals was particularly timely with so many students and teachers rebelling against an educational system which they saw as "irrelevant."

Thus two new and important forces were being felt in American education—the advocates of some form of humanistic psychology in the classroom and the advocates of "open education." What these forces lacked, in my opinion, was a person or group to pull together the different innovations that were being advocated, to describe these in an easily understood fashion, and to give a firm psychological foundation to the whole movement to "humanize" education. At this point, also, the Association for Supervision and Curriculum Development, under the leadership of Arthur Combs and others, which had drawn heavily on the thinking of Rogers and other humanistic psychologists, became the educational group which was probably the most influential along these lines.

Most of Rogers' educational ideas were already formed; now he had an audience to hear and read them and take them seriously: The most significant learning occurs when the content has meaning to the student. We must help students learn to set their own goals and achieve them. We must facilitate, not direct, the learning process. Education of this sort strengthens the student psychologically, enables him to deal more effectively with life, to continue to learn and solve his problems as he grows older. The primary goal of school should be to "grow persons," not merely teach subject matter. These ideas which had seemed exaggerated or irrelevant a decade before now were sought after and applauded by an increasing number of educators. Articles by Rogers began to appear in some of the largest or most influential educational journals, like the *Harvard Educational Review*, the *Yearbooks* of the Association of Supervision and Curriculum Development, the National Education Association's *Journal* with its more than one million readers, the influential *Educational Leadership*, and *Instructor* magazine reaching approximately 300,000 elementary school teachers. He became more and more sought after as a speaker for educational audiences, large and small. During 1966, for example, he spoke to audiences of four thousand members at the American Personnel and Guidance Association, three thousand at the Association for Supervision and Curriculum Development, and two thousand at the California Guidance and Counseling Association, as well as many smaller audiences.

The more Rogers wrote and spoke about education, the more teachers wrote him letters or contacted him telling him of the experiments they were conducting in their classes that supported (or contradicted) his ideas. Gradually his thinking took on greater substance as he had more and more examples and research at his fingertips to support his generalizations. By the late 1960s he had enough published articles, unpublished speeches, and new ideas and examples to gather into a new volume on education, which was published by Charles E. Merrill Publishers in 1969 under the title *Freedom to Learn: A View of What Education Might Become.*

The book was about significant, meaningful, or experiential learning. He wrote in his introduction: "Let me define a bit more precisely the elements which are involved in such significant or experiential learning. *It has a quality of personal involvement*— the whole person in both his feeling and cognitive aspects being *in* the learning event. *It is self-initiated.* Even when the impetus or stimulus comes from the outside, the sense of discovery, of reaching out, of grasping and comprehending, comes from within. *It is pervasive.* It makes a difference in the behavior, the attitudes, perhaps even the personality of the learner. *It is evaluated by the learner.* He knows whether it is meeting his need, whether it leads toward what he *wants* to know, whether it illuminates the dark area of ignorance he is experiencing. The locus of evaluation, we might say, resides definitely in the learner. *Its essence is meaning.* When such learning takes place, the element of meaning to the learner is built into the whole experience. . . .

"I believe that all teachers and educators prefer to facilitate this experiential and meaningful type of learning, rather than the nonsense syllable type. Yet in the vast majority of our schools, at all educational levels, we are locked into a traditional and conventional approach which makes significant learning improbable if not impossible. When we put together in one scheme such elements as a *prescribed curriculum, similar assignments for all students, lecturing* as almost the only mode of instruction, *standardized tests* by which all students are externally evaluated, and *instructor-chosen grades* as the measure of learning, then we can almost guarantee that meaningful learning will be at an absolute minimum. . . . But there *are* alternatives—alternative practical ways to handle a class or a course—alternative assumptions and hypotheses upon which education can be built—alternative goals and values for which educators and students can strive. I hope that these will become clear in the following chapters."

The first three chapters attempted to illustrate these alternatives through highly specific and detailed descriptions of three teachers. The first was Barbara Shiel, a sixth-grade teacher, who gradually found ways to give her students freedom to learn things that were important to them, but who was also able to remain congruent herself, not allowing the students freedom to go to extremes that violated her own feelings of comfort and well-being. The next chapter shows Dr. Volney Faw, an undergraduate psychology professor who, in a very structured manner, with requirements and grading procedures all spelled out from the beginning, managed to provide students with an enormous number of choices for learning psychology in ways that would have meaning to them—e.g., reading, writing a psychological autobiography, working with old people, taking psychological tests, receiving counseling, doing case studies, etc. The last example was "My Way of Facilitating a Class," in which Rogers described his own approach to setting requirements, establishing grades, and conducting a class or workshop. Much of the substance of *Freedom to Learn* appears in these three chapters, and I have heard many people comment that they wish he had pictured even more teachers, at all levels of education, at work with their students. It was in these chapters that all his theoretical writings on education really came alive.

In the two chapters of Part II he described in a bit more detail the role of the teacher who wants to encourage self-directed learning and specific methods for accomplishing this. He spent a good deal of time, of course, describing the conditions of congruence, empathy, and "prizing, acceptance and trust," the last being a more suitable description for teachers than "unconditional positive regard," although in most ways the concept was the same. He also went into extra detail in his discussion of congruence. "Some teachers," he wrote, "raise the question, 'But what if I am *not* feeling empathic, do *not*, at this moment, prize or accept or like my students. What then?' My response is that realness is the most important of the attitudes mentioned, and it is not accidental that this attitude was described first."

Ms. Schiel, for example, wrote in her journal that her students were not cleaning up after using their art materials and that consequently the room was looking more and more chaotic. "I find it maddening to live with the mess—with a capital M! No one seems to care except me. Finally, one day I told the children . . . that I am a neat orderly person by nature and that the mess was driving me to distraction. Did they have a solution? It was suggested there were some volunteers who could clean up. . . . I said it didn't seem fair to me to have the same people clean up all the time for others—but it would be solved for me. 'Well, some people like to clean,' they replied. So that's the way it is. . . . I used to get upset and feel guilty when I became angry. I finally realized the children could accept *my* feelings too. And it is important for them to know when they've 'pushed me.' I have my limits, too."

Among the methods Rogers regarded as the most useful to the facilitator of learning, he listed and discussed: the provision of resources; the use of learning contracts; helping students learn how to conduct an inquiry and discover things themselves rather than giving them the predigested and preorganized knowledge to merely memorize; the use of simulation activities to provide experiential learning; programmed instruction when this would help a student learn something he wanted to learn more efficiently (he even quoted Skinner, without sarcasm!); the basic encounter group; and self-evaluation.

The next section of the book was called "Some Assumptions." Here he included his short controversial piece "Personal Thoughts on Teaching and Learning," discussed above. Another short and cogent statement of his educational assumptions was "Regarding Learning and Its Facilitation." Then came "Current Assumptions in Graduate Education: A Passionate Statement." This unpublished paper, written in 1963, previously had been rejected by the APA's leading journal *The American Psychologist,* but it soon became what Rogers guessed was "one of the most widely read unpublished papers of the past decade." In it he enumerated what he saw as the implicit assumptions that seemed to guide most graduate education.

1. The student cannot be trusted to pursue his own scientific and professional training.
2. Ability to pass examinations is the best criterion for student selection and for judging professional promise.
3. Evaluation is education; education is evaluation.
4. Presentation equals learning. What is presented in the lecture is what the student learns.
5. Knowledge is the accumulation of brick upon brick of content and information.
6. The truths of psychology are known.
7. Method is science.
8. Creative scientists develop from passive learners.
9. "Weeding out" a majority of the students is a satisfactory method of producing scientists and clinicians.
10. Students are best regarded as manipulable objects, not as persons.

In trying to illustrate each of these assumptions, he used some strong language ("it seems a scandalous waste of manpower. . . .") and some vivid examples to prove his point. "If the day comes," he concluded, "when psychology wishes to make a thoughtful appraisal of its methods of professional preparation, it will, I believe, throw out most of its current assumptions and procedures." He emphasized that, though his remarks were aimed in particular at graduate education in psychology, they could be applied readily to graduate, undergraduate, and precollege education in most other areas as well. In his next chapter he proposed "A Revolutionary Program for Graduate Education," one designed to reverse the implicit assumptions he had just described. In another chapter he offered "Some Thoughts About Educational Administration."

The last major section discussed "The Philosophical and Value Ramifications" of the earlier sections. Here he included speeches, articles, or revised presentations which had already appeared in print: "A Modern Approach to the Valuing Process," "Freedom and Commitment," and "The Goal: The Fully Functioning Person." All these chapters helped put the longer-range goals of humanistic education in a broader psychological and philosophical perspective and to deal with questions like: Toward what ends are these newer approaches to education more effective or desirable? What is the ultimate goal of education? What is the Good Life? A final section of the book described "A Plan for Self-Directed Change in an Educational System," which will be discussed below.

It was a powerful book. In one of the chapter summaries he wrote, "I'm sorry I can't be coolly scientific about this. The issue is too urgent. I can only be passionate in my statement that people count, that interpersonal relationships *are* important, that we know something about releasing human potential, that we could learn much more, and that unless we give strong positive attention to the human interpersonal side of our educational dilemma, our civilization is on its way down the drain. Better courses, better curricula, better coverage, better teaching machines, will never resolve our dilemma in a basic way. Only persons, acting like persons in their relationships with their students can even begin to make a dent on this most urgent problem of modern education."

For once one of Rogers' books was reviewed in several journals. He may have wished otherwise. Of the five reviews I came across, four were mostly negative. The reviewers saw Rogers' educational thinking as superficial and adding little new to his earlier writings on the subject. Edgar Friedenberg wrote, "Like another American philosopher, Huckleberry Finn, Carl Rogers can get in almost anywhere because the draft of his vessel is so terribly shallow; it never gets hung up. It is almost eerie to read a discussion of basic existential issues affecting human life by a man who, despite an enormous range of honestly assimilated experience, seems to have no sense of tragedy, and not as much as one might expect of the complexity of human conflict."

R.S. Peters of the University of London's Institute of Education wrote, "What is surprising . . . is that an author who strongly advocates openness to the experience of others should put together a collection of papers that are meant to be of general relevance to educational problems in such a seeming state of ignorance and innocence about educational theory and practice. Freedom is fine; and so is self-directed exploration. But there are other values, both in life and in education—truth, for instance, humility, and breadth of understanding. . . . But then, as one reads on, one begins to understand the free-floating character of the book, its lack of any proper historical, social, or philosophical dimensions. It is not really an attempt to think systematically about the actual problems of teaching and learning in a concrete historical context. It is Carl Rogers 'doing his thing' in the context of education."

It was the same old story. Vocal critics in the academy tended to ignore or minimize his contribution, and thousands of individuals out in the field began buying and reading and showing their friends copies of his book. Of the entire "Studies of the Person" series which Charles Merrill published, *Freedom to Learn* was the best seller by far, with a sale of 300,000 copies by January 1978. What was it that students, teachers, and administrators all over the country saw in the book that the critics somehow missed or devalued?

In the fall of 1970 all the students in three undergraduate classes I taught at Temple University read ten chapters of *Freedom to Learn*. Although, ironically, this was a class requirement, all but two of the students responded positively to what they read. One social work major wrote: "Never before have I regretted my choice of an academic major as when I read Carl Rogers' *Freedom to Learn*. Every concept was challenging, every chapter too short. When a person reads a book from the title to the last bibliography, the book must be powerful." One of my classes was composed entirely of black students, older people who had spent years working in community agencies and who were now returning to college to get a degree. One man wrote, "In reading Dr. Rogers' book, *Freedom to Learn*, I found myself automatically agreeing in such a manner that I felt I could have written parts of the book myself, that's how real it all seemed. In particular, Rogers' comments on the two types of learning, which are experiential and by rote, struck me as falling very close to my loosely formulated hypothesis explaining my eagerness to learn while I was 'out on the street' compared to my being almost turned off since entering college." A woman from this class wrote, "Let me begin by stating that I will treasure Rogers' 'Freedom in Learning,' [sic] and I sensed his ideas, his thoughts and his learning experiences reaching out and touching the very core of one's existence. . . ."

Many of the student papers echoed the sentiment that readers have seemed to feel, again and again, in Rogers' later writings. "His way of coming across is honest and direct." "I felt as if he was talking to me and really trying to communicate." "His written words possessed character—it was as if I was being introduced not only to his theories, but to his personality as well. As I progressed through the book I became increasingly caught up in Rogers' enthusiasm and in his goals for education."

To me these quotations represent very important examples of how Rogers has become a part of the thinking of thousands of people throughout the helping professions. His research is rarely quoted. Few people are familiar with the scope of his career or his changing theories. It is more like a fantasy I have of a "Rogers railroad train" moving slowly through time. The doors are wide open and people easily jump on. Each car on the train is a book or article Rogers has written; they are all connected, yet each is somewhat different from the car behind. Up front is the locomotive, surging steadily forward ahead of the older formulations. The passenger stays a while in the particular car he has entered. He rests, but he also thinks and feels, and when he jumps down from the train he feels renewed, more strengthened and committed to keep on going under his own power in the direction of his or her own choosing. Sometime later, that same passenger may encounter the same train and get on again into a different car. The doors are still wide open; but the train is a little longer now and the locomotive is still moving on.

With his two major interests of encounter groups and educational change existing side by side for a period of several years, it is not surprising that Rogers would begin to combine these two fields of endeavor. He had worked with school personnel, especially counselors, for many years, providing experiential workshops in which they learned the skills and attitudes of the client-centered helper. In leading encounter groups, he worked with many individual teachers and administrators among the various other professionals in his groups. Individual participants would often say, "If only the other teachers in my school could have an experience like this." "If only my principal were here." It was natural that Rogers would soon become curious as to what *would* happen in such a case. What if an entire faculty or an entire school system *did* go through an encounter-group experience? Would that have any effect on the teaching and learning that would go on in the schools? Would teachers more readily become facilitators of learning?

As he was by now receiving weekly, and by the turn of the decade almost daily invitations to address or visit school systems, it was easy for him to respond to an invitation by saying, "No, I would not come to give a speech or direct a workshop for your faculty; but my colleagues and I would come for a weekend of encounter groups with your teachers and administrators." He got quite a few takers. Rasa Gustaitis described one such experiment.

"Alma College, near Los Gatos, California, is one of the two top Jesuit training centers in the country. Its students, who have lived for a decade or longer under the Society's tutelage, are used to rigid discipline with much formality and severe restrictions on personal emotional life.

"A year ago last spring, Dr. Carl Rogers and nine of his associates from the Western Behavioral Sciences Institute, a small think tank in La Jolla, California, came to Alma to conduct a weekend of encounter groups. Nearly the entire community of more than three hundred voluntarily took part in these meetings, designed to encourage people to react freely to one another. Since then, life at Alma has changed.

"In the dining room, where faculty, students and lay brothers used to sit at separate tables, all now eat together. In some classrooms where dry lectures had been customary, small groups now engage in lively discussion. One professor scrapped the notes for an entire course soon after the weekend and asked his students to draw up personal study plans. A few students left the order for civil life. One, who was inspired to explore himself and the world beyond sanctioned boundaries, was dismissed.

"The Alma upheaval is not atypical of what happens to groups and institutions that come into contact with the mild-mannered, soft-spoken Dr. Rogers. . . ."

Rogers was impressed by the kind of changes he saw occur in systems after they had experienced encounter goups. Experiences like that at Alma led him to think that if he could demonstrate the power of encounter groups to change a large school system, this "would have not only lasting impact on one school system but . . . would start a ferment which would spread throughout the country." He began seeking funding for his idea, initially without any success. He also began describing his plan to various audiences, hoping to attract attention to it in the educational community and get a school system to volunteer. He even wrote an article called "A Plan for Self-Directed Change in an Educational System," which *Educational Leadership* published in 1967. His plan called for working in a large school system, with numerous encounter groups composed first of administrators, then of teachers, then of students, then of parents, and then "vertical groups" representing a cross section of roles. Participation would be voluntary. A second stage of the plan called for training individuals within the school system to then become group facilitators themselves, to continue to carry on the intensive group experiences after the outside consultants had left the system. Rogers listed various outcomes he hypothesized would result from participation in encounter groups. These included more democratic, flexible leadership styles by administrators, more innovative teaching by teachers, more commitment and more taking of responsibility by students, and better communication throughout the school system.

Even before the *Educational Leadership* article appeared, Rogers was circulating a draft of it and letting it be known that he had such a plan, if only the school system would come forth. Several systems did indicate an interest in participating, and before long Rogers and his colleagues at WBSI had finalized arrangements with the Immaculate Heart system in the Los Angeles area, which included the Immaculate Heart College, several high schools, and many elementary schools which the Order staffed and supervised. Meanwhile, after having failed to obtain funding from public sources, Rogers and WBSI finally were able to raise money from private sources. A seventy-thousand-dollar grant from the Mary Reynolds Babcock Foundation and a thirty-thousand-dollar personal gift from Charles Kettering II enabled the project to get underway. Interestingly, both Babcock and Kettering had previously participated in encounter groups. Kettering regarded Rogers as "an absolutely first-rate scholar, educator, humanitarian, and general all-round great human being." A later grant from the Merrill Foundation and a gift from Everett Baggerly to the Immaculate Heart College helped the project continue.

Representatives of the Immaculate Heart system and from WBSI met periodically, throughout the project, to plan next steps and evaluate results. Within ninety days from the start of the project during the fall of 1967, "forty-five administrators and faculty members of the College volunteered for the first encounter sessions. They were divided into four groups, met for one intensive weekend and then these same four groups met for a second weekend. Thirty-six high school administrators and faculty members from three high schools met in small groups for two weekends. . . . Forty student leaders from a high school met in three groups for one weekend. When, a month or more later, they met for a second weekend their faculty (counted in the preceding paragraph) were now willing to meet in groups composed of both faculty and students, a mingling which they had at first avoided. They soon found themselves communicating across generations. One hundred and eighty teachers, administrative staff, and principals from twenty-two elementary schools have met in many small groups at different times for two weekend encounter groups, often separated by a month or more. In each case individuals continued in the same group in which they had started."

The initial response was mostly positive, along the lines suggested in Rogers' plan. Communication seemed to improve among many individuals and in many schools, innovations in teaching and learning and administration began, and a great deal of excitement was generated. On the negative side, there were those in the system, mostly people who had not participated in the groups (but not entirely, for a small number of the groups seemed to have been ineffective and generated their share of "informed" critics), who were skeptical or critical of the program. Many did not fully understand the goals of the program, many others simply felt excluded, though not quite ready to volunteer for the next round of groups. The WBSI staff found that their initial conception of their role as simply group facilitators was inadequate. They had to become "consultants" in every sense of the word. They were called upon to counsel individuals who wanted help in pursuing issues which had arisen in the encounter groups. They were asked to address the entire college faculty on the subject of educational innovations, as well as an assembly of Immaculate Heart students and faculty, many of whom had little idea of what the project was doing and were therefore fearful and apprehensive. They were invited by faculty to attend many classes to provide experiences for these teachers' students. They received many new requests for weekend or evening encounter groups and wherever possible these were organized. They soon came to realize that they were not simply studying, as had been Rogers' initial intention, the effects of encounter groups on an educational system; rather, as he later wrote, they were "studying the impact of a dedicated group of individuals who are interested in persons, who want to communicate with persons, and who are interested in facilitating communication between persons, upon an educational system."

By the start of 1968 two things were occurring simultaneously. While the project staff were being invited to lead groups and sessions for many different kinds of classes and groups within the College and the schools, some serious polarization was also taking place among many parts of the College and school community. This was especially true in the elementary schools, staffed partly by the Sisters of the Immaculate Heart Order. About a year *before* the project began, these Sisters had begun formulating "new and experimental ways of living, acting under the instructions of Vatican II, that religious orders should experiment with ways of living which were more relevant to modern life." The Sisters' representative to "Chapter," their council, had come close to finishing their proclamation by the time they first participated in an encounter-group workshop. Although they were moving in this direction anyway, ". . . it appears that the workshop with the Chapter delegates may have helped them in some degree to have the courage to map out new ways of life. . . . By early autumn the proclamation was made public. Among other things it indicated that the Sisters were free to wear habits or not as they desired, to choose the names that they preferred—either baptismal or religious, and in general freed them to live a much more independent life in the community, serving in the ways that they thought were most relevant and helpful."

Enter Cardinal McIntyre and a group of conservative Catholics who were deeply opposed to the changes they saw occurring. Over the next year there was much bitter controversy, resulting finally in some forty to fifty of the Sisters who were teaching in parochial elementary schools having to leave and seek employment elsewhere. Referring to these events, Rogers and William Coulson wrote, "The year has been one of crisis and reappraisal for most of the members of the Order."

Meanwhile, as the first year of the project drew to a close, there was increasing sentiment on the college campus to reject the help of the "La Jolla group," the outside consultants. Rogers saw in this phenomenon the healthy, adolescent phenomenon of "I want to do it myself." Others saw it due in part to the consultants not being willing to go far enough in entertaining alternatives to their original plan and therefore encouraging this resistance. At any rate, the number of encounter groups held seemed to drop off sharply and there was almost a feeling of relief among many on campus that the year was drawing to a close. Simultaneously, however, the Administrative Council of the College, composed of the president and her top executives and deans, was meeting with Rogers and Sheldon Davis, a TRW Systems organizational consultant, in a "task-oriented group." More work-oriented than an encounter group, they listed problems they needed to deal with, including interpersonal problems among themselves, proceeded to deal with the problems one at a time, including these interpersonal ones—which at times led to tears—mapped out action plans where appropriate, and at subsequent meetings reported on the action steps taken. By all reports this was a highly successful experience, resulting in better communication, a democratization of the way the College budget was arrived at, an impetus for one of the vice-presidents to enter a training program in organizational development, and many other constructive and lasting changes.

From the beginning the project staff and Immaculate Heart had built into the project an ongoing evaluation by outside consultants who had no other direct connection with the project. In this connection Drs. Morton Shaevitz and Donald Barr, both of the University of Michigan, made six extended visits to the College, spaced from one to four months apart and lasting over two years. They spent many hours talking with students, faculty, and administrators, gathering data to assess the extent to which changes had or had not taken place at the College. My description, so far, has drawn upon their evaluation as well as on the perceptions of Rogers and his colleagues. Shaevitz and Barr described the beginning of the second year, the fall of 1968, as a period of "minimal activity." The formal activities of the outside consultants had ceased, although they were invited to conduct a workshop for the Library Science Department which "eventually developed an independent program, using encounter technology, which is now being introduced to librarians across the country." "A lot of latent anger toward the project staff" was still occurring, however. Shaevitz and Barr called the final stage of their observations, the spring of 1969, "Gone But Not Forgotten; Internalized But Not Recognized."

"The project was being talked about in the past tense," they wrote. "A number of staff and students still felt very positively about the project and about their own experiences in groups, but generally accepted the fact that a phase was over, and they were moving in other directions. These other directions seem to include a greater emphasis on task-oriented groups, planned all-community problem solving approaches, and the utilization of consultants with more systems-oriented philosophies. . . . We believe the project intervention led directly to some of the new procedures being used in decision-making and in interpersonal relations at Immaculate Heart College."

Still a year later, three years after the project had begun, Rogers would hear reports or receive letters like that written by a professor of education from the college. "We are working on a self-initiated and self-directed program in teacher education. We had a fantastically exciting weekend workshop here recently. Students, faculty, and administration, 75 in all, brainstormed in a most creative and productive way. One outcome is that the students will immerse themselves in schools all over the city observing classes, sitting in on faculty meetings, interviewing teachers, students and administrators. Our students will *then* describe what *they* need to know, to experience, to do, in order to teach. They will then gather faculty and other students around them to assist them in accomplishing their own goals."

What are we to conclude from the Immaculate Heart Project? If we asked Rogers, the conclusion would be an optimistic one. As he wrote in *Freedom to Learn*, "I believe that the material I have cited . . . justifies the statement that in important ways we have achieved our initial objective, namely, that of initiating self-directed change in a large educational system. We have had no close working contact with the College or any other part of the system for more than two years. Yet, self-initiated, innovative changes in the direction of making the organization a more human and participative one are continuing at an exciting rate. To me it shows that if the top leadership is willing to be experimental, the encounter group and its offshoots of brief confrontation groups, task-oriented groups, and the like can be successful in helping individuals and institutions to become changing, self-renewing, and adaptive in their reactions to modern problems."

On the other hand, if we were to ask many professional, organizational consultants their opinion of Rogers' style of intervention in the Immaculate Heart system, we would probably get a very different answer. By the time Rogers and his colleagues began the Immaculate Heart Project, the National Training Laboratories had been conducting human relations training groups for twenty years. By the late fifties and early sixties many of the NTL groups were realizing that there were definite limitations to the use of "sensitivity" groups, that is, groups designed primarily to be good learning experiences for the participants. They came to believe that when working with an entire system, in an ongoing relationship, a much more sophisticated approach was necessary, compared to the simple offering of encounter groups. This broader approach would include an array of alternatives for working with a system—intensive groups when appropriate, but also "process consultation," "third-party consultation," conflict resolution, counseling, and many other helping approaches. This overall field of "organizational development," as it is generally known, had developed considerably by 1967, when the Immaculate Heart Project began. Many of the people in this field, reading reports of how Rogers and his colleagues learned that they needed to do more than encounter groups with the Immaculate Heart system, would undoubtedly shake their heads at Rogers' naiveté. They would criticize him for remaining at the sensitivity training stage when an organizational development approach was more appropriate. Perhaps all that polarization was not necessary and the conflicts could have been resolved in a more productive way.

To some extent Rogers would admit this. Several years later he wrote to one of the Immaculate Heart leaders, "Like you I recognize how naive we all were when we started the project—and by and large I'm glad of it. We weren't even adequately aware of all the intricacies of organizational development, or the problems of changing institutional systems. But I remember an incident in the task-oriented group of the Administrative Council, held I believe in 1968. President Helen Kelley was being quite critical of the project, and I felt that most of her criticisms were valid. I told her that if we were doing it all over we would certainly start much more slowly. Her response was immediate and surprising. 'Oh no! If you hadn't held all those encounter groups so quickly I don't believe we would have seen so much change!' So, as I say, I'm glad that we couldn't foresee all the consequences of some of our enthusiastic behavior."

Who is right? Rogers says their project was effective; look at the Immaculate Heart system today. His critics say he was playing with fire, it could easily have backfired, and it certainly could have been more effective. In my opinion, both positions have merit. It is interesting, though, to recognize here a pattern typical of Rogers' career. His critics call him superficial and an oversimplifier. But he seems to get results, and his tribe increases.

A few years later the public school system of Louisville, Kentucky, undertook a program, "Project Transition," similar if not bigger in size and scope than the Immaculate Heart project. In Kentucky the Louisville school district had the greatest number of low-income students, the highest number of underachievers (seventy-one percent were below the national average), the most school dropouts (second highest rate in the nation among large cities), the most delinquency referrals and apprehensions, and the highest student and teacher turn-over (twenty percent, excluding transfers within the district). There were about sixty thousand children in the district, about sixty percent white and forty percent black; 34.1 percent were from families with a two-thousand-dollar or smaller annual income or receiving welfare.

Louisville's progressive School Board, composed of three white and two black members, hired a new school superintendent, Newman Walker, who was familiar with encounter groups and with other advances in the behavioral sciences and education. Walker hired Car Foster to head his Department of Organizational Development.

Unlike Rogers, Walker and Foster were successful in obtaining substantial funding from the Office of Education. With the funding, they were able to begin a massive change effort which, like the Immaculate Heart Project, emphasized human relations training for school personnel. In addition, however, the Louisville program included the provision of funds and resources for every teacher, administrator, or school to support and encourage educational innovations on the grass roots level. As one example of this support and encouragement, they purchased some five hundred copies of *Freedom to Learn* and distributed these widely among interested teachers and administrators in the district.

The Louisville story is interesting not so much because Rogers had any great influence in its inception or execution, but as an illustration of the indirect and symbolic role he came to play in educational systems and for individual educators throughout the country. It also provides a good example of the consulting style he came to adopt in the late sixties and seventies. He came not so much anymore as a representative or salesman for client-centered counseling, encounter groups, or student-centered learning. He came as Carl Rogers—to spend some time, to talk with people, to share some of his ideas when appropriate, and to listen and learn. This is clearly indicated in Car Foster's recollections of Rogers' visits to Louisville.

"Upon his first visit here, I don't suppose that I have ever been quite as nervous about meeting a person and entertaining a person as I was with Carl Rogers. [He goes on to talk about how often he had been disappointed in meeting famous people or writers and seeing how differently they acted from what they were advocating in their writings.] I'm very happy to report that I didn't find him that way. He is the kind of person that lives his life style pretty much according to the way in which he writes, and the belief seems to be very, very deep.

"He was one of the easiest persons to accommodate as a visitor and consultant within our system of anyone I've had here. I have entertained some one hundred sixty consultants and guests in this system in the past three years, and he is, by far, the easiest one that I have had to work with. We agreed at the beginning that whenever he wanted to work he worked, and whenever he wanted to retire he retired. I never had to worry about whether I was keeping him too long or whether he wanted to have dinner with someone that night or whatever. I asked him and he replied very forthrightly and honestly with me.

"There was a tremendous interest in people when they heard that Carl Rogers was coming, and my hardest task was keeping people away from him because he would be bombarded by dozens and dozens of people that wanted to sit in and talk with him by the hour had we allowed this to happen.

"We went into school systems, he talked with people. In general the entire system was open to him. In the first visit, we had a Board meeting scheduled one afternoon, and I had something else for him that I thought he might like to do. I gave him his option of that or going to a regularly scheduled Board meeting. He selected the Board meeting, reluctantly, but he said, 'I think I need to see how they operate.' This was a regular Board meeting and there wasn't anything planned, but something unusual did happen. That was some students brought a petition to the Board for the Board to consider some things; and in likestyle in terms of how our school board has been operating, they listened very attentively to the students, were very complimentary of their work and proceeded to take some action on it, of doing some things to answer to student needs. I thought it was fairly routine, although I knew it was unusual for most school boards to do this. Carl Rogers was sitting there and hadn't said anything, but was listening very intently. He raised his hand and asked permission to speak to the board, and when I looked around I noticed there were actually tears in his eyes. He told them that he had witnessed something there that afternoon that he had never seen before in his life. That was a school board that was actually responsive to students and listening to what students said and taking some action on it. He said, truthfully, he didn't think that there was another school board in the United States that would measure up to this kind of commitment.

"He spoke to several groups while he was here and appeared to thoroughly enjoy interacting with them. He visited with some schools and he asked that I take him to some of the better schools—that was where our projects were working—then he turned around and asked me to take him to some of our worst schools, and I accommodated him.

I took him exactly where he wanted to go. I think he felt like we were really being honest with him and letting him see everything that was here. Later on he spoke of this and said he didn't think we had a lot to hide and that we had problems, we *knew* that we had problems and that we were trying honestly to face up to them.

"On his second visit, he brought with him two other people from the Center for Studies of the Person, because he wanted other people . . . to verify that we weren't overrating some of the things that we were doing. . . . During this time, he did not make very many public appearances. It was strictly as a consultant to us and to talk with us.

"Most of the people within the system who still talk about his two visits here are amazed that a man of the stature and the caliber of Carl Rogers can say so often, 'I really do not know about this. I have very little knowledge in this area.' His admittance of where he has no expertise or where he does not know too much about the application of various procedures was of such a nature that, I think, people tended to believe even more strongly the other things that he did have to say."

Most of all Foster was impressed by what he saw as Rogers' ". . . fantastic modesty in his effect upon people and even his symbolic importance to people of just being able to meet him and listen to him and talk with him. . . . I think he underrates his importance with other people, when he has such a tremendous influence on people's lives. Perhaps he may have to do this, because it would be a tremendous burden to know that you are this influential with so many people's lives."

As indicated, Rogers was as impressed with the Louisville Schools as they were with him. In *On Encounter Groups,* he devoted four pages to describing "Project Transition," calling it "the boldest and most promising venture I know of in education systems at the present time."

In almost every chapter of Rogers' life I have included a section on his "growing reputation." This chapter is no exception. If one were to plot his rising esteem and influence on a graph, there would be a steeply rising curve covering the three periods of Rochester, Ohio, and Chicago, a leveling off or even a slight decline during his years at Wisconsin, and then another rapidly rising curve to cover his California years, a steeper rise, in fact, than at any previous point in his career. The ten years or so described in this chapter have, indeed, been "a Rogers decade."

It began with the publication of *On Becoming a Person* in 1961, when a larger audience than ever before could identify with Rogers' theories and methods, now expressed in a less technical form. Then, in addition to his psychological writing, which continued to appear in the journals of the psychology and psychotherapy professions, his educational thinking began reaching an ever widening audience as many of his articles appeared in some of the most popular educational journals and magazines. So, too, did his articles start appearing in the new *Journal of Applied Behavioral Science,* published by the National Training Laboratories group of human relations trainers and community and organizational development specialists. Both the *Newsletter* and the *Journal of Humanistic Psychology* also publicized his thinking among the members and followers of the Association of Humanistic Psychology. The new popular magazine *Psychology Today* recognized his stature and published an interview with him and two of his articles within a two-year span. In addition CRM Books, put out two large, attractive volumes meant to serve as interesting and contemporary textbooks for psychology courses. Although the authors were listed as "contributors" in the back of these volumes rather than next to their articles, Rogers wrote chapters for these books. They have sold very well and have been read widely in psychology courses across the country. He even wrote a piece which was circulated in major newspapers across the country. The *Minneapolis Star* called the piece " 'Process' People Replacing Those With Timeless Goals," and the editor introduced it by saying, "This is the ninth of 20 essays by leading men in the world's academic community. Today's writer discusses many issues concerned with what we call 'the good life.' "

Aside from *On Becoming a Person,* Rogers wrote four other books during this period which contributed substantially to his reputation. Of these, three have already been discussed—*Man and the Science of Man,* which sold hardly any copies at all, and *Freedom to Learn* and *On Encounter Groups,* both of which sold very well. The fourth was *Person to Person: The Problem of Being Human.* Barry Stevens, a woman who was born the same year as Rogers and who had experienced great emotional turmoil and many interesting experiences during the course of her life, approached Rogers, whom she knew only a little, and proposed that they compose a book together. Rogers is first to admit, "It was entirely her idea. *Person to Person* is her book. The one thing I regret about the book is that she talked me into putting my name first on it, because she knew it would help to sell the book. And I shouldn't have let her do that, because it's a damn lie. It's her book, and I never feel good about seeming to author something that I really didn't." On the other hand, he later wrote that, "When Barry Stevens learned that I was annoyed because my name was first on her book she was indignant. She said my name should be first on the book because it would never have been written without me, that she would bring in a batch of her free-floating stream of consciousness material expecting me to be very harsh about it and I always encouraged her to do more. So, perhaps, I did have more to do with the book's creation than I give myself credit for."

Anyway, Stevens took four essays previously written by Rogers and three written by Rogers' former colleagues (Gendlin, Shlien, and Van Dusen) and very skillfully wove her own experiences around these essays. Her free-flowing memories and associations came across with a great deal of power and often served as a vivid case study of what the professionals were talking about. The style of the book was so unusual, though, that she was unable to find a publisher. Some chapters were highly technical, others were more in a diary or train-of-thought style. Publishers wondered who would buy such a book. Finally, as a last resort, John Stevens, Barry Stevens's son, who was also interested in psychology, set up a publishing company just to publish his mother's book. This type of small, individual publishing venture is almost always doomed to failure; yet, for whatever reasons—Rogers' name on the cover probably being a primary one—the book was a great success. At one point it was selling about two thousand quality paperback copies a month, successful by any publishing standards. Stevens went on to publish another book by his mother and two by the Gestalt psychologist Fritz Perls. Eventually these books were doing so well on the market that Pocket Books, one of the biggest publishers of paperback books, bought the rights to some of them. *Person to Person* then reached an even wider audience, and Rogers' name became still better known by the layperson interested in psychology.

He also made an increasing number of personal appearances, often before large assemblies. In 1965 and 1966, for example, he spent 142 and 148 days, respectively, away from home. This included vacation periods; but considerably more than half the time was spent conducting encounter groups, giving speeches and workshops, and consulting. From 1967 through 1970, partly because Helen's health was getting worse and she could not travel with him as much as before, he spent 112, 96, 83, and 70 days (and usually nights) away. Even this last figure, however, is substantial, especially for a man of sixty-eight, and all this traveling over many years served to bring him into personal, often intimate, contact with many thousands of people across the country.

Beyond his writings, the various films and tapes mentioned earlier —mostly on encounter groups and mental health—served to give Rogers a wider public viewing. An increasing number of people came to know him as a three-dimensional person, not the nondirective caricature often portrayed by psychology professors. This and his ever more personal writing style brought him much closer to thousands of people in psychology, education, and other helping professions and accounts for the kind of aura about him which Car Foster described in the previous section.

Another indication of his stature in the intellectual world at large is that during the late fifties and the sixties he participated in dialogues with three of the outstanding thinkers of our time. His association and public dialogue with Michael Polyani has already been described. In 1957 he held a dialogue with Martin Buber, the world-renowned Hebrew philosopher. They spent a good deal of time in discussion and in comparing the person-to-person relationship Rogers strived for in therapy and other settings with Buber's concept of the "I-Thou" relationship. In 1966 he held two taped dialogues with theologian Paul Tillich. Again they spent their time comparing and contrasting Tillich's theological concepts—the essential nature of humans, the ground of being, forgiveness, grace, acceptance, freedom, the demonic, and so on—with concepts and experiences that Rogers drew from psychotherapy.

And, of course, there were more awards. In 1964 he was named "Humanist of the Year" by the American Humanist Association. "For Outstanding Contribution to the Understanding of World Affairs," he was made a Fellow of the Institute on World Affairs of San Diego State College. He received in 1967 the Distinguished Contribution Award of the American Pastoral Counselors Association, an ironic accolade for a man who had left the seminary a half-century before. He was awarded his second, third, and fourth honorary doctorate degrees from Gonzaga University in 1968, Santa Clara University in 1971, and the University of Cincinnati in 1974. He served on the editorial boards of the *Journal of Humanistic Psychology,* the *Review of Existential Psychology and Psychiatry,* and *Voices,* the journal of the American Academy of Psychotherapists. In 1968 he received the Professional Achievement Award from the American Board of Professional Psychology, the certifying board for the American Psychological Association. The citation read, in part, ". . . Carl Rogers, wise and gifted student of the human psyche, has helped to shape the theory and practice of human relations at home and abroad. . . . As professor of Clinical Psychology, as psychotherapist, as author and consultant, and now in all these roles at the Western Behavioral Sciences Institute, you have shaped the scientific outlook of specialists in various fields from psychiatry and education to political science and industrial management. . . . Your brilliant formulation of the principles of non-directive therapy and your outstanding contributions to ways of dealing with interpersonal and intergroup tensions are counted as landmarks in the psychological sciences and are signalized by their humanitarian as well as professional outlook."

Then, in 1972, he received the first Distinguished Professional Contribution Award from the American Psychological Association, thereby becoming the first psychologist in history to receive both the APA's Scientific Contribution Award and their Distinguished Professional Contribution Award. Again the citation explained the reason for this tribute.

"His commitment to the whole person has been an example which has guided the practice of psychology in the schools, in industry, and throughout the community. By devising, practicing, evaluating, and teaching a method of psychotherapy and counseling which reaches to the very roots of human potentiality and individuality, he has caused all psychotherapists to reexamine their procedures in a new light. Innovator in personality research, pioneer in the encounter movement, and respected gadfly of organized psychology, he has made a lasting impression on the profession of psychology."

His former colleague from Chicago, Rosalind Dymond Cartwright, said of him, "Carl provided a role model for a couple of generations of therapists, clinical psychologists, counseling people and others . . . he is a living example of the theory. He is a man who has continued to grow, to discover himself, to test himself, to be genuine, to review his experiences, to learn from it, and to fight the good fight, which means to stand up and be counted, to stand for something, to live honestly, fully, in the best human sense."

He had achieved almost every honor and award possible in his own profession and a good many in other professions as well. As our century entered the seventies, so was Carl Rogers approaching his seventies. Surely it was time to retire.

CHAPTER 11
Past, Present, and Future

"At ten o'clock on the morning of June 7, 1969," reads a Sonoma State College publication, "some 1500 friends and relatives of the Class of 1969 gathered by the side of a beautiful little lake to share in the Eighth Annual Commencement exercises." Rogers was present to deliver the commencement address. He began by explaining, "As an undergraduate I majored in medieval history. I have enormous respect for the scholars of the Middle Ages and their contributions to learning. But I want to speak to you as Carl Rogers, in 1969, not as a medieval symbol. So I hope I will not offend you if I remove these medieval trappings—this nonfunctional cap, this handsome but useless hood, and this robe, designed to keep one warm even in the rigors of a European winter." He proceeded to remove the garments and to address the graduating class on "The Person of Tomorrow."

This picture of sixty-seven year old Carl Rogers stepping out of the past to speak to young people and their parents about the future aptly characterizes Rogers' concerns in the latter years of his career. For Rogers was a pioneer. And where does a pioneer go once he has opened the field of psychotherapy to scientific investigation; formulated and popularized a new method of psychotherapy, the client-centered approach; established nondirectiveness and the facilitation of growth through therapeutic conditions as a leading school of thought throughout the helping professions; developed a major theory of personality and of personality change; been one of the pioneers and leaders in the humanistic psychology movement; been one of the most influential popularizers of the intensive group or encounter-group experience; given psychological support, credibility, and concreteness to the growing movement toward a humanistic, open education in the United States and elsewhere; and, by presenting a personal example of his theories and methods, served as a model for thousands of people to emulate?

His concerns broaden, and he looks toward the future.

In my first interview with Rogers he told me, "I hate old people who reminisce." He has frequently made comments like, "We could count on the fingers of one hand the people our own age we really enjoy. The rest are all too stuffy." When he worked on his "autobiography" in 1965 for a collection of autobiographical essays by well-known psychologists, he said it took him and Helen months to recover from spending that much time looking in the past. Both the scientist and the artist in him were operating here; both sides needed new challenges and could not be content with past accomplishments. Beyond this, for Rogers, an interest in the future also went hand in hand with his association with young people. He had always valued his contact with graduate students, and this continued after he left the university setting. As he described it: "Probably the major factor in keeping me alive as a growing therapist is a continuing association with young people on a thoroughly equalitarian basis. I have always worked with young staff members; I have never found people my own age stimulating except for rare and fortunate exceptions. I find that younger people are full of new ideas, exploring the boundaries of our disciplines and raising questions about any sacred cows which I hold dear. This keeps me stimulated, moving, and I hope growing."

His friends and colleagues at the Center for the Studies of the Person especially had this effect on him. Here were forty or so people with whom he attended weekly meetings and social gatherings, and with whom he often worked very closely, as on the Immaculate Heart Project. When CSP was formed in 1968, most of them were in their twenties and thirties, with a few older members, Rogers being the oldest. Many of them were involved in exciting projects in drug abuse education, black-white encounter groups, film making, inventing and marketing humanistic products, and dealing with all sorts of issues and areas and client populations. Both directly and indirectly Rogers was involved in all this and profited from it.

He also profited in a more personal way, as several of his CSP colleagues explained to me at one of their meetings. "He has a truly caring community around him," said one. "I think this has been a very good support group mechanism for him. It has allowed him to experience kinds of freedom—personal and cognitive—that he might not have had if it weren't for the existence of this organization." Another member told of how Rogers' fame typically creates a distance between him and other people. "Rogers and I and some others had conducted a day-long workshop for school administrators in Reno, Nevada—he was talking and I was helping lead the small groups. We had a really good day and I was excited about it. We were eating dinner and I was saying something to him like, 'You know, I really think what you did today was great. I was really excited about it.' And he turned to me and he looked me in the eye and he said, 'You know I've heard enough of that bullshit not to want to hear any more of it today.' And I almost fell off the seat, I was so surprised. And then I thought to myself that he's really telling me where he is. I've heard him talk a number of times about how that putting him up on a plateau and making him more special or talked about is really a problem he's had to face more and more." In contrast, explained another member, "most people here feel free to tell him things, both positive and negative. I can remember at the annual meeting this year, there were a couple of times that people got mad at him and felt free about doing that. I think there are few places he can really go where he's treated pretty much like other people, where he's not put on a pedestal. In effect, if we think he's full of shit one of us will say that."

Many of the CSP members impressed me as having an almost paternal or maternal attitude toward him. They were pleased about "how far he's come along in the last few years." They were proud of his growth. And they were amused by his idiosyncrasies. One member recalled the first summer he met Rogers at the Center. "I was very excited about the fact that here I was and here he walked these halls and that kind of thing. And, as I was talking to someone, in walks this fellow. He's sort of balding with a few hairs on his head, in a sports shirt, with shorts on, none of which matched, black socks on and tennis shoes, with a heavy, heavy briefcase. And he sort of stumbled in and looked like he knew where he was going." And the other CSP members, hearing this story, nodded their heads and smiled, as if to say, "Yes, that's Carl."

While Rogers placed the highest value on his relationships with his friends and colleagues at CSP, the relationships were also reciprocal. Betty Meador saw him as "always ready with compliments when you've done something that he is favorably impressed with. Unlike many people who don't really bother to give expression to whatever favorable feelings they have toward you, Carl, in my experience, has always taken that extra bit of trouble to write the memo or the note or call you and tell you that you did a particularly good job on something." Others commented on how much they learned from his example as a critical thinker with an open mind. "That's what's so amazing to me," said one. "He continues to *really* change his mind. The whole thing about his openness to psychic phenomena and so on. I think it takes a lot more to get me to change my mind than it does Carl. He really got excited about a film which showed the faith healers in the Philippines. He saw it at Sonoma State and he brought it here to show to us. He had a very open mind about it and wanted to check himself out in the presence of us." Another commented on his courage in getting involved with encounter groups. "When he could have continued being the grand old man of one thing, he moved into the forefront of another thing." Another referred to his "will power." "If he was taking a wagon across the western United States, he'd be one of those who would make it." "Particularly if Helen went along," added one of the women members.

In 1971 *Voices,* the publication of the American Academy of Psychotherapists, printed several longer reactions to Rogers by members of the Center for Studies of the Person. What strikes me about these descriptions is that they are similar to statements made by his colleagues and students at Chicago—his ability to listen, his faith in the individual, the respect, care and understanding he communicates. But in addition I detect a sense of closeness that was not there as much before. Beyond the professional benefits many of the younger CSP members derived from being associated with Rogers, they also valued their personal relationship with him. He seems in these descriptions more approachable, more self-disclosing, more fully a person. Even in his "stuffiness," as two of the three comments point out, there is a passionate, feeling person clearly visible. To Tom Gillette:

> Carl helps to provide the courage for me to be. The guy really does accept me for who I am! Incredible. And he even likes me, even though

he knows me. He sits back on the psychological horizons of my mind and when I get in a tight spot, like trying to really be me when I teach, I can conjure him up and hear him say, "Now damnitall, Tom, you've got to be you." And so I do. He sees things about me that I used to think were undesirable, like being aggressive and liking to start things but preferring not to finish them in favor of going off and starting something else. But he has helped me to convert those liabilities into assets. Another thing about Carl, he really is all those things he is supposed to be. At least most of them. He believes in what he stands for and translates that into the action of everyday life. My friendship with Carl has made it more likely that I will become many of the things I want to become. He's kind of stuffy and straight, but he's also a little mad in the right direction. Although I couldn't see myself asking him to go down to TJ for a couple of pitchers at the Long Bar, I can pass a bottle around with him and others and we can *all of us* talk freely about such things as "Extra Marital Sex I Have and Have Not Had." That's kind of mind-blowing for me. One of the most important things I have learned from him, and perhaps the most important thing I have ever learned period, is that it is O.K. for me to be me, and that I am a person of some real value.

To Bruce Meador:

Carl has high professional and artistic standards for himself and he does not let that get in the way of his being a doer. He is tolerant of others: their lower standards, their uncertainties, their inaction. He is intolerant of other men of action who impose themselves on others, who claim too much, who use people. He does not like to be shoved around except on his own terms. He comes across as stable, strong, kind but not soft. He brings this kind of strength to his professional relationships.

Carl is a passionate person. How he manifests this strength (and that he has this strength) says a lot about him. There is nothing flamboyant about his appearance or life style. He does not raise his voice above a clear conversational level. He is not colorful. He is well organized, invariably arrives at the airport 30 minutes before flight departure, and carefully prepares for any public presentation. The only thing he really flirts with is being stuffy. But he doesn't make it. His passion shines through. . . .

There is a touch of recklessness in the way he assigns responsibilities. Untested individuals are given important tasks and are seldom checked up on. There are exceptions, but this happens frequently enough to lend an air of confused excitement to his personal commitment to careful planning. . . .

Carl is not indifferent. While watching him listen to therapy training tapes or teach a class, it is always apparent that he cares what happens. When he tells his students to write on any subject they wish, there is no hint that he is indifferent to what they do. He cares a great deal, but he wants the student to make the decision. This ability to communicate caring and freeing at the same instant is an important characteristic of

Carl's. He encourages clients and colleagues alike to take more responsibility for themselves, and he does this by communicating a confidence in their ability to take responsibility for their own lives.

Betty Meador wrote:

> When I think of who Carl Rogers is as a person, two characteristics come immediately to mind which seem to be almost mutually exclusive. One is his rigorous, strong willed, self-demanding, opinionated side, and the other is his almost childlike openness to new possibilities and to persons. To me the genius of Carl is the balance which he intuitively maintains between these two, not letting either subdue the other. To grow in interaction with this man is to have him as a model of excellence, discipline, and rigor which he does not impose on me, and to receive from him, as only he can matter-of-factly give it, his utter confidence that I can do whatever I set out to do, usually communicated by a look of sincere surprise that I should doubt myself. His strong faith in an individual's capacity to stretch his imagination of himself beyond ordinary bounds is made believable by his own example. . . .

Tony Rose, also a CSP member, later offered a somewhat different perspective on Rogers:

> Suppose there were a special looking glass that always presented you with an image of yourself that you could accept and prize. How would you respond to a stranger's request for a description of that magical mirror? Would you simply say that it is square, flat, sometimes cold to the touch, and has a smooth, hard surface with a slightly rosy-silver hue? Or would you describe the images you've seen reflected there?

In addition to his younger friends and colleagues at CSP, Rogers' work in encounter groups also brought him into contact with many young people from different walks of life. Out of all his new experiences in unstructured interaction with young people, he developed a style of informal interaction with small groups which he utilized with increasing frequency. Instead of giving a speech or presentation, he began to enjoy more the chance simply to sit down with a small group of about twenty to one hundred people and chat. Often a formal speech would be combined with a smaller, informal meeting. His eminent stature in the fields of psychology and education undoubtedly made this possible. If Carl Rogers told an inquirer, no, he would not give a presentation, but he would be glad to talk with them informally, there was little chance that they would miss that opportunity. And these informal contacts seemed to have as much impact on the group, if not more, than his formal presentations did. In one cross-cultural communication workshop, with ninety-eight students from the United States and around the world, the evaluations indicated that "the sessions with Carl Rogers were reported to be of great value for most of the participants. Students and educators reported that the interaction encouraged them to put their own thoughts and experiences into perspective. By either agreeing or disagreeing with the opinions of Dr. Rogers, many were helped to define and evaluate their own reactions and impressions. A final session with Carl Rogers interacting with the total community was mentioned as especially important by 90 of the participants."

I have seen this phenomenon operate when Rogers talked with a group of some fifty undergraduates at the Irvine campus of the University of California, and when he met with thirty-five teachers at the National Humanistic Education Center in New York State, and on several other occasions. Excitement, of course, existed before he even arrived. There would be no agenda, no presentation. Usually on a tight schedule, he would be ushered in by someone responsible for his visit, he would sit in a comfortable chair up front, he would be introduced, and taking a few minutes, he would tell a little bit about himself or perhaps tell of his current interests. He did not seem to assume that anyone knew who he was, but he seemed to enjoy being there. He would invite the group to make any comments or ask any questions which interested them. The kind of effect this tended to have is well illustrated by a letter written by a young man to a student of mine, who shared it with me.

> My Dearest Terrill,
>
> It's Saturday night; nine o'clock, and I decided to stay at home tonight and spend at least the first part of the evening with you. I feel like I'm on top of the world, and there's no particular reason except that I'm turned on to psychology and life. . . . I must confess that while things in general are turning me on, one experience in particular is responsible for my present mood. Today I spent six hours with Carl Rogers.

He goes on to explain how he managed to sit in with a group of twenty-five students at United States International University.

> The group was excellent both because Carl Rogers is brilliant and so were the students. . . . Anyway, it was not an encounter group in the typical sense of the word; it was more of a seminar about encounter groups. But the big story is Carl Rogers. He is magnificent!!! To look

at him and talk to him you might think that he was the nice, old man next door—not the most influential figure in psychotherapy today. He is kind, sweet, gentle, honest, congruent, humble, sincere, attentive, endearing. . . . And at the same time when he opens his mouth and discusses anything about people, his subtle genius is almost obvious. And yet, if I didn't know that he was Carl Rogers I may have walked away thinking that he was all of the above mentioned qualities but never realizing that he was either a psychologist or famous. To me, that is the highest mark of genius and greatness. I guess that in spite of the many superlatives I used, I still may have left out his greatest attribute: he is human through and through.

Maybe I could sum up my feelings in the simplest way possible: I think that I love him. Now, my only problem is how to explain why I feel this way after being with the man for only six hours in a large group. I guess what it is about him that makes him so instantly charming is that he represents the finest of human beings at a time in my life when the need for "real" people is so desperate. Here I am trying to understand myself and the world and as a result in an emotional state varying (from minute to minute) between ecstasy and dread-filled depression; I walk into this strange room and discover a man so *deeply* human that you want to cry for joy. Yes, Mrs. Robinson, there is a Colonel Sanders! He has the kind of overflowing warmth and compassion that makes you feel like going over to him, telling him all of your problems, and then lying on his lap. . . . He is the father that every child wishes he had. For me, he is the supreme hope for humanity. . . .

Rogers makes you feel important because he listens to you with a genuine concern. And more important, he does this in a completely natural way; no technique was perceptible to me. Like I said, you feel like you're talking to the guy next door, or better yet—to your best friend, as opposed to feeling like you're talking to an authority figure, a therapist, a teacher, a wise man, etc.

Beyond this young man's superlatives, I think he shows real insight into why young people often respond to Carl Rogers so positively. I would add one more explanation. Young people, these days, are so often isolated from old people. Those they do come in contact with are too often depressing models of joyless, monotonous, and useless living. An older person with whom young people can identify is very rare. Rogers is that sort of rare person—not only thinking about topics of interest to young people, but thinking about them in "youthful," even radical ways. As one young person who has been in contact with Carl Rogers, I feel more *hopeful* about my own old age, as a result. It is very exciting to think that forty years from now I might be as alert and vital as he.

As indicated above, the relationship was reciprocal. Young people "turned on" Rogers as much as he them. The more these contacts continued, the more enamored he became with what he called "The Person of Tomorrow" and, later, "The Emerging Person."

Amidst all the problems in his own country and throughout the world, Rogers saw this "emerging person" as a source of evolutionary-revolutionary change. He found emerging persons in many places. "I find them among corporation executives who have given up the gray-flannel rat race, the lure of high salaries and stock options, to live a simpler life in a new way. I find them among long-haired young men and women who are defying most of the values of today's culture to form a counter culture. I find them among priests and nuns and ministers who have left behind the dogmas of their institutions to live in a way that has more meaning. I find them among women who are vigorously rising above the limitations which society has placed on their personhood. I find them among blacks and chicanos and other minority members who are pushing out from generations of passivity into an assertive, positive life. I find them among those who have experienced encounter groups, who are finding a place for feelings as well as thoughts in their lives. I find them among creative school dropouts who are thrusting into higher reaches than their sterile schooling permits. I realize too that I saw something of this person in my years as a psychotherapist, when clients were choosing a freer, richer, more self-directed kind of life for themselves."

Read again the sentence above that describes the emerging women in our society. Four years earlier, when Rogers had first written of his "person of tomorrow," he frequently described this person as "the new man." Four years later he had dropped this terminology and was writing, "He (or she)—I wish someone would provide us with a bisexual set of pronouns. . . ." More important than the change in wording is that, in those four years, Rogers had been aware of and open to one of the most important liberation movements going on around him. Here, at seventy-one, he was struggling to wrench himself free from one of the basic language conventions he had lived with all his life.

What are the characteristics of this emerging man or woman whom Rogers perceived? First was a "desire for authenticity," a freedom from facades, an aversion to "hypocrisy, deceit, mixed messages . . . doublethink and doubletalk." Second was a belief that "institutions exist for people," an opposition to "all highly structured, inflexible, bureaucratic institutions." Beyond these two major qualities, he noted: "the unimportance of material things"; "a nonmoralistic caring"; "the wish for intimacy"; "a skepticism about science"; a fascination with "the universe within" the person—from one's feelings to "esoteric and transcendental religious" experience; a desire to live "in balance with nature"; a person "in process"—always changing; and finally, one who lives by "the authority within"—having "a trust in his own experience and a profound distrust of all external authority."

Acknowledging that few individuals possessed all these characteristics and that their proportion to the whole population was small, he still believed that the emerging person stood the chance to have a revolutionary impact upon society. Of course, there would be opposition by those whose position could be characterized by slogans such as: "The State above all. . . . Tradition above all. . . . The intellect above all. . . . Man should be shaped. . . . The status quo forever. . . . and Our truth is *the* truth." These forces might slow down the "emerging evolution," Rogers thought, but would not likely be able to stop it— not when it was already being lived in the daily lives of so many people. And what if the emerging person gained influence and changed the culture? Rogers concluded his article: "This emerging person would not bring Utopia. He would make mistakes, be partially corrupted, go overboard in certain directions. But he would foster a culture which would emphasize certain trends, a culture which would be moving in these directions.

"Toward the exploration of self, and the development of the richness of the total, individual, responsible human soma—mind and body.

"Toward the prizing of the individual for what he *is*, regardless of sex, race, status, or material possessions.

"Toward human-sized groupings in our communities, our educational facilities, our productive units.

"Toward a close, respectful, balanced, reciprocal relationship to the natural world.

"Toward the perception of material goods as rewarding only when they enhance the quality of personal living.

"Toward a more even distribution of material goods.

"Toward a society with minimal structure—human needs taking priority over any tentative structure which develops.

"Toward leadership as a temporary, shifting function, based on competence for meeting a specific social need.

"Toward a more genuine and caring concern for those who need help.

"Toward a human conception of science—in its creative phase, the testing of its hypotheses, the valuing of the humanness of its applications.

"Toward creativity of all sorts—in thinking and exploring—in the areas of social relationships, the arts, social design, architecture, urban and regional planning, science.

"To me these are not frightening trends but exciting ones. In spite of the darkness of the present, our culture may be on the verge of a great evolutionary-revolutionary leap. I simply say with all my heart— Power to the emerging person and the revolution he carries within."

Of all the aspects of the "person of tomorrow," the one which most fascinated Rogers was the attempt of younger people to develop intimate relationships and growth-producing living arrangements with what he called members "of the other (I refuse to say opposite) sex." This led, in 1972, to the publication of his thirteenth book, *Becoming Partners: Marriage and its Alternatives,* published by the Delacorte Press, with Delta and Dell paperback editions.

He had not originally intended to publish a book on marriage. It actually began with an invitation by Scott, Foresman and Company to write a textbook for introductory psychology courses, written from a humanistic perspective. At first Rogers was not interested, feeling that even though it would be a worthwhile book and he could probably do it, it was not a book that really came from within himself. He didn't want to feel obligated to "cover" the field. It wouldn't be *his* book, coming from the deepest parts of himself and his experience. After much urging, however, he agreed to the assignment. His plan was to take some of the key issues of concern to young people and write about these from his own perspective, referring also to the work of others and suggesting further readings and activities for readers to pursue. The topics would be: finding oneself; relationships with others—parents, siblings, intimates; communal living; urban problems; minority groups; drugs; and so on. He would call it *Being Human.*

He wrote six chapters, the first three entitled: "Can We Be Human in the Classroom?" "Who Am I? How Can I Find Myself?" and "Am I Alone?" The next three were on the subject of marriage: "Shall We Get Married?" and two chapters based on the unusual yet in many ways typical experiences of two married couples he interviewed. The chapters pleased him, especially the last three, but he was finding the going very tedious and slow. While writing usually came easily for him, it was now often painful and anxious work. At times he gave up on the book, only to resume it again for another few weeks and months before the discouragement returned. As he told an audience in 1971, "It has made me sharply aware of the fact that every previous book I have written has been written because *I* wanted to say something. I have not written for a particular audience, or to serve some significant purpose." And he quipped: "So—will Carl Rogers finish this book? Will he be able to meet its enormous challenges? Tune in next year to hear the latest installment of *Being Human."*

Not only did the chapters on marriage give him the most satisfaction, they seemed to excite the several people to whom he showed the early drafts of his completed chapters. Just at the time when he was beginning to conclude that he had the kernel of a small book on marriage aimed at a general audience, Donald Cutler, the Harper & Row editor who had helped *On Encounter Groups* reach publication and who was now a literary agent in a respected New York City agency, also contacted Rogers to say he thought the marriage chapters he had read could, with some additional material, make "an attractive short book on the subject for trade publication." Thereupon Rogers freed himself from his contract with Scott, Foresman, quickly completed the volume with a great deal of enthusiasm, allowed Cutler to place the book for him, and within a year *Becoming Partners* had reached publication.

In his introduction he explained how he hoped his book might be unique. "I know," he wrote, "that you can find out anything you want to know about the *externals* of marriage and partnership. You can find out the differences in male-female sexual needs and timing. You can read books on how to improve the sex act. You can study the history of marriage. You can find out what percentage of young people of college age are living together without marriage. You can read lists, compiled from questionnaires, of the major sources of satisfaction and dissatisfaction in married couples—and on and on and on. We are inundated by data. But rarely do we discover a true picture of what a partnership is like, as perceived and lived and experienced from the *inside.* That might be the new element I could add."

His first chapter, one of those from "Being Human," was "Shall We Get Married?" and in it he acknowledged that ". . . the trend toward greater freedom in sexual relationships, in adolescents and adults, is likely to continue, whether this direction frightens us or not. Many elements have conspired together to bring about a change in such behavior, and the advent of 'The Pill' is only one of these. It seems probable that sexual intimacy will be a part of 'going steady' or of any continuing special interest in a member of the opposite sex [sic]. The attitude of prurience is fast dying out, and sexual activity is seen as a potentially joyful and enriching part of a relationship. The attitude of possessiveness—of owning another person—which historically has dominated sexual unions—is likely to be greatly diminished. . . . [Along with this,] In my contacts with young people, it has become clear to me, beyond the shadow of a doubt, that the contemporary young person tends to have a distrust of marriage as an institution. He has seen too many flaws in it. He has often seen it fail in his own home. Instead, a relationship between a man and a woman is significant, and worth trying to preserve, only when it is an enhancing, growing experience for each person."

His comments on marriage, though timely and perhaps admirably contemporary for a man of seventy, were not original. His own contribution came with his particular ability to have people trust him with their intimate feelings both about themselves and about their relationships. Throughout the book he provided short vignettes and longer case studies telling, in the words of the participants, the experiences of many different couples. Some of these came to him through lengthy letters, but most came through tape-recorded interviews. One woman, for example, shared the story of how she happened to get married.

. . . At the time it was the thing to do. "Here are all my friends getting married, what am I gonna do? I'm a senior in college, that's pretty old. I better start thinking about marriage. I don't know what else I can do. I can teach but that's not enough."

The person that I married was a very popular man and I was a very insecure person, *very* insecure; and I thought, well, golly, I'm going with this person and everybody likes *him,* so maybe if I marry him, everybody will like *me!* The man that I married, I didn't feel he really listened, but I did feel security. That, and not knowing what I'd do when I graduated —that's why I got married.

The reason why I got engaged was because a very good friend of mine had gotten engaged and she had a very pretty ring, and was making all these wedding plans. My friends were saying, "God, Joan, when are you and Max getting married? You've been going together for three years now. You better not let him get away. If you let *him* get away, you're stupid!" My mother said, "Oh, Joan, when are you going to find another person like Max? He's so outstanding and responsible and mature and secure." I felt, "This is the one I should marry because my close friends, my roommate, my mother all say it," and although I had these doubts going on inside me, I thought, "Well, you're so insecure and so stupid that you don't know your own feelings." I thought, "They know what's best for you and you don't so you had better follow their advice."

I had guts enough to tell Max why I was doing it and I said I was really kind of scared to get married and said, "I don't know if this is really right for me." And he said, "Don't worry. You'll learn to love me." I did learn to love him in a brotherly way, but it didn't go beyond that.

When the wedding gifts were unwrapped and all the newness wore off, and the newness of having a baby wore off, then I really started feeling, "Oh you stupid idiot, you should have listened to yourself." Because I had been saying those things to me, but I just wouldn't listen because I thought I was too screwed up to know what was best for me. So I was right after all.

Along with this type of self-revelation came Rogers' comments, scattered throughout the various couples' narrations. His sensitive empathy and years of experience helped him identify and elaborate on the major themes. In the case of Joan, for example, he wrote:

"There are several elements which, for me, stand out in Joan's experience. First of all, it shows how prone we all are to yield to social pressures. A female college senior should be planning to get married, and socially that's *that*.

"The dangers of advice stand out so very clearly. Out of love and caring and concern her mother and her good friends all know what is best for her to do. How easy it is to direct the life of another and how very difficult it is to live your own!

"The fear of squarely facing one's own problems. Joan knew she was insecure. She knew she was frightened of the future. She realized she couldn't get to her own feelings. But instead of facing those inner problems squarely and directly, she did what so many of us do; she built the illusion that she could find the solution outside herself—in another.

"Finally, what impresses me is that Joan, as is true of so many others, experiences no trust in her own feelings, her own inner unique reactions. She is dimly aware of the doubts she has about the relationship, of the lack of a feeling of deep love, or her unreadiness to commit herself to this man. But these are only feelings. *Only feelings!* It is not until after marriage, and after having a child, that she realizes what reliable guides her gut reactions were, if she had only *trusted* them enough to *listen* to them."

Besides Joan's experience and two others described in the first chapter, Rogers chose to include a nine-page section on "My Own Marriage." Here, with surprising candor, he told of his and Helen's earlier sexual problems during their first year of marriage, of the one-year period in his forties when he was unexplainably impotent but from which he recovered thanks in part to Helen's confidence and patience, of the way Helen helped him through his unhappy experience with the schizophrenic woman and their "runaway trip," how he helped her through her mother's terminal illness, and of several other incidents and themes in their marriage. In one tender paragraph, he shared how "in the middle of some event or scene Helen may say to me, 'Do you remember when we. . . .' and I say, 'Of course,' and we both laugh together because we know we are both thinking of the same experience. And while our sex life is not quite the same as in our twenties and thirties, our physical closeness, our 'snuggling,' and our sex relationships are somewhat like a chord which is not only beautiful in itself, but also for its many, many overtones which enrich it far beyond the simple chord."

This section of the first chapter had an effect similar to his "This Is Me" introduction to *On Becoming a Person*. It turned the book into a personal as well as a social document. Describing his forty-seven years of marriage in such frank terms, he became more credible to the reader, became a vital person, and the book communicated in a more personal way and with more impact.

The next several chapters described the experiences of several different couples. One couple had lived together several years before getting married. They were rather immature about relationships, and in fact got married as a result of an argument in which he told her to get out, she said no, he said, "Okay. Then do you want to get married?" and she said, "Okay." At various times in their recounting of their experiences, Rogers would interrupt to comment, as when he noted, "One fascinating bit of insight is Dick's dawning recognition that resolution of a conflict is not an instantaneous magic thing. He is beginning to realize that it may take "work and time" to achieve a better relationship, a more harmonious living together. Here is a man of twenty-four who has learned math and history and English literature and yet has scarcely a beginning knowledge of interpersonal relationships. How irrelevant can our education get?"

Another couple, married over ten years, was attempting a marriage in which both partners were free to pursue their own interests and growth and experience other relationships, even sexual ones; yet in which they were making great efforts to keep their communication with each other open and honest, and to continue working on improving their own emotional and sexual relationship. Psychologically they were much more mature than the previous couple, yet the outcome of their marriage was also in question. Commenting on their honest portrayal of all the emotions—fear, jealousy, joy, love, hate, excitement, and so on—that continually played a part in their marriage, Rogers wrote: "When I was a boy, I loved to read stories about the early frontiersmen in this country, the hunters, the moccasinshod explorers who ventured into the 'trackless wilderness,' crossed the Allegheny mountains, risking their lives, facing danger openly, far out ahead of the cabin-dwellers who would follow. I get this same feeling of excitement when I read the honest statements of Roy and Sylvia about their marriage. They are just as truly pioneers, exploring the far reaches of the relationship between a man and a woman. The risks they take are just as real as those taken by Daniel Boone. They live with uncertainty and at times with fear and doubt. They too have a goal which is both vague and definite. Just as the frontiersman kept pushing on, endeavoring to open up unknown territory, so these two are exploring the terra incognita which lies ahead in a modern marriage. I do not know whether their efforts will lead to success—who *could* know?—but they have my deep respect as they open new trails through the wilderness of human relationships. They have broken many of the conventional rules of 'what marriage should be' and are striving, with real dedication to each other, to build a new model for a permanent man-woman relationship. It is built on continually growing self-knowledge, on a complete sharing of even the most painful and shameful personal feelings, on permission for each to grow and develop together or separately, on a commitment which is real but fluctuating, on a changing, flowing union which carries no guarantee except that of further change."

Another chapter described the experience of one woman who went through two unsuccessful marriages before developing her own identity and personal strengths to the point where, coupled with a kind and secure partner, she was able to discover the type of intimacy she had been striving for for so long. A sixth chapter succeeded in getting the book banned in South Africa. It presented a very sensitive portrayal of a loving marriage between a black man and a white woman, as described by the man, who also described the breakup of his unsuccessful first marriage. Another chapter described a fifteen-year-old marriage in which the partners, as in the O'Neills' book *Open Marriage*, published a short time before *Becoming Partners*, were attempting to grow as individuals at the same time they were trying to grow together. In a chapter on "Communes as Experiments in Human and Sexual Relationships" he analyzed the interpersonal issues typically arising when individuals attempted to develop new forms of intimate relationships and life styles in various types of communal situations. For him the communal experience, though different in form from the nuclear family structure, illustrated the same themes as had the experiences of the other couples he had described. He wrote: "In every one of these situations something has been learned. There is pain, distress, shock, surprise, caring, loving, and despair. But none of these is final, nor are they *finished* experiences. They are part of a *process* of living, loving, learning—all of it open between them.

"I speak of this at such length because I think it is not sufficiently recognized that this is an almost completely new mode of life. The sharing of bad feelings as well as good, of pain as well as loving, of looking inward to discover what one is *really* experiencing, is very literally a new pathway. These young people have not seen it in their parents, their schools, their ancestors. They would not find it in Oriental cultures where 'saving face' is so important. They would not find it in European tradition in which, especially in matters of love, deceit is the rule.

"No, young people and others are today trying out a genuinely new way of living. To me it is refreshing and hopeful. But I am sure that I am not enough of a prophet to say that it will be the way of our culture tomorrow. All I can say is that this open sharing of *all* of one's self nearly always, in my experience, leads to personal growth. I can also add that I believe it is very rare that a person who knows this way of living prefers to go back to living with the facade, the armor, the self-deceiving and other-deceiving 'front' which characterizes the great majority of the people. So we cannot know what the future holds for Clyde and Libby and Myra except that each one is likely to grow as a person."

In a final chapter, he summarized many of the themes that recurred in the experiences of the different couples he had introduced. He spoke of the dedication to a growing relationship, the risky communication of persisting feelings to one's partner, the abandonment of traditional role expectations and assumption of freely chosen roles, and the becoming of separate selves—all of which seemed to strengthen the relationships he had described. If these kinds of qualities and acts did, in fact, help relationships survive and flourish, what implications would this have? Here he wrote of what we, as a society, might do, if we believed these qualities were important. We would lend encouragement to the experimental attempts to build new forms of relationship. We would not allow the law to interfere; "any partnership pattern entered into by mutually consenting adults" would be legal. We would change our educational systems into institutions which would help build the skills and attitudes for better human interaction and human communication. We would especially educate our children in the skills and attitudes necessary for effective partnerships. We would, as a matter of course, institute intensive group experiences for couples, especially before marriage. Families would learn to use "family group meetings" to work through problems and hurts. We would experiment with better ways of caring for our children, especially the children of divorces, where an archaic legal system introduces so much unnecessary hurt and conflict for the child and the parents. Concluding the chapter and the book, he wrote, "I want to add that the concept of partnerships—married or not—as a vast and promising laboratory has been forced on me by my learnings from these couples. I did not start with this idea at all. I tried to choose reasonably representative people. They did not—and do not—seem to me to be unusual couples or unusual persons, except for their surprising willingness to tell of their life as it is. Only gradually did I see that here is an enormous, exploring experiment, going on all about us.

"Unheralded and unsung, explorations, experiments, new ways of relating, new kinds of partnerships are being tried out, people are learning from mistakes and profiting from successes. They are inventing alternatives, new futures, for our most sharply failing institutions, marriage and the nuclear family."

Late in 1970, about the time when he was beginning the textbook on psychology which eventually evolved into *Becoming Partners*, Rogers wrote an informal letter to circulate among his friends. Entitled "A Day In My Life," it read:

> Many of you must wonder what an elderly man does with his time; how he manages to keep himself from being bored to death. I am listing below a few of the things that happened on one day, November 5, 1970, a day when I had no appointments. I don't claim that it is a typical day but neither is it atypical.
>
> 8:00 A.M. Urgent phone call from a woman in northern California who had gotten to know me in a 1955 workshop, has heard me speak since, and *must* see me. She is coming to San Diego in two days. (In spite of my telling her I just did not have time, she *did* see me.)
>
> The morning mail arrived at home and at the office I found the following items: A letter from an educator in Suva, Fiji Islands, wanting to know my latest writings on education. He had become interested through David Williams of New Zealand who was visiting Fiji and whom I had known in Chicago in the 1930's. But the Fiji Islands! My memories of Suva are of very black policemen in white shorts and women with turbans on their heads and one of the wildest outdoor markets I have ever seen. And they want to know Carl Rogers on education!
>
> A letter—would I be interested in the presidency of a Mid-West college?

A letter from a tough black man—a convicted drug pusher and stick-up man, now in jail awaiting sentence from his last trial—wanting copies of my books! He was a member of the Pittsburgh drug group which Tony Rose and I conducted, and is a lovely person in spite of his record.

A letter saying that a course is to be offered at the New School for Social Research in New York City entitled, "Carl Rogers, Psychologist and Educator."

A fan letter regarding *Freedom to Learn*. A student had been in a course taught by someone infected by the book, who conducted his course like an encounter group. "The results were exactly the kind of experience you described in *Freedom to Learn*."

Dictated replies to these and a dozen other letters.

Received a dust jacket of *Carl Rogers on Encounter Groups* from Harper & Row with a most laudatory comment about the book by Philip Slater.

Received a copy of TIME Magazine with my picture and a quotation or two, found in a mediocre article on the human potential movement.

A phone call regarding some changes they are making in the film, "A Conversation with Carl Rogers" which is soon to be distributed.

Checked garden. Little watering needed. Snapdragons and pansies—recently transplanted—doing fine. New gorgeous flowers on my best camellia! Hanging begonia still blooming. All others gone. Acalypha cuttings (gorgeous red leaves) beginning to sprout, after dubious period. Attempt to grow mossehorn fern from spores appears failure. Can't win 'em all.

Saw Philip Slater, the author of *The Pursuit of Loneliness: American Society in Crisis,* being interviewed on the Keith Berwick show. Having never met him was fascinated to see him after his comment about my book.

11:00 P.M. Long distance phone call from a student at Plattsburgh, New York. That's 2:00 A.M. his time! He had just finished reading *On Becoming a Person* and was very much excited by it. Wanted me to know that, and also wanted to know if there was some graduate school that shared my kind of ideas.

In between times, trying to get a little writing done on my new book, taking Helen out to an enjoyable movie and dinner, and calming down from the excitement. I wish I could cut off some of the stimuli.

As you can see, it is a very boring life.

As I read this letter, I am struck by its similarity in tone to the letters which a twenty-year-old Carl Rogers wrote home from his travels to China, telling of how many pages of this or that book on the Orient he had read each day. Beyond the "objective report" of his activities one senses the pride he has in his accomplishments. I often sensed this pride in Rogers. His work was important to him and he liked to find that it was important to others. Because he wanted to make a difference, he was genuinely pleased to discover new examples of his impact.

Yet the pride stopped short of vanity. Part of this may be explained by a genuinely humble feeling he had about his place in the scheme of things. As he once wrote, "I have many fields of interest . . . my professional work is not the be-all and end-all of my existence. Somehow I have an inwardly light touch in regard to my work. It is not all there is to life. Sometimes I am struck with the absurdity of my earnest effort to help a person, complete a research, write a paper. Placed in the perspective of billions of years of time, of millions of light years of interstellar space, of the trillions of one-celled organisms in the sea, of the life struggle of billions of people to achieve their goals, I cannot help but wonder what possible significance can be attached to the efforts of one person at one moment of time. I can only do my part as one infinitely small living unit in this vast ongoing universe. But such a perspective helps to keep me from feeling too self-important."

Such a metaphysical perspective, however, is only one explanation for the humility which so often impressed people who met Rogers. To call undue attention to himself or his ideas would completely contradict his philosophy. He hated to be idealized. His whole professional life had been devoted to furthering the principle of Trust Your Own Experience. So he had little respect for would-be disciples. He said in 1971, "People are continually asking me or writing me to inquire if I have changed. Some of the letters are pathetic in their search for a guru. They say essentially, 'I hear you have entirely changed your thinking and your way of working. Please tell me it isn't so. To whom will I turn if you have changed?' " As one colleague succinctly put it: "He hates 'Rogerians.' "

In any case, Rogers' "Day in My Life" letter, in addition to illustrating the pride he took in his work, characterizes something of the flavor of the later years of his career, beginning around the 1970s. As the letter suggests, he moved into a stage that might be described as "semi-retirement," spending most of his time in La Jolla and enjoying the fruits of all his years of productive work. On the other hand, he by no means stopped working or forging ahead into new areas of thought and practice. In his semi-retirement, he accomplished more than many do in their entire careers.

As he began to slow down, he traveled less, participated in fewer encounter groups and accepted only occasional speaking invitations. Many of his articles were of a retrospective bent, which had not been typical of him before this time. He continued to prize very highly his friends and colleagues at the Center for Studies of the Person. He spent a good deal of time in his garden.

Describing his own aging process, in 1977, at seventy-five, he wrote,

"I do feel physical deterioration. I notice it in many ways. Ten years ago I greatly enjoyed throwing a frisbee. Now my right shoulder is so painfully arthritic it is out of the question. In my garden I realize that a task which would have been easy five years ago but difficult last year, now seems like too much, and I had better leave it for our once-a-week gardener. This slow deterioration, with various minor disorders of vision, heartbeat and the like, inform me that the physical portion of what I call 'me' is not going to last forever.

"Yet I still enjoy a four-mile walk on the beach. I can lift heavy objects, do all the shopping, cooking and dishwashing when my wife is ill, carry my own luggage without puffing. The female form still seems to me one of the loveliest creations of the universe and I appreciate it greatly. I feel as sexy in my *interests* as I was at 35, though I can't say the same about my ability to perform. But I am delighted that I am still sexually alive, even though I can sympathize with the remark of Supreme Court Justice Oliver Wendell Holmes upon leaving a burlesque house at age 80: 'Oh to be 70 again!' "

The years were not nearly as kind to Helen as they were to Carl. When a hip problem and her rather serious arthritis condition confined her to a wheelchair and she was experiencing a great deal of pain almost daily, he took over the major part of her care. For a period of about two years he did almost all the shopping, cooking, and cleaning for the two of them. Happily, a successful hip-joint operation in 1973 worked wonders on her condition. She began to walk about more, swim almost daily at a local health club, and they even signed up for a thirty-five day Mediterranean cruise, on a freighter, for the winter of 1974. Unfortunately, after they came east in January the voyage was delayed, then canceled. Although they enjoyed their time with Natalie and David's families out East, they were both very disappointed to miss this chance to resume their beloved pastime of traveling. Shortly thereafter Helen's arthritis worsened again, other ailments caused further problems, and she began to feel that she would never travel again. With the burden of her care, as well as his professional responsibilities on his shoulders, Carl began to feel more and more distraught, harried, and depressed than he had in many years. In one workshop in 1974 he realized that he was losing his ability to care for others, so troubled was he by his own pressures and feelings. He felt as though he was being "nibbled to death by ducks" (a phrase used by one of the participants which Rogers felt perfectly described him) and resolved, in spite of Helen's condition, to take some time for and by himself. Shortly thereafter he went to a cottage on Stinson Beach in California for ten days by himself. He went without any expectations of working. The time was just for him. He read, took long walks on the beach, and spent long hours thinking or simply being (he also placed a nightly telephone call to check on Helen). These were precious days to him. Although he took no more time like this, just for himself, for the next several years, he frequently referred back to these ten days as being so important in helping him regain his balance and feeling of well-being.

Back home he realized he would need help in caring for Helen, so they hired a young woman to work in that capacity. Unfortunately Helen's condition continued to deteriorate. For a time in 1976 it seemed as if she was dying. Carl and Natalie Rogers, working together in one workshop, told the participants on the first night that they might be called away at any time. Letters to friends during this period often expressed the unhappiness he felt in seeing his lifelong partner grow old and weaker and experience such pain in the process. Once again he began to feel the strain of it. He was feeling alive, vital, still growing in new directions, becoming an increasingly radical thinker in many ways. Helen, as her health deteriorated, was feeling increasingly conservative on various issues and emotionally dependent on Carl. Never one to handle dependency well to begin with, Carl was caught in the turmoil of many mixed emotions—love for Helen, resentment for what he felt as her "clinging" behavior, admiration for her courage in facing the physical pain she felt, frustration at feeling there was nothing he could do, depression at feeling that his life was being controlled and hemmed in. For a period he saw a therapist-friend to get some help in dealing with his confusion and discouragement. It was for him the most trying period of their fifty or more years of marriage. He felt a greater distance from Helen than he had ever felt before. And whenever he contemplated dealing with her directly about this, he would stop himself, feeling that this would be neither a thoughtful nor productive thing to do with a dying person. This contributed to his sense of helplessness even further. On one occasion when she had expressed that she really had nothing to live for except to live for him, he said, "Then I can understand why you want to die," and left the room in deep despair.

But then, again, around the latter part of 1976, Helen's condition began to improve. Not only was there physical improvement, but psychologically she came alive again. She took up painting and crafts and began to initiate projects on her own. Having thought that she would never leave La Jolla again, she took a weekend trip to San Francisco to test her strength and, when she found that she was able to get along, she accompanied Carl for three weeks, in the summer of 1977, to the rustic Sagamore Conference Center in the Adirondack Mountains of New York State.

Ironically, Helen's "rebirth" introduced new problems into the marriage. Once she resolved in her own mind that living her life for her husband was not a sufficient reason for living, and that she would have to find some additional purposes of her own, she began to experience some resentment toward him for having had the opportunity to live *his* own life as he chose, over all those years. As she voiced her angry feelings, it became clear to Carl that she could take some of his resentment as well. Consequently, there was more anger present in their relationship than ever before. To Carl this was a healthy sign. Although there were many unresolved issues to be worked out, he felt they were beginning to move closer to one another once again.

Working on one's relationship, after fifty-three years of marriage, is hardly the stereotype most of us have of the "golden years." In a paper he wrote at age seventy-five, "Growing Older—Or Older and Growing," Rogers discussed one popular conception of old age. "It is often said or assumed that the older years are years of calm and serenity. I have found this misleading. I believe I do have a longer perspective on events outside of myself, and hence am often more of an objective observer than I might have been earlier. Yet in contrast to this, events which touch *me* often evoke a stronger reaction than they would have years ago. When I am excited, I get very high. When I am concerned, I am more deeply disturbed. Hurts seem sharper, pain is more intense, tears come more easily, joy reaches higher peaks, even anger—which I have always had trouble with—is felt more keenly. I believe that emotionally I am more, not less, volatile than I used to be. The range from feeling depressed to feeling elated seems greater, and either state is more easily triggered."

He wondered to what extent this greater volatility might be a function of growing older, or of his life style, or of "the greater sensitivity acquired in encounter groups." In any event, he had these feelings and was often surprised at their intensity. This was particularly true in the area of intimacy, which he discussed in his paper on the aging process.

"In the past few years I have found myself opening up to much greater intimacy in relationships. I see this as definitely the result of workshop experiences. I am more ready to touch and be touched, physically. I do more hugging and kissing, both men and women. I am more aware of the sensuous side of my life. I realize more sharply how much I desire close psychological contact with others. I recognize how much I need to care deeply for another and to receive that kind of caring in return. I can say openly what I have always recognized dimly: that my deep involvement in psychotherapy was a cautious way of meeting this need for intimacy without risking too much of my person. Now I am more willing to be close in other relationships, and risk giving more of myself. I feel as though a whole new depth of capacity for intimacy has been discovered in me. It is a capacity which has brought me much hurt, and an even greater share of joy.

"What has this meant in my behavior? It has meant deeper and more intimate relationships with men, sharing without holding back, trusting the security of the friendship. Only during my college days—never before or after—did I have a group of really trusted, intimate men friends. So this is a new, tentative, adventurous development which seems very rewarding. It has meant much more intimate communication with several women. There are now a number of women with whom I have platonic but psychologically intimate relationships which have tremendous meaning for me. With these close friends, men and women, I can share any aspect of my self—the painful, joyful, frightening, crazy, insecure, egotistical, self-deprecating feelings I have. I can share fantasies and dreams. I receive a similar deep sharing from them. These experiences I find very enriching."

Rogers' semiretirement, then, was by no means a retirement from active and adventurous human contact. Because of Helen's health problems and his own slowing down of activities, however, he conducted most of his professional work in these later years out of his office at home in La Jolla, often inviting associates, interviewers, and students to his home instead of traveling to see them. His "fan mail" continued as usual. A writer would say, "I just read your book and I must tell you . . . ," and he would have to figure out which of his more popular books was being referred to—*On Becoming a Person, Person to Person, Freedom to Learn, On Encounter Groups* or *Becoming Partners*. Reactions to *Becoming Partners* were typical, as in this Texas woman's letter in 1973.

Dear Dr. Rogers, I want to take a moment of your time to thank you for your writings. I first became acquainted with your books through a gift copy of *Becoming a Person*. I had just entered therapy at the age of 28 and my counselor hoped that the book would help me. It did—it was a turning point on my road to indeed "becoming a person." A short time later, I became involved in encounter work—first as a participant, then as a facilitator—and your book on encounter groups was invaluable in helping me experience myself and other people. After a period of pain, I finally began to open myself up to others. Now, I have come upon *Becoming Partners* and, once more, I have learned from you and gained insight into my relationships with men. I want to thank you from the bottom of my heart for your influence on my life.

Another reaction to the book came from Logan Fox, Rogers' old acquaintance and his interpreter on their 1961 trip to Japan.

> Carl, you never cease to amaze me. You are one of the stubbornest men I have known, refusing to retreat from your own interests and your own perceptions. Some of us zig-zag all over the place, crossing and recrossing your path, while you doggedly walk one of the straightest paths I know. Yet, at the same time, I have known no one who has kept growing as you have. I especially felt this after reading *Becoming Partners,* since that was a book I really didn't expect from you. But it was beautiful; so much like you, yet with a fresh and courageous handling of material that I guess was not easy for you (not that you are "square," but neither are you a "swinger") . . . again you serve to remind me of hungers in me to which I am not always faithful. I know you don't see yourself as anybody's conscience, but in so many ways you have been one to me. Except that I don't resent this conscience as I, at times, resent the rigid superego I inherited. Thank you, Carl, for being you. . . . Affectionately, Logan.

Sitting in Rogers' study one day, I began to comprehend the range of letters that he received by noticing a little stamp collection he was saving for a friend's son. In about two or three months he had taken stamps off envelopes sent to him from: Ireland, Greece, Poland, India, United Arab Republic, Australia, Canada, Netherlands, Israel, England, Italy, Norway, Bahamas, Belgium, Japan, Argentina, Spain, Philippines, and Germany.

Then there would be the little battles or issues to clear up, and as usual Rogers would enjoy waging war with his pen, as when he told an editor, "I think you better tell your legal hacks to get off my back and write a human document and not to think they can get away with murder because they sent me a check for $50." Or when he responded to a psychology professor by writing, "I don't believe you will get the kind of person you want and I don't think you deserve him. Your department sounds incredibly smug. I think the sooner the undergraduates move out, the better off they will be. If I knew a good person who would fit the kind of post you mention, I certainly wouldn't recommend that he come to your place. Sorry." Or when he resigned from a part-time professorship at the United States International University, in a letter which received a good deal of national publicity within the psychological profession: Referring to a new set of rules governing student conduct—including search of their cars and dormitories, a "loyalty oath" to the University's rules which students had to sign, and so on—Rogers wrote, in part:

> The most incredible portion of the statement is this. ". . . The University must reserve the right . . . to deny the re-enrollment of any student when such action is deemed to be in the best interest of the University or the student." I believe that historically this has been known as the Star Chamber procedure. I have never known such a procedure to be used except under dictatorships. As I read it very carefully, it means that at the end of a term a student simply disappears. Why? He does not know, nor do his fellow students. Who made the decision? "The University." What is the effect? Obviously the effect is to cause students to distrust each other, the faculty, and the administration. Who will be the next informer? No one knows. Since he has signed a statement saying he will support all university policies and regulations, each student must keep his dissenting thoughts to himself, lest he be seen as a "trouble-maker" and caused to disappear. This, to my mind, is dictatorship.

And the little surprises. The invitations to address all sorts of groups and audiences (which he would either decline or answer with "I never make any commitments over the phone. Write me a letter and I'll think about it"). The hundreds of references to his work appearing here and there. The dissertations based on his formulations, sent to him from time to time, from universities all over the world. A very popular book of poems and reflections, *Notes to Myself* by Hugh Prather, dedicated "to Carl Rogers (whose *On Becoming a Person* showed me where to look)." New publications by former students and colleagues: *New Directions in Client-Centered Therapy, Innovations in Client-Centered Therapy,* and others. And three more honorary degrees—from the University of Hamburg, Germany, from Holland's Leiden University, celebrating its four hundredth anniversary (both institutions set precedents by sending representatives across the ocean to present the degrees to Rogers in special ceremonies held in La Jolla), and in 1978 from Northwestern University.

But this picture of a less active Carl Rogers enjoying the fruits of a rich career is only half the picture. Throughout the 1970s he continued to grow, continued to work, and continued to extend his thinking into new areas of human knowledge and concern. Primarily he began to explore the social and political implications of his life's work in the client-centered mode.

Since his trip to China a half century earlier, Rogers had been interested in social issues, economic problems, and political realities. But he chose to work in a scientific and helping profession where almost all his time was spent focused on individuals, with only occasional glances outward at the implications of his work—as in the Rogers-Skinner debate. He was "a revolutionary with a narrow focus," as he described it. Gradually the work focus broadened, as he began applying his insights to the family, the school, the work setting, and to intergroup relations.

After he left university life, however, his work at WBSI, CSP, and especially in encounter groups, brought him in much closer contact with groups and individuals who were very involved in dealing with all of society's problems. In the seventies, once his own work schedule began to slow down a bit, he had a little more time to think about these broader issues. Perhaps also he realized he was enough of an established figure, a man of stature and respect, that he could afford to speak out on social issues, without it damaging his "career." At any rate, he did begin to speak out. In one speech which he delivered on several occasions, and which was first published in the *Journal of Humanistic Psychology* in 1972, he spoke of "Some Social Issues Which Concern Me." In many of his articles and speeches during the seventies he continued to refer to one or more of the social problems he addressed in this speech. These included: overpopulation; decaying cities; the eroding institution of marriage; the problems our laws and customs create for children of separated parents; racism and minorities; our "dying educational institutions"; a growing police state; and "our obscene war" in Southeast Asia (he didn't discuss the environment because he said that was one problem we were well aware of and showing some commitment to deal with it). He minced no words.

"The Pentagon and CIA appear to be major forces in formulating our foreign policy. The CIA was training troops in Laos years ago, without knowledge of Congress or the people. Presidents seem unable to stand up to these great bureaucracies. For purposes of 'national defense' we maintain more than one and one-half *million* troops in 119 foreign countries. Is this for defense? Military and totalitarian governments are being financially and militarily supported by the United States, in numbers probably never equalled in the history of the world.

Yet we proclaim ourselves as the backers of the free and democratic world.

"Why do we not stop this incredible slaughter and waste and destruction, this sordid, interminable, and expanding war? I believe it boils down to one central reason. As a country we cannot bear to say that we have made a horrible, massive *mistake*. We cannot bear, in short, to lose face. What a reason for continuing. The one thing we might learn from this incredible tragedy is to gain a clear view of the enemy. If we peer closely through the blood and death and awful ruin we can see the enemy clearly. He is us.

". . . I believe our culture is facing a life and death crisis on many fronts, and that I have an obligation as a citizen to speak out. I am frightened about our destiny as a people, as a nation. So I want to take as clear a stand as I can on a variety of issues, including our insane wars. . . . I recognize very well that I am no expert in most of the fields I shall mention, but I shall simply voice the attitudes and views of one deeply concerned person."

In one speech in 1971 he referred to the war in Vietnam, saying, "Sometimes I think the words of one of America's favorite songs should be changed to read, 'God forgive America, our home-destroying home.' " On another occasion he said that if we would apply our knowledge of the behavioral sciences to deal with problems in race relations in the United States, and "we back that effort with a sum at least equivalent to the cost of all our B-52 bombers—then there might be a chance of preventing the bloody tragedy which faces us."

Another facet of his social concern came with a very unusual encounter group he led in 1972. Although he tapered off doing encounter groups in the seventies, this notable exception came when he and William McGaw collaborated on another encounter documentary, as they had on the Academy Award-winning *Journey Into Self*. Only this time the risks were more than psychological for the participants. At considerable expense they brought across the Atlantic Ocean, to the studio of WQED in Pittsburgh, a group of Irish Catholics, Irish Protestants, and British—including an officer in the English army, a mother whose son had been shot by a British soldier, a probable member of the Irish Republican Army (because the IRA was illegal, he couldn't admit it), a clergyman, and others, to comprise a diverse group. The group members risked their lives by participating in this experiment and then returning to Ireland to show the film in movie theatres and, in teams of two—a Catholic and a Protestant—conduct a discussion with members of the audience. Rogers and Father Pat Rice facilitated the group. Although the depth of understanding and acceptance was not nearly as great as in a typical encounter group, nevertheless the group did move significantly, though reservedly, toward viewing one another as human beings without the stereotypes and enmity associated with religion and nationality. Rogers invested some twenty-two thousand dollars of his own in the project. After the filming Rogers and McGaw tried unsuccessfully to raise an additional fifty thousand dollars necessary to distribute the film properly in the United States; consequently it has not been viewed on this side of the ocean.

In many of the encounter groups Rogers led, members would often challenge both Rogers and the field of humanistic psychology in general as being irrelevant to the more important social and political issues of the day. Some political activists would (and still do) react to psychotherapy and encounter groups as being conservative or "counterrevolutionary," insofar as they might distract people's energy from solving important social issues and turn it toward simply "getting one's own head together" or establishing a few intimate relationships. Although Rogers did not agree with this appraisal, neither did he feel moved to think deeply about the connection between the client-centered approach and the world of politics and power. His speaking out on social issues was as an individual, as a concerned citizen; he made no attempt to relate his life's work to these broader areas of concern.

The turning point came in 1973, with two related incidents. In one, Alan Nelson, a young psychologist and a colleague of Natalie Rogers, happened to ask Rogers about the politics of the client-centered approach to psychotherapy. As Rogers describes it, "I replied that there was no politics in client-centered therapy, an answer which was greeted with a loud guffaw. When I asked my questioner to explain, he replied, 'I spent three years of graduate school learning to be an expert in clinical psychology. I learned to make accurate diagnostic judgments. I learned the various techniques of altering the subject's attitudes and behavior. I learned the subtle modes of manipulation, under the labels of interpretation and guidance. Then I began to read your material, which upset everything I had learned. You were saying that the power rests not in my mind but in his organism. You completely reversed the relationship of power and control which had been built up in me over three years. And then you say there is no politics in the client-centered approach!'

"This was the beginning—perhaps a late beginning—of my education regarding the politics of interpersonal relationships. The more I thought and read, and the more I sensed the present-day concern with power and control, the more new facets I experienced in my relationships in therapy, in intensive groups, in families, and among friends. Gradually I realized my experience ran parallel to the old story of the uneducated man and his first exposure to a course in literature. 'You know,' he told his friends later, 'I've found out I've been speaking prose all my life and never knew it.' In similar vein I could now say 'I've been practicing and teaching politics all my professional life and never realized it fully until now.' "

That was the beginning of Rogers' starting to reevaluate his life's work from a political perspective. The more he thought about it, the more he began to see connections. Politics was more than "the methods or tactics involved in managing a state or government," as Webster's Dictionary defined it. When applied to human relationships, politics became, as Rogers defined it, "the process of gaining, using, sharing or relinquishing power, control, decision-making. It is the process of the highly complex interactions and effects of these elements as they exist in relationships between persons, between a person and a group, or between groups."

He went on to describe how "this new construct has had a powerful influence on me. . . . It has caused me to take a fresh look at my professional life work. I've had a role in initiating the person-centered approach. This view developed first in counseling and psychotherapy, where it was known as client-centered, meaning a person seeking help was not treated as a dependent patient but as a responsible client. Extended to education, it was called student-centered teaching. As it has moved into a wide variety of fields, far from its point of origin— intensive groups, marriage, family relationships, administration, minority groups, interracial, intercultural, and even international relationships—it seems best to adopt as broad a term as possible: person-centered."

What he saw in all these areas was the attempt to return the power, the control and the decision-making to the person and away from the authority or the institution or those with the most physical or economic power. All around him, for the previous decade or more, he had witnessed and supported various movements for human liberation— "power to the people," "participatory democracy," "the population with the problem has the best resources for solving the problem," "student rights," "Vietnam for the Vietnamese," "children's rights," "sisterhood is powerful," "patient's rights," and so on. These were the slogans of the decade, and they described on a political and social level what Rogers had been saying all along for the helping professions.

What he had been saying, essentially, was that, given a facilitative climate, the individual has the resources to solve his problems and guide his life far more effectively than any power or authority or expert can do for him. What would happen if this hypothesis were extended to all power relationships—if those with the power were to be personally congruent and genuine, if they were truly to trust those over whom they exercised control, if they were really to listen empathically to what those controlled are saying, and in the final analysis, if they were to relinquish that control in favor of more egalitarian human relationships?

At the same time that Rogers was becoming increasingly intrigued by this question, a second event occurred which moved him further in the same direction. This was a letter from his daughter. Natalie Rogers, recently divorced, was by now a skilled therapist and group leader in her own right, with a good deal of experience with alternative kinds of institutions that were experimenting with new forms of nonauthoritarian power relationships. She told her father:

> I wanted to put on paper some of my feelings about my group and individual therapy work and the thoughts I so often have about you and client-centered therapy. I feel I should write this, because I keep asking you to do things with me and/or friends and colleagues of mine and it occurs to me you may think I am one of many others who might want to use your name, etc. I do want to use your drawing power but much more important than that is how important your philosophy of therapy is to me right now. As I see individual clients and we get into tight emotional spots, I am so very glad to have a theoretical framework from which I can take a thermometer reading and do what I believe is the right thing in a relationship to the client. That's not to say that I always live up to my standards . . . but at least I know what I am *trying* to do, which gives me a solid feeling as a therapist. And when I ask for feedback from clients as to the most meaningful times we have together or moments of help for them, they inevitably come back with a statement about being really heard, or deeply understood. The most simple notion that to really understand someone emotionally helps them to come to relevant, personal, meaningful solutions or insights is an amazing one. Being a little older and a little "wiser" than I used to be can get in my way occasionally because I'm tempted to give advice. When such a feeling overcomes me, instead of giving the advice I try to share something of my experience with them and let them take it or leave it.
>
> All of this is to say that I not only love you as a father, but am more and more re-appreciating the philosophy you have formulated. It is also to say that I would like a few more occasions to work closely with you. Although we have been in a couple of things together, I don't think we've ever co-led any kind of group. I'd really be interested in thinking

up something we'd like to do together. I'm also excited about the possibility of working something out that would interest you with the Greenhouse people*; because we are good people, working in a way that is
struggling to be politically in touch yet humane—an almost impossible
task. Much love, Nat.

These two events—Natalie's letter and the conversation with Nelson
—initiated a discussion which led Carl and Natalie Rogers, Alan Nelson, and two of Carl's colleagues from the Center for Studies of the
Person, Betty Meador and John K. Wood, to offer two new workshops
in 1974. These three-week-long workshops, held at San Diego and
Santa Cruz in California, were not intended to have a particularly
political focus, but rather to explore the implications of the client-
centered approach for therapy, education, intensive groups, and other
human relationships. What happened, however, was that the workshops became political events. Although a good deal of time was spent
in ongoing encounter groups and special-interest groups, regularly
scheduled "community meetings" were also held. In these meetings
the staff and participants came to experience a closeness and sense of
community that was as powerful as it was unique in their experience.
The sixty-five or so "community members" often were able to operate
with the same intensity and openness as that which is more typically
experienced in a small encounter group. The group handled its community "business" in these large meetings, but also was able to deal
with very personal issues in a supportive way. All this was not achieved
at once, but as it evolved, Rogers and the staff reexperienced the
potency of the client-centered philosophy. Here the same principles of
congruence, trust, and empathy were operating in a large and diverse
community of people. Whereas before, Rogers had only speculated
about the broader applications of the client-centered approach, now
he and his colleagues were actually experiencing such an instance.

The Santa Cruz workshop also "had many more social radicals and
revolutionaries," as Rogers recalled. "It was one of the things which
got me focused more on politics. It had a big influence on people like
that, because I think the revolutionary people often are quite blind to
the personal factors. The workshop helped to educate the squares like
me and the fanatics like them."

Their excitement about the process and the sense of community that
they saw reoccur in both workshops in 1974 prompted them to schedule another workshop of the same type, at Mills College in California,

*A group Natalie was part of in Boston.

in the summer of 1975. Carl, Natalie, and John Wood continued on the staff, and new staff members Joanne Justyn (who had been business manager the year before), Maureen Miller, Jared Kass, Maria Bowen, David Aspy, and Dick and Marian Vittitow joined their ranks. For the first time the phrase "Person-Centered" replaced "Client-Centered" in the workshop title. Building on their experience of the previous summer, the staff decided to offer less structure and leave more of the decisions about the workshop to the entire group, which included 126 participants. They allowed participants to set their own tuition fees, commensurate with their income levels. Whereas in the previous workshops the staff had set up a regular schedule for community meetings and encounter groups, and time for special-interest groups, this summer they set the structure for the first few days only and, even then, left many hours of those days open for participants to spend as they wished. Other than some brief introductions the first evening, none of the community meetings were structured by the staff.

In the absence of any kind of typical large-group leadership style, the participants, whether they liked it or not, had to take charge of their own workshop experience. For many it was enormously frustrating. The staff, especially Rogers, received a great deal of resentment and anger for not fulfilling their role, for being "irresponsible," for being irrelevant to the pain and suffering experienced by people in many of the countries from which the participants came. Others tried to give leadership to the group, suggesting schedules to follow, offering topics for group consideration, or stating needs they hoped the group would respond to. Sometimes these attempts at directing the community's progress were successful, other times not. Rogers was particularly impressed at how the community chose to reject a small group's beautifully worked out method for having large groups, small groups, interest groups and so on, in favor of using a more intuitive method of scheduling their time. They were saying, in effect, "Back home, we always live by schedules. We know how to do that. Why don't we see if we can be together, without a schedule, and still somehow meet the needs of individuals." Sure enough, at pivotal times, the whole community would somehow come together in the meeting room, even though no one had formally announced the meeting. Midway into the sixteen-day experience the feeling of a supportive, egalitarian community was present and, with peaks and valleys, the workshop continued to be a powerful learning experience for staff and participants alike.

By 1976, at Ashland, Oregon, with 130 participants, the workshop title had become "The Person-Centered Approach: Individual Change and Its Social Implications." In 1977, with 100 participants, the work-shop was held on the East Coast, at the National Humanistic Education Center's Sagamore Conference Center in Raquette Lake, New York. Between these two workshops, Rogers and several of the staff also conducted a long and several shorter workshops in Brazil. These in-cluded three two-day workshops—in Recife, Sao Paulo, and Rio de Janeiro—attended by some 600 to 800 people each.

On each of these occasions, in Oregon, Brazil, and New York, the staff moved further and further in the direction of giving total respon-sibility for the workshop to the entire group. They set less and less structure; so that by the New York workshop in 1977 all they did was announce the first community meeting at which time they introduced themselves personally to the group. They did not even suggest the possibility that encounter groups or interest groups or community meetings might be a part of the workshop. All that eventually did occur, but it came from the members' initiation, not from the staff. At one point the chaos in the community seemed so great and group decisions so difficult to reach, that even Rogers doubted the wisdom of the staff's decision about trusting the community so totally with the direction of the workshop. "Either I had helped launch an incredibly stupid experiment doomed to failure, or I had helped to innovate a whole new way of permitting . . . people to sense their own potentiali-ties and to participate in forming their own learning experience."

As it turned out, the results were always the same—even with eight hundred people in a foreign culture and speaking a language different from most of the staff's (in Brazil a translator sat in the group next to each staff member who did not speak Portuguese). The groups *did* find a direction. The participants learned to listen to one another. The workshops allowed diversity, yet experienced a powerful sense of com-munity. And the experience seemed to have important political conse-quences which were always close to the surface of the group's con-sciousness and were at times verbalized explicitly by community members.

In Brazil the political implications of the person-centered approach were particularly apparent. As Rogers said, "We were there at the right time, in the right country, with the right approach that they were very hungry for. I think it is because democracy there is a real issue and to talk about individual freedom, self-actualization, and that kind of thing, is just what people are dying to hear in a country that they fear may continue totalitarian. Secret police were in at least one of our meetings." Issues of authority, decision-making processes, and the use of power, balancing the needs of the individual and the group, dealing with members who were "different," and so on, all were experienced by participants in very personal ways. Many connections were made between how the community resolved these issues in the workshop and how they are typically dealt with in the outside, "real" world.

In spite of the pain and frustration, disappointment and resentment experienced temporarily by many of the participants ("I came here to get something from Carl Rogers"; "People are getting hurt by others in this community and the staff is doing nothing to intervene"; "All my professional life I have believed in and used the client-centered approach. If this is what that means, then I think I have been making a great mistake"; and so on), Rogers came to believe more and more strongly in the importance of this new application of the person-centered approach. As of this writing, in 1978, he and his colleagues are still experimenting with the "person-centered community," with workshops scheduled for Brazil, Virginia, Madrid, Long Island, and two in England (so much for semiretirement!). As in the past, each probably will be somewhat different from the one before. They continue to monitor the results. More time perspective is needed to tell if this will prove to be an interesting side-trip or a major new direction of Rogers' career.

As might be expected, however, Rogers did not wait long before communicating to others his deepening appreciation of the political and social implications of the person-centered approach. Rarely one to do much new thinking without committing his ideas to paper, he made this occasion no exception. Early in 1977 Delacorte Press published Rogers' fourteenth book, entitled *Carl Rogers On Personal Power: Inner Strength and Its Revolutionary Impact.*

In the first chapter of the book he described the person-centered approach and the therapeutic setting out of which it originated. Then he launched immediately into exploring the various applications of the person-centered approach, all evaluated from a political perspective. In each chapter, he used case studies—sometimes short examples, sometimes studies as long as thirty pages—to help his ideas come alive. One chapter described "the new family" and its attempts to move away from parent-centered power and put more control in the hands of the entire family, with many decisions reached through the honest sharing of feelings, good communication, and group consensus. Another two chapters explored "the revolution in marriage and partnership." Here Rogers interpreted the new interpersonal politics between men and women fostered by the women's liberation movement. What distinguished his discussion from that in *Becoming Partners* was his greater focus on issues related to power, control, and decision-making in intimate relationships. Other chapters explored the political implications of the person-centered approach when applied to education, administration, intercultural tensions, and working with oppressed groups. In the latter area he discussed at length the similarities he saw between his own work and that of Paulo Freire, whose book *Pedagogy of the Oppressed* described how Freire had sought to help illiterate Brazilian peasants find their own power and identity and take increased control over their lives.

The next major section of the book provided some lengthy case studies to help illustrate his thesis and widen it to other areas. In one chapter he described the 1975 Person-Centered Workshop, explaining in great detail how fees were set, how participants were selected, how room assignments were made and how each aspect of the workshop was handled. In another chapter he quoted Alan Nelson describing his experience as director of a children's camp in which the "powerless" campers discovered their own power when the facilitative camp climate was interrupted with Nelson's being fired. Chapters in later, briefer sections offered a theoretical base for the person-centered approach and, again, described the "emerging person" (Rogers' "person of tomorrow") who would "spearhead the quiet revolution" which Rogers saw coming—indeed, which he saw occurring.

Since it is relatively soon after the publication of *Carl Rogers On Personal Power*, it is too early to know what kind of reception the book will receive. All signs indicate that its reception will be typical of that of many of Rogers' books. It has not yet been reviewed in any of the professional journals or major book review publications. If it is, the reviewers will probably score Rogers for gross oversimplifications about the realities of the political, economic, and social order. In some cases I would agree with them, for in departing further than ever before from the "laboratories of human relations" he knew the best —therapy, education, and the intensive group—his writing, I think, often lacks the broad and accurate perspective present in most of his other works. In addition reviewers would certainly point out that there was little new in this volume, and that it probably could have been written as a lengthy article just as well.

But, as usual with Rogers, reviewers would miss something which thousands of readers will find, and that is the personal encounter with Carl Rogers, age seventy-five, still thinking, still exploring new frontiers, and still writing lucidly and challengingly about critical contemporary issues. As one reader commented, "It has been a long time since I last read Carl Rogers. It was so refreshing to have him review his thinking and to see in what new directions he is extending his ideas."

Is there enough new material to justify a whole volume? Who can say? Whether or not this is Rogers' last book, it seems, in the context of his entire career, a fitting conclusion, a rounding-out of a full life's work. Although his work certainly has social and political implications, no one can be in a position to understand those implications fully at this time. History will provide a greater perspective on that. But in his book *On Personal Power* Carl Rogers has made a good beginning. Whether or not those forces in civilization which aim to give each person dignity, respect and control over his or her life are ultimately triumphant, Rogers will have taken a stand and played a part in the outcome. In this light Richard Farson has called Carl Rogers "a man whose cumulative effect on society has made him one of the most important social revolutionaries of our time."

How does one complete a biography of Carl Rogers, who, at this writing, is seventy-six years old, with a sharp mind, current interests, and good health? He has been invited to visit the People's Republic of China this fall.

Several images come to mind. The first is Carl Rogers, at seventy, addressing a large number of the members of American Psychological Association on the topic of "Some New Challenges."

"Dare we develop a human science" he asked his audience, "or will we continue to model psychology after an outmoded conception of physics which physicists tell us no longer exists? Can our conception of the scientific process be broadened to make room for the creative part of science and the allowance of subjective human experience as important data to study? Can our departments of psychology change to accommodate such a human science?"

"Do we dare to be designers?" he asked. "Will psychologists be willing to use their knowledge to construct the new, not repair the old? In designing educational institutions, in designing environments like cities, homes, and cultures, in working with industry, in helping society deal with interpersonal and racial problems—will we put our knowledge to the test? Will we risk? Will our universities and departments shift their priorities to help us serve the public in these crucial areas?"

"Dare we do away with professionalism?" He reminded his listeners of how he had helped establish professional standards for psychologists some quarter century before. Now he believed the drawbacks of professional certification were outweighing the advantages. Professionalism exercises a stultifying effect on the profession, freezing it in a past image. "Professionalism builds up a rigid bureaucracy." Nonprofessionals are often more competent than professionals; the population with the problem often has the best resources for solving it. We can find other creative ways to protect the public. "I have slowly come to the conclusion that if we did away with 'the expert,' 'the certified professional,' 'the licensed psychologist,' we might open our profession to a breeze of fresh air, to a surge of creativity, such as it has not known for years."

"Can we permit ourselves to be whole men and women" or will we continue to exclude our feelings from our professional work and professional relationships?

And finally, he asked, "Is this the only reality?" will we continue to deny the increasing evidence of parapsychological phenomena, mystical experience, other ways of apprehending reality than a linear, Newtonian conception of time and space? Not that we should jump on every bandwagon, but do we dare admit that these questions are worth investigating? "It is one of the most exciting challenges posed to psychology."

Each of these issues, he said, after elaborating on them at some length, "represents a possible move toward the enhancement, the deepening, the enrichment of our profession. Each one, in a word, represents for psychology a step toward self-actualization. If my perceptions have been even approximately correct, then the final question I would leave with you is 'Do we dare?' "

Here is Carl Rogers, challenging to its very roots the profession in which he has worked so successfully for half a century. However psychology responds to these challenges, it is likely that the remainder of the century will, again, confirm the clarity of his vision.

The second image is of Carl Rogers in his garden in La Jolla, explaining to an interviewer how patiently he has to work with some of his plants to provide the conditions of nutrition, water, sunlight, and temperature—sometimes for many months or even longer—before seeing his efforts reach fruition. His daughter Natalie is present and, upon hearing him use the word "patient," she shakes her head, smiles lovingly at him and says, "Such patience!" He proudly holds up one particular plant, a tree actually—a small torrey pine only several inches high. He has nursed it for a year and a half, and only now is it clear that this tiny tree will survive. How alike this image is to an early photograph of six-year-old Carl Rogers, in knickers, holding proudly and tenderly in his hand a tiny chick, newly hatched, no more than three inches high.

This, too, is Carl Rogers, who has been so important to so many people—a gentle, nurturing person with a deep faith in life and people.

And, finally, there is Carl Rogers at seventy-five, remembering, "As a boy I was rather sickly, and my parents have told me that it was predicted I would die young. This prediction has been proven completely wrong in one sense, but has come profoundly true in another sense. I think it is correct that I will never live to be old. So now I agree with the prediction. I believe that I will die *young.*"

Major Publications of
Carl R. Rogers

Measuring Personality Adjustment in Children Nine to Thirteen Years of Age. New York: Teachers College, 1931.

The Clinical Treatment of the Problem Child. Boston: Houghton Mifflin, 1939.

Counseling and Psychotherapy: New Concepts in Practice. Boston: Houghton Mifflin, 1942.

Client-centered Therapy: Its Current Practices, Implications, and Theory. New York: Houghton Mifflin, 1951.

Psychotherapy and Personality Change. Chicago: University Press, 1954. With Rosalind F. Dymond [Cartwright] (Eds.).

"The Necessary and Sufficient Conditions of Therapeutic Personality Change." *Journal of Consulting Psychology,* 1957, *21,* 95–103.

"A Theory of Therapy, Personality and Inter-personal Relationships, as Developed in the Client-centered Framework." In S. Koch (Ed.), *Psychology: A Study of a Science.* Vol. 3. *Formulation of the Person and the Social Context.* New York: McGraw-Hill, 1959.

On Becoming a Person. Boston: Houghton Mifflin, 1961.

The Therapeutic Relationship and Its Impact: A Study of Psychotherapy with Schizophrenics. Madison: University of Wisconsin Press, 1967. With E. T. Gendlin, D. J. Kiesler and C. B. Truax (Eds.).

Autobiography. In E. Boring (Ed.) *A History of Psychology in Autobiography.* New York: Russell, 1968.

Person to Person: The Problem of Being Human. Lafayette, California: Real People Press, 1968. With B. Stevens.

Man and The Science of Man. Columbus, Ohio: Charles Merrill, 1968. With W. Coulson (Eds.).

Freedom to Learn: A View of What Education Might Become. Columbus, Ohio: Charles Merrill, 1969.

On Encounter Groups. New York: Harper and Row, 1970.

Becoming Partners: Marriage and Its Alternatives. New York: Delacorte Press, 1972.

On Personal Power: Inner Strength and Its Revolutionary Impact. New York: Delacorte Press, 1977.

Further References

Scholars and researchers who wish more detailed reference information on the facts and quotations cited throughout this biography will find most of this available in the five hundred or so references and footnotes in Howard Kirschenbaum's *Carl Rogers: A Case Study of a Psychologist and Educator,* an unpublished doctoral dissertation, Temple University, 1974, available through University Microfilms.

Readers interested in a complete listing of Carl Rogers' published writings can consult two sources. The appendix of his book *On Becoming a Person* covers the years 1931 to 1961. A list available from the National Humanistic Education Center, 110 Spring Street, Saratoga Springs, NY 12866, covers the years 1957 and thereafter. The Center also has all of Rogers' books that are still in print for sale. A price list is available upon request.

INDEX

NOTE: All entries in the index, with the exception of names of individuals, refer to Carl Rogers.

Laughlin, Bill, 334
learning, theories of, 308–309
Levine, Lena, 227–28
Levy, David, 57, 81–82
Lewin, Kurt, 258, 328
Lindzey, Gardner, 219–20, 240, 255
Lloyd, Paul, 316, 322, 354–56
"Lonely Person—and his Experiences in Encounter Groups, The," 350–51
Louisville school district, 387–90
"loyalty oaths," 420

McGaw, William, 344, 422, 423
McGiffert, Arthur Cushman, 44–45
McIntyre, Cardinal, 384
Man and the Science of Man (Rogers and Colson), 326–27, 391
marriage, 405–12
Mary Reynolds Babcock Foundation, 382
Maslow, Abraham, 203, 229, 245, 256, 258, 373
Mathieu, Philippa, 282–87
May, Rollo, 257, 259, 350
Meador, Betty, 398, 400, 426
Meador, Bruce, 399–400
Measuring Personality Adjustment in Children Nine to Thirteen Years of Age (Rogers), 59
Melton, Arthur, 220–21
"mental health," 280
"Method, The," *see* client-centered therapy

National Conference on Social Work, 99
National Education Association, 328
National Training Laboratories (NTL), 328–30, 331, 335, 373, 386–87, 391
"Necessary and Sufficient Conditions of Therapeutic Personality Change, The," 200–201
"Needed Emphases in the Training of Clinical Psychologists," 99
Nelson, Alan, 423, 426, 430
Newcomb, Theodore, 50, 51, 57
Nicholas Murray Butler Medal, 225
1984 (Orwell), 263–65
nondirective counseling, *see* client-centered therapy
nondirective teaching, 364–70
  basis for, 267
  Harvard address on, 368–70
  leader and, 368

"Note on the Nature of Man, A," 249–51
Nunnally, J. C., 186, 187

Ohio State, 107–53
  appointment to, 107–108
  articles published, 146–147, 151
  colleagues at, 137–39
  impact of students at, 141, 146
  new psychotherapy at, 111–13, 115–17
  nondirective counseling at, 117–37
  relations with students, 110–11, 137–42
  teaching approach at, 139–41
  wartime effort and, 147–52
  work load at, 110–11, 113–14
On Becoming a Person (Rogers), 232, 299–314, 373, 391, 418
  applications of therapy, 308–11
  creative process and, 305
  as favorite book, 299–300
  humanistic psychology and, 313
  ideas on therapy in, 301–302
  optimum human functioning and, 302–305
  publication of, 312–14
  response to, 311–12
  viewpoints on therapy and, 305–308
  writing style of, 301
On Encounter Groups (Rogers), 344–53, 391
"open education," 373–74
operant conditioning, 253, 254
"Oscar" award, 344

Pavlov, Ivan, 252–53
Pedagogy of the Oppressed (Freire), 430
Perls, Fritz, 392
personal experience, importance of, 33, 84, 157, 158, 364–67
personality and characteristics of Carl Rogers:
  aloofness, 186–90
  anger, 333–34
  artistry, 236–37
  child rearing, 54, 101–107
  communication need, 23
  competitiveness, 56, 84–86, 100–101, 182–86
  debating ability, 21, 34, 182, 226–28, 325–26
  described, 177–94, 397–402, 431–33
  drive, 24, 154, 181–82
  energy level, 24, 154
  existentialism, 29, 350–51